BOOKS BY ABBA EBAN

Maze of Justice
Voice of Israel
Tide of Nationalism
Chaim Weizmann: Triumph and Tragedy
My Country
My People
Abba Eban: An Autobiography

THE NEW DIPLOMACY

ABBA EBAN

THE NEW DIPLOMACY

International Affairs in the Modern Age

WEIDENFELD AND NICOLSON   LONDON

First published in Great Britain in 1983 by
George Weidenfeld & Nicolson Limited
91 Clapham High Street, London sw4 7ta

isbn 0 297 78351 3

Printed in Great Britain by
Redwood Burn Limited
Trowbridge

To Suzy, Eli and Gila, with love

Contents

Introduction

A book on international relations published in 1940 would not have included the following terms: Nuclear War; Cold War; Détente; United Nations; NATO; Warsaw Pact; European Community; Organization of African Unity; Foreign Aid; Third World; North-South Relations; OPEC; Intercontinental Ballistic Missiles; Mutual Assured Destruction. There would have been little reference to "human rights" as a subject of international politics. Diplomacy would have been discussed in a predominantly European context. The United States would have been the theme of a relatively marginal chapter, emphasizing its detachment.

The proliferation of new concepts and the appearance of different alignments and power balances remind us of the speed with which the international spectacle has been transformed in a single generation. There have been so many upheavals in the international system that diplomacy reels under the shock of change. Negotiation, which used to be protected by privacy, is now exposed to public scrutiny and debate. International conflicts and military operations are enacted on television screens, with massive impact on public opinion. The collapse of reticence has had a revolutionary and, on the whole, inhibiting effect on the pursuit of agreements.

Summitry—the tendency to transact international business at the highest levels of authority—has become so habitual that it has lost its original dramatic effect. One result has been the erosion of the ambassadorial function. Multilateralism—the treatment of international problems through conferences with wide participation—existed before World War II, but not on anything like the present scale. It generates a torrent of contacts and deliberative occasions and involves thousands of participants. With the parallel multiplication of sovereign states, the numbers of those operatively engaged in international relations have expanded at an intense rate. The experience of four decades leads to a reserved judgment on the effectiveness of multilateral techniques. The euphoric hopes that once accompanied the idea of international organization have not been fulfilled.

The emphasis on publicity, summitry and multilateralism has given diplomacy a new aspect. But these methodical changes are not the whole or even the greater part of the story. There have been sharp alterations in the power balance. For the period covered by this book the United States and the Soviet Union towered above all others in the world community to such a degree that most of international politics seemed to be a function of their rivalries and accommodations. The entry of China into the active international arena has modified the bipolar structure without totally eliminating it. At the same time the international landscape has become diversified beyond anything known before, through the astonishing emergence of some ninety new sovereignties.

In the new international system, military power is surrounded by ambiguity. It has not lost its importance, but it is not the only decisive component in the strategic balance. Mankind lives in the shadow of the paradox in which power becomes less usable in the measure that it becomes more destructive. On the other hand, conventional military forces remain a fundamental instrument of policy, and the frequency with which they have been used disappoints the hopes of those who predicted that the argument of force would be increasingly discarded under the inhibiting influence of the new balance of terror. While nation-states are still the main actors in the international system, there is a tendency for many of them to form regional groupings. There is more fragmentation and also more integration than ever before. Diplomacy has expanded not only through the multiplication of national and interstate entities; there has also been a great increase of functions. The themes of diplomacy used to be politics, strategy, military balances and territorial issues. The horizons have now been broadened to include preoccupation with economic development, financial relations, oil prices and availabilities, environmental dilemmas and other matters once defined as "low politics."

The collapse of stabilities and the swiftness of change create an intellectual ferment in the study and teaching of international relations. There is a vast diffusion of dialogue and debate. University faculties, councils and institutes on international politics, area studies, think tanks, centers of strategic research and an endless succession of symposia and study conferences have taken the subject out of academic seclusion and have helped to stimulate and widen public controversy and debate. A new scholarly discipline attempts to construct systematic models for the description and solution of international conflicts.

The growth of popular interest in what used to be a specialized domain has been rapid and spectacular. In previous generations it appeared that many people would have preferred to live without such a thing as foreign policy. Whenever writers have reflected descriptively on the ideal condition of man they have imagined societies without boundaries or neighbors. Plato's "Republic" enjoys this luxury, and most of the utopias in literature are wistfully located on desert islands or in remote mountain fastnesses. It is now reluctantly understood that there are very few sectors of humankind that can afford the luxury of detachment or the indolent belief that everthing influential in their lives can be enacted within the frontiers that enclose their own nations. The sheer quantity of preoccupation with international affairs reflects an explosive enlargement of interest and concern. Along with this growth of hope and interest there is a degree of humility about what statecraft can achieve. Diplomacy does not offer salvation. It moves in a world in which the stakes of diplomacy are so high that even modest progress is worthy of profound respect. Imperfect solutions have to be compared with even less perfect alternatives.

This book is an attempt to catch and convey the rhythm of fluctuation in the international politics of the years that have elapsed since World War II. I write from a dual perspective. As an ambassador and foreign minister who had frequent recourse to diplomatic action in bilateral fields and in international organizations, I have been aware of the uniqueness and particularity of individual cases. But in trying to transmit this experience in teaching and public exposition I have had to seek generalizations that might give some degree of order and coherence to the baffling variety of international life. The gap between theory and practice is wide, and those who have lived on both sides of it are not very numerous. There may also be an element of novelty in a contemplation of the international system by an observer who is free from allegiance to any of the major powers or regional groupings which have dominated the story told in these pages.

My tribute of thanks begins with the Institute for Advanced Study in Princeton, which, in electing me to its membership, gave me my first opportunity of planning this book in an environment more serene than I could otherwise have encountered. I owe gratitude to Christopher Kojm, then of Princeton University and now Director of the Foreign Policy Association in New York, for research assistance; and to Yadin

Kaufman of Harvard University for comment and insight on European problems. Above all, I give thanks to Random House for its despairing fidelity to this book amid the collapse of successive deadlines, and especially to Charlotte Mayerson for her invaluable editorial labors.

Jerusalem, June 1983

Book I

Chapter 1

THE NEW INTERNATIONAL ERA
The Curtain Goes Up

IN THE CENTURY between Waterloo (1815) and the outbreak of World War I (1914) no more than 2.5 million soldiers had fallen in battle. Civilian populations were for the most part untouched by war. Then 100 million lost their lives in two eruptions of violence spanning three decades from 1914 to 1945. Between September 1939 and August 1945, more than 50 million people were killed in war, and the toll of maimed and wounded was beyond conjecture. Great areas of Europe were devastated, and two ravaged cities in Japan gave augury of a new age in destructive power. When World War II ended with the American atomic explosions at Hiroshima and Nagasaki, it seemed that traditional statecraft had been discredited beyond recall. The hour called not for piecemeal diplomacy but for a new and grand design.

A sense of recent disaster sometimes gives birth to lucid reason; but it just as often becomes sublimated into messianic yearning for a total, and therefore unattainable, perfection. There was more illusion than realism in the approach of leading statesmen to the problems of the postwar age.

The first illusion was that the foundations of the new international order could be swiftly laid. Everything was done prematurely, as if a new and complex structure could be erected before the debris of the previous order had been cleared away. The first phase of the reconstruction was enacted at San Francisco, where the founding conference of the United Nations convened on April 25, 1945. Hitler and Mussolini were still alive. Winston Churchill was in the last stage of his

power. The Japanese empire had still not been defeated. The victims
of Hitler's slaughterhouse were still shamefully confined to their
camps. The armies of the Western Allies and the Soviet Union had
converged toward each other on German soil. On the very day that the
conference met, American and Russian forces greeted each other on
the river Elbe. Franklin D. Roosevelt had died on April 12, two weeks
before. Nobody could predict what kind of leader his successor would
be. There was hardly a country in Europe—and few elsewhere—that
could foresee the nature of its regime a year or two ahead. The shape
of the postwar economies was an even deeper mystery. The colonial
empires were theoretically intact—but for how long? Everything on
the international horizon was murky, tentative, obscure. It is impossible to believe that the statesmen at the United Nations conference or
in their separate chanceries and parliaments could have had any accurate premonition of the future. Yet the literature and the rhetoric of
those days throw an astonishing light on their mood of certainty. They
were afflicted by few doubts about what the future held; their assumptions—especially the wrong ones—were emphatically sustained.

Four decades later it is hard to believe that rational men could have
lived in such a world of fallacies. The first of them was that the Allies
who had fought their way to victory would work in close concert for
the maintenance of the peace. The theory was that the ordeals which
they had undergone together would consecrate their partnership for
future tasks. If danger had united them in war, surely the lure of peace
would hold them together with equal force of cohesion.

One act of credulity begat another, and soon a whole chain of corollary
assumptions began to form in a cluster around the central illusion of
Great Power cooperation. It was believed that the new system would
give a large place to international organization. This time, unlike the
era of the League of Nations, there would be universal participation,
with all the major powers in the lead. There was much talk of collective
resistance to aggression. The international organization would have
the necessary armed forces to ensure respect for its decisions. This
meant that for the first time in history sovereign states would voluntarily renounce their right to determine how and where their armed
forces would be used. A world organization armed with these powers
would become the central arena of international diplomacy. How else
could one explain why the three most powerful leaders in the world
had spent so many hours at Yalta arguing about details of voting
procedure and membership? Large sectors of international decision
would be centralized in a United Nations forum, governed no longer

by the improvisations of the power balance, but by the objective consistency of a written Charter.

There was no end to the dream of a new and radiant dawn. International law would move from its peripheral status toward the center of diplomatic discourse. Subject peoples would emerge in steady evolution toward "self-government" (the Charter was cautious about "independence," which was mentioned only once). New levels of cooperation would be created to ensure an expanding world economy; the watchword here would be solidarity, not competition. As governments came to put more trust in each other and in international institutions, they would reduce their armaments, with consequent relief of political tensions and economic burdens. Diplomacy would be open, public, ecumenical, free of the conspiratorial atmosphere of the past and abundant in the production of agreements. Divergent ideologies and conflicting interests would still exist, but they would be subdued by the overriding vision of a universal order. Even if the Great Powers did not share a common hope, they would surely be united by a common fear —fear of "the scourge of war which twice in our generation has brought untold havoc to mankind."

These forecasts would for the most part be refuted by the end of the first postwar decade. Some of them would look somewhat frayed and dubious within three years of the end of the war. It may be questioned whether the immediate morrow of a traumatic experience is a good time to plan remedial measures. What is certain is that the statesmen who planned the new era of international life were seized by a shining vision which they somehow confused with reality. They had a zest for innovation. They assumed that nothing would be the same, that a new story, never heard or told before, would unfold across the human scene. And this conviction about the new age was not held by untutored idealists alone. It was shared by men of hard experience, nurtured in the wearying frustrations of conflict and war.

We now know how wrong they were. There was going to be very little Great Power cooperation. The alliance between the Western powers and the Soviet Union had been a marriage of convenience whose occasional courtesies concealed authentic divergences of interest and emotion. It was all very well for Roosevelt to say: "I think the Russians are perfectly friendly; they aren't trying to gobble up the rest of Europe or the world ... They haven't got any crazy ideas of conquest." This facile utterance begged the question whether the Russians, without coveting "the rest of Europe or the world," might firmly intend to "gobble up" a part of Europe and more of the world than the West wanted to concede. According to his own ambassador to the USSR, William Bullitt, Roosevelt said: "If I give him [Stalin] everything I possibly can and ask nothing from him in return, *noblesse oblige,* he won't try to annex anything and will work with me for a world of democracy and peace."

It would not take long for American policymakers to learn that "Stalin" and *"noblesse oblige"* were terms that did not sit well together. The Cold War was initially and specifically a head-on collision between two rival conceptions of the place of Eastern Europe in the global alignment, but this divergence was so acute and sensitive that the pain of it spread through every artery and nerve of the world community.

"Great Power cooperation" was the most spectacular fallacy to be embraced in the aftermath of the war and to be shattered in brief time. Next in line came the myth of a powerful international organization. By 1946 it would become evident that there was not going to be a United Nations force acting under the authority of a Concert of Five Powers. It was simply not true that institutions would create a sense of world community; instead, the absence of a sense of world community would weaken and paralyze the institutions. A sense of community would have to be created first, with effective international institutions as a possible ultimate consequence. The central actors in world politics would be nation-states claiming absolute sovereignty in their international relations and giving international institutions a subsidiary role in the service of their national interests. The fifty states that founded the United Nations would not even continue to be the main part of the world community. Nearly a hundred new sovereignties would join them in a great proliferation of independent national units, many of them of minute dimensions. There would not be "Five Great Powers" in any real sense. China would undergo vast transformations but would long stand in the margin, not the center, of the global system. The Great Power status accorded by the UN Charter to Britain and France was a gesture to the past rather than a reflection of present reality. Germany and Japan would develop an influence quite unforeseen by those who fashioned international institutions without them. Subject peoples would come to independence not by the orderly evolution envisaged in the trusteeship provisions of the UN Charter, but in an unorganized, turbulent rush of changing winds. Beginning with the Marshall Plan and the United States' European Recovery Program a new dimension of diplomacy would arise—the use of economic aid in pursuit of political and ideological goals. In a sharp reversal of the traditional power structure, the rich industrial world would often have to show deference to countries that are militarily weak and economically undeveloped but are endowed with basic energy sources.

The postwar world, far from engaging in disarmament, would be caught up in an arms race of staggering scope. Not a single weapon system would be abolished or reduced. International law would not celebrate a golden age. On the contrary, the jurists would have little comfort or international employment; nations would prefer to resolve their conflicts by diplomacy, or even war, rather than submit their interests to legal adjudication. Events would have more power than ideas, and pragmatic interests, empirically defined, would take precedence over written constitutions. The "scourge of war" referred to in the only eloquent phrase in the UN Charter would not recur in its full range or scope, but dozens of limited wars would prove that military power, though inhibited in its application, would still be a major element of international relations. The cherished hope of creating international solidarities in what were optimistically called "nonpolitical issues" would be frustrated by East-West and North-South rivalries. Regional institutions would abound but, with the important exception of economic institutions in Western Europe, they would not succeed in modifying national sovereignties through a meaningful degree of integration.

The disparity between what statesmen and diplomats predicted and what occurred is not merely a subject of academic curiosity or a theme for literary speculation. It raises the question whether world leaders today are guiding their policies in a similar climate of fallacy. Human beings are unable to foretell the future and, on that count, some of the inaccuracies and obscurities that marked international thinking in the mid-forties are excusable. For example, the UN Charter, with its emphasis on enforcement through the military units of the major powers, was written by people who had no idea that there was such a thing as atomic weapons. If they had known of this development they would not have seriously imagined that it would be wise to multiply the occasions on which American and Soviet armies were put into active duty in areas of tension. Pre-nuclear concepts continued to dominate international thinking for many years after they had become obsolete. Similarly, there was little indication in the attitudes of Churchill and De Gaulle that would have given prior notice of the astonishing voluntary abnegation of the imperial role—by the Attlee government and by De Gaulle himself in his second presidency. India, Pakistan and Burma were relinquished as an act of British policy, while France gave birth to more than fifteen states in Africa in a deliberate surge of decolonization. Thus the trusteeship system was overtaken by accelerated

independence, and the international map was transformed with unexpected suddenness.

But if many developments in the postwar age were inherently unpredictable, it was not intellectually justifiable at any time to believe in the
myth of the continuing Great Power alliance or in any consequences
that might flow from that premise. Historians would find it hard to
recall a parallel for such a far-reaching assumption embraced with such
little cause. Nor was there any objective excuse for believing that
international security would cease to depend on alliances and balances
of power as a result of the establishment of the United Nations. To a
great extent these two illusions were intertwined with each other. It
was because Great Power relations would be adversarial, not harmonious, that the idea of collective security enforced by a Great Power
concert would inevitably collapse.

The strange expectation of harmony between the Soviet Union and the
West was, in the main, an American error. Russian leaders had said
nothing to encourage it, and British statesmen had not followed the
United States into the utopian wonderland.

    The dialogue between Moscow and Washington had begun on a
matter in which the Soviet Union held every advantage. At Yalta, Stalin
had told Roosevelt and Churchill that for the USSR, Poland was a
matter of security and an issue of "life and death." No American could
assert that Poland and its neighbors were a matter of American security, still less of "life and death." The Russian interest was concrete
and vital. The American interest was distant, theoretical, idealistic and
not very tenacious beyond the limits of rhetoric. International history
in recent years teaches us that when two actors compete for a certain
interest, the one that feels most intensely about it is likely to prevail.
Moreover, the Soviets were in possession of the field. It is true that
the Yalta declaration committed the Soviet Union to a more flexible
attitude toward the independence of East European countries. But
Western diplomats should have questioned the value of declarations
in which Russian leaders promised things that were inconsistent with
national habits and interests. (Thirty years later the same lesson would
have to be learned about the Helsinki Final Act, in which the Soviet
Union promised to behave in a way inconsistent with Soviet conceptions. Western leaders may have an interest in eliciting such Soviet
signatures, but they have no cause to believe them.)

    Some American diplomats, while sharing Roosevelt's moral revul-
sion at the subjugation of Eastern Europe, were realistic enough to

grasp that there was no real possibility of denying Soviet ambitions. George F. Kennan admitted at the time that the best way of dealing with Russia was through "a reasonable balance of power and under-standing on spheres of influence." He has written: "I continued to be an advocate . . . of a prompt and clear recognition of the division of Europe into spheres of influence." Such advocacy was bound to be audacious and lonely since "balance of power" and "spheres of influ-ence" are forbidden phrases in the American traditional vocabulary, however consistently they are applied in American traditional practice.

This does not mean that it was wrong for the West to oppose what it might have known to be inevitable. There is a realm of diplomacy that lies beyond realism. It is a world in which nations seem compelled by their convictions to express their own vision of a human order even if there is no chance of attaining it. The Soviet idea of what Europe should look like was something that the Soviet Union could not possi-bly renounce—and that the United States could not possibly accept. If anything, the developments after Yalta made Soviet rigidity even more probable. As if the Russian sentiment of insecurity were not sufficiently inflated there came the American achievement in creating atomic bombs. This canceled the possibility of relaxed superiority in Moscow after the successes of the Red Army in the war.

Once it became clear that the international system was going to be dominated by two gigantic powers whose interests and ideals were in conflict, not in harmony, it should have been realized, however reluc-tantly, that conventional diplomacy would be more decisive than mul-tilateral diplomacy in the latter half of the century. American statesmen had a blind spot about the United Nations, and this made their subsequent disillusionment all the more painful. When Averell Harriman suggested to Cordell Hull that he should try to influence Soviet Foreign Minister V.M. Molotov on the Polish issue, he received the incredible reply: "I don't want to deal with these piddling little things. We must deal with the main issues." The "main issues" in-cluded how voting should be arranged in UN forums. The "piddling little things" were the future of Eastern Europe and the question whether Soviet power could be contained or whether it would expand into areas in which Russia had no military presence before the war! If we were to look for the most blatant case of simple-minded idealism overpowering common sense and lucidity, we should not have to look far beyond the relative weight that some governments, especially the United States, have attached to UN debates on the one hand and real issues of power on the other. What should have worried Americans in the period after the Yalta Conference was not their President's bodily health so much as the mental attitude of their Secretary of State. Hull even considered that the crisis in Eastern Europe could be solved by the UN. "I could sympathize fully," he said, "with Stalin's desire to protect his western border from future attack. But I felt that this security could best be obtained through a strong postwar peace organization."

Without Great Power cooperation or a "strong postwar peace organization," mankind has survived in a manner and mood unanticipated in any blueprint. Nearly forty years after the present era of international relations was born, diplomacy works through a disorderly network of concepts which have often been presented as incompatible with each other but which somehow coexist side by side. The ideas of power balances and spheres of influence have not been discarded, while movements toward regional integration and international community struggle for their place in the sun far more arduously than was imagined when the curtain went up. The major superpower confrontation has assumed many names, from "containment" through "Cold War" to "détente," but its contours have changed little in four decades. The nuclear anguish creates a new psychological context in which the international drama is enacted, but it has not led to any change of the mood in which the powers approach the issue of arms control. Limited wars are a sad but permanent feature of the international landscape, but they seldom give rise to apocalyptic visions of escalation or holocaust. Single "dominoes" manage to fall without bringing the whole system to collapse. The fact that problems are seldom "solved" does not mean that they must necessarily explode, sending their deadly fragments far and wide. It is easier to diagnose the sickness of the world than to prescribe cures; and it is easier to prescribe cures than to persuade the patient to accept them.

And yet the overriding impression of the international spectacle is one of change. For the rest of the eighties and beyond, the diplomatic scene will continue to be marked by tension, instability, complexity and paradox. But there are new dimensions. The drama is played out with the whole world as stage. The communications revolution has altered the tone of diplomacy to an extraordinary degree. Sovereignty is more respected and also more encroached upon than ever before. The theme of international relations must now be studied in the context of a vast expansion of its scope. There are many more actors in the drama, more issues to be wrestled with, more functions performed, more specialized skills mobilized, more methods of analysis and research invoked and put to work, more materials available than in the days when diplomacy was a compact exercise in which relatively few people in a few sovereign countries dealt with a few salient problems while the masses of humankind went on their way unheeding. The task is, as it has always been, to keep the future open for life and, if possible, for peace. But the understanding of this task requires more complex and strenuous labor by men and women who can see the soil below as well as the vistas ahead.

Chapter 2

AMERICA
AND THE WORLD

It was there that civilized man was destined to build
society on new foundations and, applying theories
till then unknown or deemed unworkable, to
present the world with a spectacle for which past
history had not prepared it.

—ALEXIS DE TOCQUEVILLE

Twenty-five Years of Primacy

Some called it "The American Century." Others spoke of a "Pax Americana." Seldom in history had any nation held such a vast predominance of military and economic power as that possessed by the United States during the quarter century after the end of World War II. There were, all in all, no more than half a million American troops scattered in various stations, but they were a symbol of a larger commitment to bring American force into the service of American interests across the world. If anybody collided with the U.S. trip wire, he knew that there could be a drastic response. From the mid-fifties onward, America no longer held the monopoly of nuclear power; but America was the only nation to have put atomic bombs to use, and it was the bombing of Hiroshima and Nagasaki in 1945 that gave credibility to John F. Kennedy's confrontation with Nikita Khrushchev over the Cuban missile crisis in 1962. More than fifty countries that the United States was committed to defend against attack believed in the validity of that promise. So did their potential adversaries. When a dangerous vacuum appeared, as in the case of British withdrawal from responsibilities in Turkey and Greece in 1947, the United States moved in swiftly and with surprisingly little domestic opposition. And when President Harry S. Truman judged that the invasion of South Korea from the North in 1950 was an unacceptable offense to American interests, he was able to send American troops into effective action without delay. He was also sustained by domestic approbation and by a large measure of international solidarity. Fifteen members of the

United Nations sent armed forces to fight under American command, fifty nations gave some measure of material assistance, and more than sixty endorsed a United Nations recommendation for an embargo on strategic commodities to the People's Republic of China. All Truman's successors could look back with incredulous envy on the smooth, unimpeded process by which a President could put American force to work in an atmosphere of international legitimacy.

During this period American power had no hard competition. The Soviet Union was constantly probing, exploring, testing and sometimes defying America's will, but its general demeanor was pragmatic and deferential. Where the United States took a lenient or indifferent posture, as in Czechoslovakia in 1948 and 1968 or Hungary in 1956, Russian power could record an advance. Where America showed vigor and tenacity, as in Turkey, Greece, Korea, Cuba and in the resolve to save Western Europe from Communist domination, Moscow invariably acknowledged realities and prudently determined to leave well or ill alone.

America for several years was not so much a superpower as a monopower. Germany, Italy and Japan would eventually recover from their defeat, but for the quarter century of American predominance their main thought was for their own rehabilitation, not for any assertion of an international role. In the traditional centers of diplomatic leadership, British and French governments might secretly believe that their wisdom and experience surpassed the naïve, simplistic perceptions of American statecraft, but politics is principally about power, not so much about experience and wisdom, and all that London and Paris could spare was an envious, nostalgic glance at their vanishing universal role before settling down to their immediate business—the recuperation of their economies and the renunciation of colonial burdens.

Nor was American mastery limited in any degree by the growth of international organizations. The United States commanded an assured majority in the UN General Assembly and the UN Specialized Agencies. In the Security Council it could afford a condescending reluctance to use its veto power, since there was little chance of a majority daring to propose a policy in serious conflict with American wishes.

If the United States could dominate the arena of strategic and political relations, its supremacy was even more marked in the economic field. It emerged from World War II and strode into the 1950s as a nation constituting 5 percent of the world's population and producing over 40 percent of the world's product. The latter percentage was unreasonably inflated by the abnormally low productivity of the European and Soviet economies after the devastation of the war; but even years later when the gap became less abnormal, America was still the only nation whose economic strength could seriously enhance its foreign policy. Economic power worked on behalf of American foreign policy in three directions: it enabled the United States to prevent adverse changes in the strategic balance by such enterprises as the Marshall Plan, which ensured stable democratic allies in Western Europe; it gave the United States an incomparable dimension of foreign policy through military and economic assistance programs which came to embrace more than half of the nations of the world; and a unique capacity of production sustained the American side of the ideological argument, emphasizing the contrast between the advantages of a free economy and the lesser achievements of the Communist empire.

By the early 1970s, this picture of American primacy no longer held true. The Soviet Union had closed the gap between its nuclear forces and those of the United States. By signing the SALT I agreements in 1972, the United States implicitly acknowledged Soviet parity. It did not even try to compete with the USSR in the size of its conventional forces; here the Soviet Union could give its foreign policy a power of flexible movement and of psychological intimidation on a global scale. The change of the strategic balance in favor of the Soviet Union was accompanied by what seemed at the time to be a similar equalization in scientific and technological achievement. The first Soviet Sputnik in 1957 had a psychological effect out of all proportion to its real scientific significance. The United States had a four-year lead over the Soviet Union in producing atomic bombs and a whole year's lead with the hydrogen bomb—and yet here it seemed to be surpassed by Moscow in outer space. It was not until the dispatch of the Atlas satellite in December 1958 that America deemed itself to have caught up with the Soviet Union's Sputnik operation. But even when Soviet space technology was overshadowed in later years by the dynamism and audacity of American successes, it remained true that the United States was never again to be alone either in nuclear technology or in space research. Instead of being a monopower, America had to settle for bipolarity. And the impression of declining primacy in the military and scientific domains was accompanied by a measure of deflation in America's economic pretensions. The first devaluation of the dollar in the early 1970s weakened the myth of American economic omnipotence. And Western Europe and Japan celebrated such swift economic recuperation that within two decades they were the competitors of the United States—no longer its clients or dependencies.

Yet none of these shifts in relative power would have so deeply shaken American self-confidence were it not for the traumatic shock of the Vietnam war. America would not have been greatly afflicted by the mere fact of losing its predominance. "Firstness" had not been a part of the early American dream. For many generations—partly because of a persistent isolationism—the United States had been content with an international influence far less imposing than its potential strength would seem to justify. If America aspired to make "a communication of freedom to all mankind," it was to be by the contagion of its example rather than by the imposition of its power.

Moreover, the loss of a total American dominance in the Western world had not come upon the United States as an unforeseen disaster. It had been the paradoxical result of America's own policy. The United States had consciously saved Europe's freedom and rehabilitated Japan's pride; their capacity to become its competitors was a symbol of America's successful altruism, not of its failure. Unlike the Soviet Union, the United States had never consciously pursued the idea of hegemony within an ideological family. Its leadership flowed from its objective strength, not from its subjective ambition. Many Americans would willingly have returned to the idyllic days during which their country sat on the sidelines of the international system, unburdened by what George Washington called "the quarrels of Europe, their mutual jealousies, their balance of power, their complicated alliances." He had said about the Old World: "They are nations of eternal war." At the lowest point in the Vietnam disaster, Americans would have keenly liked to return to their national infancy as described by Jefferson—"the new continent, kindly separated by nature and a wide ocean from the exterminating havoc of one quarter of the globe."

Expansion had been the keynote of America's early history, but it had been accomplished mainly within the bounds of a continent, not across the seas, and it did not as a rule deprive any recognized states of their territorial integrity. Excursions into the Philippines and Puerto Rico did not refute this general rule. The United States had the rare chance of expansion together with a sense of virtue and without the odium of colonialism. So the shock of Vietnam was not the loss of "firstness"; it was the myth of virtue and success that had collapsed. Americans had believed, with the weight of experience behind them, that all problems were soluble if enough good will and resolution were brought to their solution. The United States had never known the taste of military defeat. And here in Vietnam by 1976 there were more than 50,000 American dead and myriads of wounded, with vast treasure spent and a heavy blow inflicted on the nation's pride and confidence. All this without any compensating profit for the values or interests which American policy was designed to serve. Henceforward other nations would still look to America for help, but no longer for inspiration.

As the 1970s took their course, the United States was far from being a weakling. It was still stronger economically than the Soviet Union, stronger militarily than Western Europe, stronger than Japan in both respects. But it no longer towered above the rest of the world, and its capacity to evoke deference had been eroded by the domestic and international effects of a momentous failure. It faced other nations on the basis of a common fallibility. Moreover, the tidy pattern—Communism versus freedom—no longer described the international reality. France had discredited the idea of Western unity, China had made a shambles of the idea of a united Communist empire, and scores of new nations refused to align themselves within the simple mold of bipolar confrontation.

In later years many Americans would look back on the short period of primacy and ask themselves if a more skillful statecraft might have availed to give lasting stability to the international system and to America's place within it. Had America made the most of its brief but glowing hour of predominance? This nostalgia for perfection is understandable but unrealistic. In terms of historical experience it is surprising that the United States performed as well as it did. The starting point, after all, had been an instinctive revulsion against the idea of having a foreign policy at all. The American people had wrought a miracle of success in their continent, enlarging its power and prosperity without serious hindrance and, except in the Civil War, without much bloodshed. Success was measured by the growth of domestic resources and welfare; foreign concerns were a distraction to be dealt with as summarily as possible so that the country could get back to its real vocation—making Americans more wealthy, tranquil and secure within their continental sanctuary. There was also the fact that involvement in foreign affairs substantively meant involvement in Europe, and the notion of Europe evoked the oldest and deepest reservation in the history of American political thought. "Why," exclaimed George Washington in his Farewell Address, "forgo the advantages of so peculiar a situation? . . . Why, by interweaving our destiny with that of any part of Europe, entangle our peace and prosperity in the toils of European Ambition, Rivalship, Interest, Humor, or Caprice?" This theme was to be heard again and again during the subsequent decades, and its echoes linger still. In strictly objective terms those traditional references to Europe have always been churlish and unfounded. America was able to expand and flourish within its continental expanse because the balance of power in Europe neutralized it against any potentially hostile European intrusion, while British naval supremacy ensured the freedom of the seas without laying any burdens on the United States. Remote from the exigencies and compromises of power politics, Americans were able to comment on international affairs in a detached, moralistic tone. American foreign policy was, in the main, a series of reactions to emergencies provoked from outside. When a "clear and present danger" had been dealt with, the United States would return to domestic concerns.

It would be a mistake to believe that unilateralism in U.S. foreign policy is a thing of the distant past, a memory of the pastoral folklore of the early years. It is an attitude that even survived World War I, after which there came two decades of intensely inward orientation. The Neutrality Act was adopted in 1938, not in some prehistoric past. And even after World War II the cry "Bring the boys back home" reflected the rooted tendency of Americans to see involvement as an episodic interruption of their normal rhythm, not as a destiny that would have to accompany them into their future.

While it is easy to diagnose this attitude as insularity and egotism, it was, strangely, suffused with a certain modesty. Historians have observed that American nationalism was originally, by European standards, relaxed and free from self-assertion.

> *The new-made nation was as yet innocent of traditions, commitments or memories . . . It was rooted not in the exhausted soil of some remote past, but in the virgin land of a new continent; it found inspiration not in dubious mythology masquerading as history, but in a public will openly proclaimed . . . It required centuries of history to confer sanctity on the state. Centuries of history hedged monarchy about with divinity, but there was nothing divine about the office of the President.*

So America went into the new age after World War II with immense power exercised with very little pomp or panoply or self-glorification. Initially, American Presidents and their advisers tended to conduct the nation's foreign affairs without much regard for the general international system. Except for the Soviet threat, they seemed able, because of their country's economic and military power, to fashion the postwar order much as they wished. The early success of U.S. policy did not even require much diplomatic skill. The disarray of the former Great Powers created an automatic American pre-eminence. And when the Soviet Union challenged the United States' postwar role, America was strong enough to block the challenge.

The central theme was containment. This was a defensive, not a dynamic idea, but it seemed to conform with the realities of the new age. The word itself was not very heroic. It clearly implied that it was too late to roll Soviet power back from the conquests of World War II. It was not possible to reverse the stream of recent history; but it was not necessary to accept inundation. It was possible—at least—to build dikes and dams. The analysis of Soviet policy on which this policy was based made no allowance for Soviet moderation, compassion or willingness to concede. Russian obsessiveness about security, sharpened by the pathos of suffering in war, was combined with the crusading fervor of Marxism to create a double motive for expansion. Nor did the Russian political culture leave room for harmony with the West on the grounds of common values or memories. The theory of containment was pessimistic in its diagnosis, but sanguine in its definition of remedy. It assumed that Russian power would press forward without scruple as far and as fast as it could. But it also believed that if faced with convincing power and resistance Soviet expansion would know where to stop. The USSR was aggressive but not frenetic or incapable of prudence. With so much of the world lying in political and economic ruin, active leadership by the United States could still resurrect liberal democracy and capitalism in defeated Japan and Germany and in the rest of exhausted Europe. The Soviet Union could be warned off by a series of "Keep Out" notices. If these were clear and credible they would be respected.

The Awakening

The dream of an American Century behind the shield of containment was not to come to pass. It was shattered by the Soviet Union's bid for equal superpower status, by Europe's and Japan's rebirth, by anticolonial struggles, by the rise of new nationalism in the developing world, by breaches and dislocations in the Western alliance, and—for a time—by the power of OPEC. The United States did not find it easy at first to recognize how strongly these changes in the international environment constrained its own foreign policy. Buoyed by its successes in the immediate postwar era, America continued through the turbulent 1960s and part of the 1970s to speak and act as if it could still control almost single-handedly the dynamics of international life.

But by now the international system had increased in complexity. Global power had become more diffuse. In the 1970s, the Soviet Union had achieved both nuclear and conventional military parity, and China entered the world community owing no debt to America. The nature of power itself seemed to be more elusive than U.S. policymakers had understood it to be. The Vietnam failure demonstrated that overwhelming military superiority did not ensure success in regional conflicts, while the 1973 oil crisis showed that the economic strength of the Western nations could be undermined if nations, however weak in military terms, could withhold a critical natural resource.

The amalgam of American political values, myths and history has contributed to a distinctive national style that shapes the thinking of American policymakers about the international system. American diplomacy has a unique and characteristic orientation. The nation's long isolation from the power politics of the European nations has had enduring effects. This internal preoccupation with domestic affairs meant that even when America acted externally, it was responding to challenges from outside—reacting rather than initiating.

Another aspect of American foreign policy has been its claim to a higher purpose, imbued with moralism and missionary zeal. This attitude stems from America's historic sense of a special mission that made it, in Abraham Lincoln's words, "the last, best hope on Earth." America's external dealings have often been viewed at home as a metaphysical struggle between the forces of good and evil. American democracy, free from oppression and tyranny, seemed to its own people a superior political system, capable of offering inspiration to all the world. To preserve this great experiment in democracy, the United States had held itself apart from European (although not Asian or Latin American) power politics. And when provoked to external action by a perceived threat to American values, it would respond as in 1917 and 1941 with a crusade rather than a policy. Woodrow Wilson would make the world "safe for democracy," just as Franklin D. Roosevelt would fight not, heaven forbid, for "American interests" but for "Four Freedoms."

Those who watch American policy nervously from the outside may have taken the moralistic pretension too seriously. It has been vigorously criticized by American historians of the realist school. Arthur Schlesinger, Jr., speaks of "a righteous moralism that encouraged the American people to construe political questions in ethical terms, local questions in global terms, relative questions in absolute terms." George Kennan sees "the most serious fault of [America's] past policy to lie in the . . . legalistic, moralistic approach to international problems." By this he means "an attempt to transpose the Anglo-Saxon concept of individual law into the international field and to make it applicable to governments as it is applicable here at home to individuals." Hans J. Morgenthau accuses American diplomacy of moralism and legalism.

On closer observation these may be criticisms of American rhetoric rather than of American policy. There is strong evidence for the contention that American decisions are really made in terms of power; they are then justified in terms of law and morality. President William McKinley is said to have spent a whole night in prayer for divine guidance before deciding to annex the Philippines. And in 1914 President Woodrow Wilson ordered the bombardment of Vera Cruz and then piously declared that "the United States had gone to Mexico to serve mankind." But McKinley would not have accepted a negative answer; his supplications would have continued until the Heavenly Will was worn down by attrition. And Wilson surely knew that "mankind" outside America could have willingly resigned itself to the absence of American forces from Mexico. American Presidents, whatever their rhetoric, did not really enter the two world wars to make the world safe for democracy or to establish Four Freedoms. They were acting in the service of the balance of power; more particularly in tribute to a principle, unchanged since Jefferson's time, which told them that the security of the United States could not be assured if "the whole force of Europe [were to be] wielded by a single hand."

On the eve of the Cold War the American approach to foreign policy often contrasted with the conduct of other actors in the international system. Given the precedence that American leaders accorded to domestic affairs, and their intermittent dealings in international politics, the nation was ill-prepared for a continuous and realistic approach to the manifold postwar problems. There was a tendency toward extreme swings in public opinion, from righteous intervention to isolation. The concept of a battleground between good and evil obstructed the America people's view of such realities as power and interests. The traditional disdain for power politics made the United States an awkward partner for older states whose concept of power was unashamed.

The Origins of the Cold War (1945–1947)

The literature on the Cold War is largely concerned with the question of who was "responsible" for the early tensions between the Soviet Union and the United States which were to dominate the next few decades. It was a period in which America's wartime illusions rapidly vanished. The expectation of many American leaders that amicable U.S.-Soviet relations would continue into the postwar period was astonishingly naïve. It revealed a tendency to confuse dreams with facts; realities such as the objective clash of interests and the intrinsic rivalry of a bipolar system were ignored simply because they were unattractive.

Thus, at Yalta, Roosevelt and his advisers appear—incredibly—to have sincerely believed that they had established the basis for a cooperative postwar world. Stalin had seemed to make concessions on "vital issues," from the use of the veto in the United Nations to his alleged support of self-government and free elections in Eastern Europe, embodied in the Declaration on Liberated Europe. After Yalta, Secretary of State Cordell Hull characterized the mood as one of "supreme exultation." He spoke ecstatically of the revolutionary effects to be secured by the establishment of the United Nations: "There will no longer be need for spheres of influence, for alliances, balance of power, or any other of the special arrangements through which, in the unhappy past, the nations strove to safeguard their security or promote their interests." This must surely rank as one of the most absurd statements in international literature. International organization, which, after all, is a mechanism, not a principle or a policy, was being portrayed as a magic wand that would make all politics and diplomacy obsolete.

Harry Hopkins, Roosevelt's friend and envoy, took naïve innocence to even greater heights when he later confessed:

> We really believed in our hearts that this was the dawn of the new day we had all been praying for and talking about for so many years . . . We were absolutely certain that we had won the first great victory of the peace . . . and by "we" I mean all of us, the whole civilized human race . . . The Russians had proved that they could be reasonable and far-seeing and there was not any doubt in the minds of the President or any of us that we could live with them peacefully for as far into the future as any of us could imagine.

This absolute certainty had no basis except wishful thinking. The auguries of a militant Soviet attitude were already plain to see. As we look back upon the diplomacy and public sentiment of 1945, it becomes clear that the euphoria of American statesmen was not reasonable even at the time. It should have been evident that there was not going to be any "dawn of [a] new day."

This dream of postwar harmony foundered quickly as the Soviet Union used the Red Army to consolidate its gains in Eastern Europe and impose its control. In the light of the emerging bipolar system as well as of the Russian historical experience, Soviet behavior in this period seems, in retrospect, inevitable and predictable. But in the eyes of American policymakers it was an unforeseen and ruthless retreat from the promise of cooperation. That the Soviets, after the loss of 20 million men in World War II, were responding to Russian national interest by creating an extensive security buffer on their border was incomprehensible to an American leadership that refused to understand that the wartime alliance had been a partnership of convenience, not a "marriage of true minds."

As the Soviets expanded their power, first in Eastern Europe, then in Iran, and set covetous eyes on Greece and Turkey, American public opinion shifted from a view of the Soviets as a heroic wartime ally to that of a rapacious and brutal enemy. There was no cause for surprise. The glib notion that victory in war makes for continued amity among the victors could have been refuted by any serious historian. Experience could have taught that triumphant nations who have suffered greatly in war are more conscious of their previous affliction than of their eventual success. The Russians, above all, were less concerned to celebrate their deliverance from peril than to thwart any chance that they would need to be delivered from it again.

Russian anxieties began to press and throb throughout the international system with an intensity that few had wanted to foresee. The Russians first tried to overstay their legitimate military presence in Iran, and were only dislodged by a determined campaign of quiet menace on the part of President Truman. They then put strong pressure on Turkey for control of the Dardanelles and the Bosphorus, concentrating troops on the Turkish frontier and declaiming vigorously against British influence. Truman, still in his Palmerstonian mood, dispatched a naval force to the eastern Mediterranean. Stalin retreated from his threats. By now Britain, weighed down by economic stress, sought relief from its commitments to help defend Turkey and Greece. The United States, in sharp deviation from its traditions, forgot all about "nonentanglement" and entangled itself in Europe's future for good and all in 1947 with the Truman Doctrine and the Marshall Plan for European recovery. Moscow rejected participation in the European recovery program and organized the economy of Eastern Europe in a separate framework.

A year later, in March 1948, the democratic regime in Czechoslovakia was brutally suppressed by Moscow. The Western nations under American leadership established the NATO alliance in a mood of vigilant alarm. Protesting against moves by the Western powers to unite their occupation zones in Germany, the Soviet Union in June 1948 blocked all access except by air to Berlin. The West was here in a position of acute topographical disadvantage, but it made a spirited response with the massive airlift of June 1948 to September 1949. The Soviets lifted their blockade. Meanwhile Communist Chinese forces under Mao Zedong had secured control of all Chinese territory except the island of Formosa (Taiwan). Many Americans had become resigned to the domestic results of the Chinese revolution but not to a further expansion of it through what they believed to be a Soviet-sponsored invasion of South Korea by North Korea in June 1950. The United States was able to send forces against North Korea under an international flag, thanks to the obtuse absence of the USSR from its seat in the UN Security Council. Thus, five crowded years after the end of the war, the world was looking grotesquely unlike that of which Roosevelt, Hopkins and Hull had dreamed and spoken.

The main question at issue was to haunt a whole generation and is still a central theme of international life—the status of Poland. In the Declaration on Liberated Europe of February 11, 1945, the Western powers and the Soviet Union had agreed that Poland should have "democratic institutions of [its] own choice." But this promise was qualified by the condition that Poland must have a government "friendly to the Soviet Union." Moscow's interpretation was—and is

—that "friendship" can only be secured if the Soviet Union has complete control over the behavior of any Polish government.

Back in Moscow, Ambassador Averell Harriman thought that he had achieved some gain by persuading Stalin to send his Foreign Minister, V. M. Molotov, to talk to Truman in Washington. The idea that every difficult condition can be improved by high-level dialogue is one of the more persistent diplomatic illusions. When Molotov came to confront Truman in the White House on May 26, 1945, it became evident that no situation is so bad that a badly conceived summit meeting cannot make it worse.

Molotov appealed to Russian vulnerability as a reason for seeking Soviet agreement on the composition of the Polish government. It is difficult to treat this theme without eloquence and emotion, but Molotov seems to have tried—and succeeded. Truman's response was rigorously formalistic. All that the Soviet Union had to do was to carry out the Yalta accord, agree to free elections in Poland and accept the fortune of the result. Molotov said, "I have never been talked to like that in my life." Truman replied, "Carry out your agreements and you won't have to be talked to like that."

If the Creator of the Universe were setting the stage for a Cold War, he could not possibly have cast the leading actors more authentically than by the choice of Truman and Molotov.

For some years after the end of World War II, traditional thinking and literature in the West described the origins of the Cold War in moralistic terms. According to this view the fault lay exclusively with the Soviet Union, which disrupted all hope of stability by attempting to extend its control beyond its legitimate borders deep into the territory of contiguous states. In this vision of history, American leaders, especially Truman and Dean Acheson, appear as the defenders of international order against arbitrary aggression. In later years when the Vietnam trauma had inspired American thinkers with a pervasive instinct for self-criticism, a revisionist literature developed in America. Some hard questions were asked. Was Truman really justified in dealing so severely with Molotov's message about Russian security? Was the Russian insistence on a defensive ring in Eastern Europe as preposterous as it appeared? In Russia, after all, there were 20 million dead at the hands of the Germans; American losses had been less than half a million. There was nothing remarkable or new about the tendency of Russians to see their environment as dominated by aggressive neighbors bent on their destruction. The Russian sense of vulnerability has been eloquently portrayed by one of the first writers to put the origins of the Cold War in a balanced perspective:

*While America, protected by the Atlantic ocean from superior European
land powers, was expanding westward over an empty continent in relative
security against external attack, the Russian community was expanding
eastward over an empty continent, at all times exposed to, and relatively
defenseless against, external attack by major land powers of Europe. Once
free from the Mongol yoke, Russia was obligated repeatedly to fight for
national survival against formidable foes—to the north, to the west, to the
south. Disunity and weakness in the heart of Muscovy have usually led to
invasion or intervention from abroad by Swedes, Germans, Lithuanians
and Poles in the Mongol period; by Turkey, Poland and Sweden in the late
16th, 17th and early 18th centuries; by France in the early 19th century;
by Germany in World War I; by Poland, France, Britain, Japan and
America after World War I; and by Germany, Italy and their allies in
World War II. For nearly two centuries the central fact in American life
had been security. The central fact in Russian life had been danger and fear.
The Russian fear was older than the United States itself. For a thousand
years Russia had existed in mortal terror, stranded on the great plain of
Europe, lacking any defensive frontiers, and subjected to wave after wave
of invasion and devastation.*

This distrustful vision of a hostile world bent on the destruction of
Russia was not invented by the Communist regime. It was an integral
part of Russia's national memory. In reacting to this threat, the Communist leaders were following a normal thread of Russian psychological history. Communism has not caused Russia to act in terms of its
security any differently than it would have acted under another regime.
The ideology and rhetoric of Marxism determine how Russia explains
its actions; but the actions themselves are dictated by a permanent
experience. It was natural for Americans to feel that Russia was
stretching its claims to security too far to be tolerated by Western
minds. But it was unrealistic to hope that Russia would act as if it were
America and accept the fall of the dice in a free Polish election. The
American-Soviet rivalry, later known as the Cold War, was tragic in the
Greek sense: each party was acting under the compulsion of its own
nature from which there was no rational escape. It was a Greek tragedy
—a tragedy of compulsion; not a "Christian tragedy"—a tragedy of
choice.

There is no more striking example than the Cold War of the Hobbes-
ian theory of fear as the dominant impulse of social relations. Fear on
one side creates defensive reactions on the other, which in turn increase the fear which led to the initial reactions. This cycle was at work
in American-Soviet relations just as surely as it operates everywhere
else. This is the most constant element in international history. A
residue of fear and insecurity is built into any social relationship, be

it between individuals or states. Mere protestations of good faith can never eliminate it. Insecurity is as endemic to politics as is mortality to human life. It can be alleviated, mitigated, checked and sometimes transcended, but its shadow falls pervasively over the human landscape and no amount of utopian supplication will make it go away.

The Cold War was a duel. There had never been a time when two nations exerted such a dominating influence across the length and breadth of the international system. London, Paris, Berlin and Rome could not compare with Washington and Moscow in physical might or political dynamism. The decline of other nations left America and the Soviet Union in the field as the only global powers. Each of the two pursued its national goals with a sense of universal mission. America saw itself as the guardian of national liberties and individual freedoms against a new expansionist threat, while Russia assumed the glowing image of a revolutionary crusader calling oppressed multitudes to the affirmation of their equality. The conflict between them was to be enacted in an environment lacking all the attributes associated with a well-ordered domestic society. There was no community of values to moderate their contentions. Sharing no similar opinions of what is just and unjust, they competed in their different ways to impose their separate versions of the just order.

If it was unrealistic to expect the Soviet Union to respect the idea of democratic elections in a country firmly under its military control, it was similarly far-fetched to believe that any Western government in the aftermath of World War II would acquiesce in the total subordination of Polish freedom to Russian security. The war had been fought from 1939 in defense of Poland's independence; if it were to end with Poland enslaved there would be a sense of frustration and anticlimax. In the United States citizens of Polish origin urged opposition to the Soviet plan of absorbing their former homeland into its own jurisdiction.

However inevitable Russian dominance of Poland now may seem, it was natural that the United States should have objected. The American error was an error of illusion, not of policy. The expectation of a "new era of peace" was a fantasy which was totally unshared by those who had an intimate knowledge of the Russian mentality. George Kennan, looking back in 1982, recalls his own perceptions of the immediate postwar age:

> When I returned to Moscow in 1944, I was ... aware ... that the Soviet regime was not an easy one for us to have good relations with: a number of factors, such as the ideological preconceptions of the Soviet leaders, the

ingrained Russian habits of secrecy and suspicion of foreigners, the sharp differences between the two governmental and social systems, and, not least, the great cruelties the Stalin regime was already guilty of—precluded anything like a fully normal and pleasant relationship and left only a narrow area in which useful intercourse and collaboration was even conceivable. I saw, as the war approached its end, despite all the rosy pronouncements of President Roosevelt and others, no reason to expect or to hope that our relations with the Soviet regime would be any better after the war than they had been before—if anything rather the contrary . . . In short, I can give very little comfort, I am afraid, to the revisionist theses about the origins of the Cold War . . . The attitudes and behavior of the United States government were not the main factor in making the Cold War what we have known it to be . . .

The Truman Years (1945–1953)

Once it became clear to America's leaders that there would be no era of peaceful cooperation on terms acceptable to the United States, the debate on Soviet intentions and the appropriate American response became more intense. President Truman's advisers split into two camps. There were those who believed that the Soviets might actually attack Western Europe and that negotiations with the Soviets were a fruitless venture. Headed by Secretary of the Navy James V. Forrestal, this group argued for the revitalization of Germany in order to counter aggressive Soviet designs. A second group of more influential advisers, led by Secretary of State James F. Byrnes and presidential advisers Averell Harriman and Dean Acheson, felt that while a Soviet move into Western Europe was unlikely, the Russians were ruthlessly intent on consolidating their control over Eastern Europe. Negotiations with the Soviets might be successful, but only if the United States used its superior power to pry political and military concessions from them. Secretary of Commerce Henry Wallace alone believed that U.S.-Soviet relations were suffering from mutual misunderstanding in which each exaggerated the threat posed by the other. He even maintained what was then the heresy that the Soviet Union might have legitimate security interests in Eastern Europe. Two decades later Henry Kissinger could make an identical statement without sensation; the heresy of the 1940s would become the established doctrine of the 1970s. American policymakers are not rigidly closed in on "doctrines." Mobility in passing from one conception to another is a saving grace of American diplomacy.

A memorandum written by George Kennan, then an adviser to Harriman, ultimately helped to resolve the debate and to reinforce the

Administration's determination to counter Soviet power. In Kennan's view, Soviet policy was based on historic Russian expansionism, Stalin's psychological paranoia and Communist ideology—which together created overt hostility toward the West. Fearing capitalist encirclement, the Soviets would seek every opportunity to create docile client states. Too weak militarily to confront the West directly, the Soviets would attempt to undermine the capitalist states politically. Kennan proposed a major program of aid to resurrect Western Europe in order to discourage Soviet subversion. American policy would have to be one of "long-term, patient but firm and vigilant containment."

Kennan's memorandum, written with exceptional eloquence, had a profound impact on President Truman and other Administration leaders. It provided a conceptual framework for understanding and controlling Soviet behavior. Truman and his advisers took this analysis one step further (a step too far, as Kennan later claimed) when they argued that a strong military component as well as economic assistance was required to meet the challenge of Soviet expansionism.

When Britain announced in early 1947 that it would no longer be able to meet its traditional security responsibilities in Greece and Turkey, the United States stepped into the breach and provided economic and military assistance to the two threatened nations. While the new Secretary of State, George C. Marshall, argued against a dramatic appeal based on the aggressive intent of the Soviet Union in the area, Undersecretary Dean Acheson, presidential adviser Clark Clifford and the influential Republican Senator Arthur Vandenberg held that such an appeal was necessary to mobilize support for the aid package and to alert the public to the Soviet threat. President Truman went before a joint session of Congress on March 12, 1947, to deliver a message in which he used both the strategic and the idealistic arguments. He accused the Soviet Union of reckless expansionism and of seeking to impose totalitarian regimes on free peoples. Soviet policies were "undermining the foundations of international peace and hence the security of the United States." To counter the Soviets and protect the American way of life, it "must be the policy of the United States to support free peoples who are resisting attempted subjugation by armed minorities or outside pressure." This public declaration of America's willingness to provide external economic and military assistance to beleaguered governments—the Truman Doctrine—gave concrete expression to the idea of containment.

It is important to note several points about containment. First: Given Soviet goals in the immediate postwar era, and the essential bipolar distribution of power in the international system, America had little choice but to adopt a countervailing policy toward the Soviet Union. Although most Americans desired a return to domestic tranquillity, as evidenced by the rapid U.S. military demobilization, the facts of American power and responsibility required an assertive American role. Second: U.S. policy toward the Soviet Union was motivated less, in the initial stages, by anti-Communism than by the perception that the Soviets had disrupted the promised postwar order. Only later did an uncompromising anti-Communist ideology become a central element of containment. Third: While announced in typically universalist rhetoric and later applied on a global basis, containment was initially conceived as limited in its application. Containment was to be directed to the prevention of Soviet expansion into Western Europe alone. Here, the strategic imperatives of containment fitted conveniently into the advancement of America's democratic values. Containment of Russia could be equated with the defense of democracy because of the compatibility of American and Western European values. It soon became apparent that if containment was to be applied to other regions, particularly to Asia, American policymakers would face a dilemma. If the United States supported authoritarian regimes outside Europe, it would certainly help to halt Communism; but it would then be giving support to undemocratic values. This predicament has plagued American diplomacy throughout the postwar period. Strategic interests and human values seem to be in conflict almost everywhere outside Europe.

The aid program for Greece and Turkey was only a prelude to a massive commitment of economic and military assistance to the nations of Western Europe. Truman's key advisers, Marshall and Acheson, supported a program designed to nurse Europe's war-ravaged economies back to economic health. The infusion of aid under the Marshall Plan faced significant opposition in Congress from isolationists who felt that the United States was overextending its resources. However, Stalin's forcible incorporation of the only two democracies in Eastern Europe, Hungary and Czechoslovakia, was a convincing reminder of the need for a vigorous American response.

Another unintended effect of Stalin's policies in Eastern Europe was to lead Britain, France and the United States to unify the three Allied zones of occupation in Germany. Stalin, fearing a resurgent Germany, responded by blocking the land routes to West Berlin. Soon thereafter, Truman proposed the establishment of America's first peacetime alliance: U.S. membership and leadership in the North Atlantic Treaty Organization. There was isolationist sentiment in the Senate, particularly from conservative Republicans such as Robert A. Taft, who feared that the alliance could involve the United States in a war without the approval of the Congress; yet the NATO treaty was approved overwhelmingly. Thus by the late 1940s the structures of containment had been set into place and the lines of demarcation drawn between the power blocs. Within five years the great American isolationist tradition had been left behind. It is now a part of history, even if some of its attitudes still come to life in conditions of stress and perplexity.

Events in other regions of the world proved to be more fluid. They left American policymakers with only murky notions of how, when and if to apply containment in non-European settings. The Truman Administration faced its first major test outside Europe in the struggle between the Nationalist and the Communist forces in China. Initially hopeful of reconciling the two sides, the Administration by 1947 was faced with an unenviable choice between massive assistance to Chiang Kai-shek's faltering Kuomintang or acceptance of the Communists' looming triumph. When Acheson became Secretary of State in 1948, the Administration began to adopt the position that the Communist Chinese were more Chinese than Communist and might remain independent of Soviet influence. American aid to Chiang Kai-shek was accordingly lukewarm. In any case, Chiang Kai-shek headed a losing cause which no amount of American aid could have salvaged. Mao swept to victory and took full control of the mainland in October 1949.

Truman's decision not to undertake a major effort in support of Chiang Kai-shek, and the subsequent Communist victory, led to a storm of domestic protest. A group of Republican congressmen, organized in the China Lobby, became the most vituperative critics of U.S. foreign policy. They argued implausibly that the Nationalist forces with U.S. support would have been capable of saving China from the Communists. They also claimed that Mao, by aligning himself with Moscow, was creating a formidable power bloc hostile to American interests. Because of these strong domestic pressures, Truman refused to recognize the Communist regime or to support its admission to the United Nations. Moreover, the subsequent debate over "who lost China" exercised a stormy influence on the climate of public opinion and on the thinking of incumbent and future political leaders. Avoiding the stigma of being "soft" on Communism and the charge of "losing" a nation to Communist insurgency became ingrained in the conviction of American political leaders.

The rhetoric about "losing" China, Laos, Vietnam and Iran reveals one of the fallacies in American thinking about international issues. The idea of "losing" presupposes an initial degree of possession far beyond what ever existed. America has controlled and influenced many situations but has never possessed anything except itself. The legend based on the trauma of "losing China" was to distort American politics for nearly three decades.

Soon after the Communist victory in the Chinese civil war, North Korea invaded the South, in June 1950. Although there was no formal U.S. commitment to defend South Korea, domestic support for Truman's decision to send troops under the guise of a UN police action was nearly universal. When the U.S. military success at Inchon seemed to have provided the opportunity to reunite Korea under democratic rule, Truman allowed General Douglas MacArthur to advance into North Korea. In November 1950, however, the Chinese intervened across the Yalu River on a massive scale, driving U.S. forces southward. The aim of the war was changed in mid-course from the defense of South Korea to the "liberation" of the North. It was an unhappy hour in Truman's career. Neither he nor most of his advisers had anticipated Chinese intervention, but they had enough humility and resilience to return to the original goal of restoring the status quo in a divided Korea. The aim of liberating the North was then replaced by the original purpose of defending the South. This decision enraged MacArthur, who wanted a massive invasion of North Korea and strikes against China itself. His public defiance of Truman's orders resulted in his dismissal. There was much criticism of Truman from the right, but the presidential authority was asserted and strengthened with resounding force.

The stalemated Korean War dragged through mid-1953; it was to have many repercussions on future American policy. Perhaps most important, the Chinese intervention convinced most Americans that the Communist nations, as the China Lobby maintained, were a monolithic bloc threatening the security of the free world. Secondly, the defense of South Korea and the creation of a line of demarcation between the Communist zone and the South allowed American policy-makers to apply the idea of containment to an Asian setting. This misapplication of the idea of containment which had been developed in Europe was to be repeated with increasing frequency in the coming years. It contributed greatly to the overextension of American commitments, particularly in Southeast Asia. Finally, these two factors led to a "globalization" of the containment policy. The United States embarked on a missionary crusade to prevent the global spread of Communist influence. The Cold War was no longer restricted to Europe; the whole world became an arena for the gladiatorial struggle between the forces of good and evil. And the contest was envisaged as a zero-sum game. Every victory for one side was regarded, sometimes without proof, as a loss for the other. The transformation of the United States from a nation largely isolationist in its outlook to a world power maintaining eternal vigilance against the Communist bloc had occurred within less than a decade.

By the end of the Truman Administration the picture of the new postwar order was clearly drawn. Lines were fixed in Europe and Korea, and Washington had become the center of the free world's military, political and economic struggle against Communism. Militarily, the United States' commanding nuclear arsenal and its unchallenged air and naval power protected its allies against Communist aggression. Economically, it had revived the war-ravaged nations of Western Europe and had created the institutional structures—the International Monetary Fund, the World Bank and the General Agreement on Tariffs and Trade—for the postwar international economic system. Politically, the United States had seen its dream of the UN realized, and it had fulfilled a moral obligation to the survivors of the Holocaust by helping the establishment and consolidation of the State of Israel.

Truman was greatly admired during the Cold War years. In the aftermath of the Vietnam debacle and during the détente period, his presidency became subject to revisionist criticism. He was judged to have shown a greater talent for resistance than for initiative. The test came when containment had secured its objective and the adversary might have been ready for accommodation. Some believe that this moment was already reached in 1949 when the Soviet Union was sufficiently impressed by American determination to be ready for compromise. Truman and his advisers, especially the severe Acheson, never tested the possibility of a transition from confrontation to negotiation, and the Cold War was passed on to their successors with its temperature unchanged.

Another curious feature of the American people's indulgent attitude to the Truman years was the avoidance of any agonizing judgment on the use of atomic bombs against Japan. It is now a truism that the guiding principle of nuclear strategy is deterrence, not actual use of the ultimate weapons. The fact that the deterrent stage was omitted in 1945 was calmly accepted at the time and was very rarely criticized in subsequent years. In the advanced stages of a general war there was none of the acute sensitivity about human life that comes to expression when military actions erupt suddenly out of a state of peace.

The Truman years are the constitutive period in the history of modern American diplomacy. Little substantive change was to be recorded until the aftermath of the Vietnam war, and much of the vocabulary and conceptual habits of American thinking on international politics have become firmly embedded in the national consciousness ever since. The central themes are activism, responsibility, a wide vision of America's place in the world and a particular emphasis on the vocation of the United States to be the protector of democracy as a universal cause threatened by the dynamism of Soviet expansion. The notion of America as the central pillar in an enduring coalition of which Western Europe is the main partner was by no means to be taken for granted in the light of the historic experience and prejudices of the United States. Truman may be said to have established this idea so firmly that no successor has ever felt moved to challenge it. It was during this period also that the links of the United States to an alliance system were institutionalized so heavily that the option of a return to the ideas of "normalcy" and isolation was effectively eliminated.

But American society did not emerge unscathed from this revolutionary transition to a permanent world role. The Soviet Union and Joseph McCarthy in their separate ways had succeeded in involving Americans in a senseless campaign to demonstrate their own "loyalty." It is hard to think of a more flag-conscious people or one so permeated by a sense of patriotic pride. And yet here was the Truman Administration dealing in loyalty oaths, cooperating deferentially with absurdly inquisitorial congressional committees and behaving as though tens of thousands of Americans really harbored malicious intentions toward their own country. There was never the slightest basis for any belief that "disloyalty" was even a faintly marginal problem in American society at any time. Yet Truman, for all his reputation for robust defiance, never succeeded in extricating himself entirely from preoccupation with a nonexistent threat.

His virtue lay in an awesome power of clear-cut decision. His weakness as an educator of public opinion was highlighted by the defects of his rhetoric; there was never any prospect that a striking thought or phrase would illuminate the flat plains of his utterance. With all his dedication to international causes he was essentially a parochial American, living very close to his original soil and faintly suspicious of the external domain. Letters published in the first months of 1983 reveal that his sense of the world developed late in his career under the stimulus of responsibility. As a young man writing to his bride and family he would allow himself some conventional vulgarities about "niggers and Chinamen and Japs"; and he reflected on the dream of "keeping Europe and America for white men, Asia for yellow people and Africa for blacks." As with many Americans the world war broke down this provincialism and equipped him to speak and act for an America that had renounced the dream of a fortress existence. But he never overcame a visceral distrust of "foreigners"—a heading in which he tended to include his own State Department, whom he envisaged in such stereotypes as "striped-pants boys" and "cookie-pushers."

Truman left the daily conduct of diplomacy to his two successive secretaries of state, George C. Marshall and Dean G. Acheson. To the former he evinced a touching deference so strong as to blur the very fact of hierarchical rank; one would have thought that Marshall was the commander in chief and Truman his subordinate. With Acheson, Truman formed what a later generation would have called a "strange couple." Acheson was a man of many certainties and few doubts. He gave the impression of aloofness, sharpened by a conspicuous formality of dress and speech, but he had a developed sense of personality and was penetrating and, on the whole, benevolent in his amused judgment of other statesmen. His diplomacy was in the classic tradition; the emphasis was on European humanism, reticence and pragmatic bargaining based on interests and free from sentimentality. It would have been surprising to hear him express an interest in the Third World or in Latin America, and his travels were almost exclusively conducted within the European orbit that would have been familiar to the participants in the Congress of Vienna. The business at hand was to draw America and Europe together in attachment to common values and in frank but serene confrontation with the adversary outside the gates. Under his leadership the Department of State developed a strong sense of professional competence. Public opinion and the Congress, in Acheson's view, were intruders who sometimes had to be humored and placated, more out of constitutional loyalty than through any real hope that they would add enlightenment. He and Truman were the sort of people who by virtue of their style and idiom would normally find each other incompatible; yet their friendship was sustained in all circumstances and conditions throughout and beyond their memorable term of office.

The Eisenhower Years (1953–1961)

Dwight D. Eisenhower was elected in 1952, when a broad consensus had already emerged for the conduct of United States foreign policy. While most Americans wanted an end to the stalemate in Korea, they also seemed to desire an even more active posture of resistance to Communism. Indeed, the 1952 election was largely fought on the unattractive theme of "Who do the Communists fear most?"

Eisenhower received so massive an endorsement that he could afford to choose his own style without excessive deference to his campaign oratory. He quickly discarded one of the assumptions of the Truman years—that direct negotiation with the Soviet Union would be fruitless. Truman, unlike his successors, had not been an enthusiastic summiteer or a confirmed foreign traveler. He was quite content to deal with the Soviet Union by remote control, and he resigned himself to the idea that he would never set eyes on Stalin after Potsdam. Eisenhower, on the other hand, favored dialogue. He promptly overruled the skepticism of his Secretary of State, John Foster Dulles, who advocated a less conciliatory approach in dealing with the Soviets. Eisenhower's negotiating posture paid dividends. Following Stalin's death, an armistice to end the Korean War was achieved in July 1953. Face-to-face negotiations between Eisenhower and Soviet Premier Nikolai Bulganin in 1955 created the "Spirit of Geneva"—an alleviation of the Cold War atmosphere. The superpowers also managed to untangle the question of Austria and to agree on its neutralization and unification through the negotiation of a state treaty.

The thaw in superpower relations, however, was interrupted by the Soviet invasion of Hungary in 1956. It ended completely in 1958 when Soviet Premier Khrushchev began his three-year offensive against Berlin, involving the harassment of convoys from the West and demands for the withdrawal of Western troops from the city. Relations were further worsened by the shooting down of a U-2 spy plane over Soviet territory and the subsequent breakdown of the Big Four summit conference in Paris in 1960.

There were also tensions with the other leading member of what was still called the Communist bloc, China. In 1954 and again in 1958, the Chinese threatened the Nationalist-controlled offshore islands of Quemoy and Matsu. In both instances, many of Eisenhower's advisers recommended a military response ranging from a naval blockade to a bombardment of the Chinese mainland. Dulles went so far as to suggest that the United States threaten "massive retaliation" against the Chinese. Eisenhower resisted these military options and chose to downplay the significance of the islands. His cool manipulation of authority was little admired at the time, but after the hectic adventures of the 1960s and 1970s, Eisenhower became canonized nostalgically as an effective compromiser. His Administration signed a mutual defense pact with Taiwan in 1954, but his dispatch of the U.S. Seventh Fleet to the Formosa Straits was a signal intended just as much to restrain Taipei as to deter the Communists. Eisenhower also initiated low-level diplomatic discussions with the Communist Chinese at the U.S. embassy in Warsaw; this channel was later to prove useful to Kissinger in his overtures to China.

But the great cloud was already on the horizon. Vietnam first became a focus of attention during the Eisenhower Administration. In early 1954 France requested U.S. military assistance to help break the Vietnamese siege of Dien Bien Phu. Dulles, Vice President Richard Nixon and the Chairman of the Joint Chiefs Admiral Arthur Radford all supported the use of American air power and the eventual deployment of U.S. ground personnel, if necessary. While Eisenhower denied the request for immediate U.S. military assistance, he clearly hoped after the 1954 Geneva Agreements that the Communists of the North could be prevented from taking over the South. To this end, he sent 700 military advisers to help train the South Vietnamese armed forces. The snowball was to become an avalanche.

Although there was a broad consensus during the Eisenhower presidency governing American policy toward the Communist bloc nations, the Administration's policies toward the developing world were less

coherent and more subject to criticism, this time from the Democratic
left rather than the Republican right. Adlai Stevenson and J. William
Fulbright both urged greater emphasis on economic rather than military aid, and more tolerance of the neutral course that several key
developing countries sought to steer between the rival superpowers.
According to this view America, because of its own anticolonial and
revolutionary heritage, should have aligned itself more closely with
decolonization and should have given more encouragement to modernization and democracy.

Yet, in actual policy terms, few if any critics dared to appear "soft"
on Communism, wherever and in whatever form it might appear—
even after Senator Joseph McCarthy's censure by the Senate and his
downfall in 1954. Eisenhower's policy of active opposition to what
were judged to be anti-Western governments in the Third World
encountered little domestic opposition. Dulles pursued what his adversaries called a policy of "pactomania," drawing contractual lines
throughout the Middle East and Asia to mark that which "belonged"
to the West in the Cold War. It was a classic "spheres of influence"
approach. But with decolonization under way and with rising nationalism rampant in many nations in the Third World, the alliances which
the United States formed in these regions often worked at cross-
purposes with containment. American support for authoritarian and
traditional regimes frequently served as a lightning rod for anti-
Americanism, and in many instances led to increased turmoil and
unrest—in Lebanon, in Iraq, in Batista's Cuba. Revolutionary forces
seeking Soviet assistance rationalized their conduct with the assertion
that the United States was the incorrigible champion of an intolerable
status quo.

In the meantime, Eisenhower and Dulles could record what they
deemed to be short-term successes in their struggle against Communism. In Iran in 1953, the CIA aided internal opposition to overthrow
the government of Mossadeq, which had threatened to nationalize
Western petroleum companies and raise the export price of oil. In the
wider historical perspective this American intervention would be of
dubious benefit. It committed the United States to support Shah Mo-
hammed Pahlevi with an effusiveness that sometimes reached absurdly
exaggerated limits. When the inevitable revolutionary reaction came,
the United States would be on the losing side. In 1954, Guatemalan
exiles who opposed the reformist policies of President Jacobo Arbenz
were trained, financed and provided with military equipment by the
CIA. They were successful in overthrowing the Arbenz government in
an invasion from neighboring Honduras. American advisers and
matériel were instrumental in the coup. In 1958, the Congress gave
Eisenhower strong bipartisan support when he sent 14,000 Marines to

Lebanon to protect the pro-Western government threatened with internal disintegration. While American opinion endorsed these ventures at the time, it cannot be doubted that a record of American intervention was being built up and that this cast a shadow on the indignation of the United States when the Soviet Union took military action in its own "sphere of influence."

At the same time Eisenhower sought to preserve U.S. influence in the developing world, even at the risk of alienation from European allies. While he continued the general policy of support for Israel, he angrily opposed the British-French-Israeli attempt of October 1956 to topple Egypt's Nasser by military action. He would not permit France and Britain to renew their colonial hegemony. The United States even joined with the Soviet Union in a UN resolution condemning the invasion. Eisenhower compelled the NATO allies to withdraw from the Suez Canal and the Israelis to pull back from Sinai and Gaza. It was a rare case in modern history of a Great Power acting in the name of a principle against what appeared to be its own strategic interests—against its allies and in concert with its adversaries. The deviation was short-lived. Nasser proved an ungrateful recipient of American protection. He acted against U.S. interests in every part of the globe, and the landings of the U.S. forces in Lebanon in 1958 were directed against Egypt—to the sardonic satisfaction of Britain, France and Israel.

One of the most controversial policies of the Eisenhower Administration was its nuclear weapons strategy. America possessed a clear nuclear advantage even after the Soviets' successful atomic bomb test in 1949 and its hydrogen bomb test in 1954. But the United States had failed to develop an appropriate doctrine for applying the nuclear weapon to America's advantage in the containment of the Soviets. After the Korean War, American strategists sought some way to avoid fighting limited, indecisive wars around the globe. Dulles and Radford continued to advocate "massive retaliation"—threatening a large-scale attack against the Soviet homeland with a risk of nuclear escalation in order to deter Communist subversion of pro-Western nations. It was hoped that this threat would prevent future Koreas and reduce the need for the United States to maintain expensive conventional forces across the world.

Critics of the slogan of "massive retaliation" argued in the late 1950s that the policy was flawed on several counts. First, with the growing nuclear capability of the Soviet Union, a policy that could precipitate retaliation against the U.S. homeland was reckless. Second, threatening a nuclear response to a limited Communist insurgency simply lacked the credibility requisite for its effectiveness. How could threats of U.S. massive retaliation have prevented such events as the Soviet invasion of Hungary or the rise of Castro in Cuba? It was simply beyond belief. America's possession of a nuclear arsenal seemed capable—at most—of deterring a massive attack against the United States or against Western Europe. It could not counter limited aggression elsewhere. The vaster the power, the more restricted was its potential use.

After the Soviet Union successfully launched the Sputnik satellite in 1957, critics of the Eisenhower Administration became increasingly exercised about the intercontinental nuclear threat. The ostensible Soviet lead in rocket technology, particularly evident after the numerous failures of U.S. missile tests, soon led to the issue of the "missile gap," which became prominent in the 1960 presidential campaign of John F. Kennedy. It would soon become clear that the Sputnik should not have led America into such hysterical attitudes concerning its own scientific and technological capacity. Nor was the alleged missile gap a solid reality. It is instructive, however, to note that the new era of Democratic predominance in American politics began with an attack on the Republicans from the right. In Europe, parties that are more liberal in their social outlook tend to be less militant in their foreign relations. This was not true of the United States in the late 1950s and early 1960s. The Eisenhower regime was often vehement in its anti-Communist rhetoric, but careful not to translate oratory into action.

In the light of the Vietnam war, which was mainly the work of the activist school in American diplomacy, many scholars and political thinkers have become fascinated by the idea that success may be achieved not so much by doing great things as by avoiding foolish things. This notion is at the root of a more respectful appraisal of the Eisenhower era than was prevalent during his period of office. In a careful study, Robert Divine summarizes the diplomacy of the early and mid-fifties as follows:

> He [Eisenhower] ended the Korean War, he refused to intervene militarily in Indochina, he refrained from involving the United States in the Suez crisis, he avoided war with China [over Quemoy and Matsu], he resisted the temptation to force a showdown after Berlin, he stopped exploding nuclear weapons in the atmosphere.

The words "refused," "refrained," "avoided," "resisted the temptation," "stopped" do not have a heroic ring. But when Americans later came to reflect on what had resulted from the busy, energetic, daring leaders of later years they had a nostalgic twinge of affection for leaders who were capable of constructive inaction.

Stereotyped images of Eisenhower portrayed him as amiable, indolent and uninterested in domestic politics. More thorough research and recollection refute all these epithets. He was quick-tempered,

authoritative, addicted to incessant labor and so fascinated by the
internecine party politics of America that he became an electoral champion, capable of obtaining the presidency in any competition with
anyone at any time. The charge against him is that while he avoided
the kind of sensational failures that afflicted his successors from the
Bay of Pigs to Vietnam and Cambodia, he did not put his formidable
assets to work in their full potentiality. His predominance in domestic
opinion would have made it easier for him than for his successors to
seek an opening to China, to explore the possibilities of tough but
continuous negotiation with the Soviet Union and to make a serious
bid for overriding influence in the Third World. He tended to exercise
his extraordinary capacity for leadership by leading his nation in the
direction that it wanted to go, which was not necessarily the direction
that it ought to have followed. But he did not renounce any part of the
presidential prerogative in foreign affairs, or show obeisance to military advisers, or refrain from a courageous and memorable warning of
the undue influence that might come to flow from the "military-indus-
trial complex," nor did he indulge in the rhetoric of universal responsibility. The Presidents who came after him served Eisenhower's image
more than he had done himself.

His foreign policy was energetically executed by John Foster Dulles,
whose personality seemed even less harmonious with that of his President than Acheson's had been with Truman. Dulles was a man of many
gifts, which did not, however, include a capacity to win trust and
affection. It was said of him that his problem was not that he had
enemies but that his friends found it difficult to like him. His policy had
its own rationale. His "balance of power" doctrine was a familiar part
of diplomatic history, and his habit of emphasizing the adversarial
image of the Soviet Union could be defended as well as opposed on
purely pragmatic grounds. If one wants to mobilize the American
people for a policy of strength and involvement, it is no use telling
them that Soviet policy is innocuous. But what disconcerted many
Americans in Dulles was his attempt to clothe his defense of American
interests in the sanctimonious garb of a moral crusade. His experience
and professionalism were widely respected, but his claim to a particular spirituality was not taken seriously. He always managed to make his
moral principles coincide with his material aims. Whenever he wrestled with his conscience he tended to win. He also nourished an irrational belief in the power of contracts to define and systematize the
international community. His attempts to organize the "free world" by
a series of treaty signatures eventually dissolved, leaving almost no
trace behind. Middle Eastern states resented the abortive "Baghdad
Pact" as an intervention in Arab politics; the result was an Egyptian
flirtation with Moscow. In Eastern Asia a fragile grouping called
SEATO (South East Asia Treaty Organization) merely called attention

to the refusal of most states in the area to join it. Dulles's refusal to recognize the nonalignment motif in the outlook of new states prevented the United States from developing a normal relationship with Asia and Africa. His reputation in the Atlantic alliance was also varied. He was popular in West Germany as a result of his close friendship with Konrad Adenauer, but his lack of fidelity to the concerns of France and Britain led to a crisis in 1956, when he first encouraged London and Paris to resist Nasser's seizure of the Suez Canal and then turned his back on them when they resisted too strongly. He had a vision of a world in which the friends and foes of his country would face each other in neatly defined columns like the portrayal of great armies in nineteenth-century battle paintings. He seemed to have no sense of the gray, blurred ambiguities that constitute a great part of international history and reality. He brought an excessively subtle mind into the service of an excessively simplistic view of the world order.

The Kennedy Years (1961–1963)

The advent of John F. Kennedy sharpened the tone of American policy. An abrasive style toward America's adversaries mingled with a promise of tutelary protection for America's friends. Kennedy was no rebel against the idea of containment or the rhetoric of the Cold War. He could easily rise beyond moral concerns, and he held the "softness" of liberals in open contempt. He brought his country closer to the brink of nuclear war than did any other President before or after, and he took decisive steps into the Vietnam quagmire. He began with an astonishing claim to universal hegemony: "We will pay any price, bear any burden, meet any hardship, support any friend, oppose any foe to assure the survival and success of liberty." The advisers that Kennedy brought to Washington, "the best and the brightest," were infused with an activist spirit reflecting their generation's experience in World War II. They were unsentimental, muscular and not afflicted by self-doubt. The American economy was entering a period of brisk growth in the early 1960s, and this permitted the nation to watch Kennedy's daring posture in foreign affairs with relaxed docility.

He wasted little time. In March 1961 he proposed an "Alliance for Progress" for Latin America in the hope that U.S. economic aid in that region, like the Marshall Plan for Europe, would spur economic growth and contain Communist influence, particularly in Castro's Cuba. During his three years in office, Kennedy also raised the defense budget by 20 percent, began a major naval shipbuilding program and placed some 300,000 reservists on active duty. Financial cares were not an obsessive concern in Camelot.

But the Kennedy Administration, despite its optimistic mood, also knew the taste of early defeat. The abortive invasion of Cuba, at the

Bay of Pigs in April 1961, shook Kennedy's confidence in his own intelligence agency. It has been said that there are three kinds of intelligence—criminal, human and military. The Bay of Pigs was conceived by the CIA Director Allen Dulles. The purpose of the operation was to overthrow Castro by landing a group of Cuban exiles who would foment internal opposition to the regime. The exiles were captured as soon as they landed on the beaches; there was not even a hint of an uprising. This was a major humiliation for the United States. Meanwhile, in Berlin, the construction of the Berlin Wall in August 1961 demonstrated to Kennedy that even an activist American policy could not prevent actions by the Soviets within their own sphere of influence.

But a year later, the pendulum of the Cold War swung back in Kennedy's favor. The Cuban missile crisis of October 1962, in which the Soviet Union attempted to install medium-range nuclear missiles in Cuba, provided an opportunity for the Administration to recoup some of the prestige lost in the Bay of Pigs fiasco. With a decisive intercontinental advantage and superior conventional forces in the Caribbean, Kennedy was able to enforce a limited blockade of Cuba and use American leverage to force Khrushchev to remove the missiles. Significantly, Kennedy resisted pressures to respond more provocatively with an air strike against the missile sites or with an actual invasion. His handling of the crisis demonstrated his leadership abilities; it also provided evidence of the overall military superiority of the United States. But the American people watched the approach to the nuclear brink with a public anxiety that bordered on hysteria. Many asked themselves if a few missiles in Cuba really justified such a momentous hazard. Some foreign leaders shared those doubts. (For example, Israeli Prime Minister David Ben-Gurion, by no means a pacifist, believed that Kennedy was irresponsibly taking vast risks for gains of limited importance.)

The successful conclusion of the Cuban missile crisis marked the zenith of American power and influence in the postwar world. New strategies were developed to apply this power, including counterinsurgency in local, limited conflicts in the Third World. Kennedy expanded the U.S. role in Vietnam, increasing the number of military advisers to 150,000 as well as conniving in the overthrow of the Diem government in Saigon.

The flirtation with nuclear cataclysm during the Cuban missile crisis also led the Kennedy Administration to consider new strategies at the nuclear level. Secretary of Defense Robert McNamara noted that the huge arsenals of the superpowers provided for "mutual assured destruction." Nuclear war had become unthinkable; it could only lead to national suicide, and could no longer serve any conceivable political goal. Shaken by the missile crisis, the superpowers moved toward arms control negotiations. In July 1963 they signed a limited test-ban treaty.

American power abroad and a booming economy at home seemed to signal to many Americans an unending era of prosperity and peace. But illusion was to be short-lived. An assassin's bullet cut short the term of President Kennedy. His successor, Lyndon B. Johnson, inherited not only the great military and economic power of the United States but also the policies and advisers of the Kennedy Administration. One policy in particular, counterinsurgency, applied in a faraway nation, Vietnam, would ultimately shatter the illusion of American omnipotence and the consensus underlying the conduct of American foreign policy.

Before examining the tragedy of Vietnam, it is necessary to re-evaluate the practice of containment. Despite the initial inexperience of American leaders in power politics on a world scale, U.S. policymakers at the beginning of the postwar era did succeed in practicing a diplomacy of power and proportion. Extravagant declarations notwithstanding, American policy recognized limits, accepted spheres of influence and engaged in universal diplomatic discourse, even with Communist countries. But anti-Communism was still a tempting means of mobilizing support for U.S. policy. In order to arouse public opinion for external commitments, the struggle for power and security often had to be presented as a pursuit of higher values—democracy, freedom and social justice. American leaders could practice realpolitik in the world system so long as that practice could be justified and explained in terms of an idealistic purpose—anti-Communism served that purpose. In practice the strategic and ideological purposes converged. It was difficult at a given moment to decide if the United States was confronting the Soviet Union out of fidelity to anti-Communism or in defense of strategic interests. Probably both motives were at work.

A national style that responded well to U.S. domestic politics had ambiguous consequences in foreign policy. Once anti-Communism was employed to justify a more active policy to an otherwise uninterested domestic audience, it had an inadvertent feedback effect. To be "soft" on Communism amounted to near treason; to "lose" a country to the Communists was tantamount to political suicide. The hysteria of the McCarthy period and the "loss" of China introduced into the American psyche a reflexive anti-Communism. As a result, American policy was subject to overreaction and a rigid ideological approach to revolutionary change in the Third World. U.S. efforts to resist change, either overtly or covertly, were seldom successful. Ultimately, America's inability to perceive the indigenous character of revolutionary movements led to the misapplication of American power, most dramatically—and most painfully—in Vietnam.

Kennedy's impact on the international community closely paralleled his domestic reverberation. His youth and style, which separated him from the previous generation, excited the hope of innovation and initiative. Of the eight Presidents since Roosevelt, Kennedy alone did not come to his task from a small-town environment with a regional, inner-looking outlook. His was not the America of Independence, Missouri, or Abilene, Texas, or Johnson City, Texas, or Whittier, California, or Grand Rapids, Michigan, or Plains, Georgia. The birthplaces of the other Presidents were not wide open to the outside world or intimately linked with a non-American reality, so that their education in the school of international entanglements reflected high credit on their subsequent adaptability. Kennedy was born into a world of metropolitan concerns, and some of his formative years were spent in London at an embassy residence at the heart of the central international crisis. The method and atmosphere of international discourse held no secrets for him.

Three years were not a sufficient period in which to deploy these advantages, and such time as he had was so overshadowed by the single drama of the Cuban missiles that historians have little else on which to base an appraisal of what his foreign policy would have been. It would not be unjust to conclude that he was more at home in the understanding and manipulation of power than in the exploration of ideas. He accepted the international landscape that he inherited from Truman and Eisenhower as a reality not susceptible to easy variation, and moved within it in a strong, assured and assertive manner. The group that he gathered around him included men such as Adlai Stevenson, Chester Bowles and Kenneth Galbraith who would have been happy with an America showing a more accommodating face to the nonaligned world, but the dominant memory in Kennedy's mind was of how appeasement led to danger and how unchecked aggression grew from small to large arenas until it went beyond control. The mechanical application of these lessons from European history to the remote areas of Southeast Asia led to an embarrassing conclusion. America's greatest international error—Vietnam—was committed under the aegis of the presidential team most versed in the ways of the world and most at home in the concepts and traditions of diplomacy.

Johnson and the Ordeal of Vietnam

In a relatively brief period, from the Cuban missile crisis of 1962 to the Tet offensive of 1968, the United States went from a mood of supreme confidence in its power and purpose to an attitude of disillusionment, self-questioning and recrimination. Within a few years there would be domestic criticism of U.S. involvement in Vietnam, and attacks on U.S. defense spending, on military aid and on the multiplication of U.S. commitments abroad. But no such fears attended the early stages of the Vietnam involvement. When Johnson made the crucial decision in 1965 to escalate the war in Vietnam still further by sending large numbers of U.S. ground troops, it was axiomatic that Communist expansion anywhere had to be resisted even at heavy cost. Johnson confided to then U.S. Ambassador to South Vietnam Henry Cabot Lodge: "I am not going to lose Vietnam. I am not going to be the President who saw Southeast Asia go the way of China." When the failure of the French armies created a vacuum of power in Indochina, the United States moved in just as it had done when a British retreat created a vacuum in Turkey and Greece. But the analogy was not relevant. Kennedy had ignored De Gaulle's warning that Vietnam would be "an entanglement without end." It was more intelligent for France to move out than for America to move in.

The "domino theory" played a critical role in providing the rationale for U.S. involvement. It was argued that if South Vietnam were overrun it would be only a matter of time before the Communists, emboldened by their victory, would seek to spread their gains throughout Southeast Asia. Thus, the adversary needed to be stopped at the earliest possible stage in order to deny him the fruits of future aggression. Seldom was U.S. policy focused on any tangible vital national interest in Vietnam itself. The Vietnam war, paradoxical as it may now seem, had an idealistic motive. America would gain no wealth or power. It would only vindicate a principle and an idea. U.S. leaders were dominated in their thinking by habits of analogy and obsessed by the notion of contagion. They believed that any failure to defend South Vietnam would be interpreted by other allies, particularly in the Third World, as a general weakening of American resolve. This, in turn, would lead them toward accommodation with revolutionary forces. In this sense, Vietnam was fought not to end all wars, but to prevent the United States, through deterrent example, from having to fight any future wars, however limited or local.

It is important to note that this fear of an epidemic of aggression was widespread during the initial phases of the U.S. build-up in Asia. The Gulf of Tonkin Resolution, which authorized the President to use military force to prevent further aggression, showed the degree of congressional acceptance of the domino theory and the acquiescence of the Congress in the executive's decisive role in foreign affairs.

Ironically, perhaps, the successful but morally dubious use of American combat forces in the Dominican Republic in April 1965 may have contributed to the decision later that year to send combat forces to Vietnam. In response to an incipient civil war between leftist forces and the government, the United States sent 30,000 troops to ensure that there would not be "another Cuba" in the Caribbean.

An incidental result of American intervention in the Dominican Republic and in Guatemala, and of the activist policy pursued in the Cuban missile crisis, was the weakening of the moral basis of American resistance to Soviet encroachment in Eastern Europe. In theory, all states have "equal sovereignty." In practice, states who are the neighbors of a superpower exercise a sovereignty of constraint. They are "free" to have regimes which the neighboring superpower does not consider hostile to its interest. The USSR interprets this as a positive right of direct control. The United States is content with a more moderate negative criterion: the neighbor must not be "free" to align itself with America's adversaries. The general effect is to demonstrate that the idea of spheres of influence which many Americans greet with rhetorical revulsion is no more obsolete in practice than the idea of balance of power. Indeed, one of the fascinations of modern diplomatic history is the durability of old practices in an arena that is, in general, marked by a spectacular pace of change.

But Vietnam, unlike the Dominican Republic, was not on America's doorstep, and the North Vietnamese were not a disorganized band of fledgling revolutionaries. They had cast off the yoke of one colonial power in their defeat of France in 1954, and they were well skilled in the conduct of a guerrilla war. As has been demonstrated time and again in anticolonial revolts in the developing world, guerrilla warfare is an effective strategy by which a small, lightly armed insurgent force can frustrate a larger and better equipped power by means of discipline, knowledge of local conditions and, above all, a strong political motivation. U.S. forces were ill-prepared to cope with these conditions of guerrilla war in the developing world. Thus, despite the increased commitment of U.S. military forces to over half a million troops by 1968, "victory"—even defined in limited terms as the preservation of a pro-American regime in Saigon—was no closer. Secretary of Defense McNamara resigned after Johnson twice rejected his advice to halt the bombing of the North and freeze U.S. troop levels. Disillusionment grew among the public at large. By 1967, over 50 percent of the American people disapproved of Johnson's handling of the war.

Congressional opponents attacked the war from several perspectives. Some emphasized that the domestic costs of the war exceeded any potential gain. Protest and dissent were dividing the nation; inflation was undermining the economy at home and the stability of the dollar abroad; defense spending was siphoning off money better spent on ameliorating domestic social conditions. These were held to be valid justifications for ending U.S. involvement. Others in Congress emphasized the overextension of U.S. commitments abroad and the overreliance of U.S. foreign policy on military force. A more radical critique of U.S. involvement was offered by student protesters and campus intellectuals. Their greatest impact, however, was not in analyzing loss and gain but in demonstrating by moral fervor that the war did not enjoy the consensus necessary for its prosecution. Nor did the conduct of the South Vietnamese government make the American intervention more palatable. Its officials were brutal and corrupt, it had little popular support and its army was ineffectual. It was difficult to sustain an idealistic philosophy in support of "allies" such as this.

The critical turning point in America's perception of the war effort occurred in early 1968. The Communists' Tet offensive, which penetrated all major cities in the South, convinced the American public and many policymakers that the war was unwinnable without a total military commitment. The war was fought on the television screens of America, and there, at least, it was apparent that the United States was fighting a losing battle. The visual exposure of the horrors of war and of immense human suffering marked a new era in the story of armed conflict. Henceforward, those who fight wars must take into account the psychological and, therefore, the political impact of direct public contact with war's physical reality. In the New Hampshire presidential primary, Senator Eugene McCarthy, a leading critic of U.S. involvement, ran a surprisingly close race with President Johnson. This reflected the depth of antiwar sentiment even in a conservative state. McCarthy's strong showing led Senator Robert Kennedy to enter the presidential race on an antiwar platform and contributed to Johnson's decision to withdraw his candidacy in March 1968.

Soon after the Tet offensive the commander of U.S. forces in Vietnam, General William Westmoreland, requested an additional 200,-000 troops. On the recommendation of Secretary of Defense Clark Clifford, Johnson convened an informal group of senior statesmen, "the Wise Men," to study the Vietnam debacle. A solid majority of the group, including Dean Acheson, George Ball, Arthur Goldberg, Cyrus Vance and Henry Cabot Lodge, concluded that there was no way to "win" militarily short of bombing the civilian population of North Vietnam or using tactical nuclear weapons on the battlefield. They recommended that the United States send no more ground troops to Vietnam and cease the bombing of the North. Secretary of State Dean Rusk and presidential adviser Walt Rostow, whose involvement with Vietnam policy dated from the Kennedy Administration, advocated further troop commitments. But Clark Clifford was instrumental in convincing the President to accept the Wise Men's recommendations.

By the end of his term of office, Lyndon B. Johnson was a tragic figure: he had come into office with an elevated vision of a Great Society, and he left the presidency consumed by an ugly and destructive war. The war had not only consumed Johnson's vision of a Great Society, it had also caused the Administration to neglect its interests in other areas of the world. In 1967, Johnson and his advisers watched the imminent Arab-Israeli war as bemused spectators. Their main goal seemed to be avoidance of any military commitment that might affect the U.S. effort in Vietnam. In 1957, the United States, on obtaining Israel's withdrawal from Sinai, had undertaken to support Israel's right of free passage in the Gulf of Aqaba and the Straits of Tiran and to regard a renewal of the Egyptian blockade as an aggressive act which Israel had a right to resist by force. After a vain attempt to organize an international naval force to break the blockade, Johnson ceased to oppose self-help by Israel, and he gave Israel strong support in the United Nations discussions. Without having taken any risks, the United States benefited indirectly from a crushing Egyptian-Syrian defeat which weakened Soviet prestige in the Middle East and gave the United States a clear diplomatic advantage. Washington has had a monopoly of diplomatic initiative in the area ever since.

In 1967 Johnson met with Soviet Premier Kosygin and agreed to initiate arms control negotiations aimed at limiting antiballistic missile systems which both countries were on the verge of constructing. As McNamara explained, an effective ABM system might cause either side to strike first, hoping that it would be protected from unacceptable retaliatory damage by its ABMs. This would undermine the basis of mutual assured destruction. But the Johnson Administration remained preoccupied with Vietnam, and the Soviet invasion of Czechoslovakia in August 1968 effectively foreclosed any chance for successful arms control negotiations before the end of Johnson's term.

The presidential campaign in 1968 centered on public disaffection with the American involvement in Vietnam. Both Hubert Humphrey and Richard Nixon offered palliatives—hopes of "peace with honor" and "no more Vietnams." Neither had a concrete plan to end the war, and Humphrey's loyal but excessively enthusiastic identification with Johnson's war policy contributed to his narrow but inevitable defeat.

Lyndon B. Johnson receded into obscurity on a Texas ranch four years after receiving the most massive vote of confidence in American presidential history. *Sic transit gloria mundi.* The war that brought about the collapse of his leadership was his inheritance rather than his own creation, but he showed no capacity to disentangle himself from its embrace. This was surprising in the light of what was known about the elements of strength and will power in his character. In the deepest recesses of his heart he would have been glad to live without foreign affairs. His sustaining vision was of a society ridding itself of the disabilities and hardships that stemmed from ancient inequalities. He fulfilled this dream in an extraordinary eruption of legislative energy from which he was diverted by the tragedy of Vietnam. This absorbed him so fully that it is hard to remember what he and his foreign policy advisers contributed to such domains as American-European relations or Third World development.

In the light of later developments it is strange to recall that Johnson sincerely believed that his central aim of maintaining domestic unity would actually be served by support of the Vietnam war together with the patient construction of the "Great Society." For this intuition he relied on public-opinion surveys which, as most of us have forgotten, constantly expressed approval of the American involvement in Vietnam. When his assumption dissolved in the heat of domestic contention, Johnson resorted to the sulky assumption that American dissentients were under Soviet influence. "Isn't it funny," he said, "that you could always find Soviet Ambassador Dobrynin's car in front of James Reston's house the night before Reston delivered a blast on Vietnam?" This brutal defamation reveals the extent of his fall from the lofty vision of a united and free America which he had seemed to embody on the tragic day on which the assassination of Kennedy propelled him to sudden power.

Nixon, Kissinger and Vietnam

Richard M. Nixon entered the White House justifiably obsessed with the crisis of Vietnam. The issue was not whether American forces should be withdrawn; this was a foregone conclusion. The question was how the United States could best disentangle itself. If it withdrew quickly, the results that it had sought to prevent—the collapse of South Vietnam and possibly of Cambodia and Laos—would conceivably occur. This, in the view of Nixon and his National Security Adviser, Henry A. Kissinger, would weaken the credibility of other American commitments and seriously increase the prospects of further Soviet adventurism.

Thus, the Nixon Administration was opposed to any settlement perceived as tantamount to defeat—such as a coalition government in Saigon that would include Communists. It was critical to Nixon's vision of the world and to his twin goals of détente with the Soviet Union and rapprochement with China that America's reputation as a victorious Great Power be preserved. America needed to save its honor in Vietnam in order to have the necessary prestige and flexibility to normalize relations with the two Communist powers.

American policy in the postwar period has constantly sought to examine every conflict not within its own parameters but in relation to its contagious effects on other situations. The international system is envisaged as a series of interlocking chains, in which any development in a particular area sends out repercussions far afield. If there is a conflict between North and South Vietnam, Israel and Egypt, Turkey and Greece, India and Pakistan, China and Russia, Iran and Iraq, Britain and Argentina, the tendency of American policymakers is to predict a long series of effects reaching beyond the regional context into every part of the international horizon—especially those sectors of it that bear on the Soviet Union. It would need some research to elicit whether a more particularist approach, meticulously analyzing the specific conditions in the affected region itself, might not have led to easier and better decisions.

Nixon and Kissinger, concerned with the global effects of a precipitate withdrawal, devised a two-pronged strategy for ending U.S. involvement in Vietnam. First, American ground troops were to be withdrawn gradually to cut the human and political costs of a long U.S. casualty list. This step would make further hostilities more palatable to the "silent majority" of Americans who, Nixon believed, would support an honorable end to America's commitment as long as the U.S. "body count" declined each month. Once the ground troops were removed, Nixon felt, he would have a freer hand to use U.S. air and naval power against the North so as to "encourage" Hanoi to negotiate an end to the war. The second prong of Nixon's strategy was a policy of "Vietnamization," in which South Vietnam's own military forces would gradually assume the burden of national defense. It was hoped that a reasonably effective South Vietnamese fighting force, together with U.S. air and naval power, would increase Hanoi's incentive for a negotiated settlement.

Hanoi's army, however, did not stand still while President Nixon began to carry out his strategy. In an attempt to ease the military pressures which the North was applying, Nixon boldly widened the war in April 1970. U.S. forces invaded Cambodia and attacked North Vietnamese and Vietcong border sanctuaries. The invasion of Cambodia caused vehement political protest at home and abroad. There was dissension in the President's Cabinet, in the State Department and, above all, in the Congress, which had not been consulted before the invasion. The college campuses erupted. At Kent State University, the Ohio National Guard shot and killed four students, and this tragedy came to symbolize student opposition to the war.

In 1972, a spring offensive by the North across the demilitarized zone tested the policy of Vietnamization and the capabilities of the South Vietnamese army. The results were poor, and only massive American air support staved off greater losses. In a sense, the war became "re-Americanized" through the massive bombing of the North and the mining of key ports. But Nixon—and the Soviets—refused to let the flare-up in the fighting stand in the way of Nixon's visit to

Moscow in May 1972, the first by an American President. This should have indicated that the notions of contagion and linkage are not as powerful as many statesmen and scholars have come to believe. The Soviet Union was pragmatically capable of compartmentalizing its reactions. It could be audacious in one area and restrained in another.

The United States justified its bombing and mining of the North as an effort to force Hanoi to make concessions at the bargaining table. But parallel to the air strikes, Nixon offered concessions of his own: the withdrawal of all U.S. forces and a cessation of the bombing and mining of the North in exchange for a return of the American prisoners and an internationally supervised cease-fire in place. Hanoi rejected the offer. It smelled the prospect of a one hundred percent triumph. With the long war so close to achieving the expulsion of American forces, Hanoi wanted guarantees that it would control the government in Saigon. Kissinger's feeling that the domestic confusion about the war weakened his bargaining position was objectively well-founded. But this condition is endemic to the diplomacy of democratic states. To long for the protection of foreign policy from domestic criticism is a form of protest against democracy itself.

Hanoi was under a different kind of pressure. Its chief ally and supplier of arms, the Soviet Union, made known its preference for a negotiated American withdrawal, in the expectation that the North could pick up the rest of the pieces once the Americans left. In October 1972 Hanoi signaled unexpectedly that it would be willing to settle for something less than a total victory. It accepted the American formula and acceded to negotiations with the Thieu government in the South. The tentative agreement alarmed Thieu, and he tried to stall the Americans. Nonetheless, Kissinger buoyantly announced shortly before the 1972 presidential election that "peace is at hand."

Negotiations broke down after the elections, and a re-elected Nixon resorted to intensive B-52 attacks—the "Christmas bombing"—in a last effort to force the North Vietnamese into submission. Kissinger and Le Duc Tho finally reached agreement in Paris in January 1973, allowing for America's complete exit from Vietnam. The national exultation was intense, but Kissinger, not the most averse of men to praise, soberly refused to join it. He even contemplated refusing the Nobel Peace Prize, awarded to himself and to Le Duc Tho. He knew that nothing but a respite had been achieved, enough to give an illusory impression that the United States was sailing home, leaving South Vietnam with a chance of independent survival. The cease-fire in place was soon violated, and the North Vietnamese conquered the rest of the South in April 1975.

For the United States, the material cost of the war was $150 billion and more than 50,000 lives. The psychological costs were immense.

They are still being defrayed. The embarrassing flight of the American ambassador by helicopter from his embassy rooftop during Saigon's final days will long be remembered as a symbol of American humiliation. The United States had entered the war as a self-confident and purposeful power; it ended it disillusioned by military failure and plagued by doubts about its role in the world.

Lessons from Vietnam

Much has been written about the "lessons" of Vietnam: the conventional wisdom is simply that the United States should in the future avoid similar quagmires. Yet precisely because Vietnam has occurred, American leaders are unlikely ever to face a precise analogue. The United States in the future will take into account specific indigenous conditions in any contemplated intervention. It will avoid applying generalized ideological or strategic principles which have little bearing on the specifics of a local conflict. But to learn "too well" from Vietnam would also be self-defeating. The universal slogan "no more Vietnams" is no more helpful to U.S. policymakers today than the universal cry of "no more Munichs" was to leaders of an earlier generation. We might well end up with the unhelpful advice to avoid both resistance and compromise as principles of conflict resolution.

Rather than identifying "lessons," it is useful to examine how the U.S. involvement occurred. The United States mistakenly believed that both its will to fight and its commitment to democracy could somehow be imparted to the South Vietnamese, like a transfusion of blood to an afflicted patient. Yet South Vietnam's leadership had neither the legitimacy nor the ability to galvanize public support. American officials recognized too late that their goals could only be attained by the total defeat of the North and the installation of a legitimate regime in the South—two nearly impossible requirements. Total victory over the North would be unacceptable because of the domestic costs and the Soviet and Chinese reactions, while limited victory was unlikely because the crumbling government and army in the South could not take advantage of a temporary success to consolidate its authority. U.S. involvement in these circumstances had to be both limited and open-ended: in the chasm of this contradiction the American war effort sank and died.

During the 1960s and 1970s, America's leaders employed simplistic slogans and acted on unexamined policy assumptions, such as "We must stop the North Vietnamese, otherwise the Chinese will sweep throughout all of Southeast Asia." The domino theory, like reliance on analogies, has done great intellectual damage to the cause of international conciliation. It has created a conceptual escape from the rigorous necessity to explore each situation in its own context. The idea that situation A inevitably leads to situation B is just as absurd as the contention that situation A never leads to situation B. Moreover, supplies and men were shipped to Vietnam on an incremental basis, allowing the bureaucracy, under each President from Eisenhower to Nixon, to justify each succeeding step as an inevitable sequel of the previous one. Between 1965 and 1968, U.S. leaders avoided any extensive reevaluation of their original decision to send ground troups. Finally, dissent within the Administration, such as the repeated protests by Undersecretary of State George Ball, were heard politely—and promptly dismissed. The fact that dissent was expressed served only to convince U.S. policymakers that their chosen course of escalation was a carefully weighed decision, when, in fact, its chain of consequences was never methodically considered.

During the Nixon and Kissinger period, American goals in Vietnam were focused on the idea of "honorable" withdrawal; but the quest for "honor" was long and costly in blood and life. Yet Nixon and Kissinger's vision of détente with the Soviets and rapprochement with the Chinese pressed them to seek an exit. "Vietnamization" and "bombing for peace" did not work as planned, but ultimately Hanoi and Washington for contradictory reasons each sought the same goal: the withdrawal of U.S. forces. Kissinger seemed to have won for America "a decent interval" after withdrawal so that the inevitable crumbling of the Saigon government would not be too closely linked with the end of U.S. involvement or with the credibility of other U.S. overseas commitments.

While Nixon and Kissinger were shrewd enough to seek the liquidation of the Vietnam disaster, for which they had no initial responsibility, it took many years of suffering and bloodshed to end U.S. involvement. In the process, many controversial practices were employed—from the secret war in Cambodia to the epidemic of domestic wiretaps and the abuse of presidential power. The nation's constitutional process was tested, and during Watergate it met the challenge. But America's postwar foreign policy consensus was shattered; the nation would spend the rest of the decade questioning, probing and searching the causes of failure.

The paradox is that it was the United States that put itself on trial in Vietnam. None of its allies had ever asked for a new vindication of America's fidelity to its commitments or of its capacity for courageous risk. A nation that had resisted Soviet incursions in Turkey, Greece and Iran, that had defended Western Europe against the subversion of its freedoms, that had reconstructed Japan, that had sent the aggressor packing in Korea, that had carried out a successful act of nuclear deterrence in the Cuban missile crisis could well have afforded to maintain its credentials without a test of ratification in an arena as unpromising as a former French colony in which traditional American interests had never been involved. Even without a Vietnam operation, everybody would have assumed the United States to be strong if it had not flexed its muscles at the wrong place and time. As Tacitus said of one of the Roman emperors: "Everyone would have thought that he would have made a good ruler if he had not been called to rule." "Imperii Capax Nisi Imperasset."

Détente

The tragedy was that, Vietnam apart, America's foreign policy was entering a period of lucidity and resourcefulness. The conflict in Southeast Asia had left the national leadership and public opinion skeptical of anti-Communism as the exclusive principle of America's global policy. The war in Southeast Asia, justified in the name of containing the Communist threat, had undermined the consensus for fighting such wars in the future; the price seemed too high, the benefits too nebulous. The United States, many believed, should direct its attention toward resolving domestic problems and avoiding further overseas adventures. Communism was no longer viewed as a mono-lithic threat to American survival, and the bipolar world of the immedi-ate postwar era had vanished. China had become an independent world actor. A revitalized Europe was more assertive politically. In the developing world, decolonization and nationalism had become potent counterweights to superpower hegemony and intervention. By the early 1970s, the power of anti-Communism as a unifying and motivat-ing force in the conduct of American foreign policy had diminished.

Yet what could replace it? More specifically, could an American nation that had puritanically recoiled from "power politics" construct a foreign policy based explicitly on the realities of international life rather than on a moral or ideological crusade? And how could U.S. leaders avoid what had been the dominant historical tendency of oscil-lation between the poles of isolation and intervention?

Kissinger confronted a novel postwar situation: how to conduct U.S. foreign policy in the absence of an anti-Communist consensus and yet in a world from which the United States would be unable to disengage. He emphasized balance-of-power politics of the classic European school. States, even Communist states, were a reality. They had the right to exist, and they possessed legitimate national interests. In the state system, however, there was no natural harmony of interests. National interests would never totally coincide; nor need they totally diverge. "Nobody should deny the Soviet Union its legitimate security concerns. We cannot accept a definition of security for the Soviet

Union which makes everybody else absolutely insecure." Diplomacy should identify the common ground of national interest and should resolve the differences where possible. Adversaries were not to be viewed as inherently intractable or evil. Each state actor was responsible for using its power to reconcile the minimal requirements of international stability with conditions of its own security.

What did this augur for U.S. relationships with the Communist powers, specifically Russia and China, whose system of government, economic theory and values were abhorrent to the American vision of a just world? At most, American diplomacy would seek moderate and responsible international behavior. America might influence the course of Soviet policy on certain issues or in particular areas of the world, but American power was not sufficient to transform another Great Power's domestic structures. To make future relations with the Communist states dependent on such a transformation would be both useless and counterproductive, raising tensions and constraining opportunities for negotiation. No longer should America view the Soviet Union and China as inherently hostile nations whose policies needed to be challenged in every arena. In the context of power politics, these were Great Powers in the international system, and their cooperation was needed to ensure that stability was maintained. This stability, in turn, would preserve international peace, which was the highest and most urgent moral goal of international politics. Détente in these terms was an acceptance of reality. It was not a utopian vision. Détente was not friendship. It was an effort to keep an adversarial relationship under control.

The focus of the Kissinger years, accordingly, was on the Great Powers. The rest was marginal. Although the style and rhetoric of American foreign policy shifted during this period, reflecting a large vision of the world rather than domestic values and experiences, the realities of global politics gave American policy a semblance of continuity. The Soviet-American balance remained predominant; the Soviet Union was still the adversarial superpower whose influence needed to be constrained and whose behavior had to be moderated. Yet during the Kissinger years—Vietnam aside—American rhetoric and action were more nearly in accord than ever before. Policy was frankly explained in the language of power politics—balances, spheres of influence, national interest, prestige, limits of power. There was a rejection of ideological slogans and moral crusades. America perceived its role in the international system in a realistic manner, learning to live and act within the system rather than trying to change its essential structure.

Kissinger pursued the policy of détente as the most appropriate strategy for managing the conflicting relationship of the superpowers.

Détente was an attempt to secure American interests at a lower level of tension and at less cost than the policy of Cold War or confrontation. The essential balance in international politics was still bipolar, but the relationship would be affected increasingly by developments outside the superpower balance. The role of China, for example, was becoming more influential, and the United States needed to respond more flexibly to the People's Republic. In order to achieve this, however, the old Cold War assumption of monolithic Communism needed to be supplanted by a more selective approach. Similarly, superpower rivalry could be softened by negotiating certain agreements and mutual restraints.

In Kissinger's unsentimental view, a gain for one party was not necessarily a loss for the other. "Interdependence" would focus on the areas of common interest in order to moderate Soviet behavior. While maintenance of a strong strategic arsenal and conventional forces was a necessary "stick" to deter Soviet aggression, more "carrots" in the form of agreements on trade, technology transfers and grain sales would be offered to encourage responsible behavior. The United States would then seek to link the benefits from the concessions proffered to those changes in Soviet conduct which pointed in a less militant, confrontational direction.

It is important to note that détente was not just an attempt to reconstruct the postwar consensus. By the time that Nixon entered office, the Soviet Union had achieved a strategic parity with the United States and had become a global power. The risks of challenging the Soviet Union at every turn had simply become too great; the dangers of military confrontation were far in excess of any attainable objective. Soviet-American détente—especially arms control negotiations (SALT) to stabilize the nuclear balance and reduce international tensions—became essential once the Soviets had achieved military parity. The rationale for détente was that, while remaining political competitors, the superpowers, in what Nixon termed the "era of negotiations," were obliged to cooperate to avoid the ever-present danger of nuclear holocaust.

Domestically, the Nixon years saw the continued escalation of congressional criticism, especially on the subject of U.S. disengagement from Vietnam. Congressional opponents mounted successive challenges to presidential leadership over foreign policy. In 1970, the Senate passed the Cooper-Church amendment barring any future U.S. military activity in Cambodia. Throughout the early 1970s, Senate critics attempted by various "end-the-war" amendments to limit executive war-making discretion and to force a speedier withdrawal of U.S. forces from Vietnam. Primarily through public debate, but also through their power over appropriations, congressional critics demonstrated their opposition to Nixon's policies in Vietnam and sought to increase congressional control over the nation's foreign policy.

Senators and congressmen also attempted to reduce U.S. overseas commitments. In 1971 Senate Majority Leader Mike Mansfield's perennial proposal for the unilateral withdrawal of U.S. forces stationed in Europe won considerable support. And, in 1975, the Senate rejected Kissinger's pleas for continued military aid to pro-Western factions in Angola; indeed it forbade any U.S. covert intervention in the Angolan civil war.

It can be said without exaggeration that a far-reaching constitutional change has evolved in the United States in the distribution of powers between the presidency and the Congress. The presidential freedom in foreign affairs is not what it was in the mid-sixties. Most foreign nations realize that the Presidents and secretaries of state with whom they transact their business are not plenipotentiary in the full and traditional sense. At the same time, the methods of contact between foreign governments and the Congress have not been institutionalized. They tend to be improvised, sporadic and sometimes furtive. Apart from the War Powers Act (Javits-Fulbright), the constitutional change has been empirical rather than juridical. An executive can still recapture its full powers by a deployment of strong leadership.

The Nixon Administration was criticized for spending too much on defense and neglecting social welfare programs. Even on the previously sacrosanct and arcane subject of nuclear strategy, the Congress refused to remain dutifully quiescent. Secretary of Defense James Schlesinger's proposed strategy for fighting limited nuclear wars was a particular target of attack. Schlesinger argued that the threat to respond massively to a Soviet incursion in Europe or elsewhere was no longer a credible deterrent once the USSR had achieved nuclear parity. Congressional critics, on the other hand, questioned whether any conflict could be kept limited once the nuclear threshold had been breached. They expressed a deep concern about the morality of a policy which seemed to heighten the risk of the use of nuclear weapons rather than to deter it.

The emphasis on conducting a "moral" foreign policy was a consistent theme in the liberal criticism of the "power politics" practiced by the Nixon-Kissinger team. Liberals opposed siding with authoritarian Pakistan against democratic India in the 1971 Indo-Pakistani conflict. The Jackson-Vanik amendment sought to withhold most-favored-nation trading status from the Soviet Union unless it liberalized its emigration policies. The Soviet Union preferred to renounce the most-favored-nation status rather than modify its emigration restrictions. A largely ineffectual congressional arms embargo was enacted against Turkey, a NATO ally, because of its invasion of Cyprus. The congressional emphasis on idealism led to a series of investigations regarding abuses by the CIA, from assassination plots against Cuban Premier Fidel Castro and Congolese leader Patrice Lumumba, to efforts to overthrow the elected Marxist government of Salvador Allende in Chile. The Congress first exposed, then sought to limit covert activity. The Hughes-Ryan amendment, adopted as a direct result of these revelations, required the CIA to inform congressional committees of any future covert activities. At one time it appeared that the United States was denying itself even a limited use of a policy weapon which its adversaries employ without any compunction.

The most constitutionally significant assertion of congressional power to curb the growth of the "imperial presidency" was the War Powers Act of 1973. Under this legislation, the President could commit U.S. military personnel to overseas action for a period of only sixty days without then securing congressional approval. As the Watergate scandal became publicized, the idea of curbing presidential power was further strengthened.

Despite the habit of conflict with Nixon and Ford over the conduct of foreign policy, the Congress was still essentially reactive: the initiative in foreign affairs remained securely with the executive branch. On most major issues affecting the U.S. position in the world, the Congress, after a ritual period of public hectoring and carping, would usually support the President. In arms control negotiations with the Soviet Union, for example, the Congress supported the Administration's objectives after a thorough review and debate. Kissinger negotiated two significant strategic arms limitation agreements with the Soviet Union. The first (SALT I), signed by Nixon in Moscow in 1972, limited the construction of antiballistic missile systems and froze the number of intercontinental sea- and ground-launched missile systems. The second (SALT II), signed by Ford in Vladivostok in November 1974, placed ceilings on the overall number of intercontinental bombers and missiles in a preliminary agreement pending the completion of SALT II.

The most spectacular achievement of the Nixon-Kissinger period was the diplomatic breakthrough with the People's Republic of China. Both Nixon and Kissinger believed that the Sino-Soviet split was irrevocable and might encourage the Chinese to seek improved relations with the United States. Similarly, the United States could use better relations with the People's Republic of China as a means of achieving greater flexibility and leverage with the Soviet Union. Beginning in 1969, the United States sent out diplomatic feelers through Warsaw as well as through the French, the Rumanians and the Pakistanis. When the Chinese expressed their interest in a summit meeting, Kissinger made a secret trip to Peking in 1971 and assured the Chinese leaders that the United States considered Taiwan to be a part of mainland China, and that as tensions eased, U.S. defense forces would eventually be withdrawn. This understanding was made official in the Shanghai Communiqué issued when Nixon visited China in 1972. After twenty-three years, the United States had finally taken cognizance of the world's most populous nation and a significant world power. Although formal diplomatic recognition would take seven more years, the United States' opening to China enabled Washington to exploit Sino-Soviet rivalry by playing the "China card." Congress generally welcomed this rapprochement, with the exception of some conservatives who viewed it as a betrayal of Taiwan.

American policymakers have never been free from confusion about the central purpose of their dialogue with the outer world. They arduously strive to convince other nations of their moral rectitude, while the questions that other nations ask about the United States concern American strength and resolve. The doubt about the degree of America's readiness to defend its interests is felt by friends and adversaries alike. There is an apprehension that the trauma of Vietnam may have generated an atmosphere of penitence going far beyond objective necessity and coming close to a flight from the very principle of power. It is understandable and correct for Americans to feel that their commitment in Southeast Asia was not viable or capable of success, and even that America's strategic interest was not crucially at issue. But it is a false analogy to draw the conclusion that the United States is similarly inhibited from defending its position in Central America against erosion by hostile regimes. The two contexts are not comparable in any way. In Central America the United States moves in an atmosphere far more favorable than that which made its Vietnam campaign so incongruous and self-defeating. Here the strategic interests of the United States really *are* involved. There *is* a possibility of checking destabilizing movements with little risk of global escalation. And there is a traditional acknowledgment by the world community of America's right to be preoccupied by threats to its continental security. This acknowledgment goes back to the Monroe Doctrine and came to expression in the Cuban missile crisis.

The interrelation between foreign policy and domestic opinion has always been closer in the United States than anywhere else. Even in the most immaculately democratic countries in Europe, foreign policy has been a reserved domain, insulated against constant public intrusion. This is not the case in the United States. Yet since the mid-1960s no American leader has succeeded in bringing the country's international interests into harmony with its public sentiment. There can be no doubt that in the 1980s the most decisive issue for American foreign policy is American domestic policy. The United States will not have authority or confidence abroad unless it achieves more clarity and clear counsel at home. The questions that arise in the minds of foreign nations about the United States are persistent and searching: "Do you have a clear and realistic definition of your vital interests and commitments? Are you prepared to assert and defend them? Are your processes of decision sufficiently coherent and effective to give your leadership a chance to develop and sustain a comprehensible policy?" Few observers of the American scene would give resoundingly positive answers today.

In Europe, Nixon and Kissinger had taken a new approach to America's democratic allies. The 1960s and the early 1970s had witnessed a manifest deterioration in the Atlantic alliance. U.S. involvement in Vietnam, the easing of Soviet-American tensions on the continent, and the reassertion of European political and economic independence, dramatically demonstrated by De Gaulle's withdrawal from NATO in 1966, all made the alliance less cohesive and disciplined than during the height of the Cold War. Economic issues proved to be especially divisive, and some American officials began to question whether the United States could afford military forces for the defense of an affluent Europe.

Europe, so dependent in the 1940s and early 1950s on American aid, had grown to be a potent competitor on the world market by the 1970s, but it was not making what American leaders considered to be an adequate contribution to its own defense. The American balance of trade began to suffer because of increased competition from both the Common Market and Japan. Each of them established external trade barriers which the United States felt to be excessive and discriminatory. U.S. domestic inflation, brought about by unsound fiscal policies used to finance both the Vietnam war and social programs, led to a substantial overvaluation of the dollar in the late 1960s which cut further into U.S. competitiveness.

In August 1971 the Nixon Administration adopted shock tactics to correct America's international economic problems. It ended the postwar Bretton Woods system of a dollar-centered world economy. No longer would the dollar be backed with gold at a fixed rate of exchange. Nixon also opted for Treasury Secretary John B. Connally's proposal to impose a temporary 10 percent surcharge on imports in an effort to improve the U.S. bargaining position pending a realignment of world currencies. The new fixed rates negotiated in December 1971 and March 1973 did not work well, and the world slipped by default into a system of floating exchange rates. Economic conflict continued and even intensified during the 1970s, exacerbated by a series of oil crises. Beginning in 1975, the Western nations and Japan engaged in a series of annual summits on economic relations. The meetings helped to keep leaders apprised of each other's thoughts and proved useful in fighting global protectionist forces. But economic malaise lingered.

On the political front, Kissinger attempted to bring some coherence back to the Atlantic alliance in 1973 with the proclamation of "the year of Europe" and the call for a "new Atlantic Charter." The proposed charter would have subordinated diplomatic, military and economic frictions to the overriding collective purpose of defending Western interests and values. Kissinger in particular felt that without a sense of political purpose, economic rivalry and divergent political attitudes would severely cripple the alliance. European responses to this initiative showed just how disunited the alliance had become. The Common Market nations stressed cooperation on an equal basis, emphasizing their own independence.

An abrasive political and economic challenge to American interests came with the 1973 Arab-Israeli conflict and the resulting OPEC oil embargo, which further strained the Atlantic alliance. The power of OPEC to deny oil to the Western economies and to control unilaterally the price of their most vital commodity elevated the pride of the developing countries. As was to become apparent later, OPEC members were no more inclined to use their new-found wealth to aid other developing nations than were Western nations. Indeed, the precipitous rise in oil prices affected most severely those nations already at the bottom of the prosperity ladder. OPEC had shattered the illusion that the developing countries would forever remain the hewers of wood and drawers for water for the industrialized North. The "Group of 77" developing nations hoped that OPEC's action signaled a fundamental change in the rules governing international economic relations.

The OPEC embargo also exposed a major weakness of détente. U.S. policymakers had concentrated their attention on Great Power politics. They failed to take notice of the forces at work in the Third World except as they affected the rivalry of the superpowers. This rivalry provided a few Third World nations with leverage to extract aid from the superpowers, but most of them remained profoundly dissatisfied. The Third World demanded a New International Economic Order—higher and stable prices for their commodities; the indexation of these prices to the rate of inflation in the West; preferential tariffs for their goods in Western markets; increased development assistance. The North-South dialogue had begun with the South on the offensive.

Succeeding years have shown that OPEC's power is limited. It has become clear that the oil producers are as dependent on a stable world

economy as the West is dependent on their petroleum. The demands
of the New International Economic Order remain largely unfulfilled.
The rise of Third World actors represents, nonetheless, a significant
change in the postwar world. While the superpowers continue to be
locked in their bipolar military and diplomatic struggle, the forces of
change at work in the newly industrializing countries make the world
more diverse and less hierarchical than at any time in the postwar era.

Two other events need to be noted before leaving the Nixon-Ford
years: the "October war" of 1973 and the ongoing struggle in southern Africa.

In the Middle East, the Arabs' surprise attack on Yom Kippur
marked a watershed in the Arab-Israeli conflict. Israel eventually triumphed, but the war proved, to the astonishment of many, that Israel
could be caught by surprise and that Arab forces could wield sophisticated weapons effectively. The war also pointed up Israel's dependence on U.S. arms and ammunition, and Israel's increasing isolation
in the world community because of the Arabs' oil weapon. In addition,
the Soviet ultimatum and the threat of unilateral intervention on October 24 illustrated graphically the risks of a superpower showdown in
any future war in the Middle East. Each of these factors contributed
to the new U.S. perception that a resolution of the Arab-Israeli conflict
was vital to the American national interest.

Kissinger decided on a step-by-step approach in the postwar
negotiations. In his view a total settlement of all outstanding issues was
unattainable since neither the Soviets nor the radical Arab states were
playing a cooperative role. Skepticism about "comprehensive settlements" was a constant element in Kissinger's diplomatic outlook. He
now employed his characteristic personal diplomacy by seeking to
resolve the "easier" issues before proceeding to more complex matters. The initial task, as he realistically conceived it, was the disengagement of the opposing military forces after the war; next, a further
withdrawal of Israeli forces in the Sinai and on the Golan Heights; and
finally, the resolution of the two most tangled issues—the status of the
Palestinians and the future of the West Bank and Gaza. Kissinger
hoped that a resolution of the easy issues would generate momentum
and make the difficult issues more tractable. Kissinger achieved spectacular success with two unprecedented agreements between Israel
and the Arabs: the disengagement of the opposing military forces in
the Sinai (January 1974) and on the Golan Heights (May 1974). He
obtained a further Israeli withdrawal in Sinai in September 1975 in
return for an Egyptian promise to regard the military phase of the
conflict as permanently eliminated. Additional progress in Middle East
peacemaking would have to await the dramatic initiative of Anwar
el-Sadat; but the stepping stones were in place.

In southern Africa, U.S. policy was faced with several challenges—
the growing isolation of the white minority governments in Southern
Rhodesia and South Africa, a Marxist regime in Mozambique, and the
presence of Soviet and Cuban forces in Angola. American policy usually neglected Third World issues until they had a significant impact
on the relationship of the Great Powers, and Africa, for Kissinger, was
no exception. Congress shackled Kissinger's efforts to counter the
Russians and the Cubans in Angola, and the United States had no
influence on the nationalist insurgents in Mozambique and Rhodesia
who demanded majority rule. The ability of the United States to influence events in the area was thus greatly circumscribed. Kissinger was
eventually able to negotiate an agreement in principle with Rhodesia's
Ian Smith to hold free elections on the basis of majority rule. This was
an irreversible achievement; an operative breakthrough would come
with the efforts of the Carter Administration and a renewal of British
diplomacy, leading to the establishment of Zimbabwe in 1980.

Détente in the Nixon-Ford Years: An Evaluation

American perspectives on détente swung sharply from euphoria in
1972 after Nixon's visits to Beijing and Moscow to disillusionment in
the wake of the Middle East war and Soviet-Cuban adventurism in
Africa. This abrupt change in public opinion reflected an American
tendency to oscillate between idealism and dejection without an intermediate level of realism. Kissinger has rightly noted the difficulties
inherent in a democracy's conduct of a consistent foreign policy. Détente was widely perceived, and perhaps even oversold, as if it were
designed to accelerate permanent solutions to the nation's international problems. The impression was given that negotiation and mutual interest would now dominate the superpower relationship and
that Kissinger had already constructed a "stable structure of peace."
Yet clearly there were few areas where the objectives of the superpowers really coincided—and many where collision would be inevitable.

In reality, détente was always designed to be a balance of confrontation with cooperation. Détente is not friendship. It is at best a controlled adversarial relationship. The critical distinction between Cold
War containment and détente was mostly in emphasis. Confrontation
and cooperation had both existed in each period, but this subtlety
proved very difficult for the Nixon-Kissinger Administration to convey
to the general public or to the Congress. Détente was not entente; nor
was it, as the hard-line critics charged, simply the continuation of the
Cold War by other means. It envisaged the relaxation of tensions, not
their elimination. The essence of it was that the tensions should be
restrained and that military action would be shunned.

There was, however, an important strand of continuity in the American view of détente. It was an attempt to apply containment in the age of superpower parity, the Sino-Soviet schism and the increased stature of the Third World. Détente implied an effort—not wholly unsuccessful—to define a more realistic framework for American policy in a less hierarchical world.

Perhaps détente's greatest difficulty lay in its complexity. It lacked the fervor and underlying consensus that had inspired the policy of containment before the Vietnam war. In the absence of any clear and present external threat, America remains a fundamentally insular country, mainly preoccupied with domestic problems. Only a global crusade or a war can mobilize public support for an activist foreign policy. It took the failure of the anti-Communist crusade in the rice paddies of Southeast Asia for the United States to try a more subtle approach to regional conflict.

But Kissinger's dilemma was agonizing: his politics of restraint and balance ran contrary to a deeply ingrained characteristic in the American national style. What could be used to motivate and unify the American people behind a foreign policy that sought not the transformation of the world, but the employment of American power and influence in the limited and self-interested manner characteristic of Great Powers throughout history? The usual answer—the defense of peace through a careful maintenance of a balance of power—had little appeal for Americans born to greater ambitions: to "make the world safe for democracy" or to "pay any price, bear any burden" for the sake of liberty's survival. While the personal charisma and diplomatic successes of Kissinger initially elicited public support for détente, disillusionment with the policy began to grow when the Soviets failed to show restraint in Angola and Ethiopia, expanded their naval power and ignored the provision of the Helsinki Final Act on human rights and intellectual freedom. It was difficult to demonstrate that the Soviets saw détente as a process that required concessions from them in any field. The Cold War consensus had been shattered, but no compelling replacement had been found. With the tide of world events seemingly running against U.S. interests, American foreign policy was adrift again.

The Nixon-Ford-Kissinger years are the surprise story of American diplomatic history. The two Presidents came to office with a reputation for mistrust and suspicion of America's adversaries and strong reservations about America's friends. Theirs was a confrontationist mood. Kissinger's writings revealed a profound historical sense and an impulse to evolve new ideas and concepts; but his somber view of man's political nature and his skeptical attitude toward anything that could be described as utopianism seemed to augur a tenacious defense of existing stabilities rather than an impulse to look beyond them. Yet this unlikely union of disparate characters left American policy after eight years more thoroughly transformed in scope and spirit than any corresponding period before or since.

The Kissinger period begins with China as America's most implacable foe and ends with China in a posture close to objective alliance. It opens with an atmosphere of American-Soviet contention and ends with the ambiguities, hopes and frustrations of détente. It commences with tens of thousands of American troops in the jungles and swamps of Vietnam, still hoping for an outcome that might honor their sacrifice, and ends with Vietnam receding from physical view but lingering in the national memory like a nightmare from which there is no awakening. It begins with an unbridled American-Soviet arms race and ends with one Strategic Arms Limitation Agreement in legal operation and a second agreement awaiting final form and ratification. It begins with Europe wrapped in juridical ambivalence and ends with final boundary agreements that mark the settlement of World War II. It begins with almost no contractual expression to American-Soviet relations and ends with a plethora of agreements and a relative florescence of interchange. It begins with rigidly closed doors in the Soviet Union and ends with over 150,000 former Soviet citizens in Israel and North America.

Henceforward the rhythm and texture of international life would never resemble what it had been before. Richard Nixon had been the unexpected phenomenon, appointing Henry Kissinger to the central place in the fashioning and implementation of foreign policy, pursuing the opening to China against the entire trend of American national emotion and making a mockery of his own anti-Soviet past by the assiduity of his contacts with Soviet leaders. In between the achievements lurked the incredible confusion of a Vietnam-Cambodia policy that staggered from one complication to the next until it ended with disengagement, withdrawal and costly defeat.

Nixon's air of assurance as he moved in the international field contrasted wildly with his total lack of coherence in his domestic confrontations. He was by no means a man of the outer world and he never overcame a demeanor of awkwardness in his encounter with foreign leaders and emissaries. But he approached international negotiation with none of the dark fears and suspicions that accompanied him in his domestic journey. Foreign statesmen were not his competitors and were not suspected, as were most Americans, of wanting to depose him. The leaders of the Western alliance had greeted his ascendancy with initial apprehension and even alarm. But they soon abandoned the demonological picture that had been painted of him and which had already become modified during his vice presidency, when he had become known to many countries that he visited as a statesman of restrained, centralist views. Nixon in 1960 was the first sitting Vice President in this century to become his party's presidential candidate, so that the strange office had not harmed his image. When as President he moved out of the Cold War stereotypes toward a selective approach to Communist states and made a transition from confrontation to détente in U.S.-Soviet relations he became more popular abroad than at home. After his resignation under the cloud of impending impeachment in 1974, he could usually count on a more courteous reception in China, Japan and even Western Europe than in any American city.

Nixon and Kissinger appear in each other's memoirs as four distinct persons; there are the pictures that each draws of himself, and the somewhat diminished figures that each draws of the other. But even in this somewhat surrealistic mirror, they are reflected as an unusual pair, totally divergent in every attribute of personality and yet managing to find common cause in the domain of international policy. Not every President would have allowed Kissinger to take such assertive command of the nation's diplomacy, and no other Secretary of State had ever envisaged his function as ambitiously as did Kissinger.

A rare literary talent has enabled Kissinger to expose the detailed workings of his mind and to show how he traced a path through the jungle of impeding obstacles that he encountered in the international arena and, still more acutely, on his home ground. His first aim was to avoid disaster. He knew that states could die and that tragedy is endemic to history. His second objective was to bring about a measure of mobility in what had become a petrified international alignment. If these two objectives were attained, some problems would be advanced, if not toward "solutions," at least toward tolerable stability. An example can be found in the Middle East, where his efforts produced a decline of Soviet dominance, a corresponding rise in American influence and, in the Arab-Israeli conflict, a disengagement from deadlock and movement toward a first vision of territorial and ideological change.

Americans who applaud Kissinger's successes in changing the superpower alignments and breaking the ice in the Middle East have a lot to say in a censorious mood about events in Cyprus, India and Pakistan, Chile and, above all, Vietnam and Cambodia, where almost nothing turned out as he wished. Critics in other parts of the world are even more rigorously severe on these matters. The issues on which Kissinger's record is most vulnerable are those in which diplomatic realism collided with the principle of frank disclosure. Morality had become associated in the American public consciousness with overt diplomacy, and what Kissinger did in Cambodia and Chile and tried to do in Angola were the sort of actions that do not welcome the strong glare of daylight. There was nothing new in these activities in the context of history, and the Soviet Union must have been incredulous as well as gratified to observe the zeal with which Americans denied their own government a capacity of action which Moscow deploys with no inhibition at all. The covert side of diplomacy has never won full legitimacy in American opinion. A senior statesman of the United States in the 1940s, Henry Stimson, on hearing that his government received reports of what was said in foreign embassies, said memorably that "gentlemen do not read other people's letters." Nor do gentlemen usually interfere with the way in which other gentlemen govern themselves; but these metaphors beg the question whether free countries can survive against their adversaries if they apply the gentlemanly habits and restraints of a consensual democratic society to an international system in which there is no consensus about the legitimacy of actions by sovereign states. The idea that the United States should behave toward its ruthless foreign adversaries as American gentlemen behave toward each other within the domestic order is so eccentric in terms of diplomatic history that it is astonishing to note how widespread it has become. Kissinger's critics would have had a stronger position in criticizing his policies in Chile and Cambodia on the grounds of their ineffectiveness rather than on the grounds of their immorality.

To compound his culpability in the eyes of liberal America, Kissinger was manifestly apathetic about the long-term future of the Third World; and his skepticism about America's ability to impose its own concepts of human rights on its friends, let alone its adversaries, was deeply rooted in his intuition and experience. Nor did he ever embrace the myth that international organization could replace politics and diplomacy and thus illuminate a pathway to a messianic era of harmony and perfection. His refusal to embrace these dogmas of conventional American sentiment exposed him to the kind of criticism meted out to Galileo for declining to proclaim the flatness of the globe and its centrality within the solar system. In his memoirs, Kissinger solves these problems by railing indignantly against the negative effects of uninformed domestic opinion; it would have been wiser for him to admit that the duty of a statesman is to mobilize his domestic constituency on behalf of his foreign policy aims, and that failure to do this cannot be expiated by virtuosity at the negotiating table or in the public international forum.

What Kissinger's supporters and critics should join in acknowledging is his extraordinary success in creating a new climate of enthusiasm about the diplomatic enterprise. His strong historical sense, his assertive view of himself clothed in an ironical vocabulary of self-deprecation, his satirical humor, his idiosyncratic personality, his gift for aphorism, his capacity for dominating his intellectual environment and his unashamed theatricality all came together to make international politics a popular theme in American life such as it had never been before and has not become since. The notion that diplomacy is not a specialized mystery or a perpetual source of frustration, but can become an exhilarating and comprehensible adventure, flourished briefly like a summer breeze before the onset of sultriness. International politics came to arouse more public interest than ever before, and Kissinger's eruption into the arena of responsibility was one of the causes of this popularization.

Masses of people across the world who would be hard put to tell the names of Kissinger's predecessors or successors knew full well who was in charge of American foreign policy during the years of his tenure as Secretary of State. On the surface, a successful attempt to seize the world's imagination for the interplay of international interests could be written off as inconsequential. Those of us who believe that one of the sources of alienation from the diplomatic enterprise is the prevalence of public apathy and ignorance cannot easily deny Kissinger's unique achievement in making international relations a theme of concern and curiosity in millions of homes.

That his vision was not implemented in its full scope is a truth that he himself was forced to acknowledge. It is also true, as his academic critics emphasize, that he did not produce a grand design for a new international order. But the critics who make this judgment have not themselves produced such a design, despite the advantages of their detachment from the compromises of the arena. Stanley Hoffmann states negatively that Kissinger's system is no more than "a scheme for universal, permanent, and successful containment, marshalling all our instruments of power more effectively than before and aiming at 'an end to the constant probing for openings and the testing of every equilibrium.' " This begs the question whether the objective clash of interests and principles between the Soviet Union and the West realistically permits any higher achievement than "a universal, permanent and successful containment." A world in which utopia is not available may have to be content with relatively small mercies, in which case it might be better not to keep calling them small.

The main lesson that Nixon and Kissinger contributed to American thinking was unpalatable but salutary. They accepted the Soviet system as an unwelcome but immutable reality with which they had to come to terms. One of the most deeply rooted illusions of some of their predecessors and successors had been that the Soviet system can be substantially modified, either by antagonistic pressures, as advocated by the hawks, or by deferential appeasement, as proposed by the doves. A policy that rested on the assumption that Soviet policy was constant and impermeable to outside influences sounded unambitious, but it had the compensating advantage of veracity.

Carter and the New American Crusade

Jimmy Carter's vision of America's role in the world differed in significant ways from that of his predecessors. He sought to de-emphasize the centrality of the U.S.–Soviet relationship by recognizing what he diagnosed as the increased importance of the Third World in global affairs. Moreover, he sought to build support for what he believed to be a more humane foreign policy and in the process to create a new consensus for a foreign policy based explicitly on the American values of human rights and individual liberty. At the outset, the defense of these values was presented as a guiding principle of Carter's foreign policy.

Although few Americans disagreed with the importance of human rights, the implementation of that policy proved complex and difficult. Criticism of the Soviet Union on the issue of human rights easily won support from both the liberal and the hawkish wings of Carter's own Democratic Party. But it cannot be said to have improved the basis for the arms control negotiations on which Carter set so high a value. Many liberals put peace ahead of human rights as a moral imperative and refused to badger the Soviet Union into reforms which the Soviet view of society could not accommodate. China, a Stalinist society certainly no less repressive than the land of Stalin's birth, largely escaped the Carter Administration's sermons because of its strategic importance.

Carter's human rights policy foundered on the realpolitik of defense and strategy. When he announced the withdrawal of U.S. forces from Korea, motivated in part by Seoul's abject record of human rights abuse, Japan immediately felt threatened. Of what use was a human rights policy if it called into question U.S. credibility with its most important Pacific ally? Moreover, once American support for the Seoul regime was withdrawn, what leverage would the United States have to force it to improve its behavior? Finally, would not the withdrawal of American forces make the South Korean government even more insecure—leading to further repressions? These dilemmas, faced on several occasions by the Administration, caused many to question the emphasis on human rights as the conceptual focus of U.S. foreign policy.

This is not to argue that human rights should have been ignored, as was often the case in Cambodia, Greece, Chile, the Philippines and elsewhere. But the Carter Administration's defense of human rights often undercut more attainable policy goals. In Brazil, the Administration's denunciations of human rights violations created the wrong atmosphere for persuading the Brazilians to reverse their nuclear agreement with West Germany—an important aspect of the Carter nonproliferation policy. Argentina, frequently and ineffectively chastised by the White House, found little reason to support the Carter Administration's grain embargo on the Soviet Union in January 1980. Not only was American human rights policy often accused of inconsistency; it was also tainted by hypocrisy. In Iran, Carter praised the Shah of Iran lavishly in a December 1977 toast, describing Iran as "an island of stability," despite the flagrant abuses which even his own State Department documented. In his memoirs *Keeping Faith*, Carter defends his policy of emphasizing human rights in the American dialogue with foreign states, but he evades the issue of selectivity. His effusive toast to the Shah is discreetly omitted. Yet unlike all his predecessors, Carter introduced human rights as an effective theme in international politics. It is true that he ran up against the realities of life in the international struggle between nation-states jealous of their domestic jurisdiction. It is hard to point to a real alleviation of repression in totalitarian countries arising from Carter's human rights campaign. But at least he forced them into defensive postures and gave heart to dissidents and victims of persecution who would have been crushed by an atmosphere of international silence.

As a reaction to the Watergate crisis, Vietnam and the inability of Kissinger to mobilize the public behind his vision of international equilibrium, the Carter Administration's attempt at innovation was understandable and consistent with the characteristic American style. It was an honest attempt to reclaim America's heritage as a moral and revolutionary nation, to resurrect an ideology of liberalism that should have appealed more profoundly to the oppressed peoples of the Third World than Marxism-Leninism. But Carter's policy, to be effective, would have required years of consistent and careful application under several administrations. The slow pace of change in the international system did not afford that opportunity to a one-term administration. Moreover, the speed and vigor with which Carter supported the tide of change obscured an essential question. Was any regime in the world so oppressive that it was incapable of becoming more so? The dilemma was well illustrated in Iran and Nicaragua. When the United States weakened a pro-Western dictatorship, the end result was not a pro-Western democracy but an anti-Western despotism. The Ayatollah Khomeini was no improvement on the Shah. This tends to support the view that the United States should determine its relations with other nations in accordance with their contribution to stability rather than by reference to their domestic conduct.

Two other salient features of Carter's foreign policy at the outset were its effort to reduce the emphasis on the Soviet-American relationship and on military and strategic issues. The Third World had penetrated the consciousness of the Carter Administration. This was largely a result of the assertion of OPEC's economic power, but policymakers were also responding to the rise of regional powers such as Brazil, Nigeria and Iran, which could exercise considerable influence over a broad area. No longer was bipolar rivalry viewed in Washington as the single driving force of conflict in the Third World; other factors were given weight. The Sino-Vietnamese conflict of February 1979 was but one example of a dispute with implications for the superpower relationship, but one clearly beyond the power of either superpower to determine or control.

The Carter Administration's attempt to come to terms with change in the Third World had mixed results. In Latin America, the Panama Canal treaties of 1978 transferred the Canal Zone to the Panamanians, ending seventy-five years of American control. This was accomplished at enormous cost to the President in persuading a most reluctant Congress and public. In Nicaragua, the Administration allowed the dictatorial regime of Somoza to topple in 1979; it hoped to encourage a moderate alternative, although the chances of success were dubious. Yet in El Salvador, the escalating civil war in 1980 led to a tougher response by Carter, paving the way for the Reagan Administration's severe rhetoric and pressure.

In Africa, the peaceful transfer of power to the black majority in Zimbabwe was effected in April 1980, largely through American support of Lord Carrington's initiative. Progress also seemed to be made with respect to the transfer of power in Namibia. In the Horn of Africa, however, superpower rivalry was as virulent as ever. Soviet and Cuban forces reclaimed for Ethiopia the Ogaden, which had been seized by the Somali army acting through local rebels. The Carter Administration was under intense pressure from right-wing critics to intervene, to get tough, to "do something" lest the Soviets should view Administration policy as open encouragement for their adventurism. The Administration sought to steer a fine line in Africa between recognizing the local character of disputes and yet opposing any increase in Soviet power or influence. Quite accurately, the Administration perceived that any American military effort in the Horn of Africa would only have made matters worse.

In the end, it was the double defeat of the Iranian hostage crisis and the Soviet invasion of Afghanistan that doomed Carter's attempt at a more relaxed approach to revolutionary change in the Third World. The fall of the Shah, the rise of the Ayatollah Khomeini and the virulent anti-Americanism exhibited most dramatically in the seizure of the U.S. embassy and its personnel preoccupied the Administration and gripped the nation's mind for the rest of Carter's tenure in office. The events in Iran provided yet another piece of evidence that change in much of the world operated against American policy. Moreover, the fall of the Shah had severe geopolitical consequences. No longer could America expect the regime in Iran to act as the policeman of the Persian Gulf. The virulence of the revolution cast a retrospective burden of blame on American policymakers for having refused to predict any future for Iran beyond the Peacock Throne. The Iranian crisis also drew attention to the weakness of the Nixon doctrine, which had sought to rely upon regional powers as a substitute for direct American involvement. Thus, surrogates such as Thieu and Ky in Vietnam or the Shah in Iran were left to play a security role which had to be supported with American arms. In the syndrome that developed, these "permanent" surrogates then collapsed. When Britain suddenly withdrew from its protective tasks in the Gulf in the early 1970s, the traditional American reaction would have been to fill the vacuum itself, as it had done in Turkey, Greece and the Arab-Israel area. The Nixon doctrine, however, laid the direct responsibility on the Shah of Iran. When Nixon opened the arsenals of the United States to Iran, the Shah's expenditure on arms rocketed from $1.2 billion in the previous nineteen years to $19.5 billion in the seven years after Nixon and Kissinger's 1972 visit to Tehran. It has been impossible to prove that the United States has derived any benefits from this largesse.

At this psychologically vulnerable moment for American policy, the Soviet Union invaded Afghanistan. This confirmed America's darkest suspicions of Soviet behavior. The Carter Administration could do little to counter the Soviet forces in Afghanistan directly, but together with the presidential candidacy of Ronald Reagan, and Carter's own change of heart on the Soviet Union, the invasion led to a shift in Carter Administration policy. There would now be a more militaristic, confrontational approach. It was acknowledged that conflicts in the Third World could be ascribed in large measure to local influences, but it was the Soviet-Cuban interventions in Angola, Ethiopia, South Yemen and Afghanistan, all with relatively low costs and high potential gains, which had geopolitical consequences that the United States could ignore only at the peril of its crucial interests.

With Iran in chaos and susceptible to Soviet manipulation, with radical Arab regimes fundamentally opposed to any U.S. role in the region, with the moderate oil sheikdoms disturbed by the events in Iran, the Carter Administration felt that it must have the capacity to defend American interests in the Persian Gulf region. The Carter doctrine signaled that the United States would be prepared to intervene militarily, if necessary, to protect those interests, whether threatened by the Soviet Union or threatened (as added by President Reagan later) by indigenous forces. At the present stage, however, this American determination is more a matter of rhetoric than a subject of effective preparation.

The brightest success of the Carter Administration was its peacemaking effort in the Middle East. After being surprised by Anwar el-Sadat's dramatic voyage to Jerusalem in November 1977, Jimmy Carter engaged the United States as a "full partner" in the tortuous diplomacy of peace negotiations. The Camp David accords were the result of skillful and tenacious personal efforts by President Carter, and a peace treaty between Israel and Egypt was concluded in March 1979. No American President has ever had so crucial and detailed a role in a successful mediation between third parties. Egypt recovered its territories, and Israel gained peace with its most formidable foe. It was a spectacular victory for international conciliation. The terms of this treaty, however, did not unravel the Palestinian issue, which was left to future negotiation. The central idea was to institute a period of "full autonomy" for the Palestinians in the West Bank and Gaza, leaving the permanent status of those territories to be determined by agreement between Egypt, Israel, Jordan and the Palestinians themselves. But autonomy as conceived by the government of Menachem Begin—as a prelude to permanent Israeli domination—offered no inducements for the Palestinians or the Arab states to join the peace process, and the autonomy negotiations are no nearer agreement today than they were on the first day that they convened. Lack of progress contributed to Sadat's isolation in the Arab world long before his assassination in October 1981.

By the end of the Carter Administration, the intensity of cross-pressures on American interests in the Middle East was profound. America's commitment to the survival of Israel remained strong, yet that survival could be ensured in the long term, in the view of many American leaders, only by a comprehensive solution of the Palestinian issue. Such a solution would require a convergence by the Arab states and Israel toward a central position. This was not feasible while Arab leaders ruled out compromises with Israel and while the Begin government was frankly immobile on issues that required territorial concessions to Palestinian nationalism. The United States, moreover, continued to have significant interests in the stability of moderate regimes in the area, particularly in Egypt and Saudi Arabia. Washington also had a greater concern than before to prevent the spread of Soviet influence, whether manifested in future Afghanistans or by indigenous unrest that played into Soviet hands. The careful balancing of these complex interests symbolized the central challenge for U.S. foreign policy in the decade ahead. How the United States would protect its vital interests in an international arena riven by local insta-

bility was the central question at the end of the Carter presidency. Its
most dramatic illustration, as well as the most devastating for the
American people and its leadership, was the fiasco over the hostage
crisis in Iran, which was settled a few hours after Carter left the White
House. Although he took office convinced of the limits of American
power, he left the presidency having bequeathed a new major U.S.
commitment to his successor—the defense of the Persian Gulf.

American foreign policy has been directed by six Presidents and
seven secretaries of state in the past twenty years. None of the thirteen
was consumed by an intense admiration of his predecessor. Thus the
exigencies of American domestic politics have contributed to a stac-
cato rhythm of discontinuity in the recent diplomatic history of the
United States. No transitions have been more abrupt than from Nixon
to Carter and from Carter to Reagan. Carter's presidency appears as
a tangential interlude in this strange sequence. Sick of the corruptions
and humiliations of Vietnam and Watergate, the American people saw
Carter as the symbol of disengagement from the twin curses. Carter
had been so remote from the central arenas that no one could trace
any of the mud from these swamps to anything in his own public or
personal record. The Panama Canal Treaty, the normalization of relations with China, the Egyptian-Israeli peace treaty, SALT II and the
addition of an idealistic motif to the image of American policy are
achievements that ought to rescue the Carter foreign policy from the
scorching verdict implicit in his crushing electoral defeat. But elections
are fought on the headlines of yesterday and today, not on the de-
pleted credit of the day before yesterday; and the Iranian crisis on the
heels of the Soviet invasion of Afghanistan as well as other international ambiguities came together to create an image of irresolution.

What was rejected in 1980 was not so much Carter's policies as his
leadership. Americans are not worried by diverse policies so long as
each stage is conducted with a semblance of tenacity and national
pride. Carter was suspected of revulsion from the realities of power.
His constant reference to his prayers had two built-in defects. Americans do not care to be reminded of one another's religiosity; and they
reckoned that those who constantly appeal to Divine Providence reveal
a basic skepticism about their own powers. When Leonid Brezhnev
and Carter met in 1979, few Americans who watched them on television were convinced that their own man was the stronger of the two.
Above all, there was no impression of a lucid approach to the relationship with the Soviet Union. On one occasion Carter said that he and
Brezhnev had the same kind of dream for humankind; on another he
hinted that the Soviet invasion of Afghanistan had opened his eyes for
the first time to the realities of Soviet policy. Each of these extraordinary declarations aroused alarm. The evident truth is that not a single

common thought or dream passed through the minds of Carter and Brezhnev, and the idea that the USSR might have expansionist ambitions had occurred to many Americans long before the Afghan invasion. What Americans were seeking was evidence of strength, not of compassion or moral rectitude, and it was the premonition that their leader substituted evangelical hope for hard realism that sent a shiver of apprehension through their hearts.

Carter's National Security Adviser Zbigniew Brzezinski claims that Carter, like himself, rarely thought of domestic politics when making foreign policy determinations. The idea that deafness to the voices of one's own constituency is a virtue in a national leader or emissary makes its appearance very frequently in specialized diplomatic literature. It is rather like an engineer proclaiming that he pays little heed to mathematics. The outcome was that a President free from the character defects of Johnson and Nixon followed them with surprising speed into the cloud of electoral displeasure; indeed, the paradox is that neither Johnson nor Nixon ever had their presidencies defeated at the polls, while this fate struck at the morally impeccable Carter with alarming force.

Ronald Reagan's First Years

President Reagan offered the electors change—not continuity—in foreign affairs; he advocated a return to the mood and rhetoric of the Cold War. It was as if the last twenty-five years of American history had melted away. Once again the Soviet Union was openly described as an implacable, rapacious, wicked foe against whom the United States needed to redouble its vigilance. The President spoke of the Soviet Union's atheism and of how its leaders would lie and cheat to promote their goals. He warned that the Soviet Union, buoyed by its recent successes and the alleged lack of American resistance, was poised for new adventures to take over the world. While Soviet advances were apprehensively recorded, the Reagan Administration tended to ignore Soviet difficulties and failures—in China, Egypt, Poland, Afghanistan and in the declining fidelity of European Communist Parties. Outside the United States, most observers were less alarmed than Washington about the expansion of Soviet power. Indeed the American-European relationship deteriorated largely because the United States and Europe saw the Soviet threat in a different light.

To meet the Soviet menace, the Reagan Administration sought increased defense expenditures and a much tougher stance. Once again the United States seemed to embark on a global crusade to "contain Communism" in whatever guise it might appear. Whereas a common view of the Soviet Union had united America and Europe for a whole generation, they were now divided by divergent perceptions of Soviet policy. Europeans were shocked by American pressure on them to abstain from cooperating with the Soviets on a great gas pipeline across Siberia at the very moment when the United States itself was renewing grain sales to Moscow in deference to the interests of American farmers. For their part American policymakers felt that they could not count on their European allies for any show of resistance to Soviet repression in Poland or Afghanistan, or to subversion in Central America. In the second year of the Reagan Administration the NATO alliance was in danger of becoming little more than a unilateral security guarantee without any of the warmth and solidarity that the common values of its members seemed to dictate.

While there was no formal repudiation of détente, the policies of the Reagan Administration in most areas of the world seemed to hearken back to the pre-détente era; antagonism to the Soviet Union was the focal point from which all other issues were derived. In Latin America the Administration adopted a frankly interventionist policy in El Salvador in an attempt to ensure the victory of the regime most congenial to the United States. This was an understandable policy in terms of the United States' regional security, but it was unconvincingly linked to the idea of resisting a perceived Soviet intrusion. American policymakers criticized the Carter regime for its policy of encouraging "change" in Latin America out of a sincere revulsion from despotism but with little thought of whether the change was likely to be an improvement either from the viewpoint of human rights or in terms of America's strategic interest. Ambassador Jeane J. Kirkpatrick, the representative of the United States at the United Nations, wrote:

> . . . a more prudent appraisal of politics in Central America would have left policymakers a little less enthusiastic about the destruction of any even semi-constitutional ruler, not because they approved the ruler but because they understood that authority in such systems is weak, stability fragile, and order much easier to destroy than to reconstruct.

In other words—Somoza is bad in Nicaragua, but in what respect, from the viewpoint of international stability, are the Sandinists any better? The trouble with this realism was that it left the United States identified with support of regimes, such as those of the Shah, Somoza and Marcos, which aroused strong reservations in American public opinion as well as abroad.

In Africa the Administration was inclined to reduce American harassment of South Africa on the issue of apartheid or in the matter of independence for Namibia. It tended to support any foe of Libya but to take no more interest than its predecessors in other African problems. In Asia the new Administration still nourished some nostalgic affections for Taiwan and even endangered relations with China by dalliance with the supply of arms to the Formosan authorities. But the major disquiet of American policymakers lay in more crucial areas. There was no atmosphere of consensus in the Western alliance on how to meet the challenge of Soviet competition and expansion. The shifts in American tactics and rhetoric contributed greatly to this confusion.

The American electoral system has laid particularly heavy burdens on foreign policy, often depriving it of coherence and giving it a spasmodic character. This fact came to expression in intense form after the 1980 contest for the presidency. The fact that the United States Constitution requires a quadrennial election campaign does not necessarily mean that conditions are objectively ripe for changes in the international system on the third Tuesday in January every four years. Yet when Presidents of different parties succeed each other, they are usually committed in advance to institute changes in conformity with their party pledges and platforms. It is rare for a political party to admit that its predecessor was acting in a normal or sane fashion in the conduct of the nation's foreign relations. The Carter presidency was naturally followed by criticism of its foreign policy, since, despite achievements in some domains, its last months were overshadowed by two traumatic events—the hostage crisis in Tehran and the Soviet invasion of Afghanistan. American countermeasures were patently ineffective in both cases. Ronald Reagan was undoubtedly assisted to victory by his virile promise of strong action against anyone offending American pride or interests. He pledged himself not to be satisfied with the text of SALT II, which the Carter Administration had intended to present for congressional ratification, and his campaign rhetoric was unprecedented in the virulence of its assaults on the Soviet Union. Although his election was supported for various motives by Nixon and Kissinger, the architects and fashioners of détente, Reagan was not a fervent supporter of the détente idea or its cautious rhetoric.

Thus the beginning of 1981 was tense with general denunciations of the Soviet Union and with energetic, if somewhat unspecific, promises of a new attitude and style. SALT II was suspended without a clear alternative being offered, and Secretary of State Alexander Haig embarrassed his country's allies by a vigorous campaign to prove that the testing ground for allied solidarity in defense of freedom and in resistance to Soviet expansion lay in El Salvador, where the United States interpreted the savage civil war as a Soviet plot to create a new Cuban situation with the aid of the leftist Sandinist regime in Nicaragua. None of America's allies attached such primary importance to El Salvador; some of them, especially in France after François Mitterrand's acces-

sion to power at the head of his Socialist Party, believed that the El
Salvador insurrection was primarily the consequence of social conditions in that country and that even without Soviet influence the situation would not be far different from what it had become. The Reagan
Administration, unable to do more than its predecessors about Afghanistan, repeated the familiar language of denunciation, and when
the Polish government under Soviet pressure intensified its persecution of the Polish Solidarity movement, the American reaction, although more stringent than anything that European countries were
willing to emulate, was far short of anything that would intimidate or
even disquiet anyone in Moscow or Warsaw.

In the Middle East alone the new Administration struck out in new
directions. For over a year it abstained from any initiative designed to
carry the Camp David accords beyond the Carter Administration's
achievement in sponsoring a peace treaty between Egypt and Israel.
The assassination of President Anwar el-Sadat and the early efforts of
Husni Mubarak to consolidate his rule contributed to this American
passivity. Secretary Haig made a visit to the Middle East in an attempt
to persuade friendly states that the central issue was Soviet expansion.
This effort was a failure, partly because Arab states showed more
concern about Israel than about the Soviet Union, and partly because
the thesis about the primacy of the Soviet threat was not borne out by
any evidence. The Soviets were strangely passive in the Arab-Israeli
dispute and had little part in the eruption of war between Iraq and
Iran. They seemed to have limited aims, falling short of total commitment in the region.

An American-Israeli memorandum of understanding on strategic
cooperation with Israel was proposed and later withdrawn when the
Begin government formally annexed the Golan Heights against American advice. But when Israeli forces moved deep into Lebanon in June
1982 to destroy the infrastructure of the PLO, the United States illustrated its ambivalence in a series of changing attitudes. It began by
opposing the expedition but then drew attention to the "opportunities" that the invasion had opened for a stable Lebanon and a Palestine
movement shorn of the PLO's radical and militant leadership. The
U.S. representative, Philip Habib, negotiated an agreement for the
PLO to leave Beirut, but the United States expressed strong opposition to the bombardment, shelling and siege of Beirut which the Israeli
government considered vital as a means of pressure on the PLO. Yet,
later, when many Israelis were expressing opposition to their government's militant policy, the United States was giving the impression of
acquiescence. In the end, the United States emerged as the winning
party as against the Soviet Union, which had patently failed to aid its
Palestinian and Syrian allies. Militant, radical anti-American move-

ments had again suffered defeat. But American popularity in the Arab world had further declined, and the Egyptian-Israeli peace treaty had been reduced from the promise of a new regional harmony to something like a coldly formal armistice. Reagan's attempt to move the Camp David negotiations forward in September 1982 was well conceived, and initial Israeli opposition was not likely to endure. Reagan had proposed a resumption of the Camp David negotiations for the purpose of establishing a regime of "full autonomy" for the Palestinians in the West Bank and Gaza; he had added that in such negotiations the United States would advocate a permanent solution under which the Palestinians in the West Bank and Gaza would form part of a Jordanian-Palestinian state, while secure boundaries between Israel and the Jordanian state would be fixed by negotiation. This proposal had been rejected by the Begin government almost before it had been promulgated, since it conflicted with the aim of maintaining all the territories under Israeli rule. The large sectors of Israeli opinion that were favorable to a compromise praised Reagan's initiative, but internal Israeli contention became irrelevant when the PLO, under Yasir Arafat's frightened leadership, declined to give King Hussein of Jordan the necessary authority to lead a Jordanian-Palestinian delegation in a peace negotiation with Israel. This episode illustrated one of the paradoxes of the American position in the international system. The United States has immense importance for Israel's security and economy, is the chief mainstay of Jordan, and ensures the defense of Saudi Arabia, but in a crucial test it was unable to enlist any of those three governments on behalf of an enlightened diplomatic initiative that would have brought no harm to any of the three and would have advanced the interests of regional stability. While Lebanon, Israel, Poland, El Salvador and Afghanistan periodically occupied the headlines, the two gravest frustrations for American policymakers lay in their relations with the Soviet Union and with America's European allies.

The Reagan Administration's early policy on the nuclear issue was based on a perceived need to expand and modernize the American nuclear arsenal while holding back on definitive negotiations with the Soviet Union. It was the familiar notion of "negotiation from strength." But the American nuclear strategy also required the cooperation of the European allies, who were asked to accommodate medium-range missiles and launching structures in their territory. There was vehement European resistance to this approach, reinforced by strong public revulsion from further advances in the nuclear arms race. All the European governments attached more importance to détente and arms control talks than to nuclear arms escalation. In Britain, the Labour Party, which had established Britain as a nuclear power during its period in office in the forties and fifties, adopted resolutions in favor of a unilateral abandonment of the nuclear option. Even confirmed Atlanticists who understood the logic of a nuclear balance could not grasp why the United States insisted on a numerical superiority: a capacity to destroy the planet one hundred times over is not effectively different from a capacity to destroy it two hundredfold. The logic of nuclear deterrence is fulfilled if a country possesses a measure of invulnerability for its retaliatory forces together with a capacity to inflict damage that an adversary in his right mind would find unacceptable. To harp on the need for numerical superiority seemed to be little more than a fallacious transfer of the logic of conventional arms races into the nuclear field.

The question whether degrees of superiority can confer ascendancy after a certain capacity of overkill had been reached has been a subject of debate in the United States defense establishment for many years. It was Henry Kissinger who uttered the memorable outburst: "What in the name of God is superiority? What is the significance of it politically, militarily, operationally? What do you do with it?" Later he pointed out that "imbalances of military power had historically been of great significance but that this was no longer so between nuclear powers." Not since the Cuban missile crisis of 1962 had asymmetries of nuclear power affected the outcome of any conflict between the Soviet Union and the United States. According to this view, "degrees of nuclear power were meaningless, always provided, of course, that sufficient parity was maintained to deny the enemy a disarming first strike."

It was a serious matter for the United States when its views on the nuclear arms balance were challenged abroad by its allies and at home by large sectors of public opinion. The domestic challenge did not come from peace movements and "liberals" alone. An impressive quartet of former officials—George Kennan, McGeorge Bundy, Gerard Smith and Robert McNamara—published an article in the quarterly *Foreign Affairs* in April 1982 advocating an American declaration that would renounce the idea of "first use" of nuclear weapons in an escalating conventional war. Their argument was that the first use of nuclear weapons even in an allegedly "limited" context would inevitably lead to full-scale nuclear war. Since such a threat was not credible, the unilateral renunciation would cost the United States little and might give an impetus to the halting and eventual rollback of the nuclear arms race. This approach was rejected by the Administration on the grounds that the unilateral principle would release the Soviet Union from any pressure to play its part in a balanced reduction process. The author of the détente formula, Henry Kissinger, also argued against this surprising initiative from four Americans of rigorous temperament:

A statement of no first use would leave us psychologically naked for a period that would surely extend over at least five years, even if our own government and all our NATO allies were prepared to make immediate, serious and sustained efforts to redress the imbalance in conventional weapons.

The debate would doubtless continue for many months, but the fact that American and NATO opinions were divided on the matter that should in theory unite them—the organization of an effective defense and deterrent against Soviet pressure—illustrated the growing difficulty in maintaining a Western consensus.

Simultaneously the Western front was breached at another crucial point. In order to strengthen economic links with Eastern Europe and to help solve their own economic difficulties the major European countries wished to link themselves to a gas pipeline reaching deep into Soviet territory. The Reagan Administration objected on the grounds that this would increase the dependence of European countries on Soviet good will and make them vulnerable to Soviet pressure. The United States also feared that for Europe to make this gesture would undermine the American attempt to support Polish freedom by punitive economic measures against the Soviet Union. When British, French and Italian companies nevertheless provided equipment for the pipeline project, the United States imposed financial sanctions on its closest allies. American officials were making the worst of all possible worlds. Within a few weeks the United States retreated and the European allies went on with their plans, free of American pressure.

The absence of accord between NATO countries on the central theme of an anti-Soviet strategy is certainly a failure of Western policy from which Moscow can derive satisfaction. America and Western Europe no longer face each other on the psychological basis from which their partnership grew in the late 1940s; but neither have the norms and principles of that partnership been redefined in conformity with the new balance between the allies. Paradoxically, the American deterrent has been so successful that a powerful and assertive Soviet Union today evokes less alarm in Europe than did a battered and anxious Soviet Union a few years after World War II. American policy in the 1980s is paying the penalty for its success in previous decades.

An Assessment

There is more self-criticism than self-congratulation in the American literature on the foreign policy of the United States. This severity of tone contrasts with the parallel literature in the Soviet Union which claims infallibility for Soviet diplomacy and ascribes all the dislocations and tensions in the international system to American and Western errors—or "crimes." The only agreed assumption in Washington and

Moscow is that American policy has become the central theme of contemporary international life. How America acts and how others react to America represent a very large part of modern international history; if we were to omit these two themes there would not be much to tell.

How simple it was to define American foreign policy up to World War II! There were clear doctrinal foundations going back to the earliest years: continental development; no entangling alliances; the Monroe Doctrine; equal trading opportunities; freedom of the seas; neutral rights. If these ideas are carefully examined it emerges that none of them required any commitment to other nations. They were warning notices established by the United States in defense of its own interests, with the implication that those willing to respect them need fear no penalty—nor expect any particular favor from America. "Unilateralism" would not be an exaggerated description of American foreign policy for the first 170 years of its history. America was prepared to look after itself—and after no one else. World War I was seen as no more than a temporary disturbance of this traditional rhythm, and unilateralism was resumed as soon as the troops were home. There is no evidence that the United States would ever have entered World War II had it not been forced to do so by the Japanese attack and the declaration of war by Germany. The somewhat inflated tributes by Churchill to Roosevelt before December 1941 were uttered more in flattering hope than in genuine conviction. And even when the war ended in 1945 a return to modified unilateralism was not out of the question. The naïve disposition to believe that Soviet friendship would carry over from the war to the peace and the outrageously exaggerated hopes expressed for the United Nations were subconscious excuses for renouncing an assertive individual responsibility for America in the postwar world.

Against this background, there is much to admire in the rapidity and wholeheartedness with which America reversed its passive role after realizing that Allied unity would not prevail and that the values dear to American hearts would not be ensured by a spectator's role accompanied by painless exhortations. The burdens of broadening involvement were assumed with candor and courage. After all, the cherished habits and traditions of a nation's history were being discarded beyond recall. To have brought the concept of broadening involvement to doctrinal and institutional expression by the end of 1948 illustrated the intellectual power and political dynamism of American policymakers at a turning point in their nation's history.

A general verdict about American policy must be linked to a Soviet context. It was right to resist Soviet expansionism after World War II, but it was a mistake to give that resistance such an emphatic ideological accent. Once the United States defined all Communist countries as its collective adversary it became difficult to avoid superficiality in the American approach to such diverse peoples as Yugoslavs, Germans, Koreans, Chinese, Poles, Rumanians and others. China is strictly Communist but is close to alliance with the United States. Yugoslavia and Rumania have at various times shown a capacity to take independent attitudes in international affairs. If the repressive military regime in Poland is Communist in its ideology, so also are the Solidarity leaders. American policymakers underestimated the role of diverse national interests in the formation of policy in the Communist countries.

There is a strong case for interpreting Soviet policy in its more dangerous expressions as a continuation of traditional Russian attitudes rather than as an innovation deriving from Marxist-Leninist theory. The tendency toward police-state systems, the exaltation of the state as against the individual, slave labor, a persistent pressure to extend Russian boundaries in apprehensive reaction to external threats, a somber sense of tragedy and suffering as the keynotes of national history, alienation from the habits and attitudes of Western Europe—all these features of the modern Soviet system could be diagnosed in these very words as characteristics of czarist Russia. After all, the czars had no more hesitation in occupying some Balkan countries than has the Soviet Union in imposing itself on the Baltic nations.

The possibility that the Soviet leaders have ceased to be fanatically serious about the triumph of Marxism-Leninism and its dream of a world revolution does not mean that they will ever confess a lack of deference to that ideology. The ideological dimension gives them favorable dividends among idealists abroad and a rationale for imposing strict discipline at home. But all the evidence of recent years supports the theory that they lack the frenzied element of passion that would lead them, as it led Hitler, to take action that is objectively against their national interest in order to vindicate their ideological orthodoxy.

The virtue of adopting this appraisal of Soviet policy is that it does not require any reduction of Western vigilance or defensive preparedness, while it does offer a chance of exploring accommodations, not on the naïve assumption of Soviet virtue but on the realistic assumption of Soviet self-interest. Another advantage is that it does not preclude individual definitions of American policy toward other Communist states.

It must be acknowledged that American foreign policy in the past decades has also been subject to criticism from the opposite vantage point. It has been described as inadequately demonological in its interpretation of Soviet policy, and therefore prone to "illusions," such as détente and coexistence. One of the most eloquent advocates of this theory describes it thus:

> *If . . . the aims of the Soviet Union were limited, they could be respected and even to a certain extent satisfied through negotiation and compromise . . . But what if the Soviet Union is not a "normal" nation-state? What if in this case ideology overrides interest in the traditional sense? What if Soviet aims are unlimited? In short, what if the Soviet Union bears a closer resemblance to the Germany of Hitler than to the Germany of Kaiser Wilhelm? There was no way of doing business—that is, negotiating a peaceful settlement with Hitler. As a revolutionary with unlimited aims, he offered only two choices: resistance or submission . . . What this means is that the conflict between the Soviet Union and the West is not subject to resolution by the traditional tools of diplomacy . . . Détente is not possible . . .*

Podhoretz goes on to state that "all the evidence suggests that the Soviet Union poses the same kind of threat [as did Hitler]."

"All the evidence" is an exaggeration. The truth is that the evidence is at least ambivalent and therefore places American policy before agonizing dilemmas. American foreign policy toward the Soviet Union has oscillated between the "Hitler" syndrome of the late forties and early fifties and the "Kaiser Wilhelm" model in the détente period, back to the "Hitler" scenario of President Reagan's campaign oratory, and back once more to the pragmatic assumption in the actual execution of policy. But American policy has never fully recovered from the errors of the 1950s, when it substituted a general crusade against international Communism for a detailed, empirical approach to its relations with individual Communist states.

As 1983 drew toward its close, American foreign policy had found no formula to replace détente. One of the misunderstandings about détente had been built in from the start. If détente did not mean friendship, did it at least imply stability? Kissinger would have given a positive answer: "The first necessity is to bring home to the Soviet Union that to us détente means a restrained international conduct, and if we cannot achieve that, then we will have to confront expansionism wherever it takes place." Alexander Haig as Secretary of State was more specific about the meaning of "restrained international conduct." In an interview in the New York *Times* he explained that he did not oppose what has been called "competitive coexistence" between Moscow and Washington for influence in third countries, but he was "against an arms limitation agreement that sanctions or tolerates direct military intervention by the Red Army as in Afghanistan, or by

Cuban mercenaries, financed and supplied by the Soviet Union, in Africa, Latin America or elsewhere."

If détente meant that the Soviet Union would refrain from nuclear confrontation and also from an attempt to improve its position anywhere outside the range of direct American security commitments, the result would be a Soviet dedication to the status quo no less complete than that of the United States. There can be no question that this would be a favorable development for America; but it went far beyond anything that the Kremlin had ever agreed to do under the heading of "détente." For this unpleasant realism we have the authority of a Soviet spokesman: "No one can put a freeze on the world sociopolitical development on the pretext of détente. International agreements cannot alter the laws of class struggle."

The fact that some Soviet policies are more blatantly incompatible with détente than anything for which the West is responsible does not mean that the West, and especially the United States, is immaculate in its détentist record. It was legitimate for the Carter Administration to react irascibly to the outrage of the Afghan invasion and to attempt some measures of demonstrative disapproval; indeed, it could justly be urged that these measures were not sufficiently incisive. But Carter's statement that he had learned new lessons from the Soviet action was a demoralizing confession that he had been plunged in illusion before that event.

The worst of all policies in relation to the Soviet Union is one of inconsistency. Thus the initial rigorous reaction to the report of a "Soviet combat brigade in Cuba" was made to seem foolish when the United States subsequently climbed down from its indignant posture. Reagan's severe denunciation of the Soviet system in his election campaign in 1980 would not strike any devotee of pluralistic democracy as inaccurate, but the question arose whether all that candid truth served any viable purpose. The decision to station theater nuclear missiles in Europe was taken by the Carter Administration in November 1979; it may therefore be described as a national, not a partisan policy. Kissinger's warnings against the notion that détente is compatible with a wide-ranging program of destabilization by the Soviet Union in such places as Angola, Ethiopia and Afghanistan had been echoed by Carter's National Security Adviser Zbigniew Brzezinski in a memorandum to President Carter urging that the United States should insist on a "comprehensive and reciprocal détente." The explanation of this phrase was that the Soviets were taking their own benefits from détente while conceding none to the United States. Here, too, the examples were drawn from Soviet or Soviet-sponsored military activism in the Third World as well as from violation of the Helsinki understandings on human rights.

The upshot is that American spokesmen in successive administrations have had a common view of what is wrong with détente; what is wrong is quite simply the absence of Soviet restraint. American criticism of the United States role in this dilemma has been of the usual converging variety: American reactions are "too weak" (witness the retreat from severity about the brigade in Cuba, the change of Carter's heart about the neutron bomb, the resumption of grain sales, the decision to relent in the matter of European participation in the Siberian gas project, the relatively innocuous sanctions imposed after the invasion of Afghanistan); or "too bellicose" (witness the retreat from SALT II, Reagan's verbal assaults on the Soviet system, the attribution of crises in Central America to Soviet initiative, the loud intention of organizing the Middle East against Soviet expansion and the initial suspension of arms control dialogue pending the attainment of American "superiority").

This contradictory American self-criticism reflects a genuine, objective dilemma. The truth seems to be that there are Americans who believe in the carrot and others who believe in the stick in dealing with Soviet provocations; but the American carrots are not very inviting and the sticks are not very painful. Recent American diplomacy has found it difficult to come up with incentives capable of luring the Soviets into a policy that they would not otherwise have adopted, or with threats that have deterred the Soviets from a course on which they wished to embark.

The absence of any real punitive capacity in the hands of the United States reduces the most lucid rhetoric to emptiness. Kissinger proclaimed in the heat of the Angolan crisis: "The Government has a duty to make clear to the Soviet Union and Cuba that . . . this type of action will not be tolerated again." Brzezinski advises Carter to "make it unmistakably clear to the Soviet Union that detente . . . is incompatible with irresponsible behavior in Angola, the Middle East and the U.N. (e.g., stimulation of extremist resolutions such as the one equating Zionism with racism)" and Alexander Haig, as quoted above, declares himself "against an arms limitation agreement that sanctions or tolerates direct military intervention by the Red Army as in Afghanistan."

"Will not be tolerated again" and "irresponsible behavior" are good headmaster language. But what happens when the unruly student replies with defiance and it becomes clear that the headmaster can neither punish nor expel? The sense of impotence is compounded when Washington resorts to penalties which are just as prejudicial to itself as to Moscow. Haig implies that abstention from an arms limitation agreement would be a way of "not tolerating" Soviet military activism. But an arms limitation agreement is not a favor to the Soviet Union; it is a vital interest of the West, strongly urged by American public opinion. Refusal to meet the Soviet Union at the summit seems to be regarded by the United States as an appropriate response to Soviet intransigence. But a summit meeting is a method of alleviating irresponsible conduct, not a reward for responsible conduct. To say that a summit meeting will only be held in conditions in which it is not really necessary falls short of lucidity. Similarly, the idea that economic pressure will change Soviet policy was dealt a heavy blow by the failure of the United States to secure increased emigration from the Soviet Union by a threat to withdraw economic concessions in 1974. Jewish emigration dropped by 1976 from an annual rate of 33,000 to 10,000, from which it has now declined to negligible proportions. Nor have the economic restrictions applied since the suppression of the Polish Solidarity movement and the invasion of Afghanistan had any recognizable effect on Soviet attitudes.

In these circumstances the retreat from SALT II and the denial of summit meetings have brought no benefit to American interests and can merely be adduced to demonstrate that it is not Moscow alone that has departed from the assumptions of détente. The United States has not endangered stability by any action as drastic or heinous as the military actions of the USSR and its Cuban surrogates in Angola, Ethiopia and Afghanistan, so that the principal blame for the decline of détente must attach to the Soviet Union, not the United States. But American policy since 1980 deviated at first from the style and tone of the 1970s in some major respects.

The gravest departure from the viewpoint of its effect on the Western alliance lay in the field of the central nuclear balance. The idea of suspending negotiation until the United States secured "superiority" depended rather touchingly on Soviet cooperation. Moscow would have had to accept a standstill while Washington improved its negotiating position. There was nothing to indicate why or how such altruism would be expected. In the meantime, the American observers who accused Soviet spokesmen of talking seriously about the feasibility of nuclear war were confounded by a rash of similar statements by Americans who had now reached official status. Thus, an official named Colin S. Gray announced that "the United States may have no practical alternative [!] to waging a nuclear war . . . The United States requires the capability to strike first with strategic forces and dominate any subsequent process of escalation."

A variation on this kind of rhetoric can be found in the writings of Sovietologists who tell us that the Soviet Union would not see anything particularly horrifying in a nuclear war that resulted in tens of millions of Russian deaths. Thus, Richard Pipes, a White House expert on the Soviet Union:

Soviet doctrine emphatically asserts that while an all-out nuclear war would indeed prove extremely destructive to both parties, its outcome would not be mutual suicide; the country better prepared for it and in possession of a superior strategy could win and emerge a viable society . . . There is something innately destabilizing in the very fact that we consider nuclear war unfeasible and suicidal for both, and our chief adversary views it as feasible and winnable for itself.

Mr. Pipes does not include himself among those who consider nuclear war unfeasible and suicidal for both. He is the author of the statement that "there is no alternative to war with the Soviet Union if the Russians do not abandon communism." This statement was disavowed by the United States government, but an objective outsider would now have difficulty in identifying any Soviet rhetorical extremism for which there is not an official American parallel.

If the anti-nuclear movement in Europe, which has undoubtedly weakened the negotiating position of the West, weighs heavily on American diplomacy, it would be only fair to admit that the peace movement in its present nervous mood is largely the fruit of American rhetoric. Many Europeans sincerely believe that there are Americans who harbor the idea that a limited nuclear war confined to European theaters might be feasible and, in certain conditions, the lesser of many evils. This fear has been nourished by Kissinger's Brussels speech in September 1979 urging Europeans not to rely too much on American nuclear retaliation; by Presidential Directive 59 of 1980 on limited nuclear wars; by President Reagan's statement in October 1981 to the effect that there could be a nuclear exchange in Europe without an escalation into all-out nuclear war involving the United States.

It is a relief to turn to the lucid rationality of a senior American military commander. General Maxwell Taylor, a former Chairman of the Joint Chiefs of Staff, writes: "There is no conceivable way of hedging against a failure of deterrence . . . In any major strategic exchange, the reciprocal damage would create conditions that would make victory and defeat virtually indistinguishable, save perhaps that the victors might survive a bit longer than the vanquished."

As for the idea of a limited nuclear war, we have Brezhnev's authority for the certainty that the Soviets would not accept limitation. If a nuclear missile were fired at the Soviet Union from Germany, there is no assurance that the reprisal would not be directed at South Dakota.

Some of the rhetoric of the American spokesmen on the nuclear issue since 1980 could be renounced without anything worthwhile being sacrificed. It is more difficult to make generalized prescriptions for American policy in regional disputes. In a society that is not totalitarian in its domestic structure, diplomacy tends to be complex and ambivalent. In such disputes as that between India and Pakistan, Turkey and Greece, the Arab states and Israel, and always when a Communist country is involved, the Soviet Union gives 100 percent support to one of the parties. The United States tries to ingratiate itself with both and often ends by conciliating neither and winning a reputation for inadequate fidelity. Even when a NATO ally was involved, as in the war between Britain and Argentina over the Falkland Islands (Malvinas) in 1982, the United States earned little gratitude in Britain and no appreciation for its mediating efforts in Buenos Aires.

The diplomatic handicaps which Americans should accept with greatest resignation are those that flow from the essential nature of their own pluralistic society. On the other hand, there is nothing in democratic doctrine that requires such self-inflicted wounds as those caused by the internecine conflicts of jurisdiction between State Department bureaucracies and national security advisers, or the declamation of oratory without calculating the probable effects.

The central problem in American policy is the definition of commitment. In 1961 Kennedy enunciated a doctrine of universal commitment which nobody would embrace today. After Vietnam there was a danger that the pendulum would swing back to disgruntled isolationism. In the gap between these extremes American policymakers and thinkers seek a modest role that does not go as far as total self-abnegation. George Kennan advocates an American commitment limited to Western Europe, Japan and Israel together with an eloquent admission of helplessness everywhere else. Americans are unlikely to accept the doctrine of helplessness with such totality; but it would have been inconceivable for a leading authority on United States foreign policy to have defined his country's obligations so modestly two decades ago.

Policymakers in Washington would be less than human if they were not seized by acute nostalgia for the days when they worked in a climate of public consensus and congressional deference, free from the torment of self-doubt concerning the very capacity of America to shape the Western world. In objective terms the self-criticism has gone beyond the point of rationality. Obsessed with the failure of their own highest ambitions, Americans have not wished to perceive the setbacks and failures incurred by the Soviet Union in recent years. The Soviets derived no gains from their rocket-rattling up to their defeat in the Cuban missile crisis. They have not improved their situation in the domestic power struggles in Western Europe; their cherished ideology has made very few gains; Eastern Europe is more restive and potentially turbulent than ever before; relations with China are poor; the arms race has constricted their ability to meet the pressures for a more liberal consumer economy; they are too weak in their own eyes to allow a few dissidents to express their dissent or to pierce the iron curtain for normal intellectual contact; and the display of their force against Afghanistan and the Polish Solidarity movement has brought them more trouble than glory. The American malaise may not really be a particular affliction reserved for the United States; it may only be one aspect of the new superpower modesty imposed on the two giants by the growing pluralism and complexity of modern international life.

Whatever the future American predicaments may be, there would be a stronger chance of solving them if there were a revival of the domestic confidence that was once the foundation of America's appeal to the external domain. The current rhetoric is pervaded by reproach. A widely read historian sees her country in a despairing mood and articulates it in language that evokes the Prophet Jeremiah:

> *In the United States we have a society pervaded from top to bottom by contempt for the law . . . Our government collaborates abroad with the worst enemies of humanity and liberty. It wastes its substance on useless proliferation of military hardware that can never buy security no matter how high the pile. It learns no lessons, employs no wisdom, and corrupts all who succumb to Potomac fever.*

This is carrying self-doubt too far. The transition from utopianism to cosmic gloom may have been too abrupt. In the comparative terms by which nations must be judged, the United States emerges as a nation no less endowed than others with a galvanizing tradition. America is sensitive to the stir and current of the times, and it is increasingly well versed in the harmonies and compromises demanded by an international system in which there are no universally accepted criteria of legitimacy for the actions of states. Certainly there is no other center of power in which statesmen reach more often beyond the confines of their own national interest toward a voluntary acceptance of a universal human responsibility.

Chapter 3

THE SOVIET UNION
IN WORLD POLITICS

"A RIDDLE WRAPPED in mystery inside an enigma." The fact that Churchill's epigram is witty does not make it true. The policies and actions of the Soviet Union are no more incalculable than those of any other major actor in the international system. In many ways the Soviet Union offers smooth ground for the analyst and observer. Alone among the Great Powers it has a dual international personality. It appears both as a state with clearly defined national interests and as the center of a revolutionary movement with a self-appointed mission to work for the triumph of its idea on a universal plane. In its national capacity the USSR inherits a vision of Russian interests which does not deviate sharply from what Russian leaders have asserted under previous regimes. These interests are dictated by unchanging facts of geography and historical experience that point in a single direction. And in its revolutionary capacity the Soviet Union acts in accordance with a fixed system of ideas as rigidly and passionately embraced as any set of theological dogmas. This ought to make prediction easier than if Moscow played its role in a spirit of empirical pragmatism and improvisation. Moreover, the analysis of Soviet policies and motives has now become an academic discipline engaging the activity and even the lifework of thousands of trained specialists. Since a great part of world politics consists of reaction to what Soviet policies are, or are considered to be, it may be deduced that Russian foreign policy is among the most heavily documented themes in contemporary international and intellectual life.

The analyst of Soviet policy is also helped by the fact that Soviet leadership has undergone no more than three substantive changes in the past half century. The Stalin, Khrushchev and Brezhnev epochs coincide with neatly arranged, solid blocks of time, which also coincide with whatever changes have taken place in the style and content of Soviet foreign policy. It would be salutary, therefore, for scholars and diplomats to liberate themselves from the myth of Soviet incalculability. The problem is not a difficulty of understanding. The trouble is that understanding the facts is not the same as knowing what to do with them.

One difficulty for those who examine Soviet problems from outside is the intense rhythm of change in the subjective attitude of the rest of the world toward the Soviet Union. That nation entered the affections of the West on June 22, 1941, stayed there for five crowded years, and departed to familiar unpopularity in the aftermath of the war. The brief era of euphoric embrace came in 1941 with startling suddenness. At one moment the Soviet Union was the symbol of everything that Western Europe and America had been taught to despise and fear. The single blow of Hitler's invasion exalted Moscow to a pinnacle of popularity and prestige. The transition was orchestrated by Winston Churchill on the day that Hitler's armies and planes poured over the Soviet border:

> The past, with its crimes, its follies and its tragedies, flashes away. I see the Russian soldiers standing on the threshold of their native land, guarding the fields which their fathers have tilled from time immemorial. I see them guarding their homes where mothers and wives pray . . . for the safety of their loved ones, the return of the breadwinner, of their champion, of their protector. I see the 10,000 villages of Russia, where the means of existence was wrung so hardly from the soil, but where there are still primordial human joys, where maidens laugh and children play. I see advancing on all this in hideous onslaught the Nazi war machine, with its clanking, heel-clicking, dandified Prussian officers, its crafty expert agents fresh from the tying down of a dozen countries. I see also the dull, drilled, docile, brutish masses of the Hun soldiery plodding on like a swarm of crawling locusts . . .

This extraordinary passage is a classic illustration of the capacity of war to provide sudden legitimacy for new allies and an abrupt transformation of previous images. It is certain that the Russian maidens laughed and the children played long before June 22, 1941, and that the "primordial human joys" were there all the time. The fact that the Russian cause was just, while the Nazi cause was monstrously wicked, did not create any marked differences in the way their soldiers used to "plod."

But the trauma of the Nazi invasion diffused an idyllic picture of the Soviet Union throughout the Western world, and there were to be lingering effects of profound importance for postwar diplomacy. For the five years of war, critical or even balanced appraisals of Soviet policy in the West were suspended with such rigidity that the analytical power of public opinion became almost atrophied, until Soviet actions brought it back to life when the battles ceased.

The day of the Nazi invasion is the turning point in Soviet diplomatic history; from that date onward the Soviet Union emerges out of relative solitude and becomes involved permanently in the international system as one of its decisive components. Four decades later it is not difficult to strike the balance. The Soviet Union has been a spectacular success as a state and a relative failure as a center of revolution. Its power has grown while the magnetic force of its idea has waned.

The growth of power is more easily measurable than the decline of ideological influence. From being an outlaw state on the margin of the international system, threatened by a powerful Germany in the west and a militant Japan in the east, regarded as backward in science, technology and productivity, huddled up against hostile neighbors in Central European and Baltic states, the Soviet Union has come through fire and death to the status of a world power comparable to the United States and overshadowing all others. All the contiguous states in Europe except Finland are under its direct control. Afghanistan is under its occupation. Russia's dominance in Czechoslovakia and East Germany pushes its direct control further west than the czars ever dared to penetrate. It holds world superiority in many categories of weapons, and it is one of only two participants in the research and exploration of outer space.

There was a moment in the immediate aftermath of World War II when the Soviet Union was even more predominant in Europe and Asia. Its power at that time was set in heightened relief by the temporary disappearance of Germany and Japan from the active international system and by the victory of Communism in China. It has now become apparent that the establishment of the new Chinese regime diminishes rather than enhances the Soviet leadership of world Communism. West Germany and Japan are vastly stronger than anyone could have anticipated on the morrow of the war, and not all Communist countries or parties acknowledge absolute Soviet leadership. Marxist ideology has not been able to commit all its adherents to a monolithic unity under Soviet hegemony. Nevertheless the Soviet Union now has huge nuclear capabilities and has unexpectedly emerged as a major naval power in the world. It now derives predominant status from its own strength rather than from the relative weakness of others.

In the specific terms and proportions of Russian national history the Soviet regime stands high and proud; it has recuperated all the losses of the Russo-Japanese War and of World War I with the exception of Finland. Emerging in 1918 weak and divided, threatened by external intervention and civil disorder, humiliated by territorial losses and economic depression, the Soviet Union has reached the highest pinnacle of power that any Russian regime has ever been able to celebrate. There is also a satisfying sense of psychological revenge. Russian leaders used to be received at Western European courts and chanceries with a kind of supercilious courtesy as representatives of a lower social and political culture seeking to be patronized by the European elite. Today they excite an apprehensive deference wherever they go.

Soviet expansion has been accompanied by a parallel decline in the fortunes of those who once stood at the peak of international power and prestige. Though Germany and Japan are economically sound, both they and Italy have been disarmed and shorn of empire, while Britain, France, the Netherlands and Belgium have been compressed into narrower confines. During the same period the Soviet Union has annexed 250,000 square miles of territory in Europe and Asia as well as becoming the virtual overlord of subservient states in Asia and Eastern Europe. It has intervened in the Middle East and the Caribbean, where it has established friendly regimes, and its occupation of Afghanistan, however irksome and destructive of its international reputation, has vindicated the principle that Russia has an acknowledged right or, at least, an accepted habit of determining what happens in contiguous territories. Nor does the enhanced geopolitical power of the USSR rest on unilateral and illegitimate seizure; since the early 1970s the Soviet Union has obtained world recognition of its sphere of influence in Eastern Europe, culminating in the decisions of the Helsinki Conference on European Security and Cooperation in 1975. Despite its dislike of Soviet repressions in Hungary, Czechoslovakia and Poland, the Western world, if only by default, has resigned itself to the Brezhnev doctrine announced by the Soviet government in August 1968 after the invasion of Czechoslovakia; under that doctrine the Soviet Union claimed the right to intervene by force in any Communist country which it considered to be threatened by counterrevolution, that is to say, by a change of its socialist regime. This doctrine virtually deprives Communist states of their rights under the UN Charter, including the basic right to "sovereign equality." If there is such a thing as absolute security, the Soviet Union comes nearer than any modern state to having achieved it and to having it ratified by universal recognition.

It follows that Russian citizens who are moved by nationalist fervor have no reason to be disappointed by the record of the Soviet leadership in the years since World War II. The paradox is that Marxist theory is very grudging in its approval of nationalism. It claims to be the spokesman of a universalist vision in which the separate nation-state will lose its particularity and merge into an era of brotherhood under the leadership of the workers of the world. Communists denounce the accent on patriotism as "reactionary"—unless the patriotism is that of the Soviet Union. The Marxist founding fathers could not renounce the patriotic mystique when they looked around for means of buttressing the vulnerable Soviet state. And the patriotism to which they appealed was "Russian," not "Soviet." The fact that nearly half of the Soviet Union's population is not Russian has not set any limits on the adulation of Russian traditions as the cultural and political norm. "In this role, the Soviet State manipulates patriotic symbols, commemorates national glories, venerates historic heroes (mostly tsars and generals), worships at national shrines, extols Russian culture and language, and celebrates the lofty goals and achievements of Holy Mother Russia while rationalizing and downplaying the more negative features of the Russian tradition."

There is a weakness in the Soviet Union's ideological posture here of which its rivals have taken little propagandist advantage. No Soviet diplomat will be caught saying "the Russian government," but Europeans, more frequently than Americans, habitually speak of "the Russians" when describing the Soviet state. They use this term partly out of historical and cultural habit, and partly because they see the Russian predominance from close at hand. There is no offense to truth in using the word "Russian." While Soviet rhetoric pays tribute to the multinational myth, the reality is that the leadership of the state and the party, as well as the high command of the army, the diplomatic service and the upper grades of the civil service, are manned almost exclusively by Russians. It may not be coincidental that this theme is stressed by writers such as Vernon Aspaturian, whose name betrays an Armenian lineage. (If there was anything like a similar WASP monopoly of an American public service, there would be more agonized comment than is heard in the Soviet Union about the Russian hegemony of the Soviet Establishment.) The sense of a predominant Russian identity is sharpened by the status of the Russian language with its powerful associations. In an Establishment far more monolingual than in other major countries, even the diplomatic service is alien to any external cultural influence. Thus we end up with the paradox of a country with a cosmopolitan ideology and a multinational structure displaying an intense and vehement sense of nationalist particularity.

If the success of the Soviet state has exceeded expectation, so has the relative failure of the revolutionary idea. It is not surprising to find the Soviet state emerging victorious from a contest of rivalry with the

Communist Party. The party, after all, commands the direct allegiance of only the 10 percent of Soviet citizens who are members of it, while the state affects the lives and destiny of the entire population. The state has been able to impose itself on the international system by the fact of its power, while the party has not been able to win similar victories by the power of its idea. Nearly seven decades after the initial fervor of the revolution its intellectual and emotional attraction has declined. Communism based its appeal very largely on its economic pretensions; by securing a better and more plentiful life for vast numbers of people it would atone for its denial of liberties. Yet the sorry record of the Soviet economy does not inspire envy or emulation. Soviet Communism is no longer the unchallenged leader of the Communist world. Without itself becoming a rival for such leadership, the Chinese Communist Party has effectively destroyed the Soviet monopoly. From the 1960s onward the Soviet Union could not convincingly describe itself as the only recognized central shrine of the Communist faith. There is dissidence and a quickened sense of national particularity among Communist leaders in the Warsaw Pact countries and in the Communist movements in Western Europe.

Communism as articulated by Soviet leaders does not sound like a conquering idea. Its rhetoric is stronger in denunciation of the adversary than in celebration of itself. With the passage of the years and decades it has undergone no documentary renewal. Its themes are recited with scholastic exactitude, more like a catechism than like a trumpet calling warriors to action. There seems to be no eloquence left. If Soviet society is ever eulogized, it is by pilgrims from other lands seeking to escape from their own sated societies into an imaginary Soviet Union presented to tourists in dissociation from the harsh realities of what is now a careworn and struggling nation. It is not surprising that in the international dialogue Soviet diplomats and spokesmen talk more about strength, national rights, sovereignty, security, the responsibility of Great Powers than about the magnetic pull of an ennobling society. The tone is pragmatic, not visionary.

The contrast between the success of the Soviet Union as a world power and its relative failure as the center of a revolutionary movement is not only reflected in the dissidence of sister Communist Parties. Another Soviet disappointment is the refusal of new states to embrace the Marxist-Leninist system. The resentment of the emerging nations against the Western colonial powers, the glaring disparities of wealth and status between the elites and the masses, the egalitarian rhetoric of Communism and the steadfast support of anticolonial struggles by the Soviet Union should, in theory, have combined to give Soviet Communism a good chance of establishing strong footholds in the Third World. Yet nearly all the less developed nations have listened courteously to the siren songs from the Kremlin—and passed by on the other side. They have generally adopted one-party systems with strong charismatic features but with obeisance to the outer forms of Western parliamentarianism. Third World countries have not been happy hunting grounds for Communist parties.

The disappointing record of the Soviet Union as the heart and center of world revolution is also due in large measure to the secondary role of the revolutionary struggle in the Soviet order of priorities. From Stalin's postwar leadership up to the new Andropov era, the Soviet Union has always put the state before the party. Security and influence on the international system have been more crucial objectives than ideological militance. Communist theory calls for an aggressive, uncompromising antagonism to non-Communist regimes across the world and an active and constant attempt to subvert them. But such a policy, if pursued without restraint, would have prevented the integration of the Soviet Union into the diplomatic network. The Soviet leaders have considered it more important to be accepted in the diplomatic system than to deploy their full capacity for subversion. The resultant exercise of restraint has certainly weakened the impact of the Soviet Union's role as the leader of a world revolutionary movement. Slogans like "peaceful coexistence" and "détente" may be good national policy at suitable times, but they are poor Marxist-Leninist doctrine. Since the end of World War II, Soviet policy has been more congenial to Soviet diplomats and political leaders than to Moscow's Communist theorists.

Soviet Diplomacy: Stalin's Last Years

When Truman informed Stalin at Potsdam that the United States had "a new weapon of unusual destructive force," Stalin reacted apathetically, as though nothing of great significance was being said. He replied dryly that he was glad to hear what Truman had said and "hoped that the United States would make good use of it against the Japanese." We now know that Soviet scientists were well advanced in the preparation of atomic weapons when Truman spoke to Stalin. There can be no doubt that the knowledge of a new era in military technology was one of the components that went into the making of Soviet foreign policy in the years that immediately followed the end of the war. Stalin shared none of the extraordinarily naïve illusions about the "continuing alliance" which captivated the imaginations of American statesmen in the final period of the war. He was totally unsentimental about the alliance. He knew that if the West could have reached an agreement with Germany in 1939 under which Hitler's expansionism would have been diverted eastward while the West watched the unfolding events, many leading statesmen in Britain and France would have welcomed such an understanding. In his dealings with Roosevelt and Churchill he offered no apology for the Ribbentrop-Molotov agreement which had kindled the war. In Stalin's terms this was a legitimate exercise in balance-of-power diplomacy. If the West was going to divert German aggression eastward, the Soviet Union would be wise to begin its defense from Polish, not Russian, territory. If on the other hand the West would eventually fight Hitler, the Soviet Union would have lost nothing by having insured itself against the other contingency. Thus the Soviet attitude to its allies was tinged with suspicion from the very outset. During the war Stalin referred to Churchill and Roosevelt as leaders of "peace-loving" nations—a term that he reserved for the Soviet Union alone after the war's end. But well before hostilities ceased, Soviet leaders saw their future aims with a clarity that contrasted starkly with the confusion, obscurity and unreality of Western policy. Once they were imprudently told by Roosevelt at Yalta that the United States would withdraw its forces from Europe with all possible speed, they felt that they were free to map their own security system. They regarded France as a nonpower and assumed that Britain's weight would decline sharply. Who was going to prevent them from constructing a ring of buffer states in Eastern Europe, pressing their claim for control of the Straits of Constantinople, expressing an avaricious "interest" in the Greek Dodecanese islands, prolonging their occupation of northern Iran, seeking a trusteeship in Tripolitania (Libya) and working for the victory of Communist parties in France and Italy? Territorial expansion was not a new feature of Russian history, and yet in Russian eyes it was a "defensive expansion" inspired by the lack of defensive frontiers and by the harsh experience of past generations in which invading Russia had been an endemic habit of powerful European states. From the very beginning of the postwar period the Soviet Union has displayed the classic contradictions of its image: a siege mentality combined with a sweeping audacity beyond the walls. For Stalin the war had been a mere interlude in a struggle against the capitalist world that could now be resumed in a confrontationist atmosphere. Eastern Europe had to be communized not because of ideological fervor, which had little interest for Stalin, but for the sake of Russian security, which was his single, obsessive concern.

One of the weaknesses of Soviet foreign policy planning became evident at this early phase and has persisted ever since. Soviet statecraft shows great lucidity in the definition of its aims, and tenacity and perseverance in their pursuit. But if one of the purposes of diplomacy is to keep adversaries quiet and complacent, then Soviet leaders reveal gross incompetence. It was not easy to spur a slothful America and a weakened Britain to counteraction, but the Soviet Union achieved this with total efficiency. The sheer intensity of its expansionist initiatives made the West aware that the aspirations of Moscow went far beyond a legitimate concern for security. The seizure of Czechoslovakia, the harsh pact of "mutual assistance" with Finland and the rejection of Yugoslavia's claim to national self-assertion revealed an uncompromising spirit in the Soviet Union's determination to dominate Europe. The surprising news in 1947 was not the Soviet drive for domination but the incisiveness of the Western reaction. The Truman Doctrine, the Marshall Plan, the successful resistance to the 1948 Berlin blockade, the establishment of NATO and, subsequently, the American defense of South Korea were all provoked by a Soviet drive that stirred Western energies which a shrewder Soviet diplomacy might have left dormant.

The ambiguous reputation of the Soviet Union as a chess player who makes powerful opening moves but fails to anticipate or counter the adversary's response was now to be reinforced. The Soviet Union had the opportunity to join the Marshall Plan and thus prevent it from becoming the starting point of an anti-Soviet alliance. In July 1947 it ordered Czechoslovakia to cancel its tentative agreement to send representatives to the conference at which the plan would be discussed and ratified. By proceeding with the establishment of the Cominform a few months later, the Kremlin virtually ordained the demarcation lines of the Cold War.

It may be that the Soviet leaders misunderstood the withdrawal of American forces from Europe as a reversion to the old ideas of detachment and "normalcy." They failed to understand that World War II marked the end of American parochialism. This was pardonable only because there actually was an impulse for withdrawal in the American political temperament. Many Americans hoped that their country would be able to limit its overseas commitments and leave the United Nations to deal with obdurate international problems. The expansion of United States responsibilities was unplanned. But this is precisely the basis on which Soviet policy deserves to be criticized in Soviet terms; it was the exaggerated and abrasive Soviet pressure in the early postwar years that compelled American policy to take an activist direction that was not historically inevitable. And in 1950 this Soviet error was compounded by Moscow's sponsorship of the North Korean attack on the South. All the consequences of this initiative were unhappy for Moscow. The Republic of Korea defended itself successfully, the Communist cause found no support in Seoul or in the countryside, Japan was stimulated into a revival of an international role, the Japanese treaty negotiations were expedited under American initiative, and NATO, under the guise of a United Nations command, became something like a real military alliance. Meanwhile, the increased priority for military production in Eastern Europe perpetuated the economic distress of satellite countries; there is substance in the view of some historians that this was a factor in provoking the troubles in Poland and Hungary in 1956. When Stalin died in 1953 he left behind a legacy of fallibility as well as a heritage of power.

Khrushchev and Peaceful Coexistence

It might have been anticipated that the growth of Soviet power would lead to an intensification of Moscow's ideological drive. The very opposite occurred. As Soviet and American weaponry became overpoweringly destructive, both superpowers—not America alone—defined their vital interests with greater caution. The Soviet commitment to the promotion of revolutionary Marxism involved risks which had to be taken into careful account. Nikita Khrushchev saw himself as the servant of a national constituency with relatively marginal responsibilities to non-Soviet interests such as the Communist Parties in Europe and Asia. After the brief Malenkov interlude, which heralded no changes in the direction of Soviet diplomacy, Khrushchev illustrated the normal, human desire of successors to prove that they are not tied down to slavish continuity. The most perceptible change was in diplomatic style. Stalin himself had shown no interest in summit meetings, which he had had his fill of during the war. His Foreign Minister, Andrei Vyshinsky, had treated foreign nations as though he were still a public prosecutor and they were criminals awaiting his indictment. Khrushchev, accompanied by the negligible Nikolai Bulganin, went abroad to convince the bourgeois world that it was possible to have dialogue across the barriers of ideological conflict. By the end of 1954 the Soviet leaders had initiated and attended a conference in Geneva on Indochina, visited the Eastern European capitals and even made overtures to Tito in Belgrade in an unsuccessful effort to woo him back to bloc discipline. Khrushchev also broke the deadlock on the Austrian State Treaty by inviting the Austrian Chancellor to Moscow and signing the treaty with the other three occupying powers in May 1955. This was the only occasion on which Soviet troops withdrew from an area in Europe occupied by their forces without leaving a Communist regime in power. This new phase in Soviet diplomacy culminated in the Geneva summit of 1955; the results of the conference were meager, but the habit of encounter had been firmly and emphatically entrenched. By September 1955 the German Chancellor, Konrad Adenauer, had been received in Moscow; thereafter he was no longer the wicked representative of "German revanchism." In the spring of 1956 Khrushchev visited London in a vain attempt to lure the Labour Party into a posture of dissociation from NATO and the American alliance. A few months earlier the historic Twentieth Congress of the Communist Party had endorsed Khrushchev's formulas of "peaceful coexistence," "rapprochement with all countries to preserve peace" and the expansion of international contacts and relationships.

This was nothing less than de-Stalinization. The outside world would have been even more convinced of this fact if it had secured earlier knowledge of Khrushchev's astonishing attack on Stalin in the secret speech which made the Twentieth Congress historically memorable.

There is no doubt that the Kremlin was signaling to the West that its approach to the international arena was undergoing a change. Even before Stalin's death the Soviet government had made a proposal for a unified and neutralized Germany which was conciliatory in Soviet terms, although the West naturally saw it as a device for breaking the Atlantic alliance. The possibility that Soviet policy was undergoing a substantive change was not put to the test by either superpower. The United States was busy constructing a wall of anti-Soviet pacts and agreements with the rhetoric suitable to that purpose, while the Soviet Union had barely managed to elicit a few appreciative thoughts from Western commentators when it shattered the incipient image of its moderation by invading Hungary and sending notes to Britain and France threatening "to use force to crush the aggressors and to restore peace" in response to the Anglo-French-Israeli operations against Egypt in the Suez Canal area.

The withdrawal of British, French and Israeli forces from the Suez area was actually achieved by the United States, which put direct economic and diplomatic pressure on Britain and France and gave Israel satisfaction by replacing Egyptian troops with a United Nations force and subsequently enforcing free passage through the Straits of Tiran. But the Soviet Union strengthened its international position as a result of the Suez and Hungarian debates in the United Nations. The West was caught in the tension between its vehement oratory over Hungary and its total impotence in the field of action. In the Suez debate it became evident that Third World countries were far less agitated by the agony of Hungary than by the far shorter and less drastic ordeal of a Third World state—Egypt. Moreover, the Western alliance showed greater disarray and division than at any time before or since. There was nothing in all this to convince Khrushchev that his policy was dangerous or unlikely to pay dividends.

What was his policy? His personality is deeply impressed on the history of the next decade. At the Twentieth Congress he had attacked "the cult of personality" and spoken loudly for collective leadership, but no Soviet leader has ever imposed his personal idiosyncrasies so blatantly on his country's public image. Stalin was a withdrawn character, apathetic toward the posturings of publicity-conscious politicians; but for the war, he would have shown no inclination to expose himself to the cameras, even for the awkward and contrived joviality of his encounters with Roosevelt and Churchill. He gave no outward sign that he enjoyed anything or anybody. Most of his collaborators in the Kremlin gave off a similar air of gloom. The Soviet diplomatic demeanor was forbidding and detached; there was no sense of being involved in the same human adventure as the rest of humanity. Khrushchev changed all this. He was rambunctious, aggressive, often inexpressibly arrogant and even vulgar, but he belonged to this world and this age. He relished the prerogatives of his status, the suspense that spontaneously created itself around him, and, above all, the challenge and zest of conflict. He seemed to prefer the company of adversaries to that of obedient allies. In his diaries he was to record his respect for John Foster Dulles as "an able ideological rival." One had the sense that he was born for combat and that if there were no contention he would try to invent it. But it was a form of contention that required contact and discourse; it was Khrushchev, not Stalin or Malenkov, who brought the Soviet Union into the heart of the international community.

With the confidence that he took from the 1956 controversies he went on to develop a diplomatic strategy that kept a fine balance between audacity and caution. His formula, which has still not been totally abandoned by the Soviet leadership, was strictly experimental. The Soviet Union would advance toward its own aims and interests as far as the lack of Western resistance would allow; but the range and pace of the advance would be strictly controlled. It would always be possible to draw back. There would be an invisible escape ladder built into every position.

The tactic of pressing to the limit of safety came to expression in the final years of the Eisenhower presidency. Whether or not power corrupts, the Soviet Union sees the absence of power as a form of decadence, and the lame duck status of an American President invites Soviet pressure. At the summit meeting in Paris in 1960, Khrushchev felt able to humiliate his adversary without any long-term risk. Ostensibly, he was defending Soviet honor against the "outrage" of the U-2 encroachment on Soviet territory and sovereignty. In fact he was acting on the realistic assumption that the Paris summit in May 1960 was not going to bring him any Western concessions on the issue of Berlin and Germany. In the meantime his display of militance would refute the accusations of the Chinese leaders, and perhaps of his critics in the Kremlin, who accused him of softness. He was now in full spate. He pursued his vendetta against Dag Hammarskjöld in the United Nations, demanding his replacement by a "troika" secretariat, created a sensation at the UN General Assembly by banging his shoe on the table and generally gave the impression that there was only one Great Power, not two. Kennedy's brave inaugural address did not arrest the dynamism of Khrushchev's diplomacy. He was less impressed by the audacious rhetoric than by the evidence of bungling and timidity in the Bay of Pigs fiasco. In Vienna in May 1961 he treated the power-laden Kennedy no better than he had the power-ebbing Eisenhower a year before. He gave him until the end of 1961 to settle the Berlin crisis and confer legitimacy on East Germany. If this deadline was not met he would sign a separate peace treaty with East Germany.

The deadline would come and go without the threat coming to fulfillment, nothing would change in the Soviet favor in Berlin, but Khrushchev was vividly illustrating what he meant by peaceful coexistence. The words have a compromising sound, as the word "détente" was to have a decade later. It is important to understand the semantic implications of Soviet policy statements. In speaking of peaceful coexistence the Kremlin did not necessarily seek to deceive its adversaries —unless they wanted to deceive themselves. What the Soviets were prepared to renounce under that slogan was not the pursuit of their own interests; these were no less egotistically conceived than in the era of the Cold War. All that was being surrendered was the option of pursuing Soviet interests to the point of unlimited war. They would halt "peacefully" at some point before total conflict. This itself is no triviality. But the democratic world tends to take words to the full scope of their meaning, so as to embrace their tone and spirit as well as their literal significance. In Western ears "peaceful coexistence" signifies an element of warmth. The Soviet vocabulary is less sentimental. A nation that has endured so much havoc is quite satisfied with the idea that peace is fulfilled by the absence of war. The more rhapsodic implications of peace are not much believed.

Thus peaceful coexistence is no more but also no less than an adversarial relationship kept under control. In this it is not much different from détente. It leaves a large place open for intense competition, and the point at which competition is restrained on behalf of peace is determined experimentally. It is the resistance of the Soviet Union's adversaries that makes the determination. Since this factor cannot be precisely predicted, Soviet policy must be prepared for sudden changes of speed and direction. The fact that Soviet policy is not constantly answerable to public opinion makes this more feasible for the USSR than it could possibly be for a democratic country.

The Cuban missile crisis is the decisive case history. It illustrates both the audacity with which Soviet leaders can advance to the brink and the lack of shamefacedness when they draw back from it. The Soviet proposal for ending the crisis was in fact a unilateral withdrawal:

Let us, therefore, show statesmanlike wisdom. I propose: We, for our part, will declare that our ships, bound for Cuba, will not carry any kind of armaments. You would declare that the United States will not invade Cuba with its forces and will not support any sort of forces which might intend to carry out an invasion of Cuba. Then the necessity for the presence of our military specialists in Cuba would disappear.

Since the United States had no thought of invading Cuba, least of all after the trauma of the Bay of Pigs in 1961, the only concession arising from this confrontation was the Soviet withdrawal of its "military specialists." The United States was recording one of the few victories for compellence, as distinct from deterrence. Compellence is the strategy of *forcing* an adversary to take overt action that it would have wished not to take. Deterrence is the strategy of *dissuading* an adversary from taking undesirable action, and since it is a passive concept it is impossible to prove.

Two years were to pass before Khrushchev's dismissal in October 1964, but there is little doubt that his retreat in Cuba contributed to his decline. Domestic and economic reasons had more to do with his ouster than foreign policy, and it may be that his temperamental quirks played a bigger part than Marxist doctrine would wish Soviet theorists to acknowledge. Soviet leaders assembled on balconies for military parades or state funerals have a way of being difficult to distinguish one from the other. Personal idiosyncrasy is associated with the idea of getting out of step; from this the road is short to the temptations of "personality cult." It is easy to understand why Khrushchev might have evoked envy and mockery among his colleagues, but none of them could have questioned his daring or his originality. And there was personal risk in his strategy. The more rigorous Soviet ideologists with their concern for prestige and their ambition to sustain Soviet leadership in the Communist world could convincingly complain that Moscow came out of the Cuban crisis diminished and, to some extent, humiliated. Khrushchev might well have lost his position in 1963 if Frol Kozlov, his rival and adversary, had not fallen ill. He used that year to widen the foundations of his coexistence policy. This was expressed principally in the nuclear test ban treaty, the opening of emergency communication systems with Washington and a more moderate attitude toward West Germany. When he was eventually deposed, it is remarkable to note how much of the charge against him was based on personal habits and characteristics ("wishful thinking, boasting, empty words, complacency, subjectivism") and how little on accusations related to policy and ideology.

Khrushchev had taken Soviet diplomacy out of provincialism and caused it to flow into the universal stream. In addition to his fraternization with non-Communist Europe he developed a broad network of Soviet links with the Third World. In the United Nations, where traditional Soviet policy had been concerned only with the Great Power issues centered on the Security Council, Khrushchev developed a new habit of initiative. In order to involve the Soviet Union in cooperation with other states, it was necessary to formulate proposals in the General Assembly that were not expressed in strict Communist terminology. The expansion of Third World membership with the addition of forty-five new states gave Moscow a chance of avoiding its traditional UN posture of embattled solitude against a Western "mechanical majority." The majority was no longer mechanical, and it soon ceased to be a majority.

As usual, Khrushchev pressed his advantages too far. Just when the Soviet Union was beginning to record successes in what had been an American-dominated arena, it lost two battles; the Third World was not disposed to weaken the Secretariat by wild ideas about a troika secretariat, and in the Congo crisis the Third World pursued its own interests without being drawn into the radicalism advocated by the Soviet Union. But Moscow was no longer isolating itself within its own rigid patterns and interests. It was playing the international game in its full scope and variety; there was now no issue or arena in which the United States would go unchallenged.

The variation of Soviet policy between flexibility and rigor made it difficult to define the Khrushchev period in simple terms. If one wanted to portray its mood hopefully it was possible to refer to the end of the Korean War (1953), the Geneva Conference on Indochina (1954), the Austrian State Treaty (1955), the realistic retreat in Cuba (1962) and the nuclear test ban (1963). But there was also the suppression of dissidence in Berlin, the institutionalization of the Cold War in the Warsaw Pact (1955) and the ruthless policy in Hungary (1956–57). The heritage of Stalinism lived side by side with a new trend of international accommodation. Soviet foreign policy has never lost this duality.

It was equally necessary after Stalin to show versatility in developing the Soviet role in the Communist system. At the end of World War II there was one Communist power covering 17 percent of the world's territory and comprising 3 percent of its population. Within a decade, a quarter of the earth's surface and a third of its population were under the control of Communist parties. This faced Moscow with new predicaments such as polycentrism, problems of hegemony and the clash between the instinct for centralized control and the need to satisfy national particularism in Communist regimes and among Communist parties in the West. The rise of Communist China had a profound effect on the Soviet Union. Despite the envy and rancor provoked by the unexpected rivalry for leadership in world Communism, Moscow did not take long to realize that it would be impossible to keep a quarter of the world's territory and a third of its population under a single, centralized leadership. That China would take a separate course was objectively inevitable. In any case, the international system of the early 1960s was losing its bipolar structure. The West was not simply an American bloc; De Gaulle had made this clear, and there were other evidences of pluralism in the alliance. As nuclear stockpiles grew, the superpowers found that their military preponderance was vast but not sufficiently usable to give them power of control over other nations. Bipolarity was simply out of harmony with historical, cultural and human reality; the notion that China could be a Soviet satellite was intrinsically absurd. If the Kremlin could not control, seduce or punish Tito, what chance did it have with Mao Zedong?

China had good reason to doubt the USSR's professions of solidarity. Khrushchev was unashamedly more interested in his relations with the United States and Europe than in the destiny of China, whose interests seemed parochial in his eyes. When he actually suggested to Beijing late in 1959 that China accept a separate status for Formosa, the Chinese leaders accused him of betrayal. The two great Communist powers were at daggers drawn during the 1960s both on ideological issues and on matters affecting their national interests. There were border disputes. One of these in 1969 even resulted in clashes between Soviet frontier troops and Chinese soldiers near the Ussuri River. The invective exchanged between Soviet and Chinese representatives in international agencies was more virulent than the East-West polemics at the height of the Cold War. American diplomacy, under Henry Kissinger's direction, skillfully exploited this tension. By the early 1970s the United States was enjoying the luxury of being wooed by two great Communist powers. China, which had been regarded as the more militant of the Communist countries, was asking Washington for something close to alliance, and the Soviet Union reacted by seeking détente. The Chinese Communist Party had called for improved relations with the United States in October 1968, and this led, after three and a half years of patient diplomacy, to the historic Nixon-Kissinger visit to Beijing in 1972. At the Twenty-fourth Soviet Party Congress in March 1971 there was a clear resolution calling for better relations with the United States. The shape of international politics had become transformed; there was now a triangular pattern in the superpower relationship. Soviet diplomacy was called upon for more subtlety than in the black-and-white bipolar age of the Cold War. It had to maneuver, cajole, threaten, compete and, sometimes, even compromise in order to defend its interests and its status.

The Brezhnev Era (1964–1982)

As if the Chinese issue was not troublesome enough, the leadership of
Leonid Brezhnev, having firmly consolidated itself within a year of
Khrushchev's eclipse, faced the complexities of dissidence in Eastern
Europe. Strict Communist discipline had never seemed congenial to
the Czechs and Slovaks, who, alone among the Warsaw Pact countries,
could look back to a period of democratic rule in the Masaryk-
Beneš era. When Alexander Dubček became First Secretary of the
party in 1968, he continued to emphasize his nation's devotion to the
Warsaw Pact and to the principle of Communist Party hegemony in
domestic politics. But these dutiful statements were not enough to
placate a Soviet leadership that was now tormented by the loss of its
influence in China and the memory of its crisis with Tito. A "progressive" wing was bidding for control of the Czech party, reformism was
openly advocated, and there was an anti-Moscow undercurrent in
Czech politics. Rumania's initiative in establishing relations with West
Germany had been bad enough, but a Prague-Bonn rapprochement
would be a far more serious defiance of the Soviet foreign policy
interest.

But it was the domestic deviation of the Czech leadership that
aroused most concern. If a Communist state could exist without rigid
censorship, if minorities in party organs could maintain dissenting
views, if factions could be tolerated, if secret balloting was accepted in
party councils, and if separatist initiatives in foreign policy were legitimized—what would be the essential difference between Czechoslovakia and a social democratic state? When the conduct of maneuvers by large Warsaw Pact armies in Czechoslovakia in June was not a
sufficiently potent "hint" to the reformers in Prague, Brezhnev abandoned all thought of compromise. In August 1968 Soviet forces invaded Czechoslovakia and within a few weeks Czech capitulation was
complete. Several months were to pass before a leadership fully congenial to Moscow could be finally established in Prague, but the message to Eastern European countries was clear. The maintenance of
complete Soviet control was an objective for which the Soviet leadership would renounce world opinion, idealistic pretensions, UN Charter provisions and the sympathy of Eastern European peoples. The
views and protests of liberal and progressive circles in the West, condemnation by China, Rumania, Albania, Yugoslavia—nothing was
powerful enough to avail in Soviet calculations against the absolute
aim of controlling the social systems and international policies of its
socialist neighbors. In the words of the article in *Pravda* that set out

this policy in doctrinal language: "Every Communist party is responsible not only to its own people but also to all the socialist countries and to the entire Communist movement."

The Czech crisis of 1968 is a momentous definition of the nature of the Soviet system. It makes it clear that in a conflict between national sovereignty and Communist solidarity, Warsaw Pact countries must give precedence to Communist solidarity. Russian power and security come first, and separatist policies that conflict with those interests must be renounced on pain of forcible suppression. To ensure that this scale of priority is respected, the Communist Party in each of these states must be the exclusive repository of power. The world of the Warsaw Pact is a one-way street; once entry has been established there is no way out.

The repercussions of the Soviet invasion of Czechoslovakia in other parts of Eastern Europe were so severe that a full year elapsed before the Kremlin could convene a world conference of Communist Parties; even then the conference was ignored by the parties in China, Yugoslavia, Albania, North Korea and North Vietnam. China was virulently attacked by those who attended, but it was victorious in its absence since the conference celebrated the formal end of the Soviet claim to exclusive hegemony. It adopted the important declaration that "there is no leading center of the international Communist movement." Once this degree of leniency was articulated (if not acted upon) toward separatist policies in Communist states, it could not be expected that Communist Parties in capitalist countries would show a greater docility in their acceptance of Moscow's ideological dictatorship. Eurocommunism was an inevitable sequel to the weakening of Soviet authority among ruling parties in Communist countries. Since the Moscow Conference of Communist Parties in June 1968, there has not been a single crisis or controversy involving Soviet military action or repression in which all the world's Communist Parties have given unanimous allegiance to Moscow's will. The Afghan and Polish crises found the Communist family split between those who supported Moscow, those who opposed it and those who watched in stony silence and apathy.

Brezhnev and the Détente Era

Khrushchev's abrupt deviation from the Stalinist postures in foreign policy has obscured the significance of his reformist initiatives in other fields. It was this that contributed as much to his downfall as did his failures in the Cuban missile crisis and other foreign policy issues. His rhetoric had legitimized the popular demand for consumer goods, but his management of the economy turned out to be a failure. So long as the collective farm system was sacrosanct and centralization in industry was mandatory for ideological motives, there was not much room for experimentation. The rate of productivity was declining, and the sensation of defeat in the economic effort converged with the humiliation of the Cuban missile crisis to create a hard resolve by the post-Khrushchev leadership to assert Soviet interests in the future with more tenacity and less risk of losing the struggle. The important task was to make the Soviet Union weigh more heavily in the scales of comparative power with the United States. This required a period of consolidation. Military parity with the United States and a more dignified economic performance could not be achieved overnight.

Détente corresponded with a long series of converging interests among the leading actors in the international system. It came into existence because it suited everybody.

The Soviet acceptance of détente was primarily dictated by its disquiet about China. The disparity between Soviet and Chinese power was so vast that this Soviet concern might seem obsessive. Yet the reflection of China in the Soviet consciousness during the early 1970s gave a convincing impression of peril. The Chinese leaders spoke with ghastly serenity about a nuclear war in which the sheer demographic vastness of China would enable it to survive a nuclear holocaust in which both America and Russia would be decimated. China threatened the ideological leadership of the Soviet Union, made no secret of its claim to boundary changes and was now involved in such a subtle flirtation with the United States that Dobrynin, the Soviet ambassador in Washington, was discreetly asking American leaders to keep him informed of the evolution of U.S.-Chinese relations.

By the time of the Nixon visit to Beijing in 1972, Moscow could see the signs for itself. Adam Ulam has cogently pointed out that in the Soviet mind the United States presents itself as a nation that offers little threat to the USSR on the bilateral level (because of the restraints of its democratic system), but which often tends to be "incited" against the Soviet Union by a third party. The role of the "inciter" had been played, according to Soviet mythology, by Britain in the late 1940s, by Adenauer's German "revanchists" in the 1950s, and now by China.

In addition to this powerful motive, the Soviet Union was impelled toward détente by its need for Western trade and technology and by its desire to cool the inflamed atmosphere after the alarms of the Cuban missile crisis. Moreover, the Soviet Union had most to gain and nothing to lose by an arms control negotiation that would inevitably acknowledge its equality of status with the United States and possibly relieve its economic burden.

The American interest in a new definition of its relationship with the Soviet Union was no less compelling. After the Cuban crisis, the United States, despite its taste of victory, was eager to find a less explosive and precarious basis for its dialogue with the Soviet leadership. Nobody in America had an ambition to go through the "Russian roulette" experience again. Indeed, Kennedy's instruction had been to avoid any gloating, celebration or crowing over the defeat of the USSR in the 1962 confrontation. Lyndon Johnson had tried the technique of personal contact in his conference with Kosygin at Glassboro in the summer of 1967. But it was not until the advent of the Nixon-Kissinger Administration that a new approach to Moscow became urgent as well as prudent. Kissinger had large ideas for a new sweep and direction in United States policy, but nothing could be achieved or even attempted without an end of the Vietnam war.

There was pressure for détente in Europe. De Gaulle had despaired of his capacity to serve as a central bridge between the Soviet Union and the West. Moscow had politely indicated that it really did not need Paris as a mediator between itself and its main interlocutors—the United States and Germany. Russian policy since World War II has been obsessively concentrated on the United States and relatively apathetic about less formidable centers of power. But if any third party could interfere with the autonomous flow of American-Soviet relations, it would not be France but West Germany with its embarrassing pressure for German reunification. In the Adenauer era, Germany might have been a serious opponent of détente. But it was just at this time—toward the end of the 1960s—that Willy Brandt was leading his countrymen away from the old rigidities. The *Ostpolitik* was a drastic break with the German diplomatic past. Instead of insistence on reunification there would be the formula of "two states within one nation." Instead of regarding reunification as a precondition of détente, Bonn now accepted that reunification would come, if at all, as a consequence of détente. And instead of a futile show of insistence on changing the postwar boundaries of Poland and Germany, Brandt began to prepare for the Helsinki Conference at which recognition would be given to the frontiers created by World War II.

Although all the main actors in the international drama contributed to the détente era, the Soviet Union must be regarded as the key character. The idea of a relaxed relationship between the powers had been a part of Western thought since the tempestuous days of World War II. The United States had imagined the possibility when Soviet leaders were blatantly pursuing a Cold War campaign. It had taken the Western countries some time and much painful experience after 1945 to admit that the wartime alliance was not in full vigor. They had imagined détente before it existed. It was the Soviet leadership that was called upon for a far-reaching modification of rhetoric and attitude if détente was to have any credibility. If they wanted détente they could not go on describing the non-Communist world as a villainous gang of bloodthirsty plutocrats subjecting every human interest and value to their insatiable private greed. They would now have to admit that people outside the Soviet Union could be "peace-loving." Soviet society would have to be less hermetically closed. There would have to be foreign journeys for Soviet musicians, artists and scientists, despite the risks of flight with requests for asylum. Soviet diplomats would have to emulate the bonhomie and conviviality of Khrushchev rather than the frigid hostility of Stalin and Molotov. It was in this atmosphere that more than 100,000 Jewish émigrés could be allowed to leave Russia in the years following 1972. Above all, the Soviet Union would have to reconcile its ambition for military parity or superiority with the image of a Great Power seriously interested in arms control.

Brezhnev applied himself to this task with tenacity and a talent for flexible adaptation. Soviet leadership had to develop a sharper sense of the outside world; it had to learn what was possible and what was not possible for the West to concede. In a significant move, Andrei Gromyko, the veteran Foreign Minister, was appointed to membership of the Politburo in 1973 without the usual period of candidacy. He has since been promoted to higher national rank, as a First Deputy Premier. The simultaneous elevation to the Politburo of the military leader Marshal Andrei Grechko and the head of the secret police, Yuri Andropov, in 1973 indicated a growing respect for specialized and professional skills. Gromyko had been Foreign Minister for nineteen years and was thus the most experienced negotiator in the international community. His appointment to the Politburo was seen as proof of the rising importance of diplomacy in the Kremlin's priorities. There is no doubt that foreign affairs have stood higher in the scale of Soviet urgencies during the 1970s and early 1980s than at any time before.

The results were a brilliant success for Soviet diplomacy. Within a few years the Brezhnev Administration had secured international (including West German) recognition of the new boundaries in Europe, thus establishing the Oder-Neisse line as Poland's western frontier and ensuring the separateness of the East German Republic. These principles were first established in negotiations by the European governments most closely concerned, but they later secured the formal sanction of the entire Western world by being ratified at the Conference on European Security and Cooperation with United States participation at Helsinki on August 1, 1975. This was the most tangible result of an assembly so crowded with heads of powerful and influential states that it exceeded the Congress of Vienna and all other historic summit meetings in the range and weight of its representation. No progress was registered or even prepared on arms control, and the only price that the Soviet Union was called upon to pay for its gains was the acceptance of obligations involving the guarantee of human rights for all Europeans, in the east as well as the west of the continent.

The signature of these human rights provisions was regarded at the time as a heavy concession by the Soviet Union, and some enthusiastic commentators in the West spoke of a Soviet "capitulation." The Helsinki Final Act in Basket One and Basket Three committed the Soviet Union to

> respect human rights and fundamental freedoms, including freedom of thought, conscience and religion; to facilitate free movement and contacts for persons individually and collectively; to permit travel for family visits; to permit family reunification; to facilitate the free and wider dissemination of information of all kinds; to improve dissemination of newspapers and publications from other states; and to grant accredited journalists multiple visas. Basket Three gave concrete expression to these undertakings by specifying measures of contact and accessibility.

If the Soviet Union had carried out these provisions, it would have become a totally different kind of society from that which it has always been. Basket Three virtually asked the Soviet Union to replace its Communist system by a Western-type democracy. It never had any intention of doing this. Indeed it is hard to think of a single activity or domain in which the individual rights of Soviet citizens are more flexibly interpreted now than before the Helsinki Conference. It is certainly not the case that the closed character of Soviet society has been modified or that the attitude to dissidents bears any resemblance to what is explicitly required by the Helsinki Final Act. The most spectacular development of the 1970s—the large facility for Jewish emigration —was first diminished and thereafter virtually canceled by the early 1980s. The monitoring conferences that followed the Helsinki Final Act in the early 1980s were charged with acrimonious exchanges between Western and Soviet representatives. It is now evident that Basket Three is empty.

This raises the question whether détente has brought any gain to the West in return for the Soviet achievement of legitimacy for the post–World War II territorial status. Kissinger gave an emphatically positive response in his address to the Senate Foreign Relations Committee in 1974. He drew up an impressive list of Western gains: The potential of Berlin as a flashpoint had been reduced through the quadripartite agreement of 1971. NATO and the Warsaw Pact were negotiating the reduction of their forces in Central Europe. There were active discussions of a European security conference. There had been an "honorable termination" of America's direct involvement in Indochina and a "substantial lowering of tensions." America's principal alliances had proved their durability, and incipient crises with the Soviet Union had been contained or settled without ever reaching a point of public clash. A series of bilateral agreements on cooperation had set American-Soviet relations on a new course. America had achieved unprecedented agreements in arms limitation and measures to avoid accidental war. New possibilities for positive American-Soviet cooperation had emerged on issues in which the globe is interdependent, such as science and technology, environment and energy.

This was not a fanciful picture. In a single week in Moscow in 1972 —from May 22 to May 29—Nixon and Brezhnev had signed agreements on strategic arms limitation; on environmental protection; on joint scientific and technological endeavors; on the prevention of incidents on and over the high seas; on medical science and public health cooperation; and on the creation of a joint U.S.-USSR commercial commission. Later in 1972 there was a most-favored-nation treaty signed in Washington under which Soviet trade with the United States would enjoy greater facility, and the credit status of the Soviet Union in the United States was enhanced by a generous settlement of its debt under the Lend-Lease Act of World War II.

Nobody could have imagined such a rich harvest of American-Soviet agreements in the acrimonious atmosphere of the 1950s and early 1960s. When the second Nixon-Brezhnev summit meeting, in Washington during October 1973, added an agreement on the prevention of nuclear war which included a provision for urgent consultation in times of crisis, it seemed that talk of a new era was not farfetched. Nixon did not even sound incongruous when he indulged in Churchillian rhetoric on signing SALT I in 1972: "The historians of some future age will write of the year 1972 . . . that this was the year when America helped to lead the world out of the lowlands of constant war to the high plateau of peace." Apart from the intrinsic value of the 1972–73 agreements themselves, there was the added dividend of personal rapport between Nixon and Brezhnev the like of which was never established between a Soviet and an American leader before or since. On June 24, 1973, Brezhnev's broadcast to the American people praised Nixon as a leader whose "administration united his efforts with ours to lead Soviet-American relations to a really new path." There cannot be many Soviet statements in which anybody outside the Soviet leadership has been credited with a contribution to world peace.

It will be seen that the question of human rights played so small a part in the original détente dialogue that the disappointments in this field after the Helsinki Conference were not likely to constitute the final verdict against the détente idea. Kissinger, at any rate, has never seen the human rights issue as the main testing ground for détente. He was far more interested in its potential effects on the control and containment of conflicts. The question was not whether Soviet society would change, but whether Soviet foreign policy would allow relief from the constant sensation of peril arising from such abrasive initiatives as the Cuban missile crisis or the attempt to seize virtual control of Angola. The West seemed to have no real sanction with which to retaliate against the Soviets for offenses to the Helsinki agreement on human rights. It was quite an achievement to get a Soviet signature on the human rights provision of Basket One and Basket Three; to have the signature honored would have been a double victory. It would, in fact, have been too good to believe.

It might at least have been expected after Helsinki that Western intellectuals would have been in the forefront of the struggle to pressure the Soviet Union for flexibility and openness in its domestic structure; but some of them were, in fact, more preoccupied with international conciliation than with the dream of liberalizing the Soviet system. A typical reaction came from the American sociologist David Riesman:

> I am in a position of deep moral ambiguity because, on the one hand, I admire enormously the courage of the Soviet dissidents . . . but at the same time I have consistently refused to sign petitions or in any other way to lend my name to criticisms of the treatment of these dissidents. In a bipolar nuclear world we cannot afford to hold to a simple, straightforward universalist moral standard such as one might hope for in a world free from the threat of mass annihilation . . . It is because I see the nuclear question as always foremost that I cannot be sanguine about the human prospect in the long run, unless the human rights issue in this country is made less salient.

In similar terms George Kennan, after expressing sincere support for the dissidents and sensitive devotion to individual rights, went on to declare that he saw no point in constant "incantations" about the violation of fundamental freedoms in the Soviet Union. The implication is that criticism is likely to irritate the USSR and interfere with the larger objective of securing agreements on arms control or on the relaxation of tensions.

The notion that there is an inherent conflict between the campaign for human rights and the promotion of East-West agreement on matters affecting world peace has paradoxical results. If the intellectuals and the liberals are silent or lenient about Soviet persecution of dissidents, they leave the human rights field open to the opponents of détente. This helps the USSR portray the campaign for human rights as a mere veil for anti-Soviet sentiments that exist quite independently of the human rights issue. When Senator Henry M. Jackson sponsored legislation in the United States Senate that would have made economic concessions to the Soviet Union depend on an improvement of Soviet policy on the emigration of those wishing to leave, the Kremlin canceled its request for economic concessions so as to prove that it was impossible to dictate or "purchase" changes in the Soviet domestic system. The Soviets developed the theme that the vocal defenders of human rights were more concerned to destroy détente than to help dissidents in the USSR. This was palpably unfair; it is objectively possible to be against the escalation of the arms race and also to be censorious in condemnation of Soviet treatment of Jews and other minorities. The criticism of Soviet policy on human rights is by no means confined to the opponents of détente. Yet the feeling that incessant harping on Soviet violations of the Helsinki accords may simply "irritate" Moscow and thus create a climate unfavorable to arms control agreements has never been fully laid to rest, and George Kennan and David Riesman are not the only writers to have expressed themselves in this way. There is an inhibited approach on the part of liberal-minded statesmen as well. President François Mitterrand and Willy Brandt have given vigorous diplomatic aid to imprisoned scientists, intellectuals and dissidents, but when a Conference on Soviet Jewry was convened in Jerusalem in March 1983, militant messages were read out from President Reagan and Prime Minister Margaret Thatcher, and not from Mitterrand or Brandt or Bruno Kreisky, the Austrian Chancellor, or Olof Palme, the Swedish Prime Minister.

The impression that human rights protesters in the West are recruited mainly from those who are not enthusiastic about détente is strengthened by such comparisons. The natural solution would be for those who take the lead in advocating détente with the Soviet Union also to be in the forefront of the campaign for human rights. It is frivolous to fear that the Soviet position on the central nuclear balance would be negatively affected by pressure in Western countries on behalf of a better Soviet record in human rights. The USSR is guided in strategic matters by a cold appraisal of its own interests and anxieties. Yet with all its ostensible imperviousness to external pressure, the Soviet Union maintains a degree of sensitivity to world opinion, especially to that part of it which it defines as "progressive" or "peace-loving." Kennan underestimates the positive effects of "incantations"; these might be self-evident and repetitive for those who declaim them, but they are essential if we wish the dissidents to retain their capacity of resistance. What is certain is that the absence of "incantations" can only demoralize those in the Soviet Union who strive to humanize the regime within the limits of feasibility. Western silence can all too easily become a form of intervention on behalf of the KGB and against the Soviet intellectuals and dissidents. There is also the corrosive effect on the democratic cause of an unwillingness to celebrate its own values in loud and clear tones. Communist ideology never seems to suffer from such inhibitions.

But despite the attention devoted to Basket Three of the Helsinki Final Act, the main test for détente comes not in the field of human rights but in the prospect of mitigating conflicts that are liable to result in breaches of the peace. What became of Kissinger's emphatic verdict in 1974 in favor of détente as a transaction in which the West came out with advantage and not with loss?

By the time that he drew up his balance sheet in 1974, the détente idea had already been tested in the Yom Kippur War, which broke out in October 1973. The verdict here is more ambivalent than the critics of détente would have us believe. It has been asserted that when the Soviet Union received knowledge of the impending attack by Egypt and Syria it should have passed the information to the United States. This would have conformed with the spirit of the 1972 "Basic Principles of Relations between the U.S. and the USSR," which is the Decalogue of the détente idea.

It is more cogent to argue that this was an unrealistic expectation. The Soviet Union was an ally not of Israel but of Syria and the Arab world. If it had given information about an Egyptian-Syrian military operation, it would have destroyed its position in the Arab world. The truth is that just as the Helsinki Final Act exaggerated the limits of potential Soviet concession on human rights, so did the Moscow Declaration of 1972 and the subsequent declarations at Washington and San Clemente in June 1973 give an unrealistic picture of the lengths to which the USSR was prepared to go in order to win the confidence of the United States. Soviet and American leaders meeting at the summit are no more immune than lesser mortals to the temptations of overoptimistic rhetoric, which has been a feature of diplomacy in all ages. Personal warmth, conviviality and the normal desire of guests and hosts to be amiable toward each other add a measure of effusiveness that goes beyond genuine intention. There is also the mutual desire at summit meetings to convince the media that the eminent negotiators have achieved great personal success. It is important to take summit communiqués with enough pinches of salt to offset the sugary taste of their rhetoric. If we were to write diplomatic history in accordance with communiqué texts at summit meetings, we would conclude that all governments are in excellent relations with all others and that all meetings of heads of state are a total success.

The USSR, free from the intrusive scrutiny of its own public opinion, is more able to sign far-reaching commitments without the necessity of fulfilling them than is a Western-type democracy. The Western countries had gained a tactical advantage in securing Soviet commitments to human rights policies even if Moscow was unlikely to honor them. But anyone who studied the basic principles of social organization in the Soviet Union should not have been surprised by the gap between promise and performance. Similarly the Soviet undertaking in the 1972 communiqué to avoid competing with the United States in regional conflicts was heartwarming but not credible.

The overall picture of Soviet behavior in and after the Yom Kippur War gives a more accurate impression of the Soviet interpretation of détente than do the idyllic declarations of 1972–73. The attitude of the Soviet Union to the United States during the Middle East crisis of 1973–74 was neither cooperative nor totally adversarial. There is some evidence for the belief that the USSR did not encourage Egypt or Syria to launch their attack on October 6, 1973. When the attack unexpectedly won initial success the Soviets supported the Arab belligerents with a heavy airlift. It also proposed a cease-fire on terms predictably unacceptable to Israel and the United States. Its proposal was that Israel should return to the pre-1967 lines as a condition for the cease-fire! Two weeks later, when the United States made a totally different proposal for a cease-fire based on the existing positions, with Israeli forces deep into Egypt, and with an additional provision for a negotiation of a peace settlement, the USSR accepted the American proposal. Later, when fighting continued west of the Suez Canal and came within 101 kilometers of Cairo, the Soviet Union alarmed the United States with a veiled threat of unilateral military intervention. When the Nixon Administration responded with a nuclear alert and a stern warning, the Soviets retreated from their militant position and accepted the innocuous idea of participation in an unarmed UN observers' team. The Soviet Union joined the United States in sponsoring a Middle East peace conference at Geneva and allowed Kissinger to negotiate an Egyptian-Israeli disengagement agreement. A similar disengagement between Israel and Syria was witnessed jointly by the United States and the USSR at a signing ceremony in Geneva. It is possible that Syria would have been unable to conclude this agreement without Soviet acquiescence. In the discussions at Geneva the Soviet Union opened a line of communication to Israel by talks at foreign minister level. It also, for the first time, acknowledged Israel's 1967 boundaries as legitimate; until then the Soviet doctrine on Israel's boundaries had been less favorable to Israel. The Soviets were clearly not exercising their maximal capacity for mischief.

What can we make of this Jekyll and Hyde performance? It seems to illustrate a constant tension in Soviet policy between two opposing pressures. On the one hand, Moscow would vigorously compete with Washington in the Cold War tradition in an effort to win the support of third parties, especially in the nonaligned camp. On the other hand, if its pressure on the United States provoked dangerously sharp antagonism with Washington, the Soviet Union knew how to retreat. It clearly regarded its fundamental relationship with the United States as a higher interest than fidelity to its Arab or other Third World friends. If there was a possibility of joint action with the United States in the Middle East, the Soviets attached great value to such a posture. In the 1973 Middle East war the Soviet Union challenged the United States —but only up to the point at which further tension would endanger the entire notion of détente and peaceful coexistence. We come back to the Soviet idea of détente as a competitive relationship held under control.

If the Soviets had everywhere pursued the complex but tolerable diplomacy that they had adopted in the Yom Kippur War, the United States might have reluctantly regarded détente as workable. But in the next three years Moscow pursued a policy which made it difficult for the devotees of détente in the West to pretend that the word had any meaning. The USSR supported the invasion of North Yemen by South Yemen in violation of the Paris agreement on Indochina. It encouraged Cuban forces in the attempt to transform Angola into a Communist-controlled state. It supported a militant regime in Ethiopia at the price of its relations with Somalia. It encouraged the united Vietnam in its attack on Cambodia. And just when the Western supporters of détente were reassuring themselves and others that the USSR had never used its own armed forces outside Europe, the Soviet invasion of Afghanistan in 1979 descended on them like a clap of thunder. This action alienated the sympathies of the pro-détente forces in the West as well as those of the Third World. There is no doubt that the turbulent dynamism of the Soviet Union in Afghanistan, Southeast Asia and the Horn of Africa helped to create the atmosphere in Washington against senatorial ratification of SALT II.

By the beginning of the 1980s there were few people in the West who confidently used the word "détente" as an accurate description of the Soviet relationship with the West, and particularly with the United States. In an important study, *The Soviet Union and the Arms Race*, David Holloway sums up the dilemma:

> *In the mid 1970's a shift of emphasis took place from détente to activism. This prompts the question: might Soviet policy have developed differently if the West, and particularly the United States, had pursued détente more vigorously, giving the Soviet Union more to hope for from cooperation (and perhaps also more to fear from conflict)? The question cannot be answered on the available evidence, but the existence of different currents in Soviet thinking makes it worth asking.*

The Soviet leadership has still not agreed to regard détente as dead and buried. At the Twenty-sixth Party Congress in February 1981, it restated the principle of détente and hailed the USSR as the defender of world peace. While defending all the dynamic irruptions of the Soviet Union in recent years, Brezhnev pleaded unavailingly for direct dialogue with the United States at the top level. He frankly avowed the enormous build-up of Soviet arms but asserted that this was for Russian security, not for international aggression. When he died in the last weeks of 1982, he left behind a strange foreign policy legacy: the Soviet Union was not committed to stability, but neither did it want chaos.

The Soviet need for a relatively moderate relationship with the outside world became intensified during the Brezhnev regime as a result of growing economic embarrassment. No conservatism in Soviet society has been more extreme than in the domain of economic organization. The economic structure remained stagnant for the entire post-war period, centralized to the point of strangulation, inefficient in production and unable to keep up with the growing public demand for consumer goods. Industrial production increased in trivial percentages, while agricultural production actually diminished by 10 percent in the two-year period 1979–80 and has not recovered since. When the Soviet Union, which had once been the world's greatest grain exporter, became the world's greatest grain *importer* by the early 1980s, the traditional pride of the Communist regime in its agrarian achievements was sorely eroded.

It would be rash, however, to assume that this condition will necessarily modify basic Soviet policies in a direction favorable to the West. Soviet citizens have a tradition of stoicism and docility, and their government does not have to answer to them every month for an adverse index in the definition of economic trends. The most that can be expected to flow from Soviet economic hardship is an openness to arms control ideas that do not threaten the present balance and an interest in a severely controlled form of détente which the Soviet partner would interpret only as the avoidance of a direct assault on America's vital security interests.

The best case for détente is that no party seems to be gaining from its eclipse. While it lasted it gave the United States a broader field of diplomatic maneuver and an improved relationship with European allies. It helped the Soviet Union in its economic development and decreased its isolation. It was strategically useful to China. It served Eastern European states by giving them greater security from overt Soviet repression than they might otherwise have enjoyed. Above all, it contributed to the preservation of world peace, without dangerous regional wars such as those in Korea and Vietnam which are often described as "peripheral" but which were far from marginal in their overall international effects. Coral Bell has pointed out that during the Cold War years

the margin of safety . . . was very low; at one stage during the 1950's the
CIA were allegedly refusing to predict the avoidance of central hostilities for
more than five or six weeks ahead. It is inevitable that the level of risk should
be greater in a high-tension strategy than in a détente strategy. Tension
begets frictions, frictions beget crises, crises beget wars.

Did the Soviet leadership really believe that the United States would
accept Russian policies in Vietnam, Cambodia, Yemen, Angola, Ethiopia, the Horn of Africa, Afghanistan and Poland? It is more likely that
on cold calculation the Soviet leaders considered that the promotion
of their own interests was more important than the preservation of the
détente formula. A situation in which there is no authorized theoretical
definition of Soviet-American relations and in which no summit meeting has taken place for five years is sufficient to inspire international
nostalgia for the condition that prevailed before the Soviet drive in the
Third World between 1974 and 1979. The least that can be said on
behalf of détente is that the situations that preceded and came after
it were not better in any respect—not even in the matter of human
rights.

Does the West have any cause for self-reproach about the decline of
détente to a degree that would substantially counterbalance the Soviet
responsibility? All that Soviet apologists can convincingly claim is that
there was a great deal of anti-détente rhetoric in America (although
very little in Western Europe, even from right-wing movements). But
when Governor Reagan and Senator Jackson and former Defense Secretary Melvin Laird spoke suspiciously of détente, especially during
the American presidential campaign in 1976, they were indirectly
drawing attention to the fact that détente was actually being upheld by
the Administration, even at some domestic risk. Moscow was affronted
by American support of dissidents such as Aleksandr Solzhenitsyn and
by the continuation and intensification of broadcasts to the Soviet
people. There was no easing off in NATO's military reinforcement, but
détente had never promised unilateral disarmament.

The Carter Administration began its career in 1977 with an increase
in military spending and a more insistent pressure for human rights.
Its posture in arms control talks was by no means any more flexible
than that of its predecessor. But all this taken together could not
compare with the military actions taken or supported by the USSR in
a purposeful effort to change the regional balance in many sensitive
areas. In short, the American interpretation of détente was compatible
with stability; the Soviet interpretation was not. The Soviet Union had
never given anyone reason to believe that it would refrain, in the name
of détente, from competing with the United States in those areas which
were outside the range of American security commitments. The
United States abstained from attempting to alter the global orientation

of Third World states, not because of détente but because its own policy and interests required no such action. Similarly, there was no need for détente in order to ensure that the United States would be an open society in which pluralism of opinions would be maintained and protected. Basket Three weighed exclusively on the Soviet Union. There is thus no symmetry in the demands that the détente principle makes on the two parties. It must be objectively acknowledged that détente, if taken seriously, requires more change and adaptation from the Soviet Union than from the United States. It does not impose any modification of basic American attitudes. This may be one of the reasons why Moscow was the first to cast off its restraints.

The habit of dividing the course of Soviet foreign policy into three epochs under the heading of Cold War, détente and post-détente makes life easy for the student and the analyst, but it is open to serious reservation. The transition from one of these eras to another has no fixed chronology, no signposts and no definite lines of demarcation. There were many acts of accommodation and restraint during the Cold War and many moments of tension and explosive suspense during the years of détente. These decades cannot rationally be demarcated like the reigns of kings or the transition from the French monarchy to the French republics. The habit of giving a label to an age in terms of its central attribute is safer if it is practiced retrospectively. The Age of Enlightenment was not totally enlightened, the Age of Reason was reasonable only in parts, the Dark Ages were not without light for those who were on top of the power structure, and those who lived in the Middle Ages had no consciousness of medievality. They thought that they were as modern as could be. Whether détente will be an appropriate label for the present age of international relations will only emerge in a larger perspective than is available today.

The experiment of détente, whatever its ultimate outcome, has taught the world some clear and hard lessons about what the USSR will not do in return for a relief of tensions with the West: it will not abandon its quest for growing military strength; it will not agree to stabilize the distribution of influence in the international system at a level of American predominance; and it will not willingly renounce the idea that its own security requires it to dominate the policy and the social regimes of its contiguous neighbors in Europe.

The Quest for Military Power

The obsession with military strength is intensified by the trauma of 1941. This is still the most powerful component of Soviet thinking about security. Russians speak of the Great Patriotic War and evoke the memory of the 20 million dead in two contexts: as an explanation of the need for total security and as proof that the Soviet Union cannot possibly be accused of wanting another war in the present or the future, so that its peace-loving character should be taken for granted and regarded as axiomatic.

Many stages of progress in the Soviet military build-up have been reactive; they have been direct consequences of United States initiatives. The first Soviet atom bomb test came in August 1949, four years after the American atomic bombardment of Hiroshima. The Soviet activity in building thermonuclear bombs came close on the heels of American progress in that field. Soviet missile development has been closely linked in timing and quality to innovations achieved or projected by the United States. But it would be a mistake to regard Soviet military policy as nothing but a trial of physical strength or a guarantee of national security. The Soviet Union was second only because it could not be first. The Soviet Union has always had a clear conception of military power as an instrument of foreign policy. The central aim of its diplomacy is to secure worldwide recognition of its status as one of two superpowers, with a capacity equal to that of the United States to impress itself on the international order. Its chance of achieving equality with the United States in economic power and productivity or in technological innovation is remote; but the prospect of maintaining military parity is feasible if it is pursued with single-minded intensity. Historical experience has shown that transformations of a military balance can be realized quickly without much relation to other factors of power. In the Soviet view, defeat in the Cuban missile crisis might have been avoided if the USSR had projected a more convincing impression of equality in military strength. Moscow is not prepared to be a regional power centered on Europe while the United States alone wields global responsibilities. The most deep-seated yearning of the Soviet Union is to be regarded as America's equal in the world power balance. The pursuit of a strong nuclear posture was inspired by a passion for status as well as by military considerations. It is not certain that the achievement of a strong military status will induce a relaxed mood in which arms control agreements can be negotiated with the United States. What is certain is that no such agreements could ever have been realistically envisaged from a situation of pronounced Soviet inferiority. It is instructive to note that once the Soviet Union lost its sense of nuclear inferiority, it ceased to indulge in hopeless formulas of "general and complete disarmament" and became interested in such pragmatic notions as limitations on the testing and deployment of nuclear weapons.

The crucial question is whether the Soviet Union, now endowed with unchallenged military power, will deploy its enhanced status in the diplomatic arena, or whether it is capable of believing in the potential utility of nuclear war. The pessimists point to studies such as that of

Marshal Vassily Sokolovsky, who was Chief of Staff from 1952 to 1960 and who wrote with a sense of cold realism about the possibility of a nuclear war:

> *Military strategy in the conditions of modern war becomes the strategy of deep rocket-nuclear strikes in combination with actions by all services of the armed forces, with the aim of simultaneously striking and destroying the economic potential and the armed forces on the whole depth of the enemy's territory and for attaining the objectives of the war in a short time.*

This sounds infinitely alarming. It becomes less so if we understand that generals have a professional commitment to anxiety; it is their duty to think in terms of worst-case contingencies. Moreover, these words were written in the late 1950s when the Soviet Union was obsessed by a sense of its nuclear inferiority. In 1965, when the USSR was more relaxed about its strength, the same Sokolovsky was writing that "general nuclear war would be immensely destructive; hundreds of millions would perish not only in the West, but in the Soviet Union and throughout the world. The main aim of preparing for a general nuclear war was to prevent it." By September 1963 the Soviet government was sternly reproving Chinese leaders including Mao Zedong for their cold invocation of nuclear war as a feasible contingency:

> *Thermonuclear war will have catastrophic consequences for all peoples, for the whole world. All countries, even those that survive the war, would be thrown back in their development by decades, if not centuries.*

The top Soviet leadership has also deprecated the idea that nuclear war is feasible. In a speech in January 1963 Khrushchev said that "according to calculations of scientists the very first strike in a nuclear war would destroy between 700 and 800 million people. All large cities, not only in the United States and the Soviet Union, the two leading nuclear powers, but also in France, Britain, Germany, Italy, China, Japan and many other countries would be razed to the ground and destroyed." Brezhnev was even more incisive: "The existing stockpiles of nuclear weapons are capable of blowing up the entire planet." For the past two decades Soviet official rhetoric has emphasized the inconceivability of nuclear war, not its feasibility. Nuclear preparedness is presented as a device for avoiding war, not as a prelude to waging it.

The most recent pronouncement on this theme came from Brezhnev at the Twenty-sixth Party Congress held in Moscow. He was pouring scorn on comment in Washington asserting that the USSR believed that it could use its nuclear strength to win a war. Brezhnev retorted:

What is this Soviet superiority about which they talk? The danger of war hangs over the United States just as it confronts every other state in the world. We are ready to struggle against this real danger, combat it arm and arm with America, with the European states, and with all other countries on our planet. But it would be sheer madness to try to outdo one another in an arms race, or to count on achieving a victory in a nuclear war.

He then proposed a freeze on the deployment of new intermediate-range missiles by NATO and the Warsaw Pact.

Georgi Arbatov, who appears to be the USSR's accredited spokesman to the American public, has also referred to the evolutionary aspect of Soviet thinking. Confronted with the question whether articles, speeches and books by Soviet military writers may not legitimately be invoked as proof that "the Soviet Union believes in fighting and winning a nuclear war," Arbatov responds: "These quotes are ten to twenty years old . . . Awareness of the consequences of nuclear war has increased in this time span." He then goes on to quote statements by General Curtis LeMay and former Secretary of Defense Melvin Laird to the effect that "the United States must develop the willingness to wage total nuclear war." Arbatov adds inaccurately: "You will not find anything of this kind written or said by Soviet military leaders, or by anyone in the Soviet Union."

The crucial question is whether Soviet protestations about the insanity of nuclear war can be believed. The case for skepticism can be sustained by many quotations about the feasibility of nuclear victory, but these are nearly always taken from old technical military publications. Arbatov has not found it difficult to quote American parallels by searching out the literature in which U.S. military leaders analyze contingencies without committing themselves to their degree of probability.

The case for Soviet credibility on the particular issue of avoiding a holocaust does not involve a generalized naïveté about Soviet policy; it rests on the impression that Soviet leaders were sincerely traumatized by the World War II experience, which all of them are old enough to be able to recall, while their younger successors may be less ideologically minded and more prone to a pragmatic acknowledgment of Western power. To assume that Soviet policymakers prefer being alive to being blown up or shriveled into nothingness does not seem to be an excessively generous tribute to their sense of human vulnerability. It is not necessary to be "soft on Communism" to believe that Soviet leaders prefer to be alive rather than dead. Another, more pragmatic consideration is that the Soviets have no reason to feel so frustrated by their present condition and prospect as to be impelled toward courses of action that proceed from desperation. The Soviet Union is not a dissatisfied irredentist power. In the last resort, it is a salutary habit, when confronted with two alternative possibilities of belief, to avoid choosing the one that leads to paralysis of hope and action. The idea that the Soviet Union has no particular aversion to a nuclear holocaust in which it would be consumed together with the rest of us takes us nowhere and leaves us with nothing to do, except to prepare for embattled resistance or abject surrender. It is a contingency for which diplomacy holds no answers. On the other hand, the contingency of Soviet sincerity in the egotistical wish to avoid self-destruction does leave ways open for active response. It does not condemn us to dull, despairing inertia. And it does not conflict with the known laws of human nature.

The real effect of the Soviet Union's nuclear power lies not in its military results but in its psychological support of Soviet diplomacy, especially in Europe. The purpose is to detach European countries from strategic cooperation with the United States. Western and especially American diplomacy was so obsessed by the problem of the central nuclear balance that it was somewhat late in coming face to face with the problem of intermediate-range missiles in Europe. Here the matters at issue belonged more to politics and image-making than to strategy in the technical sense. The question was which of the two superpowers would convince European opinion that its rival was responsible for the deadlock? At first the propaganda advantage was with the Soviet Union; the United States merely stated its implacable resolve to station the cruise and Pershing missiles on European soil and gave no satisfaction to European anxieties. In the second stage, the United States recovered the initiative to some degree with President Reagan's "zero option" proposal of November 1981. But Moscow had little difficulty later in persuading the Europeans that this idea was unworkable; the Soviet Union was not going to renounce something that existed (its SS-20 missiles) in favor of something that was only intended (the cruise and Pershing II missiles). Reagan recovered the initiative again with his declared willingness at the end of March 1983 to compromise on the "zero option" by a gradual policy of mutual reduction. In a sense, Europe was virtually mediating between American and Russian interests by alternately pressing each of the two sides to draw nearer to the other. President Reagan's compromise on his "zero option" may not have initiated a turning point in the arms control discussion, but it was a signpost in the journey of the alliance; for the first time in many years the NATO countries applauded an American posture toward the Soviet Union in a matter related to the nuclear balance.

Negotiating with the Soviets

The question of how to deal with the Soviet Union occupies such a large area of modern diplomacy that nobody can act effectively in the international arena without some conception of the USSR's negotiating techniques. There is now a profuse literature about national styles in negotiation. Raymond Aron considers that British negotiators believe in discussion and argument while their French counterparts "create obstructions from which to retire." Harold Nicolson idealizes British negotiating techniques as the norm from which all other styles are deviations. Thayer writes that all states except the Soviet Union use the same habits and techniques. Fred Ikle makes a salutary effort to bring the discussion down to earth by arguing, convincingly, that Soviet negotiators are just as prone to failure as their Western counterparts. "Contrary to a popular image in the West, Soviet negotiators are bold rather than shrewd, brazen rather than cunning. It is not the skills attributed to a Talleyrand that the West must fear from Communist diplomats nor are the Russians brilliant disciples of Machiavelli." Kissinger, who has more empirical experience than any other writer, has pointed out that "the Soviets always leave room for bargaining; I knew no instance where a Soviet opening position was anywhere close to the final outcome. Once the principle had been conceded, the gap would almost certainly be subject to improvement through negotiations." Edward L. Rowny, who has negotiated with Soviet representatives on strategic arms limitation, contends that "the Soviets have a basic approach to negotiations that differs from ours and they utilize a different set of techniques in conducting such negotiations."

What distinguishes the Soviet negotiator from his Western counterpart is his tight subservience to centralized authority, with an absence of any latitude even in matters of formulation. The fear of violating instructions commits him to the endless repetition of positions without any sign of being influenced by the argument of the other side. Soviet diplomats are reluctant to suggest modifications of policy or even of formulas to Moscow lest they be regarded as casting doubt on the omniscience of their superiors. Kissinger is almost certainly right about the Soviets leaving room for "eventual" moderation of their positions, but the word "eventual" embodies a terrifying ordeal of intermediate attrition for the non-Soviet partner. Soviet negotiators must be prepared to uphold original positions in detail and for long periods. Unlike the representatives of democratic societies, they do not feel free to comment immediately on new proposals heard in the course of negotiations. While Western negotiators are committed to the substance of their positions but have wide discretion in explaining them, Soviet negotiators must always assume that there is deep ideological significance in the specific words in which their instructions are couched. They are thus deprived of the capacity to soften the reaction of their negotiating partners by a more amenable interpretation of what they are submitting. On the other hand they are quick to seize on semantic obscurities or ambiguities in their rivals' stated positions. In 1942 the Soviet Union and Britain had promised to withdraw their troops from Iranian soil "six months after the conclusion of hostilities." At that time the Soviet Union had been at war with Germany, not with Japan. The meaning of the phrase "conclusion of hostilities" must have been clear. But at Potsdam in 1945 the USSR insisted that the six months must be counted from the surrender of Japan, which at that time seemed likely to take place in early 1947! The delay in the Soviet withdrawal from Iran provoked the first East-West crisis after the end of World War II and played a part in the creation of the Cold War atmosphere.

There are some stereotypes in Western thinking about diplomacy which the Soviet Union has never embraced. The idea that it is normal to solve disputes by splitting the differences between the parties "down the middle" has no place in Soviet diplomatic theory. Philip Mosely has pointed out:

> One of the difficulties of Soviet-Russian vocabulary is that the word "compromise" is not of native origin and carries with it no favorable empathy. It is habitually used only in combination with the adjective "putrid" . . . Therefore any point which has finally to be abandoned must be given up only after a most terrific struggle. The Soviet negotiator must first prove to himself and his superiors that he is up against an immovable force.

This tenacity is not always successful. One of its results is that the Soviet Union may often have missed chances of securing a partial gain by insisting on a total victory.

Western negotiators often waste a great deal of time and credibility by obeying a moral necessity to explain and justify their positions to Soviet representatives. In Soviet eyes what is important is to understand what a Western position is, not why it has been adopted. Negotiation in the Soviet scheme of thought is a clash of wills and interests, not a competition to discover who has the most cogent arguments. When Western negotiators strive to prove that their positions are more logical or more humane or more objectively reasonable than those of their Soviet interlocutors, they are addressing themselves to their own domestic constituency or to their own allies rather than to the Soviet negotiator.

This brings us to an essential difference between Soviet and non-Soviet negotiation; it is a difference that overshadows and explains many others. Soviet negotiators hold their dialogue not only with the representatives of democratic states but also, and perhaps mostly, with the public opinion in the constituencies of their rivals. Non-Soviet negotiators—because of the nature of the Soviet political system—have no such duality of purpose; they are dealing with the Soviet government alone. This lack of symmetry has pervasive effects, and Soviet policymakers are fully conscious of their advantage. In 1960 the State Publishing House for Political Literature in Moscow published a "diplomatic handbook." With more veracity than tact its authors wrote:

> [Communist diplomacy] is invariably successful in exposing the aggressive intentions of the imperialist governments . . . [This] is one of the important methods of socialist diplomacy by means of which it mobilizes democratic social opinion and the masses of people all over the world against the aggressive policies of the imperialist governments.

Realistic Western negotiators are frankly aware of this distinction, and the awareness itself is helpful to them even if it does not weaken their sense of discrimination and "unfairness." Kissinger includes among the advantages enjoyed by Soviet diplomacy the fact that "[it] has one great asset . . . It has no domestic pressures impelling it constantly to put forward new ideas to break deadlocks. It is not accused of rigidity if it advances variations of the same proposals year after year. There are no rewards in the Politburo for the exploration of ever-new schemes, which turns so much of American diplomacy into a negotiation with ourselves." Soviet and Western representatives engaged in a negotiation are not involved in the same kind of dilemma. The Soviet negotiator asks only: "How can I advance Soviet interests?" The Western negotiator asks: "How can I advance my country's interests and also reach an agreement?" Nobody has heard of a Soviet negotiator having to face critical domestic opinion if he comes home without a signed accord; nor will the Soviet press ever distribute the censure equally between Soviet and Western governments.

Yet it would be inaccurate as well as self-defeating to assume that Soviet diplomacy, laden with these tactical advantages, is "invariably successful," to use the modest words of the Moscow handbook. Soviet policymakers and negotiators have made costly errors for which their Western counterparts would have had to pay a heavy price in discredit or dismissal. The USSR erred in rejecting membership in the Marshall Plan (1947); in absenting itself from the Security Council in 1950, thus enabling the United States to obtain UN authority for its campaign in

Korea; in provoking an intensified Western commitment to Turkey in 1946 and 1968 by bellicose rhetoric; in weakening credibility by ultimative deadlines about Berlin in 1961 (which were not honored); in encouraging Egyptian and Syrian pressure on Israel in 1967 without being ready to back them in the consequent risks; in adopting such an arrogant stance in Cairo as to alienate Egyptian nationalism (1970–72); in sacrificing the sympathy of the Third World by the invasion of Afghanistan in 1979; and in alienating European liberals by a repressive policy toward the Polish Solidarity movement in 1981. Towering above all other errors was a clumsy diplomacy in the Cuban missile crisis (1962), in which Soviet threats went beyond any real intention to carry them into effect. Nor can any objective observer of the Soviet scene understand how the persecution of the Soviet scientists Andrei Sakharov and Anatoly Shcharansky can have been so compelling as to prejudice the larger objectives of Soviet policy in the tense dialogue with the non-Soviet world.

Those who negotiate with the USSR must respect its strength and understand the somber sense of tragedy that pervades its national experience, but they have no need for self-abasement. It is not the case that Soviet diplomacy is a precise cybernetic exercise immune to the dislocating gusts of passion, injured pride, personal exhaustion and other human frailties that prevent a negotiator from acting in strict accord with well-defined interests. Moreover, the first condition of a successful negotiation is that the parties should have a clear and lucid comprehension of each other's way of reasoning and decision. Here the exotic view of the non-Communist world imposed by Soviet propaganda inhibits Soviet representatives from understanding those with whom they are negotiating. For example, the USSR is committed to the view that when a Great Power has a close connection with a small state, it is the Great Power that dictates the policy of its "client." The repeated and manifest failure of the United States to impose its will on European allies, on states in Southeast Asia and on Israel is simply not believed; it is genuinely regarded by the Soviet Union as mere hypocrisy.

The difficulty of mutual understanding flows from a deeper source than can be found in an isolated study of the diplomatic enterprise. It is rooted in a history of separation. In theory, the Soviet Union is a part of continental Europe. But this is a geographical, not a cultural, truth. When Russia was dominated by the Eastern Orthodox Church and Europe by Catholicism and Protestantism, the religious schism corresponded with a profound gulf in thought and belief. The two parts of the continent were divided from each other as sharply as if great distances and oceans stood between them. The liberalizing winds of European political culture never found an echo across the chasm.

Russians became endemically attached to the idea of authority, discipline, obedience, national unity and docility. For two hundred years under the Tartars the Russian people developed a habit of authoritarian rule which has never lapsed. Whether the rulers of Russia have been czars or commissars, the central principle of the social order has always been the subjection of individuals to the state. Even when contacts with the West were permitted or even encouraged—as by Peter the Great—they were carefully confined to a small artistic or diplomatic elite. Distrust of foreigners is a universal attribute of all nation-states, but in Russia this emotion has a special intensity.

Another barrier to normal negotiation is the conviction of Marxists that they possess a superior insight into the laws that govern the social order. It is difficult for them to admit, by concession, that their adversaries can reach valid conclusions without accepting the revealed truth of the Communist prophets. The upshot is that a negotiator involved in transactions with the Soviet Union must understand that he is entering a special world of experience for which other kinds of negotiation have not necessarily qualified him.

There is even an element of uncertainty about the institutional procedures by which Soviet foreign policy is formulated; the non-Soviet negotiator cannot always be certain about the degree of authority vested in his negotiating partner. In theory, the Supreme Soviet is the final resort and the ultimate authority, and after the death of Stalin some reality was given to this fiction. The Supreme Soviet joined the Inter-Parliamentary Union in 1955 and began a routine of addressing itself to other legislatures and sending parliamentary missions abroad. But the real power lies with the Presidium, which is itself subordinate to the directives of the Politburo. There is some obscurity about the overlapping functions of the Presidium and the Council of Ministers, whose Chairman corresponds to the Prime Minister in a parliamentary country. However, when Bulganin held the rank of Chairman in 1955–58 it became apparent after a short time that real power had moved to the General Secretary of the party, Khrushchev. When Kosygin became Chairman of the Council of Ministers in 1964, he was thought to be pre-eminent in the formulation of foreign policy, but by 1968 it was clear that his power in foreign affairs had passed to Brezhnev, who had been elected as General Secretary of the party in 1966. As against these fluctuations at the summit of power, those who have negotiated with the USSR at foreign minister level since the 1930s have encountered only four foreign ministers in fifty-five years—Maxim Litvinov (1929–39); Vyacheslav Molotov (1939–49 and, later, 1953–56); Andrei Vyshinsky (1949–53); and Andrei Gromyko (1957–?). The technical nature of this office is revealed by the fact that the USSR found nothing incongruous in using Molotov successively as its representative in a pact with Nazi Germany and, a few years later, as its spokesman in relations with American and British allies in a war to the death against Hitler. Soviet diplomats are men for all seasons. Because of their inevitable exposure to external influences it is likely that more care is taken to ensure their Communist orthodoxy and party loyalties than with any other sector of Soviet officialdom.

Continuity and Change in the 1980s

Given these complications, it may seem rash to predict the course of the Soviet Union for the remainder of this decade. Yet recent and current trends are sufficiently clearcut to make the exercise feasible:

—Soviet military parity with the United States is an established reality which cannot now be rescinded. Whether the arms race will continue or be restrained by arms control, the end result will not be Soviet inferiority. The USSR has the will and the economic and technical capacity with which to sustain its hard-earned status as a military and naval power.

—While the United States and the Soviet Union have each lost a measure of control over their respective alliances or power blocs, their strength exceeds that of other actors in the international system so greatly that they still command the arenas of world strategy. Bipolarity is not an outworn myth.

—The social systems, political ideas and national values of the United States and the Soviet Union are so divergent that their interests are bound to be in conflict in many parts of the world. On the other hand, there is a mutual interest in controls and restraints. Therefore, categorizing their relationship at any particular time as "Cold War" or "détente" is excessively simplistic.

—Though the two superpowers have the capacity either to escalate local conflicts to global crises or to moderate them and keep them localized and limited, the future outlook is that they will tend to be moderate and not take them to the level of the Berlin crisis or the Cuban missile crisis.

—The Soviet economy will be weaker than that of the United States, Japan and Europe, so that the military power of the USSR is not paralleled on the economic front. But the dependence of the Soviet Union on trade and technology from the West will not be acute enough to induce Moscow to modify its policies to a substantial degree. On the other hand, declining growth rates and increased pressure for consumer goods will create an interest in negotiating balances and restraints in arms development if United States attitudes encourage this trend.

—Nationalism is the strongest impulse at work among the USSR's neighbors in Eastern Europe. Memories of recent Soviet repression in Hungary, Czechoslovakia and Poland show how powerful that impulse is. It is unlikely that another decade will pass without further attempts in Eastern Europe to loosen the Soviet hold. But the West will not have much power to influence the outcome of this struggle.

—Criticism of the repressive elements of the Soviet system will be heard in the West and sometimes in the Third World, but there is no reason to believe that the Soviet system will change or evolve toward Western versions of democracy with greater freedom of opinion and dissent.

—There are probably two trends in Soviet politics and society: modernism and orthodoxy. Modernists call for optimism, scientific progress, relative openness to the world and a more relaxed view about the USSR's perceived vulnerability. The orthodox school will stress vigilance, centralized bureaucratic discipline and a rigorous defense of ideological purity. Which of these alternative trends will prevail depends, in part, on whether the West opens arms control options or whether it concentrates on escalating the arms race. In the latter case, the orthodox school is more likely to be strengthened in the USSR.

—Soviet policy in Europe will be focused mainly on West Germany, where the USSR will strive to recover from the negative influence (from its point of view) of the Christian Democrat victory under Helmut Kohl in March 1983. Moscow will work on German public opinion in order to restrain cooperation between the Federal Republic and the United States on the location of medium-range missiles.

—The Third World will be marginal, not central in Soviet diplomacy. The USSR will be immeasurably inferior to the United States in the dimensions and scope of its aid programs to the South. (The Soviet aid to Africa is only 7 percent of that of the United States and is not likely to increase.)

—Efforts will be made to defuse the ideological conflict with China and to intensify cooperation with Japan. Soviet policy toward Japan will be devoted to avoiding any intensification of the Japanese defense effort and to benefiting from Japanese technology, which may be less linked to political attitudes than is that of America and Europe.

—The USSR has not reconciled itself to its exclusion from the diplomatic process in the Middle East. It will use its influence in Syria and elsewhere to obstruct American-sponsored settlements unless the United States renews cooperation with the Soviet Union to promote joint policies. The Soviet Union will support Arab causes, but not to the point of challenging Israel's existence, and will endeavor to improve its position in Iran.

A third of the way into the 1980s the Soviet Union has not substantially modified the two central impulses that have inspired its policies since the beginning of the postwar age. The central themes are security and equality. The first of these has been achieved to the point at which nobody of sane mind can imagine an attack on the USSR or its vital interests from any quarter. The emphasis now is on the legitimization of Moscow's status as a world power center in no way subsidiary to Washington's. This task is not yet complete. It is still common to speak of "growing American *influence*" in Egypt or Lebanon, and of "Soviet *penetration* or *expansion*" in Syria or Ethiopia. The implication is that the USSR should be satisfied to be a regional power with vital interests in Europe and on its own Asian borders, while American diplomacy is naturally free to roam across the globe in the service of a universal vocation. This is an attractive idea for those who are repelled by the harsher elements in Soviet society and policy, but there is no chance that the Soviet Union will accept the implied discrimination.

This inevitably strengthens a military emphasis in Soviet policy for the simple reason that beyond its military power the Soviet Union has a surprisingly limited weight in relation to its size and resources. Its basic economic self-sufficiency is an asset from one point of view, but its economic failures and its insignificance as a trading power reduce the weight of its diplomacy. Its network of international relations does not compare in range or weight with that of the United States. The two distinguishing features of Soviet society are military strength and economic weakness. The first of these is the more spectacular, but the latter is no less decisive in its effects. On the positive side, Soviet economic weakness creates a salutary dependence on tolerable relationships with the West and gives a powerful incentive to arms control. On the negative side, a lack of pride and self-confidence about its economy reinforces the decision of the Soviet Union to insulate itself as much as possible from external contact and scrutiny and to inhibit free movement between Eastern and Western Europe.

The four power centers that lie outside the Soviet orbit—America, Western Europe, China and Japan—may have no alternative but to combine in the deterrence or containment of Soviet military force. These words—"containment" and "deterrence"—have a depressingly familiar ring. But there is something to be said for the idea of an international balance that may induce the USSR to limit the use or demonstration of its military power to aims that fall short of aggression. The choice before the non-Soviet world is clear: Should there be an effort to deny the Soviet Union a sense of particular status? Or are there domains in which this ambition can be partially fulfilled without the unappealing consequence of a two-power domination of the entire international system? The logic of détente was that the Western-Soviet relationship needed a broader and more variegated context than could be provided by a dialogue focused exclusively on the strategic balance. Though this idea was lost from sight in the late 1970s, nothing more rational or prudent has yet taken its place.

There are no generalized, ready-made prescriptions for the understanding of future Soviet policy, still less for dealing with it. The Andropov era is too young for responsible conclusions to be drawn about its direction; for example, how far did Soviet passivity in the Lebanese war reflect a general view of the subsidiary nature of Soviet interests in that sector of the Middle East, as against the possibility that Soviet decision-making was under temporary constraint during Brezhnev's period of physical decline? Is it prudent, as some observers have done, to determine at this early stage that the new Soviet leadership will be less rigorous and more pragmatic than its predecessors?

What is certain is that Soviet policy is variable, not predetermined, and that one of the influences that may help to fix its course is the subtlety and clarity with which Western statesmanship approaches it. Here there have been two favorable developments: American policy in the early 1980s has been more rational and less virulent than American rhetoric, and Western Europe under Kohl, Mitterrand and Thatcher is far from accepting a posture of abjectness in the shadow of Soviet power. Beyond this, many Western analysts express a longing for a more coherent Western policy toward Moscow. Some would like Western and especially American policy to rise above the complex interrelationship between domestic and foreign policy. "Using outside events in even limited ways for internal purposes will neither solve domestic difficulties nor serve our [U.S.] external aims." There is also the advice to Western Europe to reduce the area of its diversity: "Western Europe's inability to sustain the momentum toward political integration" is cited as "the source of military imbalance between the Soviet Union and the West."

The trouble with such remedies and reproaches is that they come close to advising America to stop being American and Europe to cease being European. The tendency of the United States to link its foreign policy to its domestic consensus and of Europeans to safeguard their individual interests and judgments are a deep-rooted expression of their social histories and their political personalities. Those who advise the West to face the Soviet reality as it is, not as one would want it to be, cannot escape the implications of their counsel in relation to the diversity and pluralism of the democratic world. Foreign policy specialists should heave a deep sigh and accept this diversity and pluralism for what they are.

Apart from divergences of ideology and interest, the dialogue between the Soviet Union and the West is complicated by a lack of symmetry on the diplomatic-tactical level. The Soviet Union is a unitary actor with a single center of decision. "The West" is a complex notion, fragmented at two levels: at the level of domestic divisions and at the level of divergent policies and attitudes among separate states. This condition implies a profound tactical disadvantage for the non-Soviet world. Yet if diversity and pluralism in democratic countries are handicaps in the diplomatic arena, they are, after all, the very principles that give Western diplomacy its redeeming values and its sense of vocation.

Once the ambivalent character of the relationship between the Soviet and the non-Soviet worlds is fully grasped, it will be possible to avoid extremes of confrontation without yielding to a hopeless utopianism. It may well be possible to reach agreement with the Soviet Union on some things without reaching agreement on everything.

Chapter 4

THE NEW EUROPE
AND THE ALLIANCE

Decline and Recovery

For many centuries Europe had been the center of the world. No
region could compare with it in wealth, productivity, military power or
political influence. At the turn of this century all the Great Powers were
European states. Europe's predominance was even greater in the
world of ideas than in the domain of material power. There are few
institutions or movements that have exercised an important influence
on world civilization which cannot trace their origin and impetus back
to Western Europe. Catholic Christianity, Protestantism, parliamentary democracy, Marxism, the Industrial Revolution and modern science are all the result of European imagination or research. As Barbara
Ward has written: "What superlatives should one use to describe the
vitality of a society which within a few hundred years produced Dante,
Shakespeare, St. Francis of Assisi, St. Teresa of Avila, Leonardo da
Vinci and Michelangelo, the music of Bach and Beethoven and master-
pieces of Gothic and Baroque architecture?"

There was too much vitality here to be confined to a small continent.
Europe has never been inward-looking. It has always sought its destiny
in association with others. European energies surged beyond Europe
itself and founded new societies in the European image in the Western
Hemisphere and elsewhere, while the immense commercial activity of
Britain laid the foundations of the first coherent economic system in
world history.

The psychological consequences of this supremacy included a deep
sense of pride and self-esteem. Everything that was not European was

deemed by much of mankind to be parochial. Thus, the shock was correspondingly sharper at the end of World War II when Europe found itself suddenly reduced to the status of a bankrupt suppliant facing political disintegration and urgently needing $4 billion to save its credit and ensure the rhythm of its life. That was its condition in 1945.

The most urgent weakness came from economic crisis. But there were also the traumatic rancors of the war, the sense of instability that pervaded political institutions, the threat of Communism and the haunting sensation that European countries would have to seek new forms of interaction and relationship. It was an astonishing change of fortune. The shock was compounded by the speed with which it had come. The decline of empires has usually been slow; Roman civilization took centuries to fall from unchallenged predominance to collapse, but here no more than seventy years separated Western Europe's nineteenth-century peak from what threatened to be its resounding decline.

The years of war had shattered the pattern of Western European commerce. Britain had spent most of its foreign assets, had incurred £3 billion of war debts and had worked its machines to a standstill, without thought of obsolescence or replacement. France had been bled white by the German occupation, while its fertile soil had been devastated in battle. The Dutch countryside had been flooded for military defense, and the people of Holland had known starvation. Belgium and Norway had suffered less physical damage, but they had lost their traditional markets. The Ruhr area of West Germany was scorched earth during the war, and its development after the fighting was inhibited by the Potsdam agreement, which limited German industrial activity to minimal levels. German agriculture had been largely concentrated in the Eastern zones, which were lost to Germany through the decision to make the Oder-Neisse line the permanent German frontier. With this new border Germany lost nine million people together with a third of its pre-1937 territory. Production of German coal and steel was drastically short of what it had been in 1939.

The European response to these adversities was to embark on a great spurt of production as soon as the war came to a formal end. But here Nature completed a disaster which human conflict had begun. The coldest winter for a century was succeeded in the summer of 1947 by a drought which cut French agricultural production by 50 percent, with lesser but important damage everywhere else on the continent.

Happily for Europe's welfare but unfortunately for its pride, America had experienced an immense growth of productivity during the preceding years and was able to bring the New World to the rescue of the Old. There are few if any precedents in economic history for the growth of the American economy between 1939 and 1944. There were no battlefield wounds to heal, and the needs of the war industry had stimulated prodigious demand. In five years American production and income rose by 100 percent! What had been created in eighty years was doubled in four. Immense quantities of food, coal and manufactured goods poured out of the United States, so that within a few years the European economic crisis had become a crisis of payment, not of supply. The pattern of Europe's dependence on America with its accompanying political and psychological effects was firmly fixed in the immediate aftermath of the war. With the advent of nuclear weapons, economic dependence was compounded by a similar relationship of inequality in strategic defense. It seemed that America was becoming everything that Europe had once been.

After absorbing the reality of its new situation for a few years, Europe went on to celebrate a phenomenal display of resilience. Between 1950 and 1960 the nations of continental Europe experienced a rate of economic growth double that of the United States in the same period. American policy, through the Marshall Plan, was paradoxically transforming Western Europe from a poor dependent to a vigorous competitor and was thus the primary agent in the weakening of American hegemony. In later years even American leaders who chafed at Europe's recalcitrance at following American policy would have admitted that this embarrassment was much preferable to the possibility of a communized Europe putting itself at the service of Soviet national ambitions.

But no amount of external aid would have had a revitalizing effect if there had not been a swift consolidation of political stability. Britain led the way with economic and social reforms initiated by the Attlee-Bevin government, applying the egalitarian principles of the British Labour movement to the acute lassitudes and dislocations of the wartime economy. National health legislation was passed in 1946, and the coal industry, public transport, steel, electricity and gas were brought under governmental control. Whatever their long-term efficacy might prove to be, these measures seemed revolutionary at the time. Italy, on the morrow of the war, was able to cover 80 percent of its 1946 deficit by direct American aid. Although the 1946 elections brought a strong Communist Party into the open arena with 19 percent of the vote, it was clear that real control would be shared by the Christian Democrats with 35 percent and the Socialists with 21 percent. Under the leadership of Alcide de Gasperi and Carlo Sforza, Italy exchanged its lost, unhappy colonial career for a partner's role in the European movement toward integration.

France was in a desperately weak economic position after its liberation. Because of chronic inflation and low industrial output, by the summer of 1947 the average French worker was spending 75 percent of his income on food. Economic and social reforms by the coalition government in 1946 included nationalization of coal mines, electricity and gas as well as of much of the banking system. An extensive social security network gave the population serious protection from the uninhibited working of the free market system, and Jean Monnet's General Planning Commission, founded in early 1946, devised a plan to concentrate investment in certain vital sectors of the economy.

But in France the mark of interrogation was poised on the political outlook. France was the only big power to have suffered defeat by Hitler's armies. The shame of the capitulation set up crosscurrents of self-doubt which were not totally assuaged by the pride of the Resistance. The assertive period of De Gaulle's leadership was to come later, after his return from Colombey-les-Deux-Eglises in 1958, but his role in the immediate sequel to the war was even more crucial. His brief postwar leadership was sufficient to ensure France's place as a permanent member of the UN Security Council, with consequent recognition as one of the Great Powers. By inaugurating a new parliamentary epoch in France, De Gaulle had done democracy in Europe great service, which was all the more remarkable in view of his personal distaste for democratic procedures. The idea that there could be more than one side to any question was foreign to his imperious nature, but he was prepared, for his country's sake, to give the multiparty idea a new chance to vindicate itself.

Another of De Gaulle's early legacies to French political thought was the idea that France need not adapt itself to the polarization of the Cold War. He fiercely resented France's exclusion from Yalta, Dumbarton Oaks and Potsdam, and it was in order to avoid such humiliations in the future that he signed a mutual aid agreement with the Soviet Union in December 1944, two months after granting amnesty to the Communist Party leader Maurice Thorez. In addition to the handicap of his country's dependence and weakness he had to cope with a cool American attitude inspired by his reputation for dictatorial leadership. He replied by the simple formula of intransigent response whenever American and French interests were in conflict. After leading the coalition government to an impressive victory in October 1945, De Gaulle resigned three months later when the left-wing parties sought to limit his authority. He departed to self-imposed exile where he brooded on the need to give France a more authoritative system of government than the parliamentary system allowed. The Fourth Republic was to see twenty-six prime ministers in its twelve-year existence.

If France had secured a status that went beyond its geopolitical strength, the contrary fate befell Germany. The speed of its subse-

quent recovery could not possibly have been foreseen from the vantage point of its condition at the end of the war. A quarter of its
territory had been ceded to Russian and Polish control, and what was
left was divided into five sectors, each controlled separately by the
United States, France, Britain and the Soviet Union, with Berlin split
among the four countries. Three principles for governing Germany
laid down at Potsdam were denazification, demilitarization and demo-
cratization, but their application was at the discretion of the four occupying powers. Within a few years the Soviet Union had converted East
Germany into a society totally alienated from the West.

The Gulf Widens

The strengthening of the Soviet grip on East Germany was met by a
stern anti-Communism in the West. The two major West German
parties created a solid and stable democracy. The Social Democratic
Party (SPD) led by Kurt Schumacher stood for radical social programs
but also for democracy and public order. The Christian Democrats
(CDU) under Konrad Adenauer advocated a federal structure, laissez-
faire economics and close cooperation with the Western powers, including France, the "hereditary enemy" to the southwest. The liberal
Free Democrats were the third party and were to play an important
coalition role in future West German governments. Conditions were
now ripe for the reintegration of West Germany into the Western
world.

There is no rational explanation for the speed with which the Soviet
Union ensured that the renascent nations of Western Europe would
seek their destiny together in overt confrontation with the East. The
memories of the war had left behind a large deposit of sympathy for
the Russian people. Britain remembered the half year from June to
December 1941, in which the Soviet Union had been its only ally.
Other European peoples associated the Soviet Union with their own
liberation from the Nazi yoke. There was enough social radicalism in
postwar Europe to create a fund of hope in the possibility of Soviet-
Western coexistence. Yet within two years of the end of the war,
Moscow had virtually rejected this option without even giving it a trial.
The Soviet Union sought reparations for its vast losses in the struggle
against Nazi Germany. It went on to adopt attitudes and policies which
would have been understandable only if the division of Europe into
East and West had been its cherished ambition. In 1947 and 1948 all
opposition to Communist rule in Eastern Europe and the Balkans was
eliminated, the Czech regime was overthrown, Berlin was blockaded
and the Soviets refused participation in European recovery through
the Marshall Plan. The Soviet Union then supported Communist pres-

sure in Greece despite the fact that Greece had been understood to lie in Britain's sphere of influence and a majority of the Greek people had voted in a plebiscite for the restoration of the monarchy. In the meantime the Soviet Union maintained its troops in northern Iran beyond the agreed date, and Moscow adopted a policy of threat and intimidation against Turkey.

The Soviet drive for domination of all neighboring territories was so drastic that many scholars have wondered if it was fully calculated. It should have been clear that the West was being pushed beyond the limits of its indulgence and that a reaction was bound to come. The likeliest explanation of the policy is that the Soviet pressure was more traumatic than rational. The nightmare of constant attack from neighboring countries, most recently experienced in the tragedy of 20 million Russian dead at the hands of the Nazis, had hardened the Soviet resolve to be satisfied with nothing less than total control of all contiguous territories. By any realistic standard the idea that a battered and divided Germany, totally disarmed, could renew its threat to Soviet security seemed remote. But the Russian leadership was not thinking in short categories of time. Here was an opportunity to build a deep moat around the devastated homeland. Since the chance might be fleeting and was unlikely to recur, the Kremlin was resolved to build Russia's defenses and was ready to bear any Western opprobrium or resistance. Nazism might seem dead in the Western mind, but the specter of "German revanchism" still obsessed the Russian consciousness, and the suspicion that those in the West who opposed Hitlerism yesterday would regard the USSR as the enemy of tomorrow was sustained by enough Western anti-Communist rhetoric to seem credible in Russian eyes. But there was more at issue than historic fear. The Soviet Union evidently believed that the new balance of power could be conceived in purely European terms and without taking the United States into account. The idea that American intervention in Europe had been episodic and transitory was nourished by the speed of United States troop withdrawals from European soil to the applause of massive public opinion in America itself. If Western Europe's limited power was all that stood in the path of Russian continental domination, it seemed quixotic not to take the opportunity.

The Soviet Union had assumed that America would disengage from Europe. In terms of historical experience what was surprising was not the Russian assumption but the American resolve to refute it. There was to be no repetition of 1918–39. Europe no longer had its frontiers within the continent. Its fate would not be determined by its own interior equilibrium, and the United States was not prepared to leave the Old Continent to its fate. The Truman Doctrine of March 1947 and the Marshall Plan, announced in June 1947 as a vow to fight "hunger, poverty, desperation and chaos," created a new alignment that would characterize American and European politics for a whole generation.

The American-European alliance did not rest on a foundation of affection; it was a covenant of mutual necessity, and so it continues to be. The same was true of European unity. This was a dictate of necessity. In Raymond Aron's words:

> As long as the Soviet bloc exists, as long as the Red Army is stationed two hundred kilometers from the Rhine, as long as the western fringe of the Eurasian land-mass owes its liberty to the protection of the maritime powers, the former enemy nations [in Europe] are doomed to live together in an alliance imposed by events. The real question was whether this alliance would be borne as a cruel fate or accepted as a challenge to be met by the will to construct.

The "will to construct" was not lacking in the economic sphere. The spectacular achievements of the Marshall Plan should not make us forget that some of Europe's most acute economic wounds had been healed before the plan came into effect. By 1948, the output of European industry and agriculture was almost as high as before the war. There were severe balance-of-payment problems and a prospect of social disorder. Winston Churchill could ask rhetorically in 1947, "What is Europe now? a rubble heap? a charnel house? a breeding ground of pestilence and hate?" But Europe's economic growth showed amazing resilience and continued almost unabated through the late 1960s, well beyond the dreams of the most optimistic observers in the earlier postwar years.

The tendency to attribute Europe's recovery exclusively to American aid does flagrant injustice to Europe's own record of vitality. Europe had many reasons to despair, but accepted none of them. Many across the world questioned Europe's capacity to survive with dignity in a world dominated by American and Soviet power. Europe proudly rejected this theory. Throughout the 1950s, Europeans showed more self-confidence and resilience than they or anyone else had predicted. Together with swift economic growth there came an extraordinary impulse of political and social innovation. Europeans were no longer the captives of their past. The past was too tragic to be a point of reference for the future. Within a few years of their darkest memories, millions of Europeans were inspired by an exceptional buoyancy.

It could well have been otherwise. Europe, after all, was incapable of defending itself, and its reliance on American protection was absolute. This situation had no precedent in European memory. Nobody could doubt the profound psychological effects of this disability. And it was aggravated by another blow no less wounding to Europe's pride.

Until the Second World War most major breakthroughs in science or technology owed a large debt to European scholarship or imagination. By the mid-1950s it was clear that the resources needed for participation in the technologies of space were beyond Europe's reach. Europeans were called upon to be junior partners both in the modern military enterprise and in the adventure of outer space. Together with the loss of vast overseas territories these new limitations might have been expected to shatter European self-confidence. Yet thanks to the realism inherent in its own intellectual tradition and to exceptional good fortune in the quality of its leadership, Europe was able to come to terms with the truth of its own capacities. It looked at itself hard and straight. It gave up the idea of military domination, imperial possession and technological supremacy in order to devote itself to those spheres of action in which large opportunities still beckoned. No external influences or initial poverty of resources could prevent Europe from testing its own qualities in two fields: social and economic construction and the exploration of the European idea.

The Search for European Identity

It is commonly believed that integration is a more advanced stage of social evolution than national separatism. This is not true historically of Europe. The concept of a single European society is older than the division of the continent into separate national states. Until the late eighteenth or early nineteenth century the leadership of the European world was in the hands of men who thought of themselves as Europeans first and Frenchmen, Germans, Dutchmen or Englishmen second. They were brought up on a common cultural heritage deriving from Latin and Greek literature. They listened to the same music. They attended the same theaters. Gibbon, in viewing this culture, could speak of Europe as "one great republic." All the leaders of European nations were the products of a Western civilization firmly grounded in the "Corpus Christianum."

Gibbon's idea of Europe as a great republic had been familiar to Voltaire. This is what he says in his biography of Louis XIV:

> One could regard Christian Europe except Russia as a sort of great republic divided into several states, some monarchical, others of a mixed character; the former aristocratic, the latter popular, but all in harmony with each other, all having the same substrata of religion, although divided into various sects; all possessing the same principles of public and political law unknown in other parts of the world . . . In obedience to these principles, the Europeans do not make their prisoners slaves. They respect their enemies' ambassadors. They agree as to the preeminence and rights of certain princes

such as the emperor, kings and other lesser potentates, and above all, they
are at one on the wise policy of maintaining among themselves, as far as
possible, an equal balance of power, ceaselessly carrying on negotiations
even in wartime and sending each other ambassadors or less honourable
spies who can acquaint every court with the designs of every one of them,
give in a moment the alarm to Europe and defend the weakest from inva-
sions which the strongest is always ready to attempt.

Voltaire is an example of a man who could feel himself to be both
an ardent citizen of France and a citizen of Europe. He seemed able
to think about both with equal pride and was ultimately incapable of
separating one from the other.

Across the Channel, Edmund Burke, a British Member of Parliament
who had made his name at Westminster largely through defending the
interests of individual nations and peoples—the American, the Irish
and the Indian—was just as disposed as Voltaire to think of himself in
terms of European identity:

Nothing is more certain than that our manners, our civilizations and all
the good things which are connected with manners and with civilization,
have, in this European world of ours, depended for ages upon two principles
and were indeed the result of both combined. I mean the spirit of the
gentleman and the spirit of religion.

The equation of religion with gentlemanliness might seem superficial and ill-considered. But what is important is that Burke spoke of
Europe in the first person: "this European world of *ours.*"

The strength of the European consciousness was attested by its
capacity to transcend national allegiances. A Frenchman or Dane serving another European government had no sense of guilt, still less of
treachery. Statesmen, diplomats and generals felt a stronger affinity
with people of similar class in other countries than they did with the
masses of their own countries. They were able to transfer their loyalties with a promiscuity which would seem astonishing to those of us
brought up in the age of separate nation-states. Military and diplomatic personnel moved from one monarch to another. A French diplomat or officer would enter the services of the King of Prussia and
further the aims of Prussia, or fight in the Prussian army against
France. Shortly before the outbreak of the Seven Years War in 1756,
Frederick the Great sent a Scottish Earl Marshal as his ambassador to
Spain in order to get information about Spanish intentions. This Scottish ambassador of Prussia had a friend in Spain, an Irishman by the
name of Ward, who happened to be the Spanish Foreign Minister and
who told him what he wanted to know. The Scot who "happened" to

be a Prussian ambassador transmitted this information to the British Prime Minister, who in turn passed it on to the King of Prussia. As late as 1792, shortly before the outbreak of the war of the First Coalition against France, the French government offered the supreme command of the French forces to the Duke of Brunswick, who, however, decided to accept a better offer from the King of Prussia to lead the Prussian army against France.

The extraordinary lengths to which this permissive sense of allegiance could be taken is illustrated by Hans J. Morgenthau in a reference to Bismarck:

> Bismarck's experience in 1862, on the occasion of his recall as Prussian ambassador to Russia, is significant for the persistence of this international cohesion of the aristocracy. When he expressed to the Czar his regret at the necessity of leaving St. Petersburg, the Czar, misunderstanding this remark, asked Bismarck whether he was inclined to enter the Russian diplomatic service. Bismarck reported in his memoirs that he declined the offer "courteously."

Morgenthau goes on to observe:

> What is important and significant is not that Bismarck declined the offer —many such offers had certainly been declined before and perhaps even a few had been since—but that he did so "courteously" and that even his report, written more than thirty years after the event, showed no trace of moral indignation. Only a little more than half a century ago the offer to an ambassador who had just been appointed Prime Minister, to transfer his loyalties from one country to another, was considered by the recipient as a sort of business proposition that did not at all insinuate the violation of moral standards. Let us imagine that a similar offer had been made in our time by a Russian Prime Minister to the American ambassador or by the American President to any diplomat accredited in Washington and visualize the private embarrassment of the individual concerned, and the public indignation following the incident and we have the measure of the profundity of the change that has transformed the ethics of foreign policy in recent times.

The erosion of Christian authority and the resulting secularization of government removed what had been Europe's unifying force. Until the seventeenth century the national states of Western Europe had regarded themselves as parts of the same Christian entity, and that entity was seen as something higher than any of the national divisions into which Europe was splitting up. National policies were pursued with Christianity as the universal allegiance to which all European

statesmen made their obeisance. Policies became legitimate only by
reference to the common source of all life and all purpose. It was only
much later that princes became more powerful than the Church and
that nationalism supplanted religion as the main focus of human solidarity.

The remarkable fact that Europe was unified first and fragmented
afterward is not merely a matter of historical curiosity. The leaders of
postwar Europe who became the architects of the European Community, Konrad Adenauer, Alcide de Gasperi, Robert Schuman, Charles
de Gaulle and others, were all practicing Catholics, familiar from their
school days with the idea of Europe as a "great republic." It is true that
by the time of their birth, Europe had been irreversibly secularized and
de-Christianized, but ideas, like matter, are indestructible. The recollection of an epoch in which allegiance to Europe was greater than any
national loyalty was built into the consciousness of educated, observ-
ant Europeans so deeply that the revival of the European idea in our
generation came without any sense of radical innovation or shock.

Today the European Community is tangibly expressed in economic
institutions of growing cohesiveness and power. In the political realm,
national sovereignty is closely guarded. De Gaulle's return to power
in 1958 had been the major barrier to the development of a federal
spirit in Europe's political structure, but in recent years the French
campaign against supranationalism has been strongly espoused by
Britain. Thus European integration has been impeded by two of the
strongest national particularities in world history. But if the European
Community today has more of an economic than a political significance, we should not forget that this is contrary to its original purpose.

The modern European Community is not a response to any compul-
sive historical necessity. Nobody can say that it was born because there
was no alternative to its birth. By the time that negotiations for the
Treaty of Rome began in 1957, European recovery was making excellent progress within national frameworks. There was also great accessibility across boundaries and a disposition to renounce protectionist
trade policies in the hope of stimulating the growth of a broad regional
market. The community idea took concrete form when it did largely
because of original and imaginative leadership. It happened that Robert Schuman and Konrad Adenauer were gripped by an intense vision
and were in a position to carry it to fulfillment. It also happened that
Jean Monnet, who had done more than any man to win intellectual
attention for the European idea, was not a mere academic philosopher
wasting his wisdom on the desert air; he was firmly plugged in to the
French economic establishment and had a wide network of contacts
across Western Europe and Britain. In other parts of Europe, De
Gasperi of Italy and Paul Henri Spaak of Belgium were confirmed

Europeans in positions of influence and power. The aging Winston Churchill belied his stereotyped reputation as an inveterate nationalist by spreading the message of European unity across the world with authoritative and thunderous eloquence. Thus an idea that could have withered took firm root as the result of vigorous personal intervention by men who had large powers and large opportunities of using them. Since few of them were afflicted with excessive reticence, we know directly what they were trying to do. They were not particularly interested in a customs union or in a device for regulating the prices of agricultural crops. They used the economic argument in order to clear the way for a political idea. Their strategy was set out by Robert Schuman's declaration of May 19, 1950:

> The contribution which an organized and active Europe can make to civilization is indispensable for the maintenance of peaceful relations. Because Europe was not united, we have had war. The uniting of the European nations requires that the age-old opposition between France and Germany be eliminated. The actions to be taken must first of all concern France and Germany.

Jean Monnet has described the original purpose of the community in the following words:

> This proposal has an essential political objective: to make a breach in the ramparts of national sovereignty which will be narrow enough to secure consent but deep enough to open the way towards the unity that is essential to peace.

Nothing could be clearer. The first aim was to eliminate the most deep-rooted antagonism in European history—the conflict between France and Germany. Beyond this, the objective was to build a foundation for permanent peace by creating a structure which would inhibit European powers from ever going to war against each other. It was only when they saw that the slogans of supranationalism encountered obstacles of nationalist sentiment that the "Europeans of the first hour" retreated in their rhetoric to more pragmatic economic and fiscal justifications. If coal and steel were the first issues on which nation-states were prepared to make a renunciation of sovereignty, Schuman was quite prepared to begin there. This does not mean that he cared very much about coal and steel. But from 1958 onward, it was clear that the only way of securing De Gaulle's acquiescence in the development of the community was to present it as a device for economic progress and to understate its federal and supranational implications. Thus the "Europeans of the first hour" concealed their political flag as a matter of tactical prudence; they never abandoned the dream which it embodied.

Robert Schuman's plan for a European Coal and Steel Community (ECSC) was proposed in early May 1950. Those who embraced it had diverse motivations. Germany saw it as the concrete evidence of reconciliation with France that was not much evident in other fields. Italy seized upon it as the first symbol of its own integration into European life and politics. Sforza and De Gasperi were convinced that the Italian economy would benefit from continental cooperation, but they were captivated mainly by the political dream. The Benelux countries believed that integrative efforts such as the Schuman Plan would guarantee the participation of the smaller countries in European decision-making processes. The United States wished Europe to adopt the American bias in favor of liberalized international trade and overlooked the prospect that its European protégés would soon become its competitors.

The successful establishment of the ECSC was followed by an exhilarating multiplicity of new institutional structures. The 1957 Treaty of Rome created the European Atomic Energy Community (Euratom) and the European Economic Community (EEC), with goals of high employment, a higher standard of living, price stabilization and regulation of the disordered balance of payments. Some observers believed that these modest beginnings represented "the first stirring of European patriotism."

Yet there can be little doubt that these stirrings would have remained very dim and parochial if they had not received the impetus of shared political anxieties. The apprehensions generated by the overthrow of Czech democracy in 1948 and the 1950 Korean War worked strongly in favor of the European integrationists. The Soviet-Western tensions drove the European states toward a more intimate cooperation than they would have achieved in a more serene climate of global relations. Some enthusiastic Europeans such as Albert Camus came out strongly and urgently for an integrated federal Europe. Others, more prudent, like Jean Monnet, advocated a "functionalist" approach. They sought a new international order in Europe based on a network of specialized agencies without attempting a direct assault on national sovereignties.

It was one thing to build a community structure devoted to economic cooperation and the breakdown of interstate protectionism. It was far less simple to define the European role in defense. With the onset of the Korean War the United States began to press for an integrated European force with a centralized command and increased German participation. NATO was less than two years old, and the United States with its endemic distrust of fragmentation and its love for large areas of power did not believe that the European Community needed six separate centers of decision in matters of defense. It was here that Washington, not for the last time, failed in its perception of European sensitivities. For several years the European policy of the United States was based on German-American solidarity, which Dulles and Adenauer pursued without much regard for Soviet denunciations or French reactions. French Gaullists and Communists joined hands in torpedoing the Pleven Plan for a European Defense Community (EDC) in August 1954. Dislike of supranationalism and dislike of Germany converged in this obstruction. The practical difficulty was overcome by German admission to NATO (May 1955), but the defeat of EDC gave salutary warning of the limitations which historic memories still imposed on European integration.

The early 1960s marked the peak of greatest hope for the future of the European Community. Everything seemed to be flowing in its favor. The economies of the six original members were growing into a common system from which separation would soon be inconceivable. The EEC was becoming the world's greatest single market. It was fashionable to cite statistics of population, production, steel supplies and average per capita income to prove that Europe was on the same level of power as the United States and the Soviet Union. The network of departments in Brussels constituted a bureaucracy so labyrinthine and populous that it might have had a century of history behind it. (I heard Willy Brandt speak in 1968 of a "United States of Europe" destined to arise within ten years.) Britain, together with the Scandinavian countries, Austria, Portugal and Switzerland, formed a free trade area (EFTA) innocent of political aims or federalist heresies. But it was Europe of the Communities that called the tune and excited the hopes of those across the world who dreamed of an age in which the nation-state would be transcended by larger loyalties. In British politics the aim of joining Europe was the single most exalting vision in a nation which, in Dean Acheson's words, had lost an empire and not discovered a vocation. The Six would inexorably grow to nine or ten in the early future.

Nor was the European Community a success story in the mercantile sense alone. It was the second pillar of an alliance dedicated to withstanding aggressive designs in Europe. There were many tensions between the United States and European nations, but it was not until the mid-sixties that many began to wonder if the alliance deserved its name.

The Tormented Alliance

What went wrong? The question is dictated by the title of this section, which has many parallels in the literature of the 1960s. In 1965 Henry Kissinger called his book *The Troubled Partnership* and the relevant chapter of his memoirs "The Uneasy Alliance." Theodore Draper's somber and penetrating study is headed *The Western Misalliance*. Many years have passed since a serious scholar or statesman wrote of the alliance without an epithet signifying skepticism, nostalgia or gloom. The same is true of the community adventure; but even those who would deny that there is an existential crisis write and speak about the European Community without the old rhapsodic overtones.

Like many confusions this one is aggravated if not actually created by a lack of precision about words and facts. The popular myth, attested to by the word "alliance," tells us that the United States and Western Europe originally entered into a contractual undertaking to help each other in every predicament, to support each other in every confrontation and to build a comprehensive relationship inspired by solidarity and mutual support. If this were really the gist and content of the alliance, both Americans and Europeans would be justified in accusing each other of flagrant departures from their pledged word.

The trouble is that no such word was ever pledged. The only engagement that the United States and Europe ever undertook toward each other is contained in the North Atlantic Treaty of April 4, 1949. The heart of the treaty is the agreement of the parties "that an armed attack against one or more of them in Europe or North America shall be considered an attack against them all" (Article 5). In Article 6 the territories of the parties are strictly defined. The attack against which common action is pledged is to be against "the territory of any of the parties in Europe or North America, on the Algerian Departments of France, on the occupation forces of any party in Europe, on the islands under the jurisdiction of any party in the North Atlantic area north of the Tropic of Cancer, or on the vessels or aircraft in this area of any of the parties."

None of these contingencies has arisen, which may be taken as evidence that the deterrent purposes of the treaty have been fulfilled. But the NATO text said nothing about an alliance such as that which brought Roosevelt and Churchill into global support of each other's positions during World War II. The geographical limitation in the treaty's text is too tight to be inadvertent. The conclusion is plain: there is no alliance obliging European states to support American policies or actions in Cuba, Vietnam, Cambodia, Iran, Afghanistan, Poland, Nicaragua or El Salvador. Nor does the alliance necessarily require the United States to take account of European advice in the Middle East or to applaud Europe's tendency to cooperate economically with the Soviet Union and to compete with the United States. All these are matters to be resolved empirically in the light of each party's view of its interests or values. They are not to be settled by invocation of a contract, and the world "alliance" is no substitute for diplomacy.

There seems to be an ideological implication in the treaty's preamble to "safeguard the freedom, common heritage and civilization of their peoples, founded on the principles of democracy, individual liberty and the rule of law." But this does not resolve the question whether Salazar's Portugal, the former Greek colonels' regime or the military administration in Turkey interprets "democracy" and "individual liberty" in the same way as other signatories. Kissinger's description of the relationship in 1965 as "a unilateral American guarantee" may have been abrasive, but this does not mean that it was inaccurate. (He used the phrase in the book *The Troubled Partnership*, which helps to explain why the partnership was troubled.)

Much of the trouble arises from the drastic change in the relative power and self-confidence of the two partners since the United States and Europe first established the procedures and institutions of the NATO system. In the beginning there was no atmosphere of reciprocity or equality. Europe needed America for its own defense, while America did not need Europe to defend America. This part of the truth remains valid to this day. In effect, the European members of NATO are allies for their own self-defense; they are not allies in any other sense. The language of mutuality in the North Atlantic Treaty is a gesture of tact, not an expression of reality. The American expectation of European solidarity arises from this consciousness of imbalance between the weight of commitment which the two parties have accepted toward each other. To this, Europeans have two answers, both of them crystallized during De Gaulle's presidency but surviving in growing strength in the ensuing decades. First, if the United States complains that the treaty is too narrow and specific, it would do well to remember that it was American vigilance and caution which lay at the root of that condition. Dean Acheson has recorded that the Canadians wanted the treaty to speak of cultural, economic and social cooperation so as to hint at evolution toward Atlantic community. It was the United States Senate, in a typical expression of its suspicious nature, that insisted on a strictly functional military formulation.

Beyond this formal response to American pleas for total solidarity, the Europeans have another sentiment which is more generally felt than De Gaulle's lonely invocation of it would indicate. It is true that the United States protects Europe, but it does this in response to American, not European interests. Why, then, should Europe have to pay for what it can obtain free? This feeling is nurtured by the tendency of American leaders to seek congressional and public support for the alliance in terms of hardheaded egotism. "It's good for America," proclaim Administration spokesmen in a tone that indicates regret for any incidental advantage that the recipients of the aid may derive. A similar disavowal of idealistic motive dominates some U.S.

Administration pleas to the Congress for aid to less developed countries. It is a rare case of human beings pretending to be less generous than they really are.

The result is that while Europeans attach crucial importance to the American military shield, they do not regard it as an altruistic gesture that invites gratitude or reciprocity beyond the mutual advantage that the United States shares with Europe. And if the United States guarantee, like the quality of mercy, is something that "blesseth him that gives and him that takes," it becomes a closed chapter and not an opening to European attitudes of generosity or warmth.

Thus a qualified observer was able to write in the summer of 1979 that "unlike the fifties and to some extent the sixties, there is today almost an absence of distinctly pro-American political parties in Western Europe and anti-American feeling is more differentiated than in the past." It would be reasonable to point to a similar and reciprocal lack of affection for Europe in the American public, even including Establishment circles which had been nurtured on the idea of the Western alliance.

The literature of recrimination is profuse, but so repetitive that it lends itself to fairly easy summary. First, the American bill of complaints against Europe:

> You want and accept our protection but you do not give us your solidarity. Our capacity to help you depends on our overall strength and deterrent capacity, across the water, but you do not support us or even refrain from criticism when we move to defend our interests outside Europe. The defense of our oil interests in the Gulf area is even more crucial for Europe's economy than for ours, but we get no understanding from you of our efforts to resist Moslem fundamentalism in Iran or Soviet aggression in Afghanistan. When we try to make a show of strength, as against the Soviet Union in Poland, you decline to join us even in a limited sanctions policy, and you even reinforce your economic links with the Soviet Union by participating in the Siberian gas pipeline project. In the central issue of defense we have two complaints: Europe is so obsessed with its own financial ambitions that it does not bear a commensurate part of the financial burden for NATO operations; and although you welcome our nuclear umbrella you sometimes follow a policy of maximum protection with minimum risk by reluctance to station our medium-range missiles in your territories. When we try to assert the credibility of our commitments, as in the airlift to Israel at a time of danger in the 1973 Yom Kippur War, you even deny us the use of your airspace and landing grounds. When you speak of "independence" you mean only independence of the United States,

and you interpret this as a right to isolate us in international agencies by voting with or, at any rate, not against the Soviet Union. While you accept our concept of détente in theory, in practice you are more indulgent of Soviet violations of the dé-tente spirit than supportive of American indignation and protest when the violations occur.

These resentments find expression in different combinations and are addressed to different European destinations as conditions dictate. Once the chief target of American discontent was France, whose leaders seemed to have made an automatic, self-regulating decision to refuse support for anything that the United States proposed or desired. More recently Germany, under Willy Brandt and Helmut Schmidt, was seen in Washington as unduly self-assertive and independent in its approach to European security problems.

The American sense of grievance is not assuaged by close contact with European leaders. On the contrary, Americans who are deferential to European traditions and interests as a matter of instinct and origins become exasperated when they enter the operational field. Dean Rusk became haunted by the disparity of burden:

We have taken over 600,000 casualties in dead and wounded since the end of World War II, and it hasn't been very collective. We put up 90 per cent of the non-Korean forces in Korea, 80 per cent of the non-Vietnamese forces in Vietnam. We've carried some significant burdens virtually alone during certain crises, such as the crisis over Berlin. . . . So if cousins of mine in Georgia say to me: Look, if collective security means 50,000 American dead every decade, and it is not even collective, maybe it's not a very good idea. I have a profound respect for that reaction.

Henry Kissinger before taking office constantly urged his countrymen to come to terms indulgently with European independence.

A united Europe is likely to insist on specifically European views of world affairs—which is another way of saying that it will challenge American hegemony in Atlantic policy. This may well be a price worth paying for European unity; but American policy has suffered from an unwillingness to recognize that there is a price to be paid.

Nothing could be more large-minded than that. What ensued is similar to what happens when a learned writer on child guidance himself becomes a parent. The generous theory dissolves into irascible frustration. Kissinger as Secretary of State fretted anxiously about German policy, describing it alternately as too assertive and too flexible:

*There is also the historic danger that a Germany conducting a totally
separate or "special" policy in the center of the continent could so disquiet
everybody as to bring on all the dangers that it is seeking to avoid . . .
whether it is the Hallstein doctrine which ran the risk of confrontations, or
the Ostpolitik which ran the risk of excessive negotiations.*

Here is an eminent American statesman uttering the same kind of
generalized apprehension that Europeans direct to American policy.
When the United States is not blamed for timidity it is blamed for
recklessness. When Europe is not criticized for abjectness it is censured for being provocative.

It is difficult for anyone outside the alliance to pass judgment on
the validity of the American charge sheet against Europe, although it
is easier for us who are not on either continent than for those directly involved in the intricacies and delicacies of the relationship.
The strongest American case is related to the growth of European
parochialism. As soon as the United States seems to be preoccupied
with an issue outside Europe, it finds European statesmen either
bored (as with El Salvador) or skeptical of success (as with Vietnam).
American indignation is most justified when the supposedly "non-
European" issues really involve European interests no less than
those of America. When Europe asks itself whether it should "support America" in Iran, Afghanistan or Poland, there is a tendency to
forget that all those areas are much closer to Western Europe than to
America and that American vulnerability is perceptibly less than that
of Europe. In strict rationality, Europe should be clamoring for
America to engage its responsibility in these concerns while America
would be showing tendencies of disinterest and detachment. But
even this complaint is much weakened when American leaders themselves seem to allot Europe a limited role and then accuse Europe of
limited vision! How else can we interpret Kissinger's concise generalization: "The United States has global interests and responsibilities.
Our European allies have regional interests"? The question is
whether this is a regretful description of fact or an exhortation to
European modesty. When Europeans take the restrictive definition
seriously they hear American voices demand, "Where are the Allies?" To be accused of parochialism and intrusiveness at one and
the same time is the obverse side of Europe's own habit of submitting its American allies to mutually exclusive criticism.

We now come to formulate the European bill of complaint against
America. The most striking conclusion is the symmetrical nature of the
dialogue. Europe's complaints largely take the form of a counter-
balancing response to American grievances:

You seek our solidarity but not our advice. You listen to our ideas about Europe, but you claim our support for your ventures outside Europe, in which we have no opportunity of expressing our views in advance. What you did in Cuba, Vietnam, Cambodia, El Salvador was done on your own responsibility. Where we thought that your action was essential, as in Cuba, we gave our support. We did not believe that our interests—or yours—really necessitated the involvement of your strength and prestige in the Indochina wars. For centuries you have claimed under the Monroe Doctrine that the Western Hemisphere should be remote from European influence; why, then, seek our endorsement of your view—which we do not share—that Central American crises are the proper arena for asserting Western interests against the Soviet Union? By initiating détente you indicate that commercial relations with the Soviet Union are a useful brake on Soviet militance. Why complain if the effect is that West Germany has become the USSR's biggest trading partner? If our banks and economic agencies develop their own dynamism in trade with the USSR, that is the case with your private interests as well; witness American refusal to include grain sales in the sanctions against the Soviet Union over Poland while urging European countries to abstain from large purchases of gas from Soviet pipelines. Above all, we find American policy hard to follow in the central issue of the West's relations with the Soviet Union. From the anti-Soviet ideology of the fifties you passed, through détente, to President Carter's warning against "inordinate fear of Communism," thus defusing the West's ideological tension. A few months later, after one of your elections, you were accusing the Soviet Union of being the source of all international tensions (1981), including those tensions such as in the Gulf and Central America which manifestly have large non-Soviet components. While you determine many parts of our destiny by arms control negotiations, you insist on negotiating SALT agreements bilaterally.

Running through these attitudes and grievances we can detect a uniting thread; it is the suspicion that the United States, while claiming hegemony, could not be trusted in a last resort to fulfill its pledge to protect Europe's security. In that case, it is natural for Europe to invest in a second line of defense by reducing Soviet motivation to move against European states. This involves a more deferential attitude toward Moscow than the United States can reconcile even with détente. Not all Europeans would endorse De Gaulle's ringing affirmation in a talk with André Malraux in 1969: "The desire of the United

States, and it will satisfy it one day, is to desert Europe. You will see."
But no European leaders believe that American protection of Europe
against Soviet attack is so certain that it can be Europe's only reliance.
There is a lingering resentment at America's most costly psychological
error: the attempt in the 1960s to be the sole possessor of nuclear
weapons in the alliance. In opposing the British and French nuclear
programs—without success—America is regarded as having revealed
its ambition of reserving to itself the definition of what constitutes the
vital interests of the entire alliance. "The strategic debates," writes
Kissinger, "were thus only the tip of the iceberg. The deepest challenge was that after centuries of Europe's preeminence, the center of
gravity of world affairs was moving away from it. For nations to play
a major international role, they must believe that their decisions matter." If this diagnosis is true, it follows that Europe's crisis is not
military or political as much as psychological. It revolves around
Europe's quest for a sense of identity and relevance in a world in which
it no longer controls the ultimate decisions.

The United States, being the stronger and still the less vulnerable
partner, is less sharp in defining its disappointments about Europe.
But their depth should not be lost from sight. They are cogently stated
by Theodore Draper:

> What [the founding fathers of the alliance] did not anticipate was that after
> more than thirty years Europe would still not be able to defend itself but
> would use its increasing unity and recovery to make itself more independent
> of the United States at the expense of American influence and prestige
> throughout the world. European independence from the United States is
> only one side of the coin; the other side is American independence from
> Europe. American isolation can make a comeback via isolation.

With phrases like these flying through the diplomatic and academic
air, nobody can say that it is an exaggeration to believe that "the
alliance continues to fade away even while it endures." And one of the
deepest underlying causes for the decline is rarely stated for fear of
tactlessness and embarrassment. The alliance was founded in an atmosphere of exceptional European deference to American strength.
America had secured the defeat of tyranny, had blocked the expansion
of Soviet power into Western Europe, had created enormous surpluses
of capital and productive capacity, had stabilized a shattered Europe
by sustained economic growth and had patiently fostered European
attempts at integration and unity. If the United States did not inspire
affection, it certainly excited envy and emulation. This sentiment
began to erode in the late 1960s under the impact of an embarrassing
impotence in Vietnam and of a falling dollar. When America was

forced to accept Soviet military parity and to confront the rise of OPEC oil power, the legend of U.S. omnipotence suffered further disillusion. In the late 1970s and early 1980s, Europe winced at evidences of American weakness and vacillation—the cancellation of the B-1 bomber, the wavering over the neutron bomb, the sharp fluctuations of the dollar, the delays over SALT II and, above all, the fiasco in Iran. If American opinion was agitated by these developments, it was unreasonable to imagine that Europe would be unaffected in its willingness to accept America's leadership. The assassinations and scandals of the turbulent 1960s and 1970s were America's own business only in the formal sense. They sent their repercussions far and wide into the international system. Europe lost confidence in the ability of the United States to manage the international order. In general, the United States' image in Europe is determined far more by what America is and does than by what America says.

The idea that the preponderant power of the United States in the European system gave it a capacity of leadership in the alliance was refuted in the test case of the trans-Siberian pipeline. The effort of the United States to apply sanctions against French, British and Italian firms which cooperated with the Soviet project collapsed in late 1982 in the face of tenacious European defiance. It is plain that the United States cannot effectively tell Europeans where their economic interests lie. Nor do European countries regard the United States as more authoritative than themselves in analyzing and defining Soviet policy. Western Europe is de-demonizing the Soviet Union. It regards Moscow not as the center of a powerful and diabolic conspiracy of conquest, but as the capital of a struggling country laden with many burdens and unable to solve its most elementary economic and social problems. In military and strategic issues Europeans are aware of their relative impotence, but as economic performers they face the Soviet Union in a mood of self-confidence, conscious of their superiority in technology and productive capacity. Even in times of recession Europeans can feed themselves; the USSR cannot even do that. Since the Soviet Union is less formidable than it once appeared it is not perceived as a threat to Western Europe.

In its turn, the Soviet Union is losing its traditional fear of Western Europe. Its own military strength excludes the possibility of the Soviet Union regarding itself as vulnerable, and its links with Western Europe have taught it that it does not face a monolithic hostility in the West.

It must be admitted that the Western alliance flourished when there was a sense of deep alarm concerning Soviet power and intentions. Without a new demon the alliance loses the tension and urgency which once held it together.

The United States played a large role in encouraging movements of

integration among the countries of Western Europe, and its approval
of the Treaty of Rome was generous and authentic. Americans are
commanded by experience and instinct to prefer large units of government and to deplore fragmentation; their leaders have also hoped that
a united Western Europe would be stronger than the sum of all its
parts and would thus counterbalance Soviet predominance in Europe.
The prevalent American mood today is disappointment, tactfully concealed by lowering the threshold of expectation. Europe has not manifested its united strength by a strong, self-reliant defense posture, as
the United States would have wished; and Europe's strength as an
economic unit has worked against American economic interests by
virtue of the protectionist character of the EEC as a market in which
non-members do not have access on equal terms with members. In the
only political issue on which the EEC ever took a stand, namely the
Arab-Israeli conflict, Europe was competing with the United States,
not cooperating with it.

The notion that security would be the focal point of harmony between the United States and Western Europe was based on a superficial reading of the psychological background. It is true that Americans
and Europeans are both apprehensive of Soviet intentions, but when
this fear is broken down to its detailed components there emerges a
genuine divergence of perspective. The United States fears only a
nuclear attack by the Soviet Union, and it meets that threat by deterrent nuclear power. Americans do not have to fear a Soviet invasion
aimed at the conquest of their territory and the subjugation of their
people. Europeans fear both a nuclear attack and a Soviet invasion by
conventional forces, and the latter fear—which Europe does not have
in common with America—is more realistic and less fanciful than the
fear which Americans and Europeans have in common. It is thus objectively inevitable that Europeans should have a more intense need to
look carefully at their relationships with Moscow and to strive with
greater zeal to avoid abrasiveness. Since their fear of a conventional
military invasion occupies their minds more than the improbable contingency of a nuclear assault, Europeans are haunted by the question
whether the American umbrella would really protect them. American
policy and diplomacy seem to have been carefully calculated to nourish
the apprehensions of Europeans at their highest pitch. They suspect
quite candidly that there is an American design to confine the next
nuclear war to Europe, leaving the United States unscathed.

On this issue the unintentional war of nerves by America against
Europe has passed through many stages. First, Kissinger in his Brussels speech of September 1, 1979, virtually told the Europeans that all
their worst fears were justified. It is worth recalling the text:

*Our European allies should not keep asking us to multiply strategic assur-
ances that we cannot possibly mean, or if we do mean, we should not want
to execute, because if we execute, we risk the destruction of civilization
. . . We must face the fact that it is absurd to base the strategy of the West
on the credibility of the threat of mutual suicide.*

This statement also contained a recommendation for "theater nuclear
weapons" in Europe, with the implication of limited nuclear war in
Europe and unlimited nuclear safety for the United States. The Soviet
Union has always made it clear that it would not cooperate in a distinction between the use of intermediate nuclear weapons in Europe and
the avoidance of escalation that would destroy civilization. In an interview with *Der Spiegel* on November 21, 1981, Brezhnev said bluntly that
"if a nuclear war breaks out in Europe or in any other place, it would
inevitably and unavoidably assume a world-wide character." But the
fact that Americans who dream of a limited nuclear war are seeing false
visions does not mitigate the effect of their rhetoric on European
nerves.

Europeans do not blame Kissinger for expressing his views; they
blame the United States government for secretly harboring them.
Their awareness of the predicament that Kissinger articulates drives
them, however, not to the development of their own independent
defense system but to a diplomacy based on the appeasement of the
Soviet Union rather than on resistance and deterrence. Subsequent
speeches by Reagan and Haig strengthened Europe's fears about a
possible United States strategy for limited nuclear war on European
soil from which continental America would somehow be insulated. It
was this wave of rhetoric in 1981–82, together with the fierce Cold War
oratory of American leaders against the sin and horror of the Soviet
system, that drove European leaders to Washington in an attempt to
set American policy on a new path. The attempt did not fail. President
Reagan, from his first "zero option" onward, was at last engaged in
discussion of arms control techniques and bargaining, instead of
merely calling for American superiority as a prior condition of such
bargaining. European leaders responded by supporting the United
States on the stationing of intermediate-range missiles in their countries, although public agitation against these plans continues to re-
sound. Anti-American sentiment escalated particularly in Germany in
the first Reagan years, since the United States was suspected of seeing
Germany as the future battleground with the Soviet Union. The
American ambassador in Germany, Arthur Burns, joined the public
exchange: "There may well be a growing sentiment in America," he
said, "to turn back upon itself and let Europe depend for its security
and freedom upon its own resources or upon Soviet good will. . . ."

The American-European tension reached its height in early 1982 and has been partly alleviated by Helmut Kohl's leadership in Bonn, with its greater emphasis than that of Helmut Schmidt on a pro-American strategy. Relief also comes from the fact that the Reagan Administration is taking arms control more seriously than in the early rapture of its first year in office. But it would be misleading to suggest that America and the European Community have gone far enough beyond the principle of a joint strategy of defense to reach viable agreements on how to put such a strategy to work.

Europe is also distanced from America by its more intimate involvement in relations with Eastern Europe. The volume of trade is immensely more important for Western Europe than it is with the United States. Beyond this, Western Europeans are intellectually and emotionally engaged in the prospect of developments in Eastern Europe that might open wider gaps in the Iron Curtain—a term, incidentally, that is rarely heard in the West European vocabulary these days. The hopes of Western Europeans may be exaggerated, but they are not quixotic. There is evidence that Marxism is less popular in Eastern Europe than nationalism, that religion has not lost its hold and that the eruptions of national self-assertion at various times in Hungary, Czechoslovakia, Poland and Rumania in recent years reflect a real and tenacious emotion. Nobody doubts the ability and intention of the Soviet Union to suppress these impulses if they go too far, but Western Europeans are not prepared to see the Eastern parts of their continent as a distant, unknown and inaccessible world. Empires have an experience of decline and fall, and the fact that the Soviet domination of foreign peoples has had such extraordinary success is not held in Western Europe to be a final word.

Nor is Western Europe confined to hopeful observation alone. Whether the tendencies for pluralism and individual liberty continue to grow in Eastern Europe will depend to a large extent on whether Western Europe offers hopeful visions of progress and economic security. If the economy of Western Europe is marked by unemployment and inflation, few people in Eastern Europe will find much to envy or emulate in social-democracy or parliamentary procedures. The populations of Eastern Europe lack self-expression and do not breathe free air, but their basic subsistence is assured with growing success. The superiority of a free economic system has to be proved, not merely asserted. The nostalgic longing for a Europe not scarred by a hermetic, impenetrable frontier works more powerfully on the imagination of Western Europeans than on that of Americans. All in all, it would be prudent to cool the more ardent ambitions that once glowed around the European Community, both in respect of the federal dream and in relation to the vision of a unified Atlantic consciousness.

. . .

Thirty-three years after the alliance became formalized it has not moved far beyond its original, limited purpose as a security guarantee. Today the only thing that Europe wants of the alliance is that the United States should defend it, if necessary by nuclear arms. The only thing that the United States asks from the alliance is that Europe should support American global policies outside the area of the treaty on which the alliance rests. This discord does not exclude the survival of the alliance within its constricted terms, nor does it rule out ad hoc empirical, concrete agreement on matters as they arise. The common traditions of the parties as well as their exposure to common threats are more likely to bring them together on crucial issues than to keep them apart. But it is a far cry from this cold realism to the bright vision of a free, harmonious Atlantic community that illuminated the hopes of Europe and America three decades ago.

The Mood of Europe

Enclosed by two world powers whose shadows fall over every corner of its life, Europe finds itself without anything beyond Europe to emulate or admire. "Neither superpower is an inspiration. The United States is not viewed as a social model, both because of the old continent's cultural snobbery and because of the different experiences and ideologies that separate the continents." This judgment by Stanley Hoffmann reflects the disappointment of American Europophiles who dreamed of a spiritual compact that would span the Atlantic and create a new age of enlightenment. There are no utopian models that have been found to work and that might have been imitated by Europeans. "To Europeans, America is a supermarket, not a religion; one turns to it for recipes and goods, not for its spirit or its values."

If America never became an ideal, the Soviet Union has ceased being one even to its erstwhile zealots. The French, Spanish and Italian Communist Parties have all shown a heretical dissociation from the first "socialist homeland," while non-Communist Europe recalls that Russia was never included in its notion of the European idea. Separated from the main currents of European thought by the barriers set up by the Eastern Church, Russia stood outside the culture of Christian Europe long before the 1917 revolution. Its slogan was authority, not freedom, and the idealization of dissent and diversity in European liberalism found no echo or response in any Russian political system. The attitude of Western to Eastern Europe has been condescending when it has not been overtly hostile. The idea of looking up to Russia is foreign and offensive to "the real Europe," and Eurocommunism is the first stage in a return to the tradition of Western superiority. Some Western European intellectuals flirted with the idea of a Chinese utopia, but the Cultural Revolution dampened their incipient ardor, which never developed into a movement. In these conditions, the time might have been ripe for Europe to seek inspiration within itself.

This prospect has not come to fulfillment. Neither respect for the state nor any cultural élan seems able to give Europe a sense of power and innovation. The appeal of the nation-state has been weakened by its failure to seem relevant to the transnational compulsions of the modern age. On the other hand, the state has also been weakened by a growth of regionalism, in Spain (Basques), France (Corsicans and Bretons) and even Britain (Scottish and Welsh separatist movements). There is still no European culture in the sense of one that extends beyond national cultures; nor have national cultures been noticeably affected by political and economic cooperation between European countries. Literature in Europe is still distinctively English, German and French; writers in these languages are still preoccupied with their own national issues, not by European or universal concerns. It would be difficult for a historian of culture to discern anything that could be called a specific European idea. When the searchlight moves away from problems of economic relationships and political coordination, it does not illuminate any transnational area of creativity. English writers do not send their gaze beyond the Channel, and French and German writers seldom look across the Rhine to the other side.

It might have been otherwise if the community structure had exerted a more compelling hold. But after its glittering successes in the first decade following the Treaty of Rome, the European Community became blocked in its evolution, and its supranational pretensions were consciously repressed. When the first president of the EEC Commission, Walter Hallstein, began receiving permanent ambassadors to the EEC in elaborate credential ceremonies, making him look like a head of state, the cautionary word went forth from De Gaulle, and the commission subsided into bureaucratic grayness, with the Council of Foreign Ministers becoming the decisive organ. This meant that the community directorate was little more than a permanent diplomatic conference, with a brief six-month rotating presidency as a further deterrent to charismatic fantasies. Worldwide tariff reductions diminished the particularity of the Common Market; whatever was happening in the EEC was also happening elsewhere, so that its sense of specialness was dimmed. Even on economic issues the Ten governments debate in a competitive spirit; each of them defends a particular interest against damage that might threaten from his colleagues. Since the golden age of the first treaty negotiation and the establishment of the community institutions, there have been few largely conceived initiatives on matters affecting Europe as a whole.

If this is the picture in the economic domain where nationalist sensitivities seemed less acute, it is not surprising to find even stronger inhibitions against the development of common foreign policies. There has been some symbolic progress. The diplomatic missions of the Ten members concert their action and representations on matters of community concern, and missions of the EEC are spreading lavishly across the diplomatic corps of many countries. There is a tendency for the Ten to vote together in UN agencies, provided no particular national interest of any of them arises, but there is an unwillingness of governments to commit themselves more deeply to common decisions about foreign policy, as opposed to consultations which have no binding effect. The absence of a central secretariat to make "neutral" decisions and the limited authority of the presidency of the European Community also prevent the diplomatic personality of the EEC from becoming sharply defined. The EEC governments aspire to present a collective policy in international organizations, but for the time being there is a confusing intersection of community and national policies, and the salient impression is one of fragmentation. The community has formulated general principles for a solution of the Arab-Israeli conflict, but this plan was speedily jettisoned as soon as an American initiative was taken by President Reagan in September 1983. There is no sign of a federalization of European foreign policy such as would vindicate John F. Kennedy's hopeful comparison with the American Founding Fathers.

As the 1970s progressed, one objective circumstance after another seemed to conspire against the florescence of the European idea. The resistance of France to community institutions that could conceivably override national sovereignty became only one of the inhibiting influences. The community's parliamentary institutions were formed with such parsimonious powers that membership in them hovered narrowly on the margin of intellectual dignity. The EEC had always taken pride in its economic supremacy, but in the mid-seventies with the growth of Japanese economic vitality the balance of world economic power began to tilt away from the countries of northwest Europe. This followed a dramatic shift over the last decade in the consumer-producer relationship in the field of energy. The oil crisis reinforced the failure of integration for it evoked no EEC consensus. Britain and France wished to deal with Arab producers bilaterally, and the Netherlands and Britain were reluctant to share sovereignty over their own resources. The upshot was that energy policy continued to be in the hands of national governments. When the United States sought to form a consumer bloc in order to protect the West, to conserve energy and develop new resources, Michel Jobert of France rejected "any notion of a new Atlantic structure that would tie French and European policy to the United States and open the way to renewed American dominance in Europe."

Another diplomatic implication of the energy crisis was the increased importance of economic relations between Europe and the Middle East oil countries. Overall EEC exports to the Middle East jumped 85 percent in 1974, and the trend has continued ever since. Relations of the EEC with the Third World seemed to offer a new arena for common action; but the effects are more important for the Third World than for Europe, whose major trading problems are still those that involve the community, the United States and Japan. There is still an atmosphere of marginality in the treatment of the Third World by most European governments.

Even though the political aims of the European Community have become less ambitious, the membership continues to expand. The EEC looks good from the outside. But the increase of members is counterbalanced by a dilution of character. With each new entry the community loses something of its integrative quality or of its common experience or of its economic balance. The original Six had a cohesion which is weaker with the Ten and will become further diluted with the Twelve. Britain's entry has reduced the prospect, such as it was, that the community institutions would come to transcend the sovereignty of member states. The community now has another senior member which is suspicious of supranationalism and deeply inhibited about the central vision which inspired the community's birth. Member states from southern Europe—Greece and eventually Portugal and Spain— will add numerical and demographic strength, but they give the impression of being glued on to an existing structure rather than merging with it as an organic part. All three have emerged recently from authoritarian rule, and their democratic character is less stable than that of the older EEC members. Their sense of economic inequality in relation to northern Europe causes them to draw closer to the Third World than to Western Europe. All in all, it is not clear that enlarging the community is the same as strengthening it.

The European Future

What does it all amount to? Raymond Aron pronounces the verdict with his customary lucidity: "The idea of the nation is still stronger than the idea of Europe."

Western Europe is a collection of nation-states in which individual countries have found it useful to set up a number of common institutions. The oil crisis, recession and the expansion of membership have all widened gaps within the community. Europeans of the second generation are more pragmatic than visionary. It is difficult not to endorse Stanley Hoffmann's memorable diagnosis: "Europe is a great idea that has been tamed, leashed and co-opted. The revolutionary idea of a united Europe has ended up routinized."

The routines themselves are not unimportant; they are still the only effective means yet devised for nation-states to begin the long climb toward a broader integration. There is a solid measure of interdependence among European states and a mutual agreement to preserve it. But the Europe of the second generation lacks the inspiring view of a new identity. On the contrary, there is a distinct loss of specific personality. The architecture of modern Europe is becoming homogenized on the American model, losing the intimacy of the old street and village patterns. The traditional emphasis on history and letters is yielding its priority, even in France, to the mathematical and technical disciplines in which national particularity is lost from view. The superpowers are not a source of inspiration. Yet there is still nothing that can be called a European culture, in the sense of something that transcends the separate cultures of national states. Europe gets no inspiration from outside and very little from itself.

The current sadness contrasts sharply with the buoyant enthusiasms of earlier days. Many Europeans, as well as others who share and admire Europe's legacy, may have exaggerated Europe's prospects unreasonably in the early sixties. There has been a failure both of strength and of unity. Europe has not become a power to be reckoned with beyond the economic sphere, and its unifying energies have not lived up to the rhetoric with which the European idea was celebrated in the period of the community's birth.

But if there were illusions about the capacity of European nations to merge into a new supranational structure, they were not European illusions alone. Americans were at least as optimistic as the Europeans of the first generation. What could be more far-reaching than the expectation formulated by President Kennedy in his speech at Philadelphia on July 4, 1962, when he spoke of "partnership between the new Union now being formed in Europe and the old American Union founded in Philadelphia two centuries ago"? The rhetoric of July 4 rarely finds Americans in their most lucid frame of mind, and the analogy was not well taken. The Americans who conferred in Philadelphia in the eighteenth century did not represent states of long-established sovereignty with individual cultures and a tradition of rivalry and war. The road of American states to union was far less intricate than that which Europe faces in our times. Twenty years after Kennedy's brave prediction, its tones have been muted by hard experience. No American leader today would speak of European unity in such sanguine terms. A sympathetic American scholar is forced to write:

*It is not only that Europe may have lost its sense of its past, or that it is
genuinely bewildered about its future, but that it senses its marginality, and
is desperately and rightly concerned that it is a society more acted upon than
acting . . . Indeed, a serious question must be asked: whether Europe has
not become almost peripheral to many in the world today, notwithstanding
its economic successes.*

At the heart of the predicament lies the fact that building a community is not the only task that Europeans have had to perform since the
end of World War II. The vision of integration was always confined for
the most part to the governing elites with little resonance in public
sentiment. The domestic constituencies of European states had other,
more immediate concerns. And the three major actors in the European
drama—France, Germany and Britain—have been undergoing such
drastic mutations of status and vocation that it is a wonder to find them
devoting themselves to the European idea as much as they have.

The most difficult adjustment was demanded of Britain. No other
nation has ever renounced so much in so short a time. Britain's centrality in the international system had been taken for granted when it
should have been arousing wonder. Unless special qualities were assumed it was hard to explain why a small people in a crowded island
exerted so powerful an influence over distant lands and populations
while maintaining a central place among European nations. Britain
came out of the war with great residual responsibilities which proved
to be beyond its reduced powers. But the consciousness of diminished status developed with understandable reluctance. Ernest Bevin,
the first postwar Foreign Minister, still spoke and struck attitudes
in the grand manner. When Winston Churchill returned to power in
the fifties his familiar voice and presence tended to conceal the fact
that his country was no longer playing a determining role. Anthony
Eden's habit of global diplomacy led him into disastrous illusion when
he behaved in the mid-fifties as though he were still the leading statesman of the mid-thirties. His Suez adventure in 1956 showed how little
effort he and his generation had given to the task of self-measurement.
Harold Macmillan, more realistically, sought a British vocation in close
alliance with the United States, capitalizing on his friendship with
Eisenhower and on Kennedy's deferential approach to his wisdom and
experience. But he saw the writing on the wall clearly enough to grasp
that British policy would have to operate within a compact European
framework, and before his resignation he had submitted his country's
request for admission to the European Community, only to see it
brutally snubbed by De Gaulle.

Neither pride nor experience made it easy for this gifted nation to
reconcile itself to the idea of an exclusively European role. It resented

what seemed to be a return to parochialism. It vainly sought illusory arenas, such as the Commonwealth or the "English-speaking world." These fantasies merely delayed Britain's adjustment to a modest status as one of several Western European powers. The realities of the times allowed no place for British leadership of any overseas grouping. The idea of partnership with the United States was an illusory refusal to recognize the realities of power. America alone had emerged strengthened from the war in which all the powers of Europe, including the Soviet Union, had been exhausted or mutilated. In the early 1950s America towered over the world, with a productive capacity nearly ten times that of Britain and France combined. In the 1960s American leaders, awakening to their new responsibilities, became less inclined to accept the myth of Britain's superior diplomatic skills. In 1964, when Prime Minister Harold Wilson was convincing himself that he might find a formula for American-Soviet agreement on an armistice in Vietnam, President Johnson was quietly reflecting that if the USSR had anything to say to America, it would find a way of doing so directly.

When logic demanded that Britain should seek a European identity, sentiment still pulled it into other orientations. The Labour movement was—and remains—genuinely reluctant to be associated with the EEC. The radicals saw the Common Market as a bulwark of capitalism, while the conservative-minded trade unionists resented the idea of reducing British sovereignty in favor of the Brussels bureaucracy. When Harold Wilson crossed the Strait of Dover he was very much like Samson parting with his hair. His loyalties, habits and expression were all contained within a strictly British context; he had never been a globalist, still less an adherent of the European idea. But the sheer logic of his country's status compelled him to promote the idea of membership in the European structure and to give his party's indispensable support to Conservative Prime Minister Edward Heath's battle for Britain's entry into Europe in the early seventies. Early in 1973 Heath boldly led Britain into the EEC without submitting the terms of entry to the electorate either in the form of a general election or of a referendum. Normally, a parliamentary majority is all that is required for a British act of policy, but public opposition was so strong in this case that the matter was not finally settled until June 1975, when the Wilson government won approval in a national referendum.

Leadership had triumphed over vague popular sentiment, but the fact that eight and a half million voters went to the polls to express themselves against a policy sponsored by both party leaderships indicates the strength of British doubts about the European connection. The first years of British membership in the EEC did nothing to relieve the sense of maladjustment. The Labour Party has developed an official position in favor of secession from the community, and although the repudiation of the Treaty of Rome may not be operatively feasible, Britain's colleagues in the community are strengthened in their conviction that De Gaulle may have been right after all when he saw British policy as incompatible with that of continental Europe. The Conservative government of Margaret Thatcher bargained awkwardly about Britain's inflated budgetary obligations, and none of the idealistic implications of European membership has found its way into the British political dialogue. Even when the imperial role has been discarded with as good grace as has ever accompanied the eclipse of an empire, there is still a nostalgic yearning for a context wider than continental Europe can provide. Since this dream proved to be a mirage, British politics have become provincial and inward-looking, with problems of wage levels and economic recovery occupying the whole canvas on which larger designs were once drawn. The pathos of British life now consists of a sense of contrast between the ancient glory and the unfulfilled quest for a modern role. The traditional symbols, such as the monarchy, the parliamentary pomp and the residual legacy of a hierarchical age, seem too majestic to fit the prosaic dimensions of a modern medium-sized European democracy. British history is illuminated by a talent for resilience, and this may assert itself once again, but nobody pretends that the European idea is playing much part in the national reassessment.

Germany has passed through a totally different mutation. The first postwar decade was a story of triumphant recuperation, and the stability of the new parliamentary institutions astonished the Germans as much as it impressed the outside world. The community idea occupies a larger place in the German consciousness than in that of Britain and France, but it leaves the question of Germany's place in the Western alliance fundamentally unsolved. During Adenauer's reign, the Federal Republic was the most solid European pillar in the Atlantic edifice, but with the advent of Willy Brandt and his *Ostpolitik* the eastward look began to draw Germany away from its community colleagues. Détente became something like an obsession. It enabled Germany to repair its relations with the USSR, to reopen a path to contact with East Germany and to assert a growing tendency of independence of American hegemony. Détente during the recent Helmut Schmidt era came to mean that Germany requires the United States to avoid any step that could irritate the USSR. With the advent of a Christian Democratic leadership under Helmut Kohl there is a sense of relief in Brussels and less talk of German "Gaullism."

All Western European countries in their relations with the United States theoretically seek a point of harmony between solidarity and independence, but independence comes first. Indeed its need for independence is the measure of how much solidarity Europe is prepared to give, or if it is prepared to give any at all. Germany depends on American security protection more than does any European state, but it is paradoxically in Germany that the American connection is most under challenge by peace movements seeking liberation from the responsibilities of the alliance. From being the most "communitarian" of the major EEC countries, Germany is becoming the most resolute in its dissent and self-assertion.

This leads us to an unwelcome but inexorable diagnosis of the European Community's history: the instinct for solidarity was strong when danger threatened. With the Soviet Union moving against Czechoslovakia and Hungary and fomenting Communist movements in Italy and France, European states reached out to America and to each other. There was at least a theoretical solidarity against Soviet repression of Polish freedom. But whenever the European system became stabilized, with the Soviet threat in Europe apparently contained, and whenever economic disaster ceased to be a vivid prospect, the nation-states of Europe returned to a sharpened consciousness of nationality. In a sense, therefore, the European Community, like the Atlantic alliance, is the victim of its successes, not of its failures. Its solidarities are sharpened when there is danger and blunted when danger seems to recede.

This analysis finds its strongest vindication in the record of French policies in Europe. The ideology of integration seems at first sight to run counter to all the impulses of French nationalism and culture, yet Jean Monnet and Robert Schuman were Europeans by ideology, not only by necessity. When Soviet power represented a threat to the West in the Cuban missile crisis, De Gaulle suspended his habit of dissent and gave America powerful support. By the mid-sixties France had asserted its pride by developing its own nuclear option in defiance of Washington. By now there were no signs of further Soviet expansionism outside the USSR's sphere of influence as defined at Yalta. Europe was free of servitude to the American economy and was becoming a self-confident competitor. France accordingly diminished its commitment to NATO, effectively impeded federal tendencies in the community and, in Kissinger's bitter words, "elevated refusal to consult into a principle defining European identity." Yet behind the self-assertion, France in the post-Gaullist era is coming to terms with its own limitations. Neither Georges Pompidou nor Valéry Giscard d'Estaing indulged in the Great Power rhetoric with which De Gaulle had intoxicated his countrymen. They renounced the grandiose ambition to become a "balancer" between East and West and to undermine the hegemony of Washington and Moscow. A country whose empire has disintegrated and which has suffered defeats in Suez and Algeria seems ready to seek a more limited role consistent with its reduced condition.

But French policy under François Mitterrand will continue to fascinate by its paradoxes. France will be rigorously European when facing America—and resolutely French when facing Europe. In the confrontation between East and West, Mitterand supports the West. Between North and South, he gives his sympathy to the South. And Europeans can rely on France to articulate their resentment of American hegemony. On assuming office as Foreign Minister in François Mitterand's administration, Claude Cheysson wrote several articles in the American and European press declaiming that "the Washington Treaty [NATO] is not the Warsaw Pact . . . The alliance is an association of sovereign nations. We are an alliance not a bloc . . ." He went on to decry the idea that the strongest member of the alliance should be regarded as "the leader." This was, in his words, a "dictatorial" concept. In the 1950s no one in Europe had objected to calling the United States the "leader of the Western alliance."

Europeans would have a less tortured relationship with the United States on matters of security if they aimed at two goals: greater independence and more reliance on effective conventional deterrence. The neglect of European conventional preparedness is one of the psychological mysteries of the postwar age. Soviet intervention by land against a West European state may not be a high probability, but it is less improbable than a Soviet nuclear assault. The atmosphere created by Soviet preponderance in conventional arms is a political and emotional reality with far-reaching effects even without an actual invasion. Europe's economic and technical capacity to maintain a strong defense posture is beyond doubt. We are left with the conclusion that there is a lack of will that arises in part from the undue nuclearization of defense thinking in recent decades. Some European voices can now be heard expressing a reasoned perception of this issue. Thus, Michael Howard:

> We should be doing all we can to reduce our dependence on American nuclear weapons by enhancing, so far as is militarily, socially and economically possible, our capacity to defend ourselves . . . By "defend ourselves" I mean defend ourselves in the conventional sense with conventional weapons . . .

An assertive European attempt to correct the balance of strength on the continent would have a galvanizing effect similar to that which flowed from Western Europe's extraordinary economic performance in the late 1940s and early 1950s. Western Europe has a greater population than the Soviet Union, a larger steel production and a far more sophisticated industrial and technological apparatus, yet it stands in awe of Soviet power because this superiority is not expressed in the military sphere.

In the absence of a common enterprise the tone of European policy becomes querulous and negative. It is instructive that in the four-year period 1979–1983, incumbent governments fell all over the Western world, irrespective of whether they were of the left or of the right. Carter, Giscard d'Estaing, Schmidt and Callaghan, and governments in Sweden, Denmark, Norway, Australia, Canada and Spain were all defeated in a restless search for change, as though to hold responsibility was itself a political misdemeanor. In Europe there is a growth of spontaneous antiestablishmentarianism which, coupled with nihilistic tendencies amid a young generation that does not want to hear about past glories, is likely to weaken the political culture of the most mature and reasoned sector of the human race. Europe is in dire need of an elevating adventure.

But if the dream of an integrated Europe seems disappointingly remote, the disappointment is only relative; it is a consequence of unreasonably impatient expectations. The fact remains that the countries of Western Europe have moved forward more rapidly in the direction of cooperation than in any previous period of their history. Both historical experience and modern reality are at work in support of the integrative impulse. European peoples have achieved an unprecedented mobility. They travel in the millions every year, forming associations and attachments beyond their separate boundaries. There is today little prospect of the European idea being carried forward by a group of visionary leaders such as Winston Churchill, Robert Schuman, Paul Henri Spaak, Alcide de Gasperi, Jean Monnet, Konrad Adenauer and Walter Hallstein. But a united Europe is beginning to exist at grass-roots level. Europe may be lagging behind its own vision, but it is still ahead of everyone else in the quest for an identity transcending the sovereignty of separate states.

The complaint against Europe is that it has fallen short of its highest visions of harmony. But perhaps the vision was too high and its demands too exigent. While the political leaders and diplomats in EEC countries put their emphasis on the preservation of sovereignty, there is a dynamism in functional relationships that works toward a European consciousness. There are extensive and intimate contacts between the domestic ministries of EEC member states beyond anything that is known outside Europe. Diplomats are replaced by economic ministers and officials who reach agreements of which Foreign Offices and diplomats learn after the event. Some observers believe that "the growth of an integrated international economy, the weakening of the state's security role and the emergence of politically significant transnational links have undermined the boundaries of national sovereignty . . . All major ministries in London, Paris and Bonn are involved in the formulation, management and implementation of foreign policy . . . And in all this activity, it is the government as a whole which is engaged: not simply each country's foreign ministry and two or three other departments with long established international responsibilities, but almost all the major agencies of the state."

It is quite conceivable that while Margaret Thatcher, François Mitterrand, Helmut Kohl and other European leaders strive to preserve national separatism, their ministers of agriculture, industry, finance and tourism are unknowingly laying the foundations of a federal Europe. These ministers meet their opposite numbers without the mediation of Foreign Offices; and proximity is the greatest friend of the European idea. The distance between London and Paris and between Paris and Bonn is not very different from that between Washington and New York, or Washington and Boston. When we add the effect of joint military forces and movements of working populations, it is hard to see how the national frontiers in Europe can long retain their significance despite the separatist emotions of political leaders and their constituencies.

Not even the most severe critic of the European experiment would deny its most concrete and enduring achievement. This lies in the realm of prevention. It has become totally inconceivable that there could ever again be a war between Holland and Spain, between Germany and France or between England and Germany. Although the European structure has not yet arisen in anything like its full perfection, enough has been fulfilled to liberate the most war-ridden continent in human history from its traditional scourge.

Chapter 5

THE THIRD WORLD
Asia, Africa, Latin America

L IKE "DÉTENTE" AND other terms of calculated obscurity, the term
"Third World" has a French origin. It is the English translation of
the expression *"tiers monde,"* which appeared in the political literature
of Europe during the early 1950s. The word *"tiers"* for "third" is an
archaism; to a Frenchman with a sense of history it would evoke the
"tiers état," the Third Estate of commoners, who opposed both the king
and the church. The Third World is composed of those who wish to
avoid domination either by the Soviet bloc or by the Western alliance.
It conveys the notion of a dual rejection. Nehru himself once said that
the Third World is an "anti-idea." The interesting fact about this
linguistic history is that nobody claims to belong to the First World,
and there are no candidates for the title of the Second World. Each of
the three worlds is the imaginative creation of the other two.

When the Cold War was at its height in the 1950s, both the United
States and the Soviet Union were eager to draw other states into their
lists of supporters. If anything, the United States was more zealous
than the Soviet Union in its recruiting campaign. Moscow was realistic
enough to understand that its rigorous and complex ideology was
unlikely to appeal to nations in which British and French political
cultures had struck deep roots among the dominant elites. The Soviets
concentrated their efforts among leaders who were responsive to leftist
rhetoric. The United States believed that its relatively noncolonial
record and its reputation for generosity in development assistance
would give it a wider field of opportunity. American diplomacy during

the tenure of John Foster Dulles as Secretary of State was obsessed by the idea that all states should define their position, "stand up and be counted," and, above all, avoid the "immorality of neutralism."

Both Washington and Moscow assumed, without good reason, that their own bipolar vision of the international system would be acceptable to countries that lay outside the central power context. They held the strange belief that the less developed states were seriously preoccupied with the problem of their relationship to the global alignment. When superpowers posed the question, "Which of us do you prefer?" they made no provision for the likelihood that the answer would often be, "Neither of you."

Both Washington and Moscow were striking wrong chords. The United States found it painfully hard to understand that in the eyes of the new, struggling nations it was seen primarily as the ally of the former colonial powers and the heir of their cultures and institutions. The Soviet Union was up against the fact that the newly liberated nations were haunted by an endemic distrust of all major powers irrespective of their histories or social philosophies. The effect of American and Russian pressure was to induce the nonaligned nations to seek ways of evading the unwanted embrace of each superpower. It would obviously be preferable for them to carry out the evasion with a minimum of abrasive effect and in a spirit of solidarity among all who were caught in the dilemma. In this mood the representatives of twenty-nine Asian and African nations assembled in Bandung, Indonesia, in April 1955. The occasion was called the Afro-Asian Conference and the convenors were the prime ministers of five countries, Jawaharlal Nehru of India, U Nu of Burma, Ali of Pakistan, Sastroamidjojo of Indonesia and Kotelawala of Ceylon. All of them were Asians; the tide of African independence had not yet reached its torrential flow.

The Bandung Conference is the constitutive moment in the history of what was to become known as the Third World. Not that the Bandung Manifesto said anything innovative or memorable; its ten principles were a fairly routine recitation of UN Charter rhetoric about peaceful coexistence, with the addition of the anticolonialist phraseology which gave the conference its unifying resonance. What was significant in the occasion was the fact that it had come to pass. The twenty-nine participants saw themselves and one another as partners in a common cause. Their solidarity was not inspired by a common view of the world or by any uniformity in their institutions or social regimes. They were all against "imperialism" and "neocolonialism," but they were not unanimous in defining exactly what these terms meant. The representatives of Iraq, Pakistan, Iran, the Philippines, Ceylon and Turkey attacked world Communism and Soviet colonialism in varying tones of intensity and to the deep embarrassment of Chou En-lai. When it became apparent that a resolution attacking Communism could not be filed, these pro-Western delegates, joined by Lebanon, Libya, Sudan and Liberia, drafted a compromise proposal condemning "all types of colonialism, including international doctrines resorting to the methods of force, infiltration and subversion . . ." Everybody knew what these terms meant.

These were not the only issues that disturbed the harmony to which the organizers of the conference had aspired. Cambodia and Thailand spoke of the threat of Chinese encroachment on their liberties, while the Arab delegates led by Gamal Abdel Nasser sat in sulky silence in implicit protest at the exclusion of the Palestine question; the Pakistanis had secured the exclusion of Israel from the conference in return for acquiescence in Burma's request that the Israel-Arab conflict not be raised. In one of the conferences that preceded Bandung, Pakistan had attacked India over the Kashmir problem and India had responded vehemently.

In the light of these discords one might well ask what it was that bound the members of the Afro-Asian movement together. They had different views on the global struggle, they were torn apart by conflicts among themselves, and their levels of economic development, though none were very advanced, showed great variety. Their economic and social problems could certainly not be solved by or among themselves through any serious movement of commerce or interchange. What they carried with them was the memory of long humiliation by foreign rule, a distrustful attitude toward all large concentrations of power, a determination to campaign implacably against any relics of colonialism, and an almost racial feeling that Asians and Africans were, in a sense, a separate part of humanity, long victimized and now claiming their birthright.

From Bandung with its predominantly Asian emphasis the movement broadened out. In the 1960s scores of African states entered the family of the nonaligned. The impressively charismatic gallery of Asian and African leaders expanded. Nehru, Sukarno, Nasser, Nkrumah, Kenyatta, Senghor, Sihanouk, Sékou Touré, Kaunda, Bandaranaike, Chou En-lai, Houphouët-Boigny form a glittering list. When they left the scene they would not always leave memorable successors behind. Many of the Bandung delegates were Founding Fathers of states or of regimes, and they did not conceal their fame under heavy wraps of modesty. In the speed and intensity of their emergence they transformed the international landscape and shattered its traditional structure with its heavy European and Western emphasis.

The central organizational expression became the Afro-Asian People's Solidarity Organization (AAPSO), which was founded in Cairo in

1958. Afro-Asianism became the theme and rallying point of endless gatherings: Afro-Asian Writers, Afro-Asian Youth, Afro-Asian Lawyers, Afro-Asian Railway Experts, Afro-Asian Housing Conferences, Afro-Asian Journalists, Afro-Asian Doctors, Afro-Asian Economists. There was a significant geographical expansion as well; in 1966 a Conference of Afro-Asian–Latin-American Peoples formed an organization. In preliminary skirmishes the Latin Americans were often described as "outsiders," but as radicalism developed in the southern part of the Western Hemisphere and United States hegemony became weakened, the Latin American subcontinent became increasingly accepted by the nonaligned movement. Latin America, unlike Asia and Africa, had not been injured by a lack of sovereignty; indeed when the United Nations was founded, 40 percent of its membership was Latin American. It was when the nonaligned movement took its stand on economic matters that the disabilities of Latin American societies brought them together with Asia and Africa in a solidarity of grievance and affliction. When the first United Nations Conference on Trade and Development (UNCTAD) met in Geneva in 1964, a solid bloc of 77 developing states faced the advanced countries in a mood of confrontation which has characterized the economic dialogue ever since.

The 77 have become 120. Those who call themselves nonaligned are about 95. The continental definitions have yielded in popular parlance to the Third World. The confrontation is generally, if not too accurately, described as North-South. The influence of these groupings on the international system works in three main spheres: in their interaction with the major power blocs, in their command of international voting systems and in their campaign for a New International Economic Order.

The salient trend in the Third World after the Bandung opening was a movement of sympathy away from the United States and a growing deference and indulgence toward the Soviet Union. The Cairo Conference of Nonaligned Nations in 1964 was far more hostile to the West than Bandung had been in 1955. The final Cairo declaration contained no criticism of the Soviet Union, while the United States was upbraided again and again. One reason for this discrimination lay with Washington itself; the tenor of American comment on the nonaligned movement was always more severe than the corresponding rhetoric from Moscow. The Soviet tactic was to pass in silence over formulations that could be regarded as aimed against Communism and to embrace the anti-Western statements with fervor. China was becoming increasingly prominent in the Third World, and its anti-American declarations in the 1960s were still not offset by the anti-Soviet material which was to become routine in the 1970s. At the Havana Conference in 1966 the United States bore the full brunt of Fidel Castro's denunciation. The imbalance was accentuated by the remarkable fact that the Soviet Union was actually present at Havana, where its representative made an eloquent address. The fact that the United States was heavily involved in the Vietnam conflict compounded its alienation from the nonaligned states. The conference adopted a resolution of "support of the Vietnamese people in its struggle against the aggression of Yankee imperialism."

The Third World has never found its way back to a central position in relation to the two superpowers, but its anti-Americanism became diluted after the United States withdrew from Vietnam. The more courteous Chinese attitude toward Washington also mitigated the virulence with which the Third World spoke and thought of America. Both Vietnam and China compromised their image in the Third World by the human tragedies that followed the American withdrawal. Those who had recoiled from the American alliance with the repressive regime of the Shah were embarrassed by the even worse excesses of the Khomeini regime. In Latin America, the withdrawal of American sovereignty from the Panama Canal did not fit the image of American "colonialism." And when the Soviet armies moved into Afghanistan in late 1979 most of the Third World joined the United States in resolutions of condemnation. But over these past four decades, the West has not secured sympathies in the Third World commensurate with its objective merit. After all, the Western powers have relinquished vast territories in Asia and Africa, while the Soviet Union has actually tightened its hold over subject nations in Europe. The United States, and not the Soviet Union, has sustained the agencies and institutions on which the Third World has relied for development. Yet the Soviet Union has found it far easier than the United States to form voting blocs in common with most of the Third World nations. When the Third World countries complain of their economic disabilities they seldom refer to the parsimonious record of the Soviet Union as a member of the development agencies on which they largely depend for their welfare.

While the Third World is in theory a gesture of dissociation from both superpowers, the dissent from the West is the most emphatic. There may be a positive implication from the Western viewpoint; it is because more was expected from America and Europe that the disillusion is correspondingly deeper and the criticism more severe.

From these frustrations the Third World countries seek and find consolation in their dominance of the United Nations. The UN plays a far greater role in their foreign policy systems than in those of the more established countries. Their membership in the United Nations symbolizes their emancipation; it excites and inspires their sense of sovereignty. Their voting strength gives them an illusory but comforting sense of power. Africa is not really thirty times stronger or richer or more responsible than North America; but North America in the United Nations General Assembly has two votes while Africa has sixty. Dag Hammarskjöld used to declare that the Great Powers and Europe do not "need" the United Nations, whereas for the Third World countries the UN represents a real need in terms of their pride and self-regard. One of the uses of the United Nations for the Third World is to offer a platform for talented and charismatic Asian and African leaders to deploy their leadership. They escape from provincialism and take their places on a universal stage. Many of them have enriched the international landscape in a period of grayness and mediocrity in political leadership. It may be, however, that the Third World has overplayed its hand. It has swamped the UN voting system so overwhelmingly that America and Europe have gone elsewhere for their security and political self-expression, leaving the Third World in possession of a desolated field.

It seems more probable at the present juncture that the Third World will distance itself to some degree from the Soviet Union than that it will slide further away from the West. The Soviet occupation of Afghanistan and to a lesser degree its suppression of the Polish workers have set up strong currents of alienation. An Arab scholar has written:

> An earlier generation of Third World nationalists came to learn the traumatic lesson that the liberal values of the West were not for export and that those who valued nationalism for themselves denied it to others. Now the same lesson has to be learned about Marxism. Marxist internationalism is a thin construct; behind the ideological masks can be seen the age-old desire of powerful men and societies to hoard and dominate.

If the antagonism of Third World countries toward older societies is difficult to understand, it is largely because most of it stems from roots in the past rather than from any justified grievance in the present. When the new nations denounce colonialism they are pursuing their enemy beyond the point of his own retreat. There isn't much colonialism left. The Third World simply refuses to take yes for an answer. It is true that British, French and Belgian influences are still visible in the countries where these cultures were once dominant, but it would be hard to make a case for the assumption that this is an unbearably heavy burden on the shoulders of the new states. If anything, it is the successor states themselves who cling to familiar symbols. If Ghana has red post boxes, blue lamps in police stations and bewigged judges in scarlet robes, and if Abidjan is full of open-air cafés in which Dubonnet apéritifs are sipped by French-speaking residents who receive Paris newspapers daily, it is not because anyone forces these nations to remind themselves every day of their previous servitude. The truth is that for many generations, the Westerners aroused indignation mixed with deference. Western ideologies and arrogance were not admired, but the technology and industriousness of the West were held in envious regard. So was Western power. This legend began to fade during World War II. Japan had overrun Western possessions, France had been humiliated, Britain impoverished, Germany devastated; soon the Dutch bridgehead in East Asia would vanish together with British mastery in India, Pakistan and Burma. Western men were not gods.

As this consciousness dawned, there went with it a strong retrospective indignation at what the West had done to Asian and African pride. A small coterie of advanced nations had built an international system and the beginnings of a new legal order from which the bulk of mankind was totally excluded. Those who talked of greater equality during the early part and the middle of the twentieth century meant equality within the small sovereign family. International law legitimized colonialism, for the legal order was constructed by Westerners for themselves alone. Even the liberal and progressive thinkers of the West kept their liberalism and progressiveness within the civilized family. John Stuart Mill was quite emphatic in declaring that the norms of international morality could not be applied "between civilized nations and barbarians." As for the "barbarians," said Mill, "it is likely to be for their benefit that they should be conquered and held in subjection by foreigners." Tucker, in quoting this remarkable passage from a famous liberal, goes one better in reminding us that Karl Marx took British rule in India for granted: "England has to fulfill a double mission in India; one destructive, the other regenerating—the annihilation of the Asiatic society and the laying of the material foundation of Western society in Asia."

If the so-called barbarians were to be excluded from the utopias of Western liberals as well as from any kind of equality in the imperialist system, they were left with very little to inspire or console them in Western political cultures. If sovereignty was the key to inclusion in every hopeful vision, the struggle for political independence would have to take precedence over every social and economic objective. This was the natural response of African and Asian nationalism. The emphasis was placed on institutional freedom; the monopoly exercised by a few dozen states over the status of sovereignty had to be broken before the new nations could even qualify for dialogue. In this part of their struggle the new nations were brilliantly successful in the first two decades after World War II. The Third World was on the march. It was only in the cold dawn on the morrow of their independence celebrations that they realized that their triumph was imperfect if it yielded political equality combined with economic subjection. They must now crown their juridical triumph with a parallel breakthrough in pursuit of an equitable share of the earth's resources.

It was not all that simple. It is easier to win a recognized status than to alter a deep-rooted material disability. Economic stability, unlike sovereignty, cannot be conferred in an exchange of letters or a vote in an international agency. Nor would a lavish infusion of funds suffice. The backwardness of Third World economies and societies was not merely a consequence of insufficient money in their bank accounts. The weakness lay deep in the foundations of their social structure. External financial support could at best be a supplement to domestic effort. The transition from dependence to sovereignty did not automatically improve the economic or social conditions of the new states. In the first instance it even made those conditions worse. With the continuing disparities between the advanced and the less developed states there was a feeling in the Third World that one form of colonialism had been succeeded by another. Most of the emerging states refused to believe that the developed countries did not bear the main responsibility for their backwardness. They concentrated their effort disproportionately on their demands upon the developed states and gave relatively inadequate time and attention to the reforms of their own societies which were the first condition for economic emancipation.

The gap was growing year by year. The Third World countries are mainly the exporters of raw materials and basic commodities; they are importers of manufactured goods. Prices of raw materials hardly ever rise at the same rate as those of manufactured goods. Sometimes a drastic fluctuation in the value of a single product sends a poor country's economy spiraling downward. Zambia depends totally on copper for its export earnings; when the price of copper fell by over 60 percent between 1974 and 1976, there was no way of avoiding disaster. Those Third World nations which had oil as their "raw material" saw their money supply suddenly burgeon with the worldwide increases in the price of oil. It remains to be seen how sudden drops in oil prices will dislocate their economies.

It is easy to say that foreign aid should have been more generous, but harder to prove that this would have made the crucial difference. Development assistance from the North to the South amounted to nearly $150 billion in the first fifteen years since the UN Development Decades were proclaimed in 1960. In the late 1970s the rate was $30 billion a year. In the United Nations, in UNCTAD, in meetings of the World Bank and the International Monetary Fund, the new countries called for changes in the global economic order. But these desired changes did not merely involve larger allocations of aid; they required the developed states to modify their own economic order and to abolish the free market system in favor of foreign countries. The North was peremptorily called upon to guarantee stable prices for the basic commodities of the Third World, to give free access to their own markets for exports from those countries, and virtually to subsidize the exports from the less developed nations. When the developed countries balked at these demands, they were assailed by abrasive reminders of their past tyrannies and by UN resolutions that virtually delegitimized the existing global economic order.

The prosperous North could not even pretend to be afflicted with enough sense of guilt to take the attacks from the less developed nations at their face value. It thought that in comparison to past history it was displaying great generosity; and it is true that the whole theme of foreign aid is a post World War II development. The motivation of the donor countries was mixed. Part of it was a response to idealistic and altruistic impulses at work in their public opinion. The sentiment in the wealthy states demanded that doctrines of social compassion be transposed into the international system. Governments and parliaments accepted this necessity, but in their more pragmatic way they also nourished the hope that a donor state would be able to win some influence over a recipient nation's policies. These hopes were seldom realized. The new states were able to create a curious psychological climate in which to accept aid was an act of benevolence while to accord it was a privilege for which the donors had to compete. The Western countries which gave lavish aid to Third World nations rarely secured their support or even their courteous abstention in the votes of international agencies. In the 1980s we find United States ambassadors in the United Nations addressing irascible letters to Third World delegates who had voted for resolutions full of invective against the United States. These communications contained broad hints that bilateral relations would be prejudiced by insult in the multilateral arena; but there are few examples of recipient states modifying their policies or even their rhetoric in deference to those who give them economic assistance. (One of the few case histories of a cause-and-effect relationship between financial aid and the policy of a recipient state is the announcement by the United States in January 1983 that "El Salvador has qualified for financial aid in response to its improved policy on human rights." Even here there was an impression that the desire to give the aid was as strong as the willingness to receive it, and the criteria for human rights observance may have been deliberately lenient.)

It is a strange relationship, with more frustration than harmony. When the new states intensified their campaign for a New International Economic Order their approach was frankly adversarial and coercive. The North was challenged to act out of guilt and obligation, not out of interest and a sense of common humanity. The wealthy states were to be bludgeoned, not persuaded; but the bludgeon was made of paper resolutions in the United Nations and it inflicted annoyance without pain. The first substantive injury to Western interests came when the Arab states organized an oil boycott of states which they deemed antagonistic to Arab interests in the Yom Kippur War of 1973. Oil prices, which had been too low to be fair to the oil-exporting states, suddenly became too high for the oil-importing states to pay without severe dislocation of the world economy. Since then meetings of OPEC have been pervaded by a sense of power to do injury and even cause humiliation to those who were the masters of the international system and of the world economy a short generation ago. By 1982 this satisfaction was beginning to expire. It became evident that the need of the OPEC countries to sell their oil was at least as great as anyone's need to buy it. The oil producers now show a nervous deference to their prospective customers.

The virulence with which the South addresses the North has produced a reaction. The North has lost the apologetic demeanor with which it used to approach its dialogue with the Third World. The rhetoric of sympathy for developing countries is still in vogue in liberal circles in the West, but governments are becoming more combative in resisting what they regard as Southern intimidation. It has become legitimate in Western political literature and journalism to question the assumption that the richer countries have a moral obligation to aid the poorer nations even beyond the bounds of their immediate self-interest. That mystique is still prevalent and it reaches extreme expression in statements like that of Kenneth Boulding, who writes that "people in Maine should feel the same degree of responsibility toward the people of Japan or Chile or Indochina as they feel toward California." Whatever it is that people "should feel," the fact is that there are very few people even in the most enlightened societies who are capable of projecting their sense of obligation so far afield. Practical statesmanship avoids this hyperbole and rests the case for North-South cooperation on the more prosaic grounds of common humanity. That is the approach followed by the Independent Commission on International Development Issues in its celebrated report of December 1979, entitled somewhat exaggeratedly *A Program for Survival.* The writers of the Brandt Commission Report try not to moralize or preach; they do make a strong case for the idea that nations can damage each other by their weakness, and not only by their strength, and that an impoverished region living on the outskirts of an affluent area can have the same disruptive effects as a slum in the vicinity of a prosperous town.

Even the relatively modest proposals of the Brandt Commission seem to go beyond what the consensus in Northern countries is willing to sustain. The report suggests the globalization of international development under principles that would give far greater power of determination to the developing countries. It lingers at length on the huge sums spent on armaments, thus endorsing the somewhat naïve assumption that if money were saved on arms expenditure it would be devoted to development. The same simple assumption is sometimes made in connection with space research. The truth is that it is precisely the states that spend vast sums on arms and space research that sustain the development enterprise across the world.

The major proposal of the Brandt Commission is for a massive transfer of wealth from the advanced industrialized countries to the countries of the Third World, and there is little sign that the United States, Europe and Japan are ready for such an ambitious leap into a new relationship.

It is beyond doubt that the wealthy countries have been confused and hesitant in their Third World policies and that this failure has worked against a harmonious international consensus. But it must be admitted in fairness that the new states have contributed to the deadlock and alienation. They have sought to win their case by antagonism, not by compromise. They have relied on the delusion that resolutions of international agencies couched in coercive and condemnatory terms are an adequate substitute for patient and courteous diplomacy. They have presented themselves without convincing evidence as the embodiment of the universal conscience, purer and freer from sin than ordinary mortals and ordinary governments. They have evaded their own share of responsibility by placing the whole charge for the problem and its solution on the outside world. They have not even made a convincing effort to show that transfers of wealth to the Third World would be a transfer to peoples and not only to governments and armies.

Third World leaders would be on stronger ground if they were to abandon the pretense of superior moral claims and take their stand on the notion of a common interest and an increasing interdependence between the richer and poorer nations. The Third World does not offer the other two worlds any social visions worthy of emulation or envy. The record for human rights in the Third World is often poor and sometimes horrific. Idi Amin in Uganda, the "Emperor" Jean-Bedel Bokasa in the Central African Republic, and Pol Pot in Kampuchea would enter the short list of revolting tyrannies in any age. At the Helsinki Conference of 1975 the "human rights" question was focused mainly on the Soviet Union; but there is more violence in Third World dictatorships than in the Soviet Union, not because the Soviet Union is less vigorous in its demand for obedience, but because its reputation for effective suppression has an intimidating and deterrent effect on those who might wish to rebel. In the Third World, despotic governments are cruel enough to invite rebellion and not strong enough to make the rebels despair of success. In countries such as India in which a mature leadership is sincerely opposed to domestic violence, a lack of efficiency and control makes possible such tragedies as the 1983 massacres in the election campaign in Assam.

Many Third World leaders have attracted world interest by the pathos of their struggle for national independence, but few of them have shown a consuming interest in the dull prose of economic planning. Most of them have preferred the more facile satisfactions of international and continental diplomacy. It is common to castigate the wealthy countries for spending so much of their resources on armaments, but the Third World is in the arms business more deeply than would have seemed possible two decades ago. The world as a whole spends 6 percent of the planetary product on preparation for war. Most of this expenditure is by the superpowers, but the Third World is spending nearly $100 billion a year on the purchase of arms.

There is not much for either party in the North-South dialogue to preach about to the other party. Mutual reproach for the past would be less important if there were agreement on an approach for the future. The tendency of the South to draw up an indictment of the North has opened the door to a counterattack which also errs on the side of virulence. Some writers have pointed out that far from impoverishing the new states, the West can claim that those that have had the least contact with the Western economies are among the most squalid and backward, whereas those that have been more uninhibited in their Western contacts showed better results in terms of economic levels and infrastructures. Bauer confronts the Third World proposition that "the causes of Third World poverty must be sought primarily outside the Third World itself—historically in the depredations of colonialism and imperialism, today in the consequences of an unjust international economic system which is heavily weighted in favor of the rich countries." He replies too heatedly: "Such false propositions explain why Western governments support and endorse nonsensical, groundless and offensive statements by leading Third World politicians and why the West so often abases itself before governments whose countries are usually sparsely populated by relatively small numbers of materially very backward people."

This kind of invective is not usually heard in the pronouncements of Western government representatives, but there are many who barely suppress their resentment at the assaults launched by Third World spokesmen in international organizations against their pride and self-esteem.

Much of the literature of disillusionment about development aid comes from those who have spent some years in the field and who work off their frustrations in rhetoric of excessive extremism. A recent study, tendentiously entitled *The Destruction of a Continent,* goes so far as to claim that foreign aid is not merely ineffective but positively harmful. The authors assert that international aid is "responsible" for such ills as the flight of Africans to the towns, the abandonment of agriculture, starvation and corrupt practices. The fact that these phenomena exist in countries where there are ambitious aid programs does not prove a cause-and-effect relationship. It is possible to suggest that African countries should avoid complex Western technologies and make slower progress by more traditional work processes with abundant use of plentiful and cheap manpower. This may or may not make good economic sense, but such counsel would have a patronizing sound and would be interpreted in the Third World as the essence of neocolonialism.

The foreign-aid issue has a psychological as well as an economic aspect, and in the ultimate resort the concepts, and even the complexes, of the recipient states will decide national priorities. It is reasonable for a donor country to doubt whether a Third World state suffering from financial dearth and mass penury needs a luxurious presidential palace as its most urgent priority. But if the perceptions of the recipient government tell it that its central problem is the reinforcement of the mystique of a central government and that the impressiveness of the governmental structure is one of the ways of combating tribalism and dispersion of authority, no amount of puritanical frugality in the tradition of the Western donor is going to have any echo. If the donor government recommends a public health center instead of the palace, it will be politely or impolitely advised to mind its own business and an alternative donor will be found without excessive toil. The developed countries have no option except to confer or to withhold their aid; they have no prospect of fixing the course or direction of economic and social policy in the recipient state.

There is a manifest need for both sides to revise the style and conceptual framework of their dialogue. The need for the richer countries is to understand that they are not dealing with philanthropy but with a vital element of their own stability. The Third World needs to replace confrontation, which has failed, by persuasion—which has not been tried. The colonial guilt theme is not effective. The present generation of citizens in the rich countries were born in a noncolonial age and do not feel any culpability for what their forefathers wrought, any more than present-day Swedes feel a need to repent for the excesses of the Vikings.

It would also be salutary to break out of the generalization implicit in the term "Third World." The nations grouped under that title have no common factor in terms of economic levels. They vary from the opulence of Kuwait and Saudi Arabia through the bright promise of Nigeria and Brazil to the desperate poverty of Haiti and Bangladesh. They include every constitutional structure from the traditional monarchies of Saudi Arabia and the Gulf States to the Soviet-protected state in Cuba and the dictatorships of Libya and many other African states. They are kept together more by common memories of the past than by any common destiny in the future. For the present they have more to win than to lose by suppressing their diverse views and contrary interests. But those who are not in the Third World would do well to study the essential pluralism that lies behind the misleading name. There are many different "worlds" within the Third World, and each of them deserves a separate and particular exploration. The image of the Third World as roughly equivalent to Asia, Black Africa and Latin America will become increasingly blurred as more countries in all three continents break out of the syndrome of underdevelopment or reject the doctrine of nonalignment. China is already incongruous in Third World assemblies by virtue of its dimensions. The Third World, after all, was a revolt against domination, which is not far from being a rebellion against power. A nation like China that belongs to the nuclear club and is treated by the superpowers as one of their family appears out of place in the company of the aggrieved and the dispossessed. In a speech to the Twelfth National Congress of the Chinese Communist Party, Secretary General Hu Yaobang declared that like the Third World countries, "China is still a developing country [which shares] a common destiny with the rest of the Third World"; but most of the Third World would regard the idea that they are "like China" as something close to fantasy.

Japan, unlike China, has never brandished its geographical position as an entry permit to the Third World. It disturbs the pattern of Asian continental unity by the extraordinary dynamism of its development, which has no parallel anywhere else in Asia—although Singapore, South Korea and Taiwan are drawing steadily closer to Japanese economic models and further and further away from the traditional subsistence economies of the Third World with their strong agricultural emphasis and their inability to launch themselves into the industrial and technological age.

In its economy and technology Japan is an organic part of the Western world. In its culture it has shown more success in conserving its traditional Asian character than have some of its neighbors who are strongly influenced by the customs of the English-speaking world and by the military and economic power of the United States. The peculiar mixture of serenity and intense energy that bridges the gap in Japanese culture between East and West is one of the fascinations that Japan holds for other peoples. For the Western world it is profoundly consoling that of the three giants of Asia—the Soviet Union, China and Japan —one at least rejects Communism and carries the banner of democratic pluralism in East Asia. But despite the links of Japan with Western economies, its externality to the American and European system has never been fully transcended.

For the West, Japan is both an asset and a problem. On the positive side, it combats the tendency for the international confrontation to arrange itself along continental lines. It redeems America and Europe from the suspicion of being alienated from Asia. On the other hand, the issues that demand solution within the U.S.-Japanese dialogue are extremely complex. The United States desires a greater contribution by Japan to its own defense and to that of East Asia. This pressure encounters apprehensions from Japanese liberals who see ominous visions of Japanese militarism to the peril of the Japanese democratic ethos, which has only a brief history. Japanese leaders and writers are puzzled by the idea that the United States, which was the architect of Japan's democracy, should now, however inadvertently, be exposing its own achievement to danger. The idea of a strengthened military establishment in Japan arouses even stronger tremors of memory and fear among Japan's neighbors, many of whom experienced the harsh weight of Japanese military rule in the recent past. While it is easy to understand American resentment at having to provide 53 percent of the financial burden of the alliance system, as against a Japanese contribution of 6 percent, strong inhibitions about a military role for Japan will probably prevail in American thinking.

The difficulty for the United States to argue too vehemently with Japan is aggravated by Japan's indispensability to any international system in which America has a central place. There can be little doubt that notwithstanding their fierce rivalries the Soviet Union and China would work together if necessary to prevent Japan from becoming a formidable military power. Any serious controversy between the United States and Japan would cause the Soviet Union and China to make a strong bid for Japan's friendship. The options that would face the United States in the event of a breach with Japan are uniformly forbidding. One possibility is that Japan would seek to rely on itself rather than on the United States for its security and would develop a strong military posture, including nuclear weapons. Another possibility would be an alliance between Japan and China, which would also involve the militarization of Japan and a potentially virulent Soviet reaction. Some observers have raised the hypothesis of an attitude of appeasement by Japan toward the Soviet Union, but have dismissed this likelihood in view of the heavy burden of grievance that weighs on the Japanese mind in relation to Moscow. Japan resents the retention of Japanese territory by the Soviets after World War II and has not forgotten the fate of Japanese prisoners who were in Soviet hands at the end of the war.

Even if we agree that the United States must accept the alliance with Japan for good or for ill, there is no doubt that its grievance is acute. Japan devotes only one percent of its gross national product to its own defense. A large American force on its territory gives it assurance against easy attack from the Soviet Union. The liberation of its resources for industrial and commercial activity gives it a head start in the race for competitive success. Japanese products at a relatively low price pour into the unprotected markets of Europe and the United States and threaten the industrial health of the importing countries. The United States' trade deficit with Japan was only $0.3 billion in 1967; it has now risen to $1.5 billion, and it represents about 60 percent of the total U.S. trade deficit. In 1983 the deficit could reach $20–$25 billion. The Japanese market is far less accessible to American and European products than are the American and European markets to the industrial goods of Japan.

These defects of Japanese policy from the viewpoint of the United States are balanced by a staunch Japanese fidelity to essential Western interests. There is no Third World reservation here. Japan gave stronger support to the United States on the issue of Soviet policy in Afghanistan than did many NATO countries. Tokyo joined the United States in boycotting the Moscow Olympic Games after the invasion of Afghanistan and voted consistently with the United States in international organizations on issues about which Washington and Moscow were in confrontation. The trend of Japanese policy toward the United States is to seek partnership in political and security matters and independence of the most assertive kind in the economic sphere.

What is certain is that no Third World country could conceivably be engaged in this kind of dialogue with the United States. Japan itself is ambivalent about its own role. There is an established attitude of low profile which drives Japan to the acceptance of a more modest and unassertive role than it is entitled to play by virtue of its strength and influence. On the other hand, there is now a growing disposition for Tokyo to liberate itself from the apologetic and cowed residue of World War II and to adopt an independent and activist role in world politics.

No African state has yet set itself apart from the continental pattern in a manner similar to the Japanese example. Africa is the typical testing ground for estimating the progress of the Third World toward a more confident and stable future; and here the diagnosis can only be somber. African peoples became poorer than ever in the early 1980s under the impact of high oil prices and reduced prices for African export commodities. The Organization of African Unity was paralyzed in 1982 owing to internal disputes, especially that between Morocco and the Saharan Arab Democratic Republic. And no sooner had the presidency of Idi Amin been forgotten by the OAU than the presidency of President Qaddafi of Libya presented the continent to the international community in an eccentric guise falling far short of pride. There was also a diminished sensitivity in America and Western Europe to the passionate feeling of Black Africa about South Africa, especially in relation to the unsolved question of Namibia. All in all, the Third World seems able to exercise less pressure on the developed countries than a few years ago.

The idea that the Third World could force the industrialized countries to submit to Third World influences reached its peak in 1973 when the steep rise in oil prices changed the traditional relations between an ascendant West and a subservient and aggrieved company of developing states. It seemed as if the oppressed of yesterday had become the lords of creation. The economies of America, Western Europe and Japan would tremble at every movement of wrath or contempt from OPEC meetings. A decade later the pretensions of OPEC have been brought down to earth. The glut in oil reserves and the fall of prices have been accompanied by breaches of solidarity among the oil producers, who have lost their cartel aspect. In 1980 OPEC provided 60 percent of the world's oil sales and produced 30 million barrels a day. Three years later, OPEC had to be satisfied with 30 percent of the market and was able to sell no more than 14 million barrels. It has thus been proved that in a volatile world economy there is no permanent power for the OPEC countries to lead the Third World to victories over the recumbent West by means of coercion and intimidation. There is no alternative to dialogue on equal terms.

The Third World is a memory, an experience and a moving human drama, but is not a viable framework for a concerted and comprehensive diplomacy. It is more acted upon than acting and its grievances and resentments, however well founded they may seem, are not as effective in the international arena as they once seemed to be. The Third World was graced with brilliant leadership in its struggle for independence, but its leaders have been far less impressive in the task of building modern economies. They have not perceived the potentiality of science and technology as a factor for accelerated development. In the decades of their independence they could have trained indigenous bodies of scientists and engineers instead of relying on Western expertise. They have certainly not translated their national freedom into individual liberty for their peoples. The egalitarian principles that they invoke so movingly in the relations between states find no expression in any corresponding move toward equality within their domestic societies.

A great future awaits the first generation of Third World leaders who will emerge out of the nostalgia of the past and face the developed countries on the basis of harmony, common interest and a sense of the future. None of the rich industrialized countries feels itself free from an impulse of interest and conscience that drives it to seek a fertile relationship with the Third World. This offers a unique opportunity, for the Third World cannot solve its main problems alone. The enfranchisement of scores of new nations within the international system is one of the proud achievements of this generation. But the flags are not enough. Peoples awaken on the morrow of their independence celebration to the knowledge that they may be free in every institutional sense and yet lose the essence of their freedom in the throes of starvation and want. Third World leaders are entitled to look back with emotion to their halcyon days of liberating glory. Having taken their full devotion from those memories, they must advance toward a new and more prosaic agenda.

Chapter 6

THE UNENDING CONFLICT
The Middle East

THE MIDDLE EASTERN NATIONS, despite their own rivalries and dis-
sensions, have one common attribute: they are free at last from
domination by outside forces. The region is alive with independent
energies, most of which are beyond prediction or control. There is a
sense of power, and the taste of it is especially sharp since it is a sudden
legacy of which even the most recent Middle Eastern generations
scarcely dared to dream. Arab and Muslim states now command the
voting system in international organizations on all issues in which their
own interests and convictions are at stake. Nothing can be decided
against them. Israel is lonely and weak in the world parliamentary
arena, but its military strength is out of proportion to its other dimensions and it has a proven capacity to generate reactions and apprehensions throughout the international community. Iran has weakened
itself economically since the anti-Shah uprising, but it has become the
home of a virulent passion that blows across the region like a scorching
wind. The Arab states of the Gulf, some of them small in population
and negligible in military power, can produce convulsive effects on the
oil-hungry economies of Europe, America and Japan. Europe has now
become little more than the nervous spectator of a region in which,
until a few decades ago, it used to determine everything. The United
States and the Soviet Union compete for influence, but not for domination, and neither superpower has a real prospect of achieving the
kind of hegemony that Europe once took for granted.

The emergence of the Middle East from subjection to self-assertion

has been feverishly rapid. Nothing of the sort appeared possible when
World War II came to an end. The Middle East then seemed to have
no decisive voice in its own destiny. There was hardly a corner of real
sovereignty anywhere. The North African littoral from Morocco
through Algeria to Tunisia was under the rule of France. Libya
(Cyrenaica and Tripolitania) had been wrested from Italy but was now
under British rule. Syria and Lebanon were occupied by British and
Free French forces and were juridically still subject to a French mandate awarded by the League of Nations. Palestine, including the whole
area of modern Israel, was ruled by Britain and occupied by a force of
100,000 British troops engaged in combating local turbulence. Across
the river, Transjordan was administered by the Emir Abdullah, the
grandfather of Jordan's present King Hussein, but real power still lay
with the British Resident, and the army, known as the Arab Legion, was
under a British commander. Egypt was a recognized sovereignty, but
there was a British base in the Canal area, and British forces had
recently brought about a change of government in Cairo by massing
tanks before the royal palace. Egypt's principal asset, the Suez Canal,
was owned and administered by an international company in which
French and British shareholders predominated. In the Arabian Peninsula, Aden was still a British colony, and Yemen and Saudi Arabia were
left alone principally because they were deemed to have little to offer
to a foreign colonizer. New oil wells had been discovered in Saudi
Arabia; British companies had moved out after years of unsuccessful
drilling, and American companies had struck oil almost on the morrow
of their arrival. Iranian oil already had great importance. But the
mechanics of power denied any real influence to Middle Eastern states
as a result of their oil wealth. The oil was simply not in their effective
possession. The Western corporations arranged the production, distribution and price levels with little concern for the interests of the
indigenous states, which were not even large customers for the produce of their own soil. Iran was partitioned between a British army in
the south and a Russian army in the northern region of Azerbaijan,
which was disturbingly contiguous to Azerbaijan in the Soviet Union.
There was a promise of early Soviet and British evacuation, but fulfillment depended on the unusual prospect that the Soviet Union would
withdraw its troops from an area that it occupied close to its own
borders and would not insist on controlling the political system in the
area that it abandoned. This had not happened anywhere else to that
time.

All in all, nobody could talk seriously in those days of the Middle
East as a center of influence. With no large armies of their own, with
no direct control of their own resources and with foreign armies scattered over their territories, the Middle Eastern peoples ranked low in

the hierarchy of world power when World War II came to an end. Their marginal status was reflected in the new international agencies. At the founding conference of the United Nations in San Francisco in 1945, the only Arab member states at the opening were Egypt, Iraq, Saudi Arabia, Syria and Lebanon. They were joined by Yemen in 1947. The original signatories of the Charter included only three Muslim states outside the Arab League: Afghanistan, Turkey and Iran. Pakistan would bring impressive reinforcement two years later. During their first decade it was quite possible for United Nations agencies to adopt resolutions vehemently opposed by the Muslim world. In the major confrontations between the powers on such issues as Korea and the Soviet seizure of Czechoslovakia, the voice of the Muslim and Arab states was muted and little considered, while in the dramatic debate on the partition of Palestine in 1947 they were emphatically overruled.

The present generation, conscious of Arab and Muslim strength in oil politics and in conference diplomacy, may find it hard to imagine that such a spectacle of weakness existed only a few decades ago. It was a deceptive picture even at that time. The camera of history had caught the balance of power between the Middle East and the Western world at the last moment of Western advantage. It could not register the dynamism at work below the surface, as a result of which the Middle Eastern nations would swiftly gain both the semblance and the reality of international power while Europe receded into a status of relatively little influence in the Middle East. The change was due as much to European retreat as to Arab and Muslim advance. Britain had emerged from World War II with honor but also in weakness, while France's weakness was compounded by the moral predicaments of capitulation which the Resistance had only partly overcome. When Britain yielded India in 1947 there was little point in maintaining Middle Eastern bases of which the logic lay in their being "on the way" to the Indian subcontinent. They were now not on the way to anywhere. Economic exhaustion and a sense of dwindling international power played their part in the British renunciation of the Palestine base. Other factors were the intensity of Jewish resistance and the tension provoked between Washington and London. It was only a matter of time before the British footholds in Egypt and Iraq would also crumble. France, with little cause, seemed more hopeful than Britain about the possibility of retaining imperial responsibilities, but a far-seeing statesmanship first of Pierre Mendès-France in Tunisia and later of Charles de Gaulle in Algeria would set decolonization on its irresistible course.

If the 1945 appearance exaggerated the real strength and weight of the European nations, it also underestimated the latent force of Middle Eastern nationalism. In less than four decades the tables have been completely turned. The Middle East today is not a focus of overwhelming power, but it has been redeemed from passivity and humiliation. The Arab nation, in particular, is entitled to celebrate the dawn of a new age. In an area in which hardly any Arabs lived in sovereignty and independence a generation ago, the Arab nation has achieved its independence in twenty-two sovereign states covering more than four million square miles with a population of over 100 million. The area is rich in resources; and it comprises all the centers of civilization in which Arab culture reached its highest radiance: Damascus and Cairo, Baghdad, all of North Africa, and the Holy Cities of Arabia. It is one of the greatest and swiftest success stories in the history of national liberation movements. It might have been expected that the Muslim world and, especially, the Arabs would be facing the world in a demeanor of victory, not of bitter grievance. But history moves more in paradox than in logic. An attitude of rancor and deprivation inspires the sentiment and rhetoric of the Muslim world toward the West long after the objective justification for it has passed away. Here and there, now and again, there are areas and episodes of mutual accommodation, but the salient theme of the relationship is still confrontation, not confidence.

The fluctuations in the relations between the Muslim world and Europe have dominated the life of the Middle East for most of modern history. The story is marked by prodigious reversals of fortune. It begins with a Muslim world conscious of its spiritual and secular superiority looking down on the Northern "barbarians" with frank disdain. From its spectacular conquests in the seventh century and thereafter, Islam spread from Morocco to China and expressed its political domination in monarchies (caliphates) which were never as extensive as its religious influence but which always stood at a central point in the world's power system. Islam had a view of the world that was not congenial to diplomacy because it did not acknowledge a legitimate pluralism in international life. It was not even a bipolar view, since there was only one legitimate pole. The human race was divided between the "house of Islam" (*dār al-Islām*) and the "house of war" (*dār al-ḥarb*). This partition corresponded to no geographical division. It recognized no frontiers. The believers and the infidels were destined to be locked in cosmic struggle until belief triumphed against heresy and all denial of Islam was eliminated. And there was no question of leaving this destiny to the workings of conscience and conviction. It was to be fulfilled by holy war (*jihād*) in which all non-Muslim empires would be absorbed by conquest and conversion, as the Persian Empire had been in the seventh and eighth centuries.

This deterministic view did not seem fantastic as Islam rushed headlong from one victory to another in the centuries of expansion and dominance. It was, however, frustrated by Christian Europe. At Poitiers in the seventh century, Constantinople in the eighth and Vienna in the sixteenth, Muslim military advances were repelled. There was clearly going to be a non-Muslim part of the world, after all. The response of Muslim scholars and jurists was not to despair of the global victory but merely to postpone its fulfillment to the indefinite future. Since the ultimate victory was assured, there was no point in anything but fragile accommodations with the unbelieving world. (There is a clear parallel here with the more rigorous Marxist-Leninist doctrine of the inevitable and total triumph of socialism over capitalism. If one believes that one's own particular world view is destined to be universal, there is little incentive for the compromises of diplomacy and international law.)

During the decades in which Muslims believed most fervently in their prospect of exclusive global domination, they sustained their conviction with references to their glittering achievements in culture and science and to the patent inferiority of Europeans in every domain of thought and action. In the tenth century Masūdi, an Arab geographer, had this to say about Europe: "The peoples of the North are those for whom the sun is distant from the zenith . . . Cold and damp prevail in those regions, and snow and ice follow one another in endless succession. The warm humor is lacking amongst them: their bodies are large, their natures gross, their manners harsh, their understanding dull and their tongues heavy. Their religious beliefs lack solidity. Those of them who are farthest to the north are the most subject to grossness and brutishness." Bernard Lewis quotes an eleventh-century jurist in Toledo, Said ibn Ahmed, who also adduces European inferiority from bodily characteristics: "Their bellies are big, their color pale, their hair long and lank. They lack keenness of understanding and clarity of intelligence and are overcome by ignorance and foolishness, blindness and stupidity . . ."

From the sixteenth century onward, the decline of Islam, illustrated by the growing weakness of the Ottoman Empire ("the sick man of Europe") and by the fact that nearly all Arabs were under foreign rule, made these judgments ridiculously obsolete. Europe was the hub and center of the world, and Europeans had developed the disagreeable habit of talking and thinking about Arabs in the way that Arabs had talked about "the peoples of the North" a few centuries earlier. The Arab peoples held their memories of past glory to themselves; nobody else was interested in evoking them. But the humiliation imposed by their total weakness was intensely traumatic when contrasted with their vivid recollections of a time when their power and genius were respected throughout the discovered world. If anything, they longed for respect more than for vanished power. What rankled most was not that the temporal supremacy of the Muslims had been superseded by another power, but that another religion, considered by Muslims to be inferior and illusory, riddled with false doctrine and heresy, was now accorded the highest place in contemporary thought. Muslims could forgive Napoleon for being strong enough to invade their lands; they could not pardon Christianity for its pretensions of superior truth. As the European powers set about governing the Muslim world, setting boundaries, exploiting resources, constructing bases, stationing garrisons, determining sovereignties as and when they liked, the Arabs, particularly the articulate and politically conscious among them, stored up a rancor so passionate and intense that there was bound to be an element of vengefulness when the wheel of power and fortune turned as it did, dramatically, after World War II.

The trouble was that the problem could not be solved merely by the rejection of Europe; this was feasible only for the more rigorous theologians and fundamentalists who urged the Arabs to seek their redemption by a return to ancient sources of faith and historic pride. Realism dictated another, more intricate course: to resist Europe by learning the lessons of its strength. From the end of the nineteenth century, Arabic thought and literature are dominated, to the point of obsession, by the tension between the need to reject the West—out of fear of its domination—and the need to emulate the West in order to gather strength for the rejection. Egypt has led the Arab world on this ambivalent course. Throughout most of this century it has sought to oppose the West politically and to embrace it culturally. From the earliest years of the century, Egyptian leaders have encouraged a discovery of Western literature through massive projects of translation. The study of foreign languages has been encouraged and modern Egyptian writers have often been as fluent in French as in Arabic. More recently, English has taken the leading place in the linguistic hierarchy. Ideologies based on concepts of synthesis abounded. The central idea was "Islamic modernism," an effort to reconcile ancient fidelities with Western ideas. Spiritual power would come from the old inheritance, and secular strength from the new potentiality. The West through its culture would furnish the weapons for its own political defeat by an Arab nationalism equipped with Western ideas and techniques. When Muslim modernists thought about the sources of Western strength they referred not only to science and literature but also to social ideas and principles of political organization. Democracy was not congenial to the strongly hierarchical element in Islam, but the nation-state would obviously have to be emulated. The idea of a nation expressing itself through a state was familiar at first only to Turkey, Persia and Egypt. For the rest of the Middle East, both "Islam" and "the Arab nation" were conceived as entities of wider scope than anything that could be embraced in a single political unit.

The attitude of the Muslim and Arab peoples to the West has been ambiguous to a tormenting degree. If the central idea was to oppose the West by imitating it, it was evident that imitation required an opening of doors and a broadening access. And the crucial task was not to let imitation go beyond the point at which Muslim and Arab identity would be weakened; the Arabs would admit Western ideas into their midst while keeping their own inner sanctuaries intact. The conventional theme in Arab thought about the West is that Europe and America have found the secret of power, but not of serenity and spiritual balance, which are more likely to be found in the creeds and temperament of Asian peoples.

The search for a spiritual and emotional compromise between Islam and the West has been going forward for the whole of this century. It was not until recently that Muslim fundamentalism challenged the very need for any compromise at all. The idea of a renewed and implacable insistence on Islamic purity had previously been the slogan of fringe groups such as the Muslim Brotherhood in Egypt. With the rise of Ayatollah Khomeini, Muslim fundamentalism has become a burning issue in international diplomacy. Khomeini is, in the strictest historic sense, a counterrevolutionary. The real revolution was the decision of Muslim and Arab leaders to emerge out of theological isolation and to embrace a part of the Western legacy. Khomeini seeks to take Iran—and, by example, the rest of the Islamic world—back to the days preceding the invasion of the "house of Islam" by the cultural enemy. The prospect of success for this retreat is small. One can make an omelette out of eggs, but nobody has ever reconstructed eggs out of an omelette.

The tendency of the Muslim world to be attracted by Western achievements and suspicious of Western domination creates a complex atmosphere for the relationship between the Middle East and the West. It is difficult for Western statesmen and scholars, with their pragmatic, nontheological approach to diplomacy, to grasp a situation in which religious and cultural ideas are at least as important in determining the direction of international politics as are the familiar themes of strategy, territory and military balances. The vogue among modern historians in the West is to believe that we have passed from epochs in which religion was the dominant issue of war and peace to an age in which religion counts for nothing. This view rests on the erroneous assumption that the secularization of politics is a universal trend. The truth is far different. If we look at the most burning areas of conflict of this age—India-Pakistan, Turkey-Greece, Ireland, the Arabs and Israel—it can hardly be fortuitous that the adversaries are divided not only in their interests but also in their religious loyalties. In the Middle East, more than in any other sector of the international arena, a serious study of diplomacy and strategy must include the exploration of ideas and creeds. All the peoples of the region have a self-searching tendency; they are gripped and sometimes obsessed by the question of their spiritual origin and destination.

The Arab peoples rarely celebrate their emancipation and their lavish sovereignty as a joyous achievement. They are more conscious of what they have been denied than of what they have obtained. Their demeanor of torment and unfulfilled hope afflicts them in three distinct but interrelated spheres: in their relations with one another, in their relations with the power blocs, and in their increasingly complex and diverse attitudes to Israel.

United or Separate?

The contemporary atlases and political handbooks give us a list of twenty-two Arab states, set out in separate detail, rather like the thirty states of Europe, each with its population, area and political structure. The analogy is fallacious. The individual nation-state is an invention of Christian Europe and has not yet been fully assimilated by Islam or by Arab nationalism. The structure of international agencies is favorable to fragmentation, and the Arabs do not complain about the multiple voting-power that comes from their division into separate states. But none of them would accept the idea that any Arab nation-state comes near to exhausting all their devotion and duty of allegiance, or that the Muslim or Pan-Arab solidarity which transcends the frontiers of states is of mere sentimental importance without an impact on international politics. To be an Egyptian, Iraqi, Syrian, Algerian or Saudi is also to be an Arab and, in most cases, to be a Muslim as well. This leads to an extremely complex notion of identity. Ideally, most Arabs would like to be in harmony with policies and attitudes ratified by their own separate governments, by the family of Arab states as a whole and by the entire Muslim world. Since such harmonies never prevail to a full degree, nearly all policies and attitudes of Arab governments have to be laboriously reconciled within the tension between three elements of identity: citizenship, Arabism and Muslim allegiance.

The Arabic language is the soul of the Arab nation; it is the criterion which determines whether a person is an Arab or not. The Arab mind has always been dominated by a deep sense of heritage. Its contours are formed, its spirit expressed in a language of rich and potent variety. There is a broad diversity of dialect and idiom in daily speech, but the language of books and today of radio, television, newspapers and official discourse is the lingua franca of Arab communities everywhere.

The unifying spirit in Arab life goes deeper than language. There is a cultural and psychological unity which cannot be underestimated.

There is a way of thinking, feeling, speaking, rejoicing, suffering, hating, loving that is typically and uniquely Arab. It is to this unifying ethos that Arab politicians appeal when they seek a common denominator of policy beyond the separate interests of individual states. And it is this sense of common identity that most non-Arabs have in mind when they make their sweeping generalizations affirming that "the Arabs" are like this or that, feel this or the other emotion and are likely to take this or another course.

The hope that their regional and international policies would be concerted, if not completely unified, inspired most Arab governments and peoples in the years of successful national struggle after World War II. A regional institution, the Arab League, seemed to have great influence and often became the spokesman for the interests of separate Arab states. It developed an intricate network of subordinate institutions to express a community interest going beyond diplomacy. There was a widespread assumption that Arab diplomacy would be conducted collectively. Pan-Arabism was the prevalent ideology. Citizens of separate states were more likely to say "we Arabs" than to say "we Iraqis," or Syrians, Palestinians, Transjordanians, Saudis. (The exceptions were the Egyptians, who had developed a sense of particularity as a solidly established nation-state which they would assert emphatically until the rise of Nasser in 1953.) The early postwar expectation that the Arab states would develop a markedly collective approach to international and regional politics has not been fulfilled. In general terms it can be said that the Arabs showed a great capacity to unite in their self-assertion against outside forces with which they were in conflict or in dialogue. But with every passing year the particularist tendencies in Arab nationalism have been revealing themselves with impressive strength. It is becoming doubtful whether any political statement beginning with the words "the Arabs" can have any degree of precision.

If we photograph the Arab landscape in mid-1983 we find more conflict than harmony. A savage war with thousands of fatalities is being waged between Iraq and Iran; Jordan and Egypt are supporting Iraq, while Syria is in vehement support of Iran. This means that Iraq and Syria, despite their kindred Arab and socialist ideologies, are in a virtual state of mutual belligerency. Libya is bitterly hostile to Egypt; its propaganda machine recently called for the assassination of President Anwar el-Sadat and gloated over his death. Libya's relations with Sudan and Tunisia are also strained to the breaking point. Morocco is carrying out a bitterly contested military operation to suppress the separatist Polisario movement attempting to secure independence for a South Sahara Democratic Republic. This brings Morocco into conflict with Algeria, which supports the Polisario secession. Less than two decades after an Egyptian invasion of Yemen, North and South Yemen are at daggers drawn. Syria has a large force occupying Lebanon, whose independence it has never recognized. Thirteen years ago Syria attempted an invasion of Jordan and was deterred by Israeli mobilization and American warnings. The small principalities of the Gulf, as well as Kuwait, suspect Saudi Arabia of a desire to dominate them. The PLO, theoretically cherished and supported by the entire Arab world, was violently decimated and expelled by Jordan in 1970 and suffered much death and violence from Syria on Lebanese soil in the mid-1970s. It has recently been exposed to savage vengeance by the Lebanese Christians, who deeply resent the domination of their country by the PLO since the 1976 civil war.

Amid all this violence and internecine conflict, not even Israel can unite the entire Arab family in a common policy or attitude. There are, at least, three separate approaches to the Israeli question in the Arab world. Egypt has opted for the permanent end of belligerency in a formal peace treaty involving full diplomatic relations. Lebanon has secured an Israeli commitment to withdraw from its territory after the 1982–83 war in exchange for a formal end of the state of war and for cooperation in preventing terrorist infiltration. These two agreements mark the abandonment of the traditional Arab denial of Israel's permanence and legitimacy as a state. It is commonly known that Jordan has periodically negotiated with Israeli representatives at various levels, including the highest ones, and that King Hussein would accept a peace settlement with Israel if Palestinian assent could be obtained.

Jordan represents the second or intermediate layer of Arab states which have renounced the dream of Israel's disappearance without entering into formal agreements. This category probably includes Tunisia, Morocco, some of the Gulf states and, according to some statements, Saudi Arabia, Syria, Libya, South Yemen and Kuwait are thus left in growing solitude with the doctrine that Israel is a temporary and illegitimate intrusion into Middle Eastern history. In this last-ditch stand the Arab rejectionists are spurred on by the PLO; but there are some indications, however fragile, that even in that bulwark of obduracy some cracks of doubt have begun to appear. In April 1983, a courageous PLO leader, Essam Saratawi, was assassinated by a rival Palestinian group while he was attending a meeting of the Socialist International in Lisbon. He represented what is evidently a significant minority view in the PLO in favor of greater realism about the permanence and stability of Israel.

Diversity and even conflict of interest about the Middle East are deepened in the Arab world by varying orientations and regimes. Arab states, like most of the Third World countries, are reluctant to make formal declarations about their place in the global competition between the Communist world and the West, but they are certainly spread over the entire gamut of affinities and preferences. Egypt, Jordan, Lebanon, Morocco, Tunisia, Saudi Arabia, the Emirates and Sudan are clearly closer to the United States and the European Community in their international orientation. Libya, Syria, Iraq and South Yemen are on the margin of the Soviet orbit, though not organically part of the Soviet system like Cuba. On matters affecting a Muslim state, such as the Soviet invasion of Afghanistan, the Arab states divide, with the majority on the Western side of the voting lobby. On other East-West questions the Arab "bloc" is seldom likely to vote as a united bloc.

Diversity of international orientations is matched by variety of regimes. The sociological and institutional structure of the Arab world is so fragmented that no unifying principle can be discerned. There are traditional monarchies applying Muslim law, such as Saudi Arabia and some of the Emirates. There are regimes similar to the "people's democracies" of Eastern Europe, such as the Syria of Hafiz al Assad and the regime in South Yemen. There are military dictatorships such as the Iraq of Saddam Hussein and the Libya of Qaddafi. There is the paternalistic but highly centralized monarchy in Jordan. There is even an attempt at a pluralistic parliamentary democracy in Lebanon. These differences of regime often engender hostility. When Nasser made his bellicose speech against Israel on the eve of the 1967 war, the first half of his address was devoted to a ferocious attack on the monarchies in Jordan and Saudi Arabia, which he accused of selling their Arab souls to Western imperialism. Sadat's distrust of monarchies was one of the factors in his contemptuous treatment of King Hussein, on whom the Camp David agreements conferred crucial tasks without associating him in the negotiation.

While Arab unity is not a mere fiction, it is far from being what the conventional mythology declares it to be. One of the difficulties is that one cannot seriously envisage a Pan-Arab system without raising the question of hegemony. Egypt, whose population is nearly equal to that of the other twenty-one Arab states put together, is the only serious candidate for the leading role in modern history. All Arab roads have always led to Cairo. As a center of literary and journalistic vitality Egypt has no rival in the Arab world. It is also the great communications crossroad. Egypt's military strength is indispensable to any serious war option. The Arab world has never embarked on a war against Israel without Egypt at its head. And no other Arab state could have initiated moves away from active belligerency. Without Egypt it is doubtful if the Arab world can make either war or peace.

Yet Egypt's attempts under Nasser to exercise decisive leadership had an unhappy end. Nasser interpreted his role as entitling him to enthrone pro-Nasserist regimes in all Arab countries. This involved an obtrusive intervention in the domestic systems of other states. Arab states asserted their sovereignty against this idea of Egyptian control. Nasser described any non-Nasserist regime in an Arab state as "imperialistic" or treacherous to Arab nationalism. Yet he could not impose his authority. There was no movement for the revival of the Caliphate or any other recognized framework uniting Muslims or Arabs everywhere. The general lesson of Arab history is that the Arab world accepts centralized control only if there is a military power able to enforce it. In the absence of such a power, the tendency, even in the Caliphate era, was for the outlying provinces to go their separate ways. Except for the first exuberant spasm of Arab conquest in the seventh century, Cairo, Damascus and Baghdad as well as the Holy Cities of Arabia have all declined to ascribe exclusive metropolitan status to one another. There is no consensus about where the heart of the Arab nation lies.

The consequence is that nothing has divided the Arab world more than the attempt to unite it. The particularist tendencies in Arab nationalism have been asserting themselves with impressive strength. There is almost nothing that an Arab state will not do to save itself from the unwanted embrace of another Arab state. In 1958 Jordan and Lebanon went so far as to invite foreign intervention in order to prevent an Egyptian takeover; Lebanon received American Marines and Jordan invited British troops to block what they believed was an imminent conquest by pro-Nasserist forces. Arab governments, including Iraq, laid complaints against Egypt at the UN Security Council accusing Cairo of attempting to annul their sovereignty in the name of Arab unity. Jordan, Lebanon, Tunisia and Sudan contributed to an astonishing volume of apprehension and warning directed against the possibility of an enforced Arab "unity." For a few years Syria joined with Egypt in a full-fledged federation called the United Arab Republic. Damascus soon awakened to the realization that this was somewhat like the "unity" between Jonah and the whale, and after some conspicuous failures of digestion the two separated with expressions of mutual relief.

All the major indications tend to support the prediction that there will be a weakening of federal tendencies in Arab nationalism and a steady reinforcement of particularist decision-making. Since Arab unity has a nobler sound than separate Arab sovereignties, there is great intellectual resistance to this forecast, similar to the tenacious refusal of some Europeans to recognize that the idea of a United States of Europe has receded and not progressed in the past few decades. For a time it appeared that the unresolved Palestine problem would reconstitute the cement that would hold the Arab world together. A Palestinian intellectual, Walid Khalidi, even comforted himself with the thought that separate Arab sovereignties were illusory and that the only legitimate ideas in Arab nationalism were Arab unity and uniform solidarity with the Palestinians. He wrote eloquently:

> The Arab states' system is first and foremost a "Pan" system. It postulates the existence of a single Arab Nation behind the façade of a multiplicity of sovereign states . . . From this perspective, the individual Arab states are deviant and transient entities: their frontiers illusory and permeable; their rulers interim caretakers, or obstacles to be removed . . . Their mandate is from the entire Arab Nation. Before such super-legitimacy, the legitimacy of the individual state shrinks into irrelevance . . .

The proposition is asserted dogmatically without illustration by case histories or other forms of evidence. The theological character of the dogma is instructively betrayed by the reverent capital letters with which the writer celebrates the "Arab Nation," compared with the secular humility of "the individual state." This is more like a sincere, heartrending sigh in the void of history than a rationally confirmed thesis. Within a few months after the publication of this article, the leading Arab state, through a uniquely Egyptian decision by Anwar el-Sadat, made peace with Israel. He sought no "mandate from the entire Arab Nation." He assumed that the "legitimacy of the individual state" had not shrunk "into irrelevance." He was asserting a particularism which has always been more emphatic in Egypt than in other Arab states, but which is now developing elsewhere in the Arab world. Iraq decided to fight Iran without seeking a mandate from "the entire Arab Nation." Syria sought no such mandate when it stationed Soviet missiles in Lebanon to control a part of Israel's airspace. Even Lebanon, with all its weakness and fragility, acted alone in May 1983 in accepting an American-sponsored agreement for the withdrawal of all foreign forces from Lebanon. Muammar Qaddafi would laugh at the idea that he needs a "mandate from the entire Arab Nation" to do whatever he does. Saudi Arabia sits in OPEC and determines the price of oil in the world markets in collusion with other producing countries, but without looking for Arab mandates. It would not be an oversimplification to say that the Arab states unite for rhetoric but separate for action. Their decision-making is not affected by their reverence for the same history or by the fact that the same lofty poetry stirs all their hearts. Egypt's face is toward Africa and the Nile Valley; Iraq thinks about Iran and the Gulf as Egyptians seldom do; Morocco, Algeria and Tunisia have Mediterranean thoughts, still focused on France. Syria is the most intensely parochial of states in its Arabism. Libya considers how to subjugate Africa by brandishing its wealth. Saudi Arabia has its mind fixed on oil prices and foreign-currency deposits in European and American banks. Thus each Arab state holds a part of its consciousness in common with the others—and a larger part particular to itself.

Arabs often speak of their internal relationships as those of a family. It is a useful metaphor, since it defines both the general liberty of each member and the occasional bouts of solidarity in defiance of those outside the family domain. It also explains the extraordinary rapidity with which Arab governments pass from savage rivalry to a show of reconciliation. In May 1967 Nasser and Hussein were virulently hostile at the beginning of the month—and were embracing each other as allies by the end. In 1973 Sadat and Assad joined each other in the most intimate of all unions—alliance in war. But when Sadat embarked on his 1977 peace mission to Jerusalem and was repudiated by Assad, a rhetoric of unbelievable violence flowed in both directions between Damascus and Cairo. All that realistic non-Arabs can safely do is conserve their skepticism about the durability of any Arab family emotion, whether of friendship or of rivalry.

The need for international diplomacy to deal with the Arab states as separate entities is strengthened by the fact that there is no institutional mechanism that would enable them to do anything else. Even the inadequate consultative procedures available to the European Community through the Council of Ministers and the EEC Commissioners are more than the Arab nation, with all its community aspirations, has yet been able to devise. It may well be the case that there was some artificiality in the way in which separate Arab states were carved out with their new boundaries in the aftermath of two world wars. But there is a dynamic by which a sovereignty once established in separation from others, however controversially, develops its own specific character, cultivates a devotion to its own flag, takes a liking to its own premierships, ministries and embassies, and reacts with distaste to the idea of returning to some vast unifying womb.

Another lesson from this review of Arab relationships is that scholars and practitioners of international statecraft must strive to emerge from an obsessive view of the Arab-Israeli conflict. There are good reasons to explain why this has become the most dramatic and therefore the most discussed and agitated of all Middle Eastern problems, but it is only one of many sources of regional tension. It is neither the most expensive in terms of human life nor the most explosive in its potential for the involvement of the superpowers. If the Arab-Israeli conflict were settled tomorrow, Soviet troops would not retire from Afghanistan; Iraq and Iran would not cease fighting each other; the Morocco-Algerian conflict over the South Sahara would not be affected for good or ill; Syria's claim to virtual control of Lebanon would not expire; North and South Yemen would not become reconciled; Khomeini would not abandon his anti-Western vendetta; Libya would not end its subversion in Africa; and the oil consumers would continue to be harassed by fears of escalating oil prices. There are very compelling human reasons for urgent treatment of the Arab-Israeli conflict, but this question should be approached in the sober knowledge that international tension in the Middle East has always been polycentric with most of the focal points lying outside the Israeli-Arab context. There is a strong case to be made for the proposition that international diplomacy has been too persistent and intrusive in the Israeli-Arab conflict, liberating the local governments from their own duties of initiative, and too passive and inert in other sectors of regional conflict. Above all, there have been failures arising from excessive simplification. There is no such thing as "*the* Middle Eastern crisis," no such thing as "*the* Arabs" envisaged as a unitary actor.

The Middle East and the Soviet Union

Soviet leaders and spokesmen have a ritual expression to introduce any discussion about the Middle East: they refer to the proximity of that region to the USSR and its relative distance from the United States. They go on to speak of Soviet security as the dominant factor in the USSR's Middle Eastern policy. The implication is that the sense of vulnerability which lies at the root of Soviet policy toward its neighbors in Europe is matched by a similar dilemma for Russian security on the southern flank of the USSR. Historic truth does not sustain such a fear, if indeed it is genuinely felt. Russian territories have constantly been attacked and ravaged by invaders from the West, but not from the areas of the Middle East. Yet the Russian security doctrine requires that the entire belt of territory surrounding the USSR on every side either should be in the hands of "friendly governments," which is interpreted as meaning governments under Soviet control, or, at the very least, should be free of any military bases or alliances at the disposal of the Western powers.

The obsessive dream of the Russian rulers, Catherine the Great (1762–96), Nicholas I (1825–55) and Alexander II (1855–81) was to acquire warm-water ports to the south. Little was done to put this ambition to the test of struggle, but the idea that Russia had a destiny in the Mediterranean world was never lost from the national consciousness, and the monopoly of influence exercised by France and Britain was regarded in Moscow as an intrusion of distant powers into an area crucial for Russian security. The Middle East was the first point of abrasive encounter between the Soviet Union and the West after the absorption of Poland and other East European states in 1944–45. Stalin must have been surprised by Truman's irascible reaction to his attempt to detach Azerbaijan from Iran in 1945–46. When this effort failed, the Soviet Union turned to diplomacy and propaganda in the next phase of its Middle Eastern policy. Its aim was to accelerate the disintegration of the British network of bases and positions which Moscow regarded as surrogates for the United States in its global competition with the Soviet Union. In the years immediately following World War II the Jews were more militantly opposed to the British administration in Palestine than the Arabs. The Soviet Union did not hesitate therefore to reverse and repudiate its long tradition of anti-Zionism in a specatacular campaign of support for the establishment and defense of Israel. Its delegate, Andrei Gromyko, went the whole way in this new enthusiasm. He referred to the historic roots of the Jewish people in Israel and to the suffering of Jews under the Nazi heel. "During the last war," he said, "the Jewish people underwent indescribable sorrow and suffering. No Western European state was able to help the Jewish people to defend its rights and its very existence. . . . The time has come to help these people not by words but by deeds."

The support of Israel by the Soviet Union lasted for nearly three years, which was long enough to see the British position in Palestine eliminated and the Negev in Israeli hands. The Soviet Union had feared that a British base would remain in the Negev even after Israel's establishment. Once the immediate tactical aim was achieved, the USSR turned its back on Israel and began to seek friendships in the Arab countries. The focus was on Egypt, which, after the advent of Nasser to power in 1953, had begun to develop a neutralist rhetoric. Two years later Khrushchev made his sensational decision to sell Soviet arms to Egypt, thus upsetting the balance of power to Israel's disadvantage and generating thoughts of pre-emptive Israeli military action against a growing Egyptian danger. This action was taken in 1956, when Israel, together with France and Britain, attacked Egypt across the Sinai desert and the Suez Canal.

The entry of the Soviet Union into the arena of arms supply in the Middle East is often described as an aggressive disturbance of the international equilibrium. An objective historian would have to admit that Moscow was, in fact, reacting to an American initiative. The United States had attempted to create a military alliance in the Middle East under the name of the Baghdad Pact. The original members were Iraq, Turkey, Iran and Pakistan, together with the United Kingdom. This plan had the distinction of being offensive to the Soviet Union, Egypt and Israel, in equal degree and for contrasting reasons. Israel resented the establishment of a regional organization from which it would be excluded and which would result in increased armaments for Arab states. Egypt was enraged by the American pretension to exercise strategic leadership in the Middle East and to determine the global orientation of the area in opposition to Egypt's policy. The Soviet Union had no illusions about the weakness of the Baghdad Pact in military terms; but it saw the Baghdad Pact as the expression of a principle against which it was bound to react: the principle of permissive anti-Soviet organization in an area close to the Soviet frontier and remote from that of the United States. The American-British initiative was based on the pretentious assumption that Washington and London were the only legitimate leaders of Middle Eastern policy and strategy and that the Soviet Union had no right to have its deepest sensitivities respected. It drew the USSR and the Arab world closer together.

In the ensuing decade the ties between the Soviet Union and the Arab states were strengthened by a constant stream of arms shipments and by uncritical support for the Arab side in any dispute with Israel or the West. The Soviet Union regarded its arms as a device for asserting Arab independence of the Western powers; Egypt and Syria saw them as instruments for an intensified campaign of pressure upon Israel. Terrorist attacks on Israelis from Egypt, Syria and Jordan multiplied. In 1956 Israeli, British and French forces, making common cause against Nasser, fought Egypt in Sinai and Suez. The Soviet Union reached the highest point of its influence when its threats were given credit for the withdrawal of British, French and Israeli forces from Egyptian soil.

By the early 1960s the Soviet Union seemed to have become established as a major power in the Middle East. In 1967, however, the tide began to turn against Moscow. There can be no doubt that the Soviet Union had a major responsibility for the events leading up to the Six-Day War. It had encouraged PLO attacks on Israelis by supplying the arms with which they were conducted and by preventing international condemnation of them when they occurred. It had refused to prevent Syria from giving asylum and training to terrorists and had, on the contrary, spread a shield of immunity over Syria against Israeli retaliation by brandishing the Soviet-Syrian defense alliance. When Israeli spokesmen began to warn Syria of retribution on a local scale, the USSR spread the fake notion that Israel planned to capture Damascus and had concentrated twelve brigades on the Syrian boundary. The USSR then incited Cairo to support Syria by concentrating Egyptian troops in Sinai and threatening Israel with war. It is not certain whether the Soviets wanted Nasser to go so far as to impose the maritime blockade on Israel in the Straits of Tiran, since that would inevitably leave Israel with no option but to fight a general war for the defeat of the Egyptian armies. It is possible that the Soviet intention was to intimidate rather than to kindle the fire. But it is difficult to

recall an instance in the modern age in which a major power has played
so prominent a role in fomenting conflict between regional adversaries
at the expense of the international stability that the Great Powers are
supposed to safeguard.

The crushing defeat inflicted on Egypt, Syria and Jordan by Israel
in the Six-Day War marked a turning point in the story of Soviet policy
in the Middle East. Every consequence was bleak for Moscow. American influence was strengthened by the very fact that a democracy had
defeated a Soviet-supported dictatorship. Israel had proved that it is
possible to defy Soviet threats without dire results. And Russia's Arab
allies were thoroughly disillusioned. The USSR had rashly exposed
Egypt and Syria to Israel's vigorous reaction by encouraging them to
provoke Israel beyond the limits of prudence. It was simply not reasonable to assume that Israel would absorb constant terrorist violence,
heavy concentrations of troops and tanks within striking distance of its
population centers, the dismissal of the United Nations forces stationed in Sinai and Gaza by agreement since 1967, a maritime blockade cutting it off from contact with more than half the world, and a
rhetoric threatening "the destruction of Israel"—all without taking
any drastic action in its defense. The Soviet Union and its Arab friends
were here committing the most unforgivable of diplomatic errors: they
were seeing their adversary as they wanted to see it, not as it really was.
When Israeli forces swept through Sinai, captured all the territory
under Arab control between the River Jordan and the Mediterranean,
and pushed the Syrians away from the Golan Heights, the weight and
fame of the Soviet Union as a powerful ally came under a cloud of
disappointment and skepticism in the Arab world—and beyond.

For a time the Soviet Union hoped to recoup its loss on the battlefield by diplomatic victories in the international arena. Here came
a stunning surprise: far from generating pressure on Israel to renounce its territorial positions and to give up its gains without recompense, the United Nations actually froze the territorial results of the
war! The General Assembly rejected Soviet proposals for Israel's unconditional withdrawal. The Security Council dismissed proposals for
linking the cease-fire with an immediate Israeli withdrawal to the
previous lines. The Soviet Union was being defeated in the arena of
its greatest strength. In the end it had to give its reluctant assent to
Security Council Resolution 242, which called on the Arab states to
conclude peace agreements with Israel as the condition for liberating
their lost territories. Even in that contingency the Security Council's
call for withdrawal to "secure and recognized boundaries" was vague
enough to enable Israel to hold out for limited but significant territorial changes in the event of peace and withdrawal.

The Soviet Union has never recovered from the collapse of its policy in the 1967 war. Its failure to win advantage for its Arab protégés either on the battlefield or in the diplomatic arena was compounded by its own error in breaking relations with Israel. This may have given a fleeting emotional satisfaction to Israel's adversaries, but the operative effect was to exclude the Soviet Union from a diplomatic role in the conflict and to award the United States a unique capacity to represent the international interest. Since the United States was more effective than the Soviet Union in the field of economic and technical aid, it now had the advantage in most spheres of interaction between the Middle East and the outside world.

There remained the influence that superpowers could derive from lavish arms supplies. Here and here alone the Soviet Union was predominant. The United States, constrained by public and congressional control, could never be as uninhibited as the Soviet Union in supplying arms even to its most trusted friends. After the Six-Day War of 1967, the Soviet Union reconstructed the shattered Egyptian and Syrian armories with astonishing speed. By 1968, Egypt, Syria, Iraq and Algeria had received more than 3,500 tanks, 900 military aircraft and thousands of artillery pieces from the Soviet Union. The financial value of these shipments amounted to about $3 billion. Egypt was the major recipient. There had never been such an army on the continent of Africa except under the command of a foreign occupier. The effect of this spectacular Soviet rearmament of Egypt was immediately felt in Washington. Since the United States had a commitment to what was described as a "balance" of armed strength between Israel and its potential adversaries, there had to be a vast escalation in the quality and quantity of American arms delivered to Israel. One of the anomalies created by the American-Soviet arms race in the Middle East was that small and medium countries such as Israel, Syria and Egypt came to possess the kind of military power that was traditionally associated with the great continental and imperial powers. When European governments in the early 1980s drafted documents in which they proposed to "guarantee" the frontiers of Israel against possible attack by neighboring states, they were tactfully reminded that Britain, France, West Germany and their associates might turn out to have fewer tanks, aircraft and other major categories of weapons than the countries that they sought to protect or deter.

Soviet spokesmen are reticent about what they think of their investment of weapons and political support in Arab countries. Do they feel betrayed by ungrateful clients or do they have a sense of fulfillment and reward? The objective truth is that they have not received the kind of lavish return in the Arab world that they expected, and that their Western rivals feared. The ideological gain for Communism has been small. Muslims and Arabs have not been attracted by Marxism-

Leninism. Part of this revulsion may be a reaction by a deistic culture and philosophy against a creed that decries all revealed theologies—except Marxism-Leninism itself. The contemptuous attitude of the Soviet regime to its own Muslim population is another cause for Arab reserve. Arab traditions revere such non-Marxist values as family, kinship and individual responsibility. Marxist rhetoric is turgid enough in English; in Arabic it sounds like a parody. Insofar as monarchies are renounced in Muslim countries, the renunciation has been in favor of monarchical presidencies, not of ideological parties. Thus, even when they were receiving massive military aid and intense diplomatic support from Moscow, Arab states have generally continued to suppress, persecute or, at least, despise their own Communist parties. Nor have they allowed their connection with the USSR to reach the point of accepting military bases. Above all, they have sometimes shown a rare capacity to make sudden changes of attitude toward their Soviet arms suppliers. In 1970 Nasser made a secret visit to Moscow to plead for Soviet equipment and advisers to help him construct an effective air defense system for Cairo and a new missile system for use against Israeli forces across the Suez Canal. This request came after Israeli aircraft had revealed a capacity to penetrate deep into Egypt and even to cause a demonstrative "sound boom" over Cairo. The Soviet leaders were initially hesitant about involving their military personnel so far from the Soviet defense perimeter. But they were persuaded that the effect of a refusal would be for Nasser to seek an American orientation, thus signaling throughout the Third World that the Soviet Union was a poor ally. Soviet missiles and advisers flowed to Cairo; the advisers eventually became a contingent of 20,000 men. There is no doubt that though this personnel was withdrawn in 1972, the training it provided as well as other Soviet assistance gave Nasser's successor, Anwar el-Sadat, the confident feeling that he could allow himself to conduct an assault against Israeli forces across the Suez Canal in October (Yom Kippur) 1973 with the prospect of a local success.

But over a year before Sadat was ready to launch this action he reached the conclusion that he had secured whatever he could hope to obtain from the USSR and that the presence of Soviet officers and troops had become an embarrassment. There was a strong possibility that Moscow would use its influence to restrain Sadat from his cherished venture. Moreover, the conduct of the Soviet mission in Egypt had wounded the nation's pride. It seems to have adopted a colonial manner of speech and behavior that reminded sensitive Egyptians of the former British domination. One unforgettable day in July 1972, Sadat ordered all Soviet personnel to leave Egyptian territory. It was a daring speculation; if the USSR had refused to withdraw, it is difficult to know what Sadat could have done except resign. His expulsion order and the Soviet compliance demonstrated the relative fragility of the Soviet-Arab connection. There was acrimony and a sense of grievance on both sides. Egypt felt that the Soviets were using its territory for their own strategic purposes, as a base against the United States, without even promising to support Egypt in a possible armed conflict with Israel. The Soviet Union believed that Egypt, instead of being grateful for Soviet aid, was trying to embroil its great ally in an unwanted confrontation with the United States over Israel. Egyptian indignation was strengthened by Brezhnev's conduct at the summit meeting with Nixon in May 1972; after a perfunctory verbal support of the Arab position on full Israeli withdrawal from the occupied territory, Brezhnev signed a noncommittal statement with Nixon, the effect of which was to leave the Middle Eastern situation as it was, sheltering behind an American-Soviet "agreement to disagree." Sadat's War Minister Muhammad Sadeq went twice to Moscow, desperately seeking more arms from the Soviet Union. The only explanation for Soviet coolness toward the most important Arab state is that the Soviet Union attached more importance to its détente relationship with the United States than to the satisfaction of Arab aspirations concerning Israel.

Paradoxically, the exodus of the Soviet personnel from Egypt relieved the Soviet-Egyptian relationship from a burdensome strain. The issues were clear-cut. All that the USSR had to do in Cairo was to maintain Egypt's military power, without responsibility for Egyptian policy. And all that Egypt had to do in return was to allow the Soviet Union to go on using facilities at Port Said and Alexandria so as to enable its fleet to exercise surveillance of American naval movements into the Mediterranean. In the United States and in Israel there was an atmosphere of relaxation. The conventional—and wrong—assumption in both countries was that the expulsion of the Soviet mission from Egypt signaled the eclipse of Soviet influence in the Middle East, and a greater chance of stability.

This complacency was ill-judged. The reality of global power determines that the Soviet Union, like the United States, cannot be "eclipsed" for long as an active influence on the life of the region. The Middle East has a crossroads quality which places it in the exposed path of all the currents that move human affairs. Involvement in universal issues is endemic to the region by virtue of its immutable geography and its uniquely intricate history.

The resolve of Sadat in 1973 to shake the frozen deadlock by a military shock was almost certainly an independent Egyptian decision, supplemented later by synchronization with Syria. But it provided a chance for the Soviet Union to assert its presence in successive phases of the war and its aftermath. It is clear that the Russians must have known of the Egyptian-Syrian decision for war when they began to move their families out of Cairo and Damascus. The USSR was not invited to sanction this decision but it evidently did nothing to deter or prevent it. Its calculation must have been that if Soviet arms in Arab hands secured even a limited success, this would rehabilitate Moscow's reputation as an ally of the strong, while if the Arabs were humiliated in the battlefield there would always be enough time for the Soviet Union to interpose itself and force a cease-fire. As for the possible American reaction, this was always incalculable by reason of the pluralism of American objectives, but if American concern and anger became sharp enough to threaten détente, the Soviet Union would know how to set urgent consultation on foot.

The subsequent steps taken by the Soviet Union when the Yom Kippur War erupted were all calculated to prove that large movements of events in the Middle East are not feasible without Soviet participation. In mid-October, when Israel and the United States were ready to support a cease-fire "in place" at a moment of Israeli military success, Kissinger had to go to Moscow to work out an agreed formula. The two superpowers later joined in sponsoring Security Council Resolution 338, which urged a cease-fire to be followed by negotiations for peace. When the Israeli advance into Egypt continued after the cease-fire resolution, the Soviet Union resorted to intimidatory threats that deterred Israel and impelled the United States to a two-phased policy: first, confrontation up to the point of a nuclear alert so as to convey the intensity of United States involvement; and then, compliance with the Soviet desire to be an active partner in the diplomacy of the region.

The Geneva Peace Conference on the Middle East that convened in December 1973 had the United States and the Soviet Union as its joint chairmen. This was potentially an important moment for the USSR, whose central purpose was to prevent the Middle East from becoming the unique preserve of American diplomacy. The Geneva Conference was the first occasion on which Arab and Israeli governments had sat together at foreign-minister level. But after the adoption of a unanimous conference resolution in favor of negotiating disengagement agreements, the Soviet Union paid the penalty of its unbalanced diplomatic structure. Without access to Israel, the Soviet Union could not function in a mediating role. The elaboration of the disengagement accords required negotiation of a most meticulous kind, involving constant travel between Jerusalem, Cairo and, later, Damascus. Henry Kissinger brilliantly exploited the parallel relationships of his country with the Arab states and Israel, as well as his own talent for detailed mediation. His shuttle diplomacy produced three agreements involving Israel, Egypt and Syria between January 1974 and May 1975, while the Soviet Union looked on in open frustration. Gromyko's self-inflicted inability to hold parallel talks with Israel and the Arab states ruled him out as an equal negotiator. At the worst, Moscow was able to obtain Syrian agreement to a procedure that helped to save Soviet honor. Hafiz al Assad maneuvered the negotiation of a disengagement agreement with Israel into a deadlock which only became unfrozen when the United States agreed to participation by Soviet officers in the signature of the accord at Geneva.

Yet the fact that the three accords were authentically American achievements had become embedded in the Arab and Israeli consciousness. The Arabs would now look to Moscow for arms and to Washington for diplomacy. The diminished Soviet role became even more conspicuous in 1977–79, when the United States, through President Jimmy Carter, successfully played a lone hand in mediating accords culminating at Camp David in a peace treaty between Egypt and Israel. All that the Soviet Union could do was denounce this treaty in vehement terms; but this involved the bizarre spectacle of a Great Power condemning the fact that two member states of the United Nations which had been at war for thirty years had now decided to live permanently at peace with each other. Soviet opposition to the Egypt-Israel accord was not congenial to its "peace-loving" image.

If exclusion from the Egyptian-Israeli dialogue was a source of anger and frustration for Moscow, what can be said of the Lebanese war of 1982–83? None of the parties concerned set their eyes toward Moscow; the United States mediated with mutual Arab-Israeli consent at every stage. The war officially ended in May 1983 with a Lebanese-Israeli agreement negotiated through exclusive American mediation and with no regard or reference to the Soviet Union at all. Indeed, all that the USSR could show for the war was the humiliating defeat of the Syrian air-combat system, which depended exclusively on Soviet-manufactured aircraft and advanced Soviet-made SA missiles. Apart from their disappointment with this equipment, the Syrians and other Arabs had good reason to ask what kind of ally the Soviet Union really was. Not only had it refrained from military involvement in support of Syria, it had also shown a curious diplomatic passivity. It had neither rushed to public forums such as the Security Council of the United Nations nor sought to arrest Israeli advances by the kind of menace which had been so effective in similar situations in 1956, 1967 and October 1973. The PLO could still rely on Moscow for arms, which did not, however, include tanks or aircraft; but when it came to the final reckoning at which losses and gains are measured against each other, it was the United States alone that stood between the parties, cajoling, proposing, conciliating, challenging and eventually presiding with avuncular satisfaction at triumphant compromises. Between 1974 and the summer of 1983, six agreements were signed between Israel and

Arab states, all of them with active American mediation. The Soviet Union could not avoid the impression that a Pax Americana would prevail in a region which the USSR regards as its own back yard. To achieve equality of status, if not superiority, would now become the central purpose of Soviet policy in the Middle East.

It was evident that the Soviets could not afford to acquire a reputation for ineffectiveness in this area. There had been much unwise rhetoric in America and Israel disparaging the Soviet missiles and aircraft which had easily been defeated by the Israeli air force in the Lebanese war. Soviet apathy toward Syria had also been apprehensively noted by countries that tended to rely on Russian support. A superpower cannot afford to be humiliated or downgraded, and by the early summer of 1983 the Soviet Union had replaced its SA-6 missiles in Lebanon with the more formidable SA-5 and had swiftly replenished and reinforced the Syrian air force. In a further effort to combat the impression of American dominance, the Soviets also moved in the diplomatic field; they used their full influence to support Syria in its refusal to withdraw its forces from Lebanon. This meant that Israel would also retain its forces in Lebanon and, accordingly, that the agreement negotiated by Secretary of State George Shultz for the withdrawal of all foreign forces from Lebanon would not take effect.

All that the Soviet Union could prove by this strategy was a negative capacity to prevent American policies from taking root. Moscow still lacked a positive ability to shape things its own way and the conclusion that the Soviet position has in general become weaker in the Middle East during the past decade stands intact. The senior Middle Eastern states in terms of military, strategic and economic importance are Egypt, Israel and Saudi Arabia, while Jordan and Lebanon are crucial for the peace process, and Morocco and Tunisia are increasingly influential in Arab politics. The United Arab Emirates on the Gulf are sparsely populated, but their oil resources and strategic situation are significant. In all these countries, the West has more influence and prestige than the Soviet Union; and the fact that Iran is anti-Western does not make it pro-Soviet. In these conditions, there is little consolation for the USSR in its alliances with Syria, Libya and South Yemen. The Soviet Union seems to make its strongest alliances with isolated Arab countries, while America and Western Europe hold the central ground. Unlike Southeast Asia and the Indian subcontinent, the Middle East is a region in which countries supported by the Soviet Union tend to lose their wars, so that Soviet weapons are more associated with memories of defeat than with recollections of victory. This may be an unfair deduction, since the most excellent equipment is likely to fail if it is used in an ineffective way; but impressions are no less decisive than facts in shaping popular attitudes and opinions. All that the Soviets could achieve by their arms supplies was to maintain a tenuous hold on Arab consideration. They could not compensate for other handicaps. The ideology of Marxism-Leninism does not attract those who have been accustomed to revere Muslim and Arab traditions. And the Soviet Union is not a convincing candidate for the economic rehabilitation of Arab countries; a Great Power that has difficulty in feeding its own population will find its advice and counsel received skeptically by those responsible for the management of struggling Middle Eastern economies. As if these obstacles in the path of Soviet-Arab understanding were not enough, there came the Russian invasion of Afghanistan, which alienated Muslim, Arab and Third World opinion everywhere.

The volatile nature of inter-Arab relations has weighed heavily on the Soviet Union in its efforts to win a stable position in the Arab world. Moscow has often found itself on both sides of a regional war. In the Lebanese civil war of 1976 its two friends, Syria and the PLO, fought each other with Soviet weapons. So did Egypt and Libya in their short engagement in the summer of 1977 and, for a longer period, Ethiopia and Somalia in 1977–78.

The Soviet Union has also derived little benefit from its constant support of the Arabs against Israel since the early 1950s. What the Arabs sought from the Soviets was not rhetorical sympathy but effective aid. The paradoxical situation was that the Soviet Union had been too pro-Arab to be of much use. It had no ability whatever to influence Israel in a manner that would lead to the restoration of Arab-populated territories that had come into Israel's control during the 1967 war. The Soviet Union had renounced that influence by its contemptuous attitude toward Israel, culminating in the rupture of the lines of diplomatic communication. On the other hand, the United States succeeded in the first Kissinger shuttle (1974) and thereafter in inducing Israel to yield territories to Egypt and Syria without being compelled to do so through military pressure. From that point on the United States became more important and significant in the eyes of the Arab leaders than the Soviet Union could hope to be.

A similar situation had arisen previously in relation to France. In 1956–57, when France had intimate relations with Israel, its leaders were able to play a decisive role in securing Israeli withdrawal from Sinai and Gaza after the 1956 explosion, at a time when the withdrawal negotiation had encountered deadlock. In 1967, when De Gaulle adopted an extremely pro-Arab position, France lacked any capacity to influence Israel in a direction favorable to crucial Arab interests.

The unexpected conclusion is that the Soviet Union will only become an effective friend of the Arabs when it ceases to be a virulent adversary of Israel. But the steps that it would have to take to moderate its anti-Israel posture would, in the short term, cause shock and resentment in the Arab world. To this date the Soviet Union has not shown any inclination to incur a short-term risk on behalf of a long-term goal. It is learning the hard truth that there is no real relation between military strength and diplomatic influence. The Soviet Union will always have a capacity for pressure and intimidation, and its lavish arms supplies will ensure the continuation of its conspicuous presence in the Arab sector of the Middle East. But the other factors that inhibit the full deployment of its influence add up to the conclusion that Moscow will not be the main architect of the Middle Eastern future. This does not mean that it will be possible to complete the peace process without any input by the Soviet Union. Egypt, Israel and the United States had a clear interest in the exclusion of Moscow, and Lebanon had no particular interest in broadening the mediation effort beyond the United States. But the Soviet Union has a much stronger link with the Syrian regime and the Palestinian movement. It may well have the power to obstruct any settlement involving these two peoples with whom the relations of the United States are tenuous and abrasive. It is not inconceivable that the United States will have second thoughts about its brave rhetoric proclaiming the monopoly of American responsibility in the Middle East.

The American Role

The predominance of the United States in the Middle East evolved from small beginnings. It was not the result of any deliberate ambition. The United States would have been quite content to observe the continuation of British influence in the region and to limit its own role to the support of an ally and to such activity as membership in the United Nations imposed on the Great Powers. The retirement of British power drew the United States into the center of Middle Eastern politics in a mood of reluctance. The vacuum in Turkey and Greece was filled by the United States acting under the Truman Doctrine. Oil discoveries in Saudi Arabia sharpened the sensitivities of the Pentagon and the business establishment. But more than anything else, it was the Palestine problem as it presented itself after World War II that projected the United States into the center of the turmoil. American involvement in the Middle East has become more and more intricate and compelling with every passing year. The United States is today the guarantor of Israel's security and economic viability, the protector of the Gulf oil states, the source of the region's development aid programs, the friend and supporter of Egypt, Lebanon, Jordan and Saudi Arabia, and the assiduous conciliator whenever regional tension threatens to burst into flame. To balance the picture we must recall that the United States is also the main target of Iran's passionate hostility and Libya's rancor as well as Syria's hostility. No nation in the Middle East is totally satisfied with American policy, but none of them can begin to define its own diplomatic and strategic direction without taking the United States as the central theme of its preoccupation.

American strategists began the postwar era in the conviction that their dangers flowed from the prospect of Soviet expansion. The Kremlin's starting point was opposition to Western bases. There was a period in the 1960s when it seemed likely that the USSR would come to be the predominant foreign power in the area. To be the main ally and friend of Egypt, Syria, Iraq, Libya and Afghanistan implies a formidable centrality. But Egypt and Sudan are 50 percent of the Arabic-speaking world, and when Cairo became wholeheartedly aligned with Western countries in its diplomatic, military and economic priorities, no other advance in the Arab world could balance Moscow's loss. Just when American policymakers and public opinion could become somewhat more relaxed about the prospects of a Soviet takeover, they became startled by the idea that regional "non-powers" could strike at the very heart of Western interests and that to be without military power did not prevent some of these nations from becoming dangerous to Western security. The brief but frightening oil embargo in 1973 and the anti-Western xenophobia of Khomeini's Iran were not Soviet-inspired, even if the Soviet Union drew comfort and delight from them after the event. It was evident that an American statesmanship that kept both its eyes riveted on Moscow alone would be effectively myopic and, in some cases, blind. The American gaze would now have to wander restlessly from the Soviet Union to Tehran, from Israel to Saudi Arabia, from Beirut to Amman. It could not be monopolized by the global rivalry alone.

It is characteristic of American diplomacy that it seeks to accommodate a bewildering pluralism of objectives within every definition of its interests. It recoils from sharp, exclusive alignments and thus ends up by distributing displeasure across a very broad field. Other nations complain that the United States is not a 100 percent friend; but they also acknowledge that its adversarial postures are not intense and immutable. America's allies always have something to fear and its foes have something for which to hope. There is no sector of its diplomacy in which this ambiguity is more marked than the Middle East. The United States wishes to be an ally of Israel but also of some Arab states. It wants to resist Soviet expansion but without risking war. It seeks to buttress existing regimes but also to keep a vigilant eye on new, emergent forces. It supports Palestinian freedom but objects to a separate Palestinian state. It is sincerely affronted by the violence done to Afghanistan but will not encourage any real hope that Soviet encroachment will be resisted. In the Cyprus conflict, it supports the Greeks on principle but will do nothing to end Turkish occupation in practice. It is disturbed by every expansion of Soviet influence but does not hesitate to cooperate with the Soviet Union in crisis management and in efforts to defuse explosive situations.

On the face of it, this seems to add up to vagueness and irresolution. On deeper analysis, these versatile attitudes reflect a desire to be universally present across the entire range of Middle Eastern realities and interests. America seeks a relationship not with a part of the Middle East but with the whole of it. Nothing is completely written off.

The first steps of the United States in the Middle East after World War II were reactive and not calculated. If Britain gave up its protective role in Turkey and Greece, the United States was faced with a choice between filling the gap or reconciling itself to the rise of Soviet power in the vacuum left by Britain's departure. There was thus only one possible response. When Russia explored the possibility of retaining its occupation of northern Iran, the United States had the power and the will to induce Soviet withdrawal. When Britain created another vacuum by its relinquishment of the mandate in Palestine and referred the issue to the United Nations, the United States, as the central actor in the UN system and the home of the largest of the world's Jewish communities, had to take the lead in designing a new blueprint for Western policy in the Middle East.

In the first decade after the war there was no doubt that the Middle East lay within the sphere of influence of the Western world, of which the United States was the acknowledged leader. When the Soviet Union registered disconcerting gains through the pro-Soviet attitudes of Nasser in Egypt and the growth of anti-Western impulses in other countries, the United States sought an answer analogous to its policy in Europe: it tried to establish a regional defense organization through the Baghdad Pact and CENTO. When this form of influence was revealed to be unattainable and unrealistic, United States policy sought other channels of expression. It was plain that the Middle East was not going to be "organized" in a tidy, compact framework under American leadership. Each sector of the region was a separate field to be worked and watered with dubious prospect of any harvest. The Middle East is an area on which nothing is certain but almost everything is possible. Lacking the prolonged familiarity of British and French policymakers with the intricacies and enigmas of Middle Eastern cultures, American diplomats and political leaders tended to approach the region with intellectual diffidence. They presumed that everything moved there by impulses that were different from those in other regions. It was believed that Muslim, Arab or Semitic minds were more tortuous and incalculable than the minds of other breeds of men. There was an assumption of mystery. The myth of Western Orientalism, according to which the Arabic language is less prone to exactitude and more afflicted by ambiguity than other tongues, won strong credence among those dealing with Middle Eastern problems.

The truth is that most of these generalizations are journalistic nonsense; Arabic can be as precise or as vague as the minds and intentions of those who speak and write it wish it to be. If it is true that the Arabs as the heirs of a literary civilization attach great importance to words and images, the same characteristic can be detected in Latin diplomacy and culture as well. Romantic metaphors which credit both Jews and Arabs as "Semites" with a propensity for sharp, uncompromising, fanatical, militant ways of thought have an ironic sound when they proceed from Europeans whose passions have plunged mankind in its most uninhibited orgies of violence. Western and Israeli spokesmen sometimes speak of Arabs as people who "only understand the language of force." Research would reveal that Arabs react to force much as do other peoples; they resist it when they can, and yield to it when they must. Israeli nationalism is conventionally described by its critics as excessive to the point of being chauvinistic. There is a quality of devotion to country which people call "patriotism" when they possess it themselves and "chauvinism" when they observe it in others.

Diplomacy in the Middle East is not assisted by this tendency to detach it from other areas of human experience and to portray its actors as exotic creatures subject to special laws and unique impulses. Statesmen who have dealt with European and American affairs are particularly affected by the idea that the Middle East is a special world for which their previous experience has not prepared them. Kissinger describes how he became "immersed in the ambiguities, passions and frustrations of that maddening, heroic and exhilarating region" where diplomacy was "an agonizing swamp of endless maneuvering and confusion." This is how most peoples feel when they discover new domains; after a few years Kissinger had learned, as have others before and since, that such themes as balance of power, national ambition, resistance to external control, and assertion of identity are as prevalent in the Middle East as elsewhere.

Once it had resigned itself to the idea of being the most influential external factor in Middle Eastern diplomacy, the United States developed its attitudes by a pragmatic approach based on trial and error. There was rather more error than trial in the early years. With the passage of time the United States abandoned the hope of an American monopoly; influence would clearly have to be shared with the Soviet Union. The task was to widen the areas of American influence and restrict the expansion of Soviet predominance. The Middle Eastern states would not be asked to identify themselves with the West against the Communist world; it would be enough if most of them avoided blatant anti-Western alignments. American economic aid would be available to those who sought it, but there would be no resentment against those who looked elsewhere. (The refusal of the United States to finance the Aswan Dam in Egypt, thus opening the door to Soviet entry, was swiftly regarded by the United States as an exceptional error no less flagrant than the attempt to organize Arab states in a formal defense alliance. American interests were soberly and unambitiously defined: support of the independence of the sovereign states in the region; freedom of trade and maritime passage; resistance to Communist domination, but without recourse to war; maintenance of a naval presence in the East Mediterranean as a precaution against Soviet intimidation; support of the cease-fire and armistice agreements which had ended the 1948 Arab-Israeli war; periodic explorations of the field to see if it was possible to resolve the Arab-Israeli dispute; free use of the oil resources of the area in conditions of equal trade and barter; close relations with Turkey as a NATO bastion and with Iran as a stabilizing element in the Gulf; encouragement of regional development projects such as the Jordan Water Scheme approved by Israel, Jordan and Syria; and a general if not excessively obtrusive attempt to get Middle Eastern peoples to think well of American interests and ideals.

All this is a fairly conventional list of a Great Power's interests in a region where it does not enjoy total control. What cuts across it is the addition of a unique dimension for which there is no parallel in any other realm of American concern. The relationship of the United States with Israel and its reaction to the Arab-Israeli conflict occupy a vast proportion of the time and preoccupation devoted by American policymakers to the Middle East.

There is nothing in the international system quite similar to the relationship between the United States and Israel. What makes it exceptional in the first instance is the enormous disparity of power and influence between the two partners. In theory this should result in the total subservience of the smaller partner to the will and caprice of the stronger. Soviet, Arab and some American observers are stunned when they note that this is not the case. The capacity of small countries to assert their independent interest and judgment against those of powerful allies is a feature of the modern diplomatic era, and the Israeli-American dialogue is merely the most conspicuous example of a general tendency. The huge disparity of power does not imply that the smaller partner has no independent options.

From the moment of its active entry into the domain of Middle

Eastern politics the United States carried on its shoulders a consciousness of responsibility for the outcome of the Zionist enterprise. This
has required an unceasing exercise of balance; the cultivation of relations with the Arab world has to be accompanied by a sense of obligation toward Israel's security and welfare. The circle has to be squared.

There is no single, exclusive explanation for the willingness of the
United States to incur Arab indignation in order to vindicate its obligation toward Israel. Sentiment and chivalry cannot be excluded from
the pattern of motivation. Many Americans see in Israel a re-enactment
of their own history. A people of immigrants and pioneers is constructing a new society and culture out of a bewildering diversity of origins
and identities. The founders of the American republic had recognized
their debt to the Hebrew prophetic tradition for the principles of
individual and social virtue that inspired their own struggle. Biblical
ideas and concepts flowed copiously in the literature and rhetoric of
the American Revolution. Thomas Jefferson and Benjamin Franklin
had originally wished the seal of the Union to portray the children of
Israel fleeing across the Red Sea in their quest for freedom. The seal
was to bear the slogan: "Resistance to tyrants is obedience to God."
The idea that the descendants of the ancient Israelites were celebrating a reunion with the land and language of their original nationhood
stirred romantic chords of memory. The pathos of Jewish suffering
which had reached a terrifying climax in the Holocaust deepened
American understanding of the motives that impelled the Jewish Return. The fact that millions of American Jews stood in steadfast support of Israel's rebirth ensured that Israel's cause would have a
constant and vigorous resonance in the political and public life of the
United States. By the time the United States assumed an active role in
the Middle East, it had developed an ambivalence that persists to this
day: Arab and Israeli aspirations would have to live together in the
complex fabric of America's Middle Eastern policy. Neither of them
would be denied and neither of them would be unconditionally supported.

This acrobatic quest for equilibrium between two incompatible objectives did not seem impossible or particularly awkward in the early
years of the postwar age. The United Nations majority, including the
Soviet Union, advocated Israel's statehood; the United States was taking its place within a broad international consensus. But in the 1950s,
when the Soviet Union had deserted Israel's cause and the Arab world
refused to accept Israel as an enduring reality, America's role became
more delicate. It still supported and defended Israel's legitimacy but
did little to ensure its physical survival. Instead of maintaining a balance of deterrent strength for Israel, the United States suggested that
Israel should seek its security in a policy of concession to Arab nation-

alism. Since the only "concession" that interested the Arab world was the annulment of Israel's sovereign existence, there was nothing that Israel could do to further that principle, even if it were so disposed. The American attitude to Israel in its first decade was benevolent, condescending and not especially invigorating. Having alienated the Arabs by supporting Israel's independence, American policymakers spent much of their effort in apologetic attempts to reassure the Arab states that support of Israel would not be the only or even the principal objective of United States policy. American persuasion was now devoted more to urging Israel to yield territory and to admit implacably hostile refugees than to induce Arab states to negotiate peace treaties with Israel. When this policy reached the absurdity of refusing to correct the arms balance shattered by Soviet supplies to Egypt, Israel's situation was precarious. There was a definite prospect that by 1957, Israeli propeller aircraft would be driven out of the air by an Egyptian air force that had entered the jet age. Israel's survival would then be at the mercy of its adversaries. It was objectively inevitable that Israel would take pre-emptive action. It did so in 1956 in the Suez in concert with Britain and France, which had their own accounts to settle with Nasser. The United States reacted with fury against its Western allies and with somewhat more sympathy toward Israel, which, at least, had a rational reason for expressing its concern by military action. The fact that Israel's campaign was successful while that of France and Britain was clumsily inept also played a role in mitigating American indignation. The democratic world suffers from a marked scarcity of victories and a surplus of failures, and Israel has done more than most democracies to redress this deficit.

Between 1956 and 1957 the United States was drawn into a more active role as a result of the virtual eclipse of British and French influence. The United States could not complain of this solitude, since its own exaggerated irascibility in the Suez crisis had contributed to the banishment of London and Paris from their share of responsibility in the Middle East. There is much talk about "Western policies" in the Middle East, but in all candor, there is now only America. Having told Israel, France and Britain that their fear of Nasser's power and malice was exaggerated, a red-faced United States found itself sending Marines to Lebanon in 1958 and encouraging a British military expedition to Jordan for the express purpose of restraining Nasser's alleged campaign of expansion. Soviet competition for predominance in the Middle East seemed to have a serious prospect of success. The Western world was not showing much capacity to reach a tolerable relationship with Arab nationalism; American policy was never warm enough to satisfy Israel but was always sufficiently respectful of Israeli interests to alienate the Arabs.

The Six-Day War (1967) and Thereafter

The turning point came in 1967. Believing that his own power, Soviet support and American passivity gave him the chance of changing the direction of Arab history, Nasser embarked on an extraordinary gamble. In the eleven years since the 1956 war, Israel had consolidated itself to a point where its permanence would soon be beyond serious challenge. Its population had grown to 2.8 million. The economy was less fragile. A green carpet of verdant cultivation moved across the landscape like an advancing tide. From a million acres Israel was producing 85 percent of the food consumed by its own people while also exporting $130 million worth of agricultural products to the world markets. Israeli industry was developing on the Swiss or Japanese pattern, compensating by high technology for the scarcity of primary materials. Nearly a hundred nations, including those of Africa, most of Asia and Eastern Europe maintained diplomatic links with Israel. The National Water Carrier had been completed, conveying water from the north to the parched Negev wilderness. An oil pipeline at Eilat carried Iranian oil from the Red Sea to the Mediterranean. Hundreds of Israeli scientists, doctors, engineers, agronomists and other specialists were sharing their experience with other developing nations on four continents. It was clear that the Arab view of Israel as a dark conspiracy, a rapacious colonial adventure or a temporary crusade had been rejected by the opinion and emotion of mankind. Arab leaders could not count on Israel's spontaneous disintegration or on the help of the world community to bring about Israel's ruin. If they hoped to "destroy" Israel, they would have to do it themselves. And it was now or never; a few more years of consolidation would put Israel's statehood and status beyond recall.

Nasser now played what he must have known to be his final card. His armies were bogged down in a hopeless campaign for the conquest of Yemen, and his popularity was ebbing away in many Arab lands where his radicalism was distrusted by the conservative rulers whom he periodically tried to overthrow. When he besieged Israel in May 1967, after dismissing the UN forces in Sinai and Gaza and imposing the blockade on Israel's southern coast, he was rewarded by an ecstatic outburst of Arab militancy and solidarity. He had announced his decision to impose the blockade and siege to officers at the air base at Bir Gafgafa. But far beyond his fervent audience in the baking desert heat he was appealing to the whole domain of Arabism, calling its sons to such a display of union, sacrifice, hatred, resilience and selfless passion as they had not known since the stirring and ferocious days of their early history. He brought about a deep erosion of Israeli nerves. As Israelis counted up the huge accumulations of tanks, planes, guns and troops arrayed against them on three fronts, they felt the icy wind of vulnerability. Their tragic history warned them against any temptation of complacency. They noted that the outside world took the prospect of their extinction very seriously. They could not fail to observe how foreign governments and international agencies were fleeing from the scene, abandoning Israel to a lonely fate. On June 5, 1967, Israeli air and land forces erupted into action. They were immediately triumphant. Between a single dawn and nightfall they had passed from peril to victory. Within five more days they had destroyed over 400 aircraft and 800 tanks. Nasser's dream of a Middle East, without Israel, united under his leadership lay about his feet in ruins. Israel dominated the military scene throughout the Middle East. Large territories in Sinai, Golan, the West Bank and Gaza were under its jurisdiction. The adversary had not merely been pushed into the distance; he was shorn of power.

The history of Israel as a state and, to some extent, of the Middle East as a region, is divided between what occurred before the Six-Day War and what happened after it. It was a transforming event. The changes in the global and regional balance produced by the Israeli reaction to the Egyptian-Syrian initiative have not ceased to be operative to this day.

The United States had done little to deserve any good fortune arising from the war, but it was nonetheless a major beneficiary of Israel's victory. The Soviet Union's pretensions to be an effective ally of Arab regimes had been drastically discredited. The Kremlin had made every conceivable error. It had underestimated its Israeli adversary, overestimated the military power of Cairo and Damascus, and exaggerated its own capacity to alter military realities by using its influence in UN bodies. It resembled a person who carefully examines an airline timetable for the express purpose of missing all the flights. Conversely, the United States emerged as the only potential mediator of the regional conflict. It did not call on Israel this time to relinquish its territorial gains without the recompense of a peace settlement. U.S.-Israeli consultations before the Israeli military action ensured that this mistake would not be repeated. Although Egypt and Syria broke their relations with Washington to support the pretense that the Arabs had been defeated by Western attacks, not by the lowly Israelis, it was clear that nowhere except in Washington would they find a bridge back to reality and to the recuperation of their basic interests. The Soviet miscalculations in 1967 stand as an exemplary illustration of the fact that Soviet policymakers are not the cool-headed, realistic, lucid and infallible supermen that some Western observers deem them to be. For eighteen years the United States has been in possession of the diplomatic field.

The Israeli Dilemma

But the main impact of the 1967 war was on the Middle Eastern adversaries themselves. Israel had emerged from the sharp crisis of self-confidence into which it had been plunged by Nasser's audacious challenge. It had shown the qualities that glow most brightly in adversity; and it had carried its banner forward in an atmosphere of intense world sympathy. Israel's example in 1967 seemed to have something to say to small, threatened communities everywhere. In Israel there was the consciousness of having lived a unique and elevating moment. Yet there was still a twinge of melancholy. The victory had been memorable, but the peril that preceded it vibrated even more strongly in the nation's memory than the triumph itself. Israel emerged from the war victorious but vulnerable; the Arabs were defeated but strongly assertive. Having failed to dictate a settlement from a position of strength, they sought to dictate it from a position of weakness. Their demand was that Israel should simply forget about the war and re-create the very conditions out of which it had fought its way. It was the first war in history in which the victor sued for peace while the vanquished demanded unconditional surrender.

At first sight it appeared that the crushing failure of the Arab challenge would leave no choice but that of a peace settlement. This expectation was too logical for Middle Eastern history to absorb. The unexpected factor was that Nasser's leadership survived his defeat; this is something that rarely happens to those who initiate and lose wars. The Arab leaders solved their predicament by denying that there had been any defeat attributable to leadership. They ascribed the disaster to historic causes, to defects in education and social development, to excessive subservience to Islam, to inadequate observance of Islam, to the treachery of the Western imperialists, to the apathy of the Soviet ally—to everything except to wrong decisions by Gamal Abdel Nasser. But if the basic decision to provoke confrontation was not to be repudiated or criticized, it was unlikely that a new course would be taken after the defeat. It soon became clear that the Six-Day War had not created the conditions for an early peace. Israel had occupied no Arab capitals, overthrown no Arab regimes. It could not, like the victorious allies in two world wars, bring the vanquished leaders to railway compartments or the decks of aircraft carriers to hear the terms of a dictated peace. Israel could impose its own security on them, but could not impose peace. The Arabs could not recapture their territories but they could deny a peace settlement.

And yet, in the longer run, there was more hope of peace than before. For the first time Israel had cards to play; it held something

which the Arabs wished to recover and which was therefore a basis for
an eventual negotiation. On the very morrow of the Six-Day War, in
mid-June 1967, Israel offered total restitution of Egyptian and Syrian
territory in exchange for peace treaties and also proposed a solution
elaborated by one of its ministers, Yigal Allon, under which most of
the territory in the West Bank and Gaza would revert to a Jordanian-
Palestinian federation. The Arab position was that they wanted 100
percent of the territories and would give zero percent of peace. A
decade later the Egyptian-Israeli treaty would prove that the formula
"peace for territory" was valid and realistic and that the Six-Day War
had created the objective conditions of an Israeli-Arab settlement.

Yet the absence of progress toward this goal made the first six years
after the Six-Day War a disappointing period for diplomacy. Burdened
with the leadership that had provoked the war, the Arab governments
were unwilling to modify their "all or nothing" demands; Israel had
to renounce everything and receive nothing. Many Israelis who had
begun by regarding the captured territories as cards to play at a peace
table ended up by falling in love with the cards and embracing them
so tenaciously as to eliminate their bargaining value. Yet it remained
true, as was subsequently proved, that if at any time an Arab government had offered a peace treaty to Israel, the Israeli attitude on the
retention of territories would have changed dramatically.

The period between the wars of 1967 and 1973 marked a change in
the configuration of the conflict. It had hitherto been regarded as a
contest of wills and interests between the Arab world and Israel. But
the rise of Palestinian organizations such as El Fatah and the PLO gave
a new twist to the problem. After some eruptions of military action and
spectacular and horrifying acts of terrorism, these movements added
a political dimension to their activity. Their device was to elevate the
concept of "Palestine" to a point at which Israel disappeared. So long
as the conflict was portrayed as lying between Israel and the Arab
world, sympathy went to Israel. It was enough to compare Israel's
sparse territory with the huge expanse of Arab lands in order to conclude that Arab nationalism did not have much to complain about. But
when the contest was presented as being not between Israel and the
Arabs, but between Israel and the Palestinians, the perspective
changed. All the gains of Arab nationalism in twenty states outside
Palestine were taken for granted as though they had no effect on the
balance of equity between the rights of the Arab and Jewish peoples
to independence. Previous roles were reversed. Israel could be portrayed as powerful, sated, established, recognized, while the Palestinians were, by contrast, dispossessed, dissatisfied, homeless, irredentist;
above all, their basic problem was unresolved. By this ingenuity Arab
nationalism was making an unprecedented claim to 100 percent of

self-determination. Wherever an Arab community existed, it had a right to statehood that excluded any competing right; Arabs had to have sovereignty everywhere, Jews nowhere.

The substitution of the "Palestinian" for the "Arab" image thus had a confusing effect on those sections of opinion which had traditionally supported Israel's struggle. Israel was transformed from the victim of an unparalleled hatred into the author of a great wrong. It had been converted overnight from David to Goliath. The antiestablishment current is strong in modern culture. It was now flowing away from Israel and toward its adversaries. On the other hand the pressure of hostility as well as revolting acts of murder performed by the PLO exclusively against Israeli civilians (with a special emphasis on children and air travelers) provoked a corresponding hardening of Israeli attitudes. The deadlock grew more intractable with every passing month. In August 1970, Israel, Egypt and Jordan accepted a formula for opening negotiations through UN Ambassador Gunnar Jarring. This led to a change in Israel's domestic alignment, with Menachem Begin and his party leaving the Cabinet of Prime Minister Golda Meir in protest. But so long as the parties were merely exchanging documents and "proving" each other's intransigence, there was no prospect of the intimate, meticulous comparison of interests and attitudes which only negotiation can engender.

While the lack of a settlement in the period 1967–73 has deep roots in the psychology and emotion of the contending states, there were also errors in the diplomatic field. No Arab-Israeli agreement, however limited in scope, has ever been obtained without third-party assistance; and the mistakes of well-intentioned mediators have often been just as decisive as the obduracy of the parties at issue. Thus, in 1971 Egypt and Israel responded to a questionnaire from UN Ambassador Jarring on the conditions for a peace settlement. Egypt, now under Anwar el-Sadat's leadership, expressed for the first time its readiness to conclude "a peace agreement" with Israel, but it accompanied this readiness by a refusal to negotiate, and by statements on maritime passage and demilitarization which Israel was unwilling to accept without clarification. Israel, for its part, accepted the principle of "withdrawal to secure and recognized boundaries" but had reservations about a withdrawal to the precise lines that existed before the Six-Day War. Jarring, with the support of the United States, contented himself with the statement that there was a "gap" between the positions of the parties and that accordingly he saw no chance of an agreement. An assiduous and imaginative diplomacy would have expressed satisfaction at the progress achieved and promoted a more detailed discussion of the two matters on which the parties differed. Whether a "gap" is unbridgeable or not is a question for impressionist appraisal. In the

Middle East, of all places, it is unnecessary to regard an initial position as an ultimatum. If the "gap" between the parties in 1971 had been made the subject of a persistent, nagging, unremitting exploration, like that undertaken by Kissinger in the 1974 shuttle or by Jimmy Carter at Camp David in 1978–79, there is at least a fractional possibility that enough agreement would have been reached to make the subsequent Yom Kippur War avoidable.

A similar situation arose with a proposal for a "partial agreement" discussed between Sadat's administration and Israeli Defense Minister Moshe Dayan later in 1971. The idea was for Israel to withdraw its forces some distance from the Suez Canal so as to enable Egypt to reopen and operate the Canal without fear of Israeli intervention. The issue was narrowed down to two questions: What would the required distance of the withdrawal be? and, Would Egypt insist on bringing its troops across the Canal?—thus changing the military and psychological balance against Israel, which would, after all, be making the central concession of withdrawal while Egypt would only be advancing. The American emissaries, William P. Rogers and Undersecretary Joseph Sisco, noted this divergence and abandoned their mediation. In both case histories the mediators ignored the crucial effect of time on a negotiation process.

The Yom Kippur War and Thereafter (1973–1983)

There are very few successes for threat-perception in this generation, and Israel's failure, like that of the United States, to anticipate the Egyptian-Syrian assault on Israel in October 1973 is not exceptional. Six years after the Six-Day War the region underwent an experience even more dramatic and, as it turned out, even more formative than the 1967 war. In later months Egypt would remember how the war ended, while Israel would recall only how it began. It began with a triumphant military phase for Egypt in which the Egyptian army destroyed so many Israeli tanks and aircraft that an apocalyptic sense of disaster gripped the Israeli people. It ended with such a display of Israeli resilience that Israeli forces found themselves within 101 kilometers of Cairo and 40 kilometers of Damascus. Between these two situations there was a Soviet airlift to Egypt, an American airlift to Israel, a sudden flight by Kissinger to Moscow, a joint American-Soviet cease-fire negotiation, a threat of Soviet intervention, and a United States nuclear alert.

Before 1973 Anwar el-Sadat had never been regarded as a statesman with a talent for originality. His election to the presidency had been greeted with skeptical derision in Egypt and the world. He had held nothing but representational and protocolar positions with the revolutionary regime over which Nasser had presided as the directing spirit. Yet within a few years Sadat was to shake the Middle East out of its routines and inertia with two decisions of staggering audacity. His decision to attack Israel on October 6 requires a revision of the central doctrine of deterrence. This rests on the assumption that no state will knowingly start a war unless it has a hope of probable victory. Sadat began a war which he knew he could not win in the knowledge that the war itself would serve his design, irrespective of its result. It would unfreeze a deadlock that worked solely in Israel's favor and would create a compulsion for the superpowers to address themselves to the Arab-Israeli situation on which they had begun to evince a total apathy. Once he had achieved this result Sadat made his second revolutionary decision; he would recognize that the Arabs had got nothing from Israel by war and would explore the possibility of fulfilling Egyptian and Arab ambitions by offering peace.

Both as a spectacle and as a political event, Sadat's astonishing voyage to Jerusalem and his address to the Knesset stand out as one of the climactic experiences of this generation. It was immediately clear that the Middle East was set on a new course and that nothing in the region would ever be the same again. The Arab and Israeli nations both give great reverence to the past; they are saturated with history. But the past is the enemy of the future. There is nothing in the images that the Arabs derive from their past that prepares them for the idea of a Jewish sovereign state in what they call "the Arab region." In their consciousness the Middle East is a monolith of a single Arab color, so that anything in it that is not Arab or Muslim reflects itself in their mind as artificial, transient and disruptive of regional continuity. For Israelis the Middle East is a tapestry of many colors of which the salient thread was woven by Jewish experience centuries ago. Jews appear in Arab history as subjects, members of a deviant religion, doctors, scholars, merchants—but never as the bearers of an independent political and territorial legacy. The intellectual torment of Arabs in relation to Israel's emergence is authentic and should not be taken lightly.

In similar degree, Israel's past is not conducive to easy conciliation. The Jewish historic experience is tragic; it therefore generates a traumatic reaction to any proposal or innovation that has a bearing on Israel's physical security. Sadat's immense achievement was to make a simultaneous breach in the walls of Arab rejection and Israeli suspicion. For the first time the Arab world was presented by one of its leaders with a vision of the Middle East that *did* include the sovereign state of Israel. The rhetoric and literature of rejection would live on elsewhere, but in November 1977 it lost its dogmatic force and could no longer claim to be the only normative Arab doctrine

On the same day Israelis came to look on peace not as a utopian fantasy, but as a concrete and vivid reality. The Israeli consensus about the indispensability of large territorial gains immediately underwent a sharp transformation. Sadat was the first to put this prospect to a test, and his reward was immediate and dramatic. Israel made territorial concessions that nobody would have previously imagined. It is tragic that other Arab states have not tried the same approach. Israel can be empirical about the negotiation of boundaries but not about its own legitimacy or security.

Another lesson to emerge decisively from the subsequent Camp David conference in 1978–79 was that pre-negotiation rhetoric is discarded without too much difficulty under the transforming effects of direct human encounter. At the same time, a deathblow was dealt to the theory of irreconcilability according to which the dispute between Arabs and Israelis, unlike all others, is permanent, endemic, implacable and inherently insoluble. In the Arab world this theory had become axiomatic, and in Israel it had been elevated into an academic discipline which made deep inroads on the nation's mood and policies.

The refusal of other Arab states to follow Sadat's journey and to reap similar fruits is one of the frustrations and mysteries of the years that followed the Egyptian-Israeli peace treaty. Jordan, whose monarch had been the first Arab leader to understand the unreality of policies that denied Israel's existence, paradoxically launched a campaign of criticism against what Sadat had done. Much of this acrimony was due to a diplomatic error; Carter and Sadat had drawn up a blueprint for the West Bank and Gaza involving detailed provisions for Jordan's participation without doing much to ensure Jordan's presence. The United States underestimated the factor of pride and sensitivity that affect the reactions of Middle Eastern leaders.

The opposition of Jordan and the PLO to the Camp David agreement was especially ironic, since it gave the impression that Sadat had secured Egyptian interests by the total return of Sinai while abandoning the Palestinian cause. Any objective reading of the Palestinian section of the Camp David agreement would refute any such impression. Sadat had secured the adherence of Menachem Begin and Jimmy Carter to formulations which a more lucid Palestinian leadership would have regarded as a promising launching pad for a constructive quest for a solution. The Camp David agreement treats the West Bank and Gaza as an area of indeterminate status. It goes on to make clear that the status of those territories may not be determined unilaterally by Israel or by anyone else; the final determination will have to be made by Egypt, Israel, Jordan and the elected representatives of the inhabitants of the areas. It would be difficult to conceive a body composed of four members, three of them Arabs, deciding to incorporate the Arab populated areas of the West Bank into Israel. In case this unlikely event occurs, the agreement stipulates that any accord would have to be endorsed in a plebiscite among the Palestinians in the West Bank and Gaza. The agreement lays down that the permanent solution of the problem of the West Bank and Gaza will have to satisfy the "legitimate rights of the Palestinian people and their just requirements." Pending the negotiation of the permanent status of the West Bank and Gaza, there is to be a transition period of three to five years, during which "the elected representatives of the inhabitants of the West Bank and Gaza [shall] decide how they shall govern themselves consistent with the provisions of the agreement." There must also be a "withdrawal of the Israeli military administration" and a "withdrawal of Israeli armed forces . . . and their redeployment into specified security zones."

In a discussion in which sanity had even a marginal status it would be hard to see this proposal as anything but a sharp movement toward the Palestinians. Yet it was rejected vehemently by the Palestinian organizations and by most Arab states, opposed by the Soviet Union, ignored by the United Nations and received coolly by the European governments. Instead of being hailed for creating new opportunities for Palestinian nationalism, Sadat was reviled by Arab propaganda and eventually assassinated by Muslim fundamentalists. The European skepticism toward Camp David was inspired by a strange narrowness of spirit; it was pointed out that the treaty concluded between Egypt and Israel was not a "comprehensive settlement" embracing the entire region. This came illy from a continent in which the new peace and security system were negotiated over three decades with separate treaties involving Germany, Italy, Poland and the East European states, as well as Finland and the Soviet Union. It should be evident that an Israeli treaty with one Arab state is preferable to a treaty with no Arab states, and that to make unanimity a condition of progress would be tantamount to giving a veto power to the most obdurate party and the most intransigent issue. If we have to wait until all twenty-two Arab states and the Palestinians are ready to move forward together, it will be necessary to suspend all action until President Qaddafi of Libya experiences a unique spasm of lucidity.

In the final resort the Arab cause in the West Bank and Gaza will stand or fall by the decision of the Palestinian Arabs. Their diplomatic history refutes the idea that nations usually act in their own best interest. They have never missed a chance of losing an opportunity. They have persistently rejected proposals conceived largely in their own interest, only to look back to them nostalgically when they have receded from view. In September 1983, when President Reagan made proposals based on the Camp David accords emphasizing that there must be an Arab, not an Israeli destiny for the populations of the West Bank and Gaza, the PLO prevented Jordan from forming a Jordanian-Palestinian delegation to negotiate with Israel on the basis of the Reagan proposals. This is an astonishing illustration of the tenacity with which the Palestinian movement clings to its orthodox doctrine of non-recognition. Arafat had presided over the debacle of his forces in Lebanon. He was shorn of his intimidatory power. He could do nothing but embark on a series of diplomatic wanderings which had lost all sense and meaning. Nothing concrete, solid or real lay behind the façade of red carpets and protocolar honors with which he and other PLO leaders sustained the illusion of their dignity. In the West Bank and Gaza, the Palestinians felt betrayed and abandoned, but there was nobody to carry their banner into an era of opportunity. The question now is whether the Palestinians will become capable of the daring and originality which had carried Sadat's Egypt out of deadlock into the restoration of its territorial integrity.

But the mark of interrogation is not poised over the Palestinians alone. Israel too will have to confront fateful choices in the early 1980s. In the diplomatic history of the past four decades Israel's struggle stands out as an exceptionally dramatic chapter. Israel started in the late 1940s with few bargaining assets. Its geopolitical weight was unimpressive: unlike the Arab states it had little capacity to reward friends or to penalize adversaries. Yet it scored immediate victories which changed the shape of the Middle Eastern map and the direction of Jewish history. It achieved this by successfully defending its survival and by appealing to intangible emotions of historic memory, spiritual history and chivalrous conscience in many parts of the world. Israel also benefited from the errors of its adversaries. The Arab governments took their stand on the ground that Israel ought not to exist at all. The rest of humanity was not disposed to give serious weight to this unprecedented attitude. There are dozens of sovereign states in the world today, but Israel is the only one that inhabits the same land, speaks the same tongue and upholds the same faith as it did three thousand years ago. The Arab leaders underestimated the forces at work for Israel's survival. In the words of an Arab scholar: "The Arab governments made no preparation, either for peace with its concessions or for war with its sacrifices."

But Israel's victory in the quest for world recognition was not unqualified. It rested on a contract: the international community would acknowledge Israel's sovereignty, while Israel would not push its claim to the point at which the national identity of the Palestinians in a part of Palestine disappeared. The governing principle was partition. From 1948 onward, Israel had recognized the basic fact that these two nations were marked by such strong and separate national attributes that

any unitary structure would be unauthentic, coercive and morally fragile. It would be just as incongruous to place 1.3 million Palestinians
under Israeli rule against their will as it would be to accept the grotesque idea of Israel's elimination through subjection to Arab rule in
what the PLO called "a secular, unitary state." In 1967, after the Israeli
conquest of the West Bank and Gaza, Israeli governments under the
leadership of the Labor movement kept the West Bank and Gaza
juridically separate from Israel, abstained from establishing settlements in Arab-populated areas and continued to regard the occupied
territories as negotiable in a peace settlement. The new government
established by Menachem Begin in 1977 turned its back on this doctrine. It proclaimed the whole area of the Land of Israel as an integral
part of Israel's patrimony, thus closing the door on an Arab destiny for
the 1.3 million Arabs who are the kernel and essence of the "Palestine
people," recognized in the Camp David agreements as the decisive
factor in determining the permanent status of the West Bank and Gaza.
Not a single country in the world community, including those most in
favor of Israel, was prepared to support the idea that Israel's security
required the imposition of permanent Israeli jurisdiction over a foreign nation. At least half the Israeli nation opposed the idea of the
incorporation of the population of the West Bank and Gaza into Israel.
There does not exist on the surface of the inhabited globe a single state
that resembles what Israel would look like if it were to incorporate the
West Bank and Gaza coercively into Israel. A democratic country ruling a foreign nation against its will and against the will of the world
would be a unique reality. If the 1.3 million Palestinians were to be
integrated into the central political system of Israel, they would take
the balance of power in all Israeli decisions, and Israeli politics would
become a constant, restless pursuit of their votes. If, on the other hand,
the 1.3 million Palestinians are denied the equal possibility of electing
and being elected to the Israeli parliament, Israel will face the implications of becoming a state whose inhabitants have two different levels
and categories of rights and obligations: Jews and Israeli Arabs who
can elect and be elected and, a few meters away, Palestinian Arabs who
would be held down by military force in an allegiance to which they
give no real devotion. The choice between maintaining the present
territorial breadth at the expense of Israel's democratic vocation and
accepting a more compact structure for the sake of national and social
harmony will be Israel's most fateful decision in the 1980s.

If the issue sometimes seems to be in suspense, this is because the
Arabs have not created a negotiating context. Many Israelis are reluctant to hold a painful national debate about the price to be paid for
a peace settlement with the Jordanians and Palestinians if such a settlement is not available irrespective of Israel's attitude. The solution

acceptable to Israelis would not be a separate Palestinian state inspired by the irredentist philosophy and terrorist attitudes of the PLO. A settlement along the lines elaborated by former Foreign Minister Yigal Allon envisages a Jordanian-Palestinian state to the east of Israel in which the Palestinians, east and west of the river, would join under a federal structure in what would be a union of all the Palestinians under a single Arab sovereignty. The fact that there are just as many Palestinians east of the river as there are in the West Bank and Gaza makes this a logical solution. Indeed, it is so logical that it is bound to encounter great obstacles.

In any renunciation of the bulk of the territories of the West Bank and Gaza, Israelis would seek boundary changes necessary for security and a demilitarization of the territories that would be returned to Arab sovereignty. There would have to be concession on both sides: Israel would have to give up control of territories in which it has deep emotional and historic roots, and the Palestinians would have to recognize that their national identity would have to be expressed in a more limited context than that of which they have dreamed in the past. Attitudes in which no bread is considered to be preferable to a large part of the loaf have dominated Palestinian thinking for many decades. If these can be changed, Israeli responses similar to those that occurred after Sadat's initiative are not inconceivable.

By the end of 1983 the need for a compromise were dramatized for most Israelis by the Lebanese war. After a full year of tranquillity on all borders, including that with Lebanon, the Israeli government carried out a prolonged campaign in Lebanon for the purpose of destroying the PLO as a factor capable of inflicting political and physical injury on Israel. Other objectives were the conclusion of a peace treaty with a stable Lebanese leadership based on the Christian phalangists, the expulsion of Syrian forces and the weakening of Soviet influence. After a full year, none of these objectives had been achieved. Five hundred Israelis were killed in Lebanon; this was a vast increase on any possible estimate of casualties that Israel would have suffered if the war had been avoided or—at least—curtailed. Thus the remedy was more lethal than the disease. Syria emerged from the war strengthened in military power, and Soviet involvement was far more intense and dangerous than before the war. Israelis learned how stringent are the limitations of what military power can achieve beyond its basic preventive function. There was also the incalculability of a war in full momentum; there was certainly no intention to inflict harm on the Lebanese population or on innocent Palestinian civilians in camps, but a heavy price in death and suffering was in fact exacted from both of these categories of victims, and something of the burden weighed on Israel's image and conscience. The compensating benefits for Israel were the discreditation and weakening of PLO terrorism, the possibility of a more stable climate of relations with Lebanon and a greater assurance of physical security for Northern Israel.

Many nations have suffered travail in their effort to come to terms with defeat, but Israel's predicaments are those of victory. What does one do with military victory? The modern history of the Middle East teaches us that victory and defeat are relative terms. This is because war itself is no longer a distinctive and autonomous activity of which the consequences can be measured without recourse to consequences that lie beyond its own purview.

And yet in the full perspective of the post-1945 age, the record of the Middle East is not of tragedy alone. The suffering, death, poverty and rancor are all there, naked to the eye. But there is also the moving achievement of freedom for many nations, traditionally submerged under the weight of outside rulers; Arab and Jewish civilizations face each other on terms quite different from anything that they have known in history. And the questions that most Arabs are asking today are not about whether they should negotiate with Israel, but how, when and on what terms. Time and reality have had their effect—not all of them negative.

Propaganda, which is the art of persuading others of what one does not necessarily believe oneself, has run riot in the Middle East in recent decades. But behind the outer surface of their strident contention the peoples of the region are learning truer images of one another; and with that consciousness there dawns the compulsion, however slow and reluctant, of a future to be shared in peace. It is semantically necessary to speak of the Middle East as though the implied generalization had more than geographical significance. But the outlook is for diversity. Many actors, Arab and non-Arab, will interact and compete in obedience to discrete and conflicting views of their identity and interest. The unifying factors are few and weak. Outside forces, including the superpowers, will not be able to achieve meticulous solutions of the varied problems that make the Middle East so fascinating for the student and onlooker and so despairing for those charged with diplomatic responsibilities. Those who approach the Middle East from outside would do well to be skeptical of perfect, final solutions. Diplomacy is not theology; there is no salvation in it. The best hope is that tensions can be held short of explosion and that some of the slower, unobtrusive currents flowing toward stability will be allowed to take their patient course.

Book II

Chapter 7

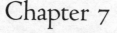

INTERNATIONAL ORGANIZATION
Myth and Reality

The Early Hope

The Secretary General of the United Nations makes a lengthy report to the General Assembly early in September each year. Like many UN documents the annual report is more often filed away than read. It rarely makes headlines. But in September 1982 Secretary General Javier Pérez de Cuéllar forced his way to public attention by an unexpected exercise in candor. He said in simple words that the United Nations is not amounting to very much, that few governments take notice of its resolutions and that the international system is marked by a "new anarchy." The background for this somber judgment was the fact that the year in review had been crowded with conflicts, and most of them had unfolded, for good or ill, exactly as they would have done if no international organization had existed. Iran and Iraq had been locked in combat in areas crucial to the world's oil supplies. Soviet troops had continued to occupy Afghanistan and to suppress guerrilla revolt. Britain and Argentina had fought each other over the Falkland Islands, with thousands of casualties. Israel had been involved in hostilities in Lebanon against the Palestine Liberation Organization and part of the Syrian army. The Polish government had suppressed the Polish Solidarity movement with the aid of threats and intimidating gestures from the Soviet Union. Savage fighting had taken place in El Salvador, with clear indications that the government forces and the guerrilla units were supplied with arms from outside. Not a week had passed without numerous clashes in Northern Ireland, with British soldiers and members of the Protestant and Catholic communities

falling dead and wounded. In most of these disputes the organs of the
United Nations had not even met for discussion, let alone action. In
some, such as the Falkland dispute and the Iraq-Iran war, the UN had
put a tentative finger into the arena of mediation, only to relapse into
passivity, letting matters take their course.

Less than forty years ago the United Nations had been born amid
ambitious claims to a controlling hand and voice in international relations. Its Charter had given it a primary role in world politics, and its
members had promised to use its machinery and procedures to the
ultimate limit of their powers. While its responsibilities were to cover
many fields of action and struggle, its major task had always been
deemed to lie in the prevention, cessation and termination of armed
conflict. The United Nations was founded at a conference in San Francisco in 1945, the largest international gathering in world history,
whose platforms resounded with slogans of redemption and hope.
Many of those who attended the sessions or followed their course in
the press and radio suspected that the expectations for the new organization were being set at an exaggerated level of optimism. But none
would have predicted that within a single generation the international
peace organization would be little more than the chorus in a Greek
drama, expressing eloquent consternation at events which it made
little effort to control.

It had been different in the beginning. The champions of international organization had rarely been content to claim that they were
merely contributing an additional technique to the existing resources
of diplomacy. They were inspired from the outset by a utopian vision.
They believed in the feasibility of perfection, and their rhetoric had a
prophetic ring. Listen to Jan Christiaan Smuts, one of the founders of
the League of Nations, writing in 1919:

> Mankind is once more on the move. The very foundations have been shaken
> and loosened and things are again fluid. The tents have been struck and
> the great caravan of humanity is once more on the march. A steadying,
> controlling, regulating influence will be required to give stability to progress,
> and to remove that wasteful friction which has dissipated so much social
> force in the past and in this war more than ever before. These great functions
> can only be adequately fulfilled by a League of Nations. Responding to such
> vital needs and coming at such a unique opportunity in history, it may well
> be destined to mark a new era in the government of man: to become to the
> peoples a guarantee of peace, to the workers of all races the Great Interna-
> tional, and to all mankind—the embodiment and living expression of the
> moral and spiritual unity of the human race.

The practitioners of traditional diplomacy have never spoken of
themselves in such inflated tones. They usually describe their role in

a skeptical, apologetic mood. They meekly resign themselves to semihumorous definitions, such as the one dating back to the sixteenth century describing an ambassador as "a man sent abroad to lie for his country." Even in modern popular parlance, to say that somebody is "diplomatic" is to hint that what he says is not strictly true. Traditional diplomacy is dominated by a sense of limitation proceeding from a somber view of human nature. It pursues relatively modest goals like stability rather than "a new era in the government of man." It accepts the notion that conflict is endemic to human relations at all levels; that the most that can be done in the international field is to keep conflict within tolerable restraint.

The movement for international organization was born in deliberate revolt against this unambitious view of diplomacy. It aspires to organize nation-states into a universal community, all of whose members are committed to mutual assistance in accordance with an objectively binding code. Its aim is nothing less than world peace under law. In this conception what each member of the community owes to the other does not depend on individual discretion according to each member's predilections, solidarities and interests. Once "aggression" is defined (which it has never been),* every member of the community is bound to resist it, even if that resistance brings it into conflict with its friends, into support of its adversaries or into the sacrifice of its particular national interest.

The UN system aspires to reconcile national sovereignty with world order. The guiding principle of the UN idea was collective security. This requires the creation of such a preponderance of power that no single state or group of states can hope to withstand it. United Nations enthusiasts, like their predecessors in the League of Nations, would be offended if we were to point out that this definition sounds very much like the idea of a balance of power. They have always thought of themselves as breakers of new ground, not as reformers of existing or previous systems. The truth is that they took the idea of a preponderance of power against aggression and gave it such a transforming twist as to earn them the claim to be innovators. In the old balance of power system, action to counter aggression was discretionary and subject to empirical decisions. It could vary from case to case. If the aggressor was your friend, or too powerful to be defied with impunity, or no more reprehensible than his victim, you might decide not to resist him at all. In that case you would probably avoid defining his action as aggression. In contradistinction to this permissive approach, resist-

*The nearest approach to an authoritative definition is the General Assembly's Resolution of December 14, 1974, but this text includes an escape clause stating that acts that appear to qualify as "aggression" may turn out to be "justified in the light of other relevant circumstances including the fact that the acts concerned or their consequences are not of sufficient gravity."

ance to aggression by an international organization was designed to be automatic, objective, universal and predictable; it was therefore to have a permanently deterrent effect. The problem of international security was not to be dealt with by casual, empirical measures; it was to be decisively solved. In the eyes of its more zealous supporters international organization was both a means and an end. It was a bright new vision that claimed to excel traditional diplomacy both in moral virtue and in efficacy.

Revolt against the Balance of Power

Multilateralism, or conference diplomacy, has had a much more dominant role in the United Nations era than in any previous time, but its ideological basis and intellectual rationalization were already fully grown in the earlier League of Nations context. It was clear at the end of World War I that international organization and collective security would become a secular religion whose devotees would look back to Woodrow Wilson as their founding prophet.

Like many religions this one had begun in rebellion against established creeds. For most of modern international history the prevalent doctrine had been that of the balance of power. The phrase itself is a metaphor derived from mechanics. It portrays a scale in exact equilibrium. The most lucid definition of its aim is by Quincy Wright: "The balance of power is a system designed to maintain a continuous conviction in every state, that if it attempted aggression it would encounter an invincible combination of the others." From this purpose there emerged a general principle that when any state became, or threatened to become, inordinately powerful, other states would regard this as a threat to their security and would respond by taking measures to enhance their own power. When the power of every state—or probable combination of states—is counterbalanced by an approximately equal power elsewhere in the system, it is assumed that aggressive action is unlikely to be undertaken or to succeed if it should be attempted.

During the century between the Congress of Vienna (1815) and the First World War (1914), the idea of a balance of power was in high repute. It seemed to be effective both as a device for describing the international system and as a means of ensuring its stability. It had always been accepted with exaggerated deference. Indeed, one of the most extraordinary features of intellectual history is the way in which the balance idea came to be compared by serious writers and statesmen to a law of nature, infallible, invariable and incapable of refutation. For several centuries, many thinkers abandoned all capacity of criticism in their reverent invocation of the balance of power. Even Rousseau had spoken of it in a pious, deterministic vein:

The actual system of Europe has precisely the degree of solidity which maintains it in a constant state of motion without upsetting it. The balance existing between the power of these diverse members of the European society is more the work of nature than of art. It maintains itself without effort in such manner that if it sinks on one side it reestablishes itself very soon on the other.

'Adam Smith,' describing the period from 1848 to 1918, wrote about balance in similar terms: "The balance of power seems to be the political equivalent of the laws of economics, both of them self-operating." Uncritical devotion to the balance of power even survived the cataclysms of two world wars, as evidenced in the statement of a skeptical modern thinker like Hans Morgenthau:

It will be shown that the international balance of power is only a particular manifestation of a general social principle to which all societies, composed of a number of autonomous units, owe the autonomy of their component parts; that the balance of power, and policies aiming at its preservation are not only inevitable but are an essential stabilizing factor in a society of sovereign nations.

This statement is the more extraordinary because it was written at a time when the efficacy of the balance principle could be empirically tested. After all, the balance concept had dominated international politics for centuries. If its aim was to preserve peace, surely the wars of 1914 and 1939 might have been expected to raise a twinge of doubt about its value.

The devotees of international organization have been more successful in criticizing the balance of power cult than in developing a convincing alternative. In their contention, the balance of power idea had not only collapsed in the test of action; it was also conceptually imperfect and obscure. It could mean almost everything or anything to anybody. Some statesmen and scholars took it for what it seemed to be by the very meaning of the word "balance"—a prescription for equilibrium. The idea was that if potential adversaries had equal force, each of them might believe it would lose in a military confrontation. Thus both were likely to abstain from an adventure that seemed to carry so much risk. On deeper reflection, however, it became obvious that if each party thought that it might lose a war, each of them had equal reason to believe that it might win it. Thus a precise equilibrium might well contain a reciprocal incentive to attempt a trial of strength.

This difficulty was apparent to the balance of power theorists. It led them to the practice of regarding the balance of power not as a quest for equilibrium but as the pursuit of superiority. Nearly every nation that spoke in favor of a balance of power really meant not equilibrium but preponderance on its own side. The relevant metaphor here is not of a scale of which the two sides are in perfect equilibrium but rather of a bank balance which normal people hope will reveal a surplus, not a zero sum. Whenever a statesman has said that "the balance of power should be maintained or restored," he has meant that it should be maintained or restored by creating a surplus of power on his own side and a deficit for his rivals. We thus reach the interesting conclusion that balance really means imbalance. This paradox does not strengthen the pretension of the balance theory to help us understand the workings of the international system.

Nor does the imprecision end there. Some writers treat the balance of power as a deliberate policy for which statesmen consciously strive. Others think of it deterministically as a condition which spontaneously asserts itself whether anybody wants it or not. To make matters more complicated there are ambiguities not only about the nature of the balance of power, but even about its aim. Some have believed that its object and vindication are to be found in the actual prevention of war. A reputable scholar, Professor R. B. Mowat, has written that dozens of wars were prevented by the balance of power in the two generations that preceded World War I. The trouble with this theory is that it can never be proved. When something does not happen there is no sure way of establishing that it would have happened if a different course had been taken. Deterrence deals with things that do not occur. Its successes are invisible; its failures cry out to heaven.

A more realistic school abandons the claim that the balance of power prevents war, and stands on less difficult ground in asserting that it enables aggressors to be defeated. Winston Churchill made no secret of his conviction that the balance of power has a better record as a prescription for winning wars than as a device for preventing them. His own country during the era of its preponderance was far more successful in victory than in deterrence. Churchill's most memorable analysis was made at a meeting of Conservative members of Parliament at the end of March 1936:

> For 400 years the foreign policy of England has been to oppose the strongest, most aggressive, most dominating power on the Continent, and particularly to prevent the Low Countries falling into the hands of such a power. Viewed in the light of history these four centuries of consistent purpose amid so many changes of names and facts, of circumstances and conditions, must rank as one of the most remarkable episodes which the records of any race, nation, state or people can show. Moreover, on all occasions England took the more difficult course. Faced by Philip II of Spain, by Louis XIV under William III or Marlborough, against Napoleon, against William II of Germany,

it would have been easy—and must have been very tempting—to join with the stronger and share the fruits of his conquest. However, we always took the harder course, joined with the less strong powers, made a combination among them, and thus defeated and frustrated the continental military tyrant whoever he was, whatever nation he led. Thus we preserved the liberties of Europe, protected the growth of its vivacious and varied society, and emerged after four terrible struggles with an ever-growing fame and widening Empire and with the Low Countries safely protected in their independence. Here is the wonderful unconscious tradition of British foreign policy.

This may be cogent as a description of a particular national experience, and the word "unconscious" is especially interesting, but it falls a long way short of validating the balance of power as a general law. The British experience rested on circumstances that were particular, not universal. It relied chiefly on the fact that during the period in which Churchill's analysis applied, there was such a diffusion of power in a pluralistic international society that it was possible to envisage a single power such as Britain determining the balance. But the fact that Britain had this capacity for so long does not necessarily prove the universal validity of the balance theory. It is hard to see how the balance principle could operate in today's world where two superpowers are so strong that there is no credible third candidate for the role of balancing the scales of world power between them. Harold Nicolson has described the particular condition of Britain up to World War I as a country "strong enough to discourage aggression in others and vulnerable enough not to practice aggression itself."

Let us therefore summarize the conceptual weakness of the balance of power theory as a general method of analysis and explanation. Its chief defects are imprecision and ambiguity. It has been taken to mean (a) a quest for equal strength among potential adversaries; (b) a quest for preponderance in favor of whoever invokes it; (c) a policy consciously calculated and pursued; (d) a spontaneous and automatic condition which is not consciously sought or pursued; (e) a device for preventing war through deterrence; (f) a method of winning wars after deterrence has failed.

A principle capable of so many diverse meanings hardly deserves the intellectual deference with which so many statesmen and scholars have approached it. An expression that means everything in general ends up by meaning nothing in particular. Indeed, "balance of power" did in effect become a cliché for describing the entire international system before the advent of international organizations. The main features of that system were changing alliances and a competitive race for predominance, with occasional periods of stability. It was a system governed by the empirical interaction of interests uncontrolled by any permanent institutionalized restraints. So many diverse policies and methods find a home in this formula that it loses its clarifying role and tends to have a confusing influence on the study of international experience.

The question is not only what the balance of power has meant but what it has achieved. Here the record is so ambivalent that it seems incredible that the theorists of the balance in the seventeenth and eighteenth centuries saw it "as a beautiful design" and that in the middle of the twentieth century a scholar like Hans Morgenthau could assert that "for a statesman not to believe in the balance of power is like a scientist not to believe in the law of gravity." If people kept seeing refutations of the law of gravity, such as apples leaping upward from the ground back to the tree, more than one scientist would express a heretical doubt.

During the centuries in which the balance of power exercised its hypnotic effects on writers and statesmen, some wars may have been prevented, but others undoubtedly occurred. Moreover, war is the ultimate sanction of the balance of power, as it is of most doctrines for preserving peace. The logic of the balance theory requires that those who uphold it must threaten to fight against those who challenge it. Like all deterrent formulas the balance of power paradoxically envisages the very contingency of war that it seeks to avoid. The potential aggressor is supposed to read the power situation so accurately as to recoil from what would be certain defeat. Alas, there is no assurance that every ambitious state will always judge the power relationship with precision and caution. Both of the world wars in this century reveal the fragility of deterrent systems based on the assumption of total rationality. The champions of international organization were quite justified in identifying the balance of power as a system which had failed to prevent wars and which even in its classical period had functioned unreliably. It was realistic and not in any sense utopian to think about replacing such a system with something more convincing.

The League of Nations Experience

The Wilsonians, like the founders of the United Nations after them, criticized traditional diplomacy for reasons quite apart from its failure to prevent the 1914 war. They did not agree that this had been an accidental failure. They were affronted by a lack of fidelity and coherence in any pragmatic alliance system. The balance of power was volatile, restless, shifting, free from any anchor of principle. States were constantly called upon to change their affections and antagonisms to meet the swaying scales of the shifting balance. Today's friends became tomorrow's enemies merely by becoming alarmingly powerful. The system was also intolerably hierarchical and elitist. Nobody could play the balance of power game with the resources of a single small state. Only a major power could ever hope to have a balancing function. Small countries were merely the ammunition which greater powers would use against their adversaries.

So when Wilson denounced the diplomatic tradition, his rhetoric was full of righteous passion. He spoke of "that old and evil order which prevailed before this war began, an ugly plan of armed nations, of alliances, of watchful jealousies, of rabid antagonism, of purposes concealed, running by the subtle channels of intrigue through the veins of people who do not dream what poison is being injected into their system." He condemned the "old reckonings of selfishness and bargaining for national advantage which were the roots of this war." His accusation was not against the Western powers or Germany or Turkey or Serbia or any country in particular. It was against the entire system whereby the world had conducted the relationships between states for over a century. The balance of power, he said, "has been tried and found wanting for the best of all reasons, that it does not stay balanced inside itself and a weight that does not hold together cannot constitute a make-weight in the affairs of men." He denied the capacity of rival alliances "to preserve an uncertain balance of power amidst multiplying suspicions."

In Wilson's eyes the system was chronically undemocratic. It was designed for the powerful; it had no rewards for the weak. One of the architects of the Congress of Vienna system, Castlereagh, had admitted frankly that he "could not harbour any moral or political repugnance against the act of handing Saxony over to Prussia," since the King of Saxony had "put himself in the position of having to be sacrificed to the future tranquility of Europe." Over a century later, the same principle—that small nations must be sacrificed for the general good—was to inspire the notorious Munich settlement.

But the champions of international organization have always been stronger in diagnosis than in remedy. It is one thing to describe the old international system as defective; it is quite another thing to prove that international organization cures the disorder that its adherents so eloquently describe. The more violently the internationalists described the dangers, the less effective did their remedy seem.

It is legitimate to ask if international organization really represents a sharp departure from the old system. Its supporters constantly lay claim to innovation, and yet they built their structure on traditional foundations. Both the League of Nations and the United Nations have accepted without illusion the fact that ultimate power lies with nation-states and not with an autonomous and overriding international authority. There has been a tendency for traditionalists to portray the devotees of international organization as vague idealists seeking to escape from such hard realities as sovereignty and power. This is untrue. While they took their ideals from the literature of the Enlightenment, the founders of the League Covenant and the UN Charter had their feet on familiar ground. They were trying to globalize the idea of a concert of sovereign states, not to discard it. Indeed, the League of Nations was so respectful of sovereignty that it gave a veto power to every member, large and small. Under Article 5 of the Covenant, any member could frustrate a resolution, simply by voting against it either in the Council or in the Assembly. The United Nations Charter theoretically restricts sovereignty by Article 25, which makes decisions of the Security Council mandatory. This provision, however, was never to be taken seriously by anyone adversely affected by it. For the founders of the United Nations, like their League of Nations predecessors, always understood that the sovereign nation-state would still be the primary actor in the international system. They sought not to deny or to suppress sovereignty, or to pretend that it did not exist, but rather to restrain its more dangerous effects by subjecting it to the obligations of an international treaty. They were not pacifists. They took into full account the likelihood that there would be violent rebellion against the new international system, and they dwelt almost obsessively on the issue of enforcement, as had Woodrow Wilson himself. "Mere agreements may not make peace secure. It will be absolutely necessary that a force be created, so much greater than the force of any nation now engaged or any alliance hitherto formed or projected. No nation, no probable combination of nations could face or withstand it. If the peace presently made is to endure, it must be a peace made secure by the organized major force of mankind." The same thought emerges from a passage which illustrates Wilson's obsession with force even more clearly. "We cannot do without force. We cannot establish freedom without force. And the only force you can substitute for an armed mankind is the concerted force of the combined action of mankind through the instrumentality of all the enlightened governments of the world."

Thus, although Wilson had claimed that he was "taking an entirely new course of action," the truth is that his doctrine was conservative about the two major realities of international politics—sovereignty and armed force. In its turn the United Nations Charter inherited this realism. It appointed five powers as a close-knit hierarchy with primary responsibility for the maintenance of international peace and security. And while the League Council had only been empowered to "recommend measures to enforce peace," the UN Security Council could theoretically "decide on the application of sanctions including the use of armed force." With this exception, the authors of the UN Charter held closely to the main features of the old League.

It might have been thought that the eruption of the Second World War would be taken as proof that the League experiment had failed. Yet even at the end of the war six years later, many were reluctant to concede that the Geneva idea had been discredited. The League in their eyes was not just an institution; it had become an ideal and a vision and its worshipers were not going to surrender it lightly. The founders of the United Nations, supported by liberals and members of peace movements across the world, gave the League of Nations a deferential burial while insisting that its immortal soul was still alive. They were convinced that the League of Nations had fallen not because of any fallacy in the idea of collective security. It had failed because it had not been universal; because the United States had never joined it; because Germany and Russia at various periods had abandoned it or been expelled; because it was so rigidly tied to the Versailles peace treaty as to make it the guardian of a petrified status quo with no instinct for reform or revision; because heads of state and foreign ministers, hypnotized by the old balance of power system and suspicious of supranational fantasies, had been unwilling to make the League of Nations the main arena of international politics. In short, there had been a failure of constancy and vision. The errors could be diagnosed and corrected and the idea itself saved from hands that had been unworthy of it.

It was not even universally agreed that the League had failed. It had known a brief hour of promise in the first decade of its existence. In that period it had taken note of some thirty disputes, most of which were resolved. It is true that these were conflicts between small or medium powers caught up in situations where Great Power interests were not at stake. The very names of these disputes have an exotic ring: the Aaland Islands, Upper Silesia, Burgenland, Jaworzina, Mosul, Leticia, the Saar. Yet there were League actions which seemed to give a premonition of real international authority. In 1925 Greek troops had invaded Bulgarian territory. The Bulgarian government had brought the matter for attention to the Council of the League. The eloquent President, Aristide Briand of France, had called for a cease-fire and a withdrawal of troops. Military observers were dispatched to the frontier to see whether the cease-fire orders had been obeyed. A commission of inquiry was set up to recommend terms for a settlement and indemnities. If only such episodes had multiplied, the prestige accumulated by the League Council and its leading statesmen might have become a potent force in international life.

Scarcely had these hopeful visions come into view than they were shattered by what were recognized even then to be the rumblings of an approaching earthquake. In 1931, the Japanese assault on Manchuria exposed the League of Nations in all its impotence. Britain and France were unwilling to apply economic and military sanctions against Japan, and the United States would support no drastic measures. When a proposal was made under Article 11 of the Covenant to establish a commission of inquiry, Japan used its power of veto. China promptly appealed under Article 15, in which the votes of disputed parties "could not block a decision." A five-member commission composed of the Great Powers under the chairmanship of Lord Lytton arrived in Manchuria nearly seven months after the first outbreak of violence. But in the meantime Japan had completed its conquest of Manchuria and had established a puppet government. The Lytton commission duly censured Japan for its military aggression, but no action was taken by the League or its members to "compel" Japan to comply with its recommendations.

The consequence was that few people across the world were surprised when the drama of impotence was again enacted in 1934 and 1935, when Italy and Ethiopia clashed in a disputed zone on the Italian Somaliland border. When Ethiopia requested an investigation, the major European powers made eloquent denunciation of Italy from the rostrum of the League Assembly, but behind the scenes they were actively condoning Mussolini's adventure. In August 1934 British and French representatives held secret meetings with Italian delegates in which they proposed a territorial settlement to Italy's advantage. Encouraged by this complacency, Italy launched a full-scale invasion of Ethiopia in October 1935. This time, at least, the League response was rapid and vehement. Italy was defined as the aggressor and the sanctions provided for in Article 16 of the Covenant were voted. Fifty-four members of the League endorsed cooperative action against Italian aggression, and a coordinating committee of fifteen states supporting the League action was formed. For the first time it seemed that international sanctions might be effective. The Italian economy was seriously injured, but when it came to blocking Italy's access to the Suez Canal or imposing embargoes on oil, steel, coal and food, the Western powers recoiled. In December 1935, Anglo-French proposals for giving Italy control of most of Ethiopia shocked opinion in the rest of the world. It was clear that Great Power interests would come before League principles. But the generosity toward Italy shown by Britain and France was not enough for Mussolini. The war went on. In July 1936 all sanctions against Italy were abandoned and Mussolini became "Emperor of Ethiopia." Ironically, one of the primary motives for Britain and France to placate Mussolini was not ignoble; it was their greater fear of Hitler, who had already alarmed them by invading the Rhineland and who was manifestly the primary danger to world stability. The Great Powers were anxious not to isolate Italy and thus drive Mussolini into an alliance with Hitler.

The spectacle of Haile Selassie of Ethiopia vainly appealing in Geneva for international support became deeply inscribed on the memory of a whole generation. So also was the apathetic response of the League and its major members. The guiding principle of international relations was obviously not going to be collective security but individual national interests. By the time the Ethiopian crisis ended, the idea of effective collective response to aggression was virtually dead. The League, because of its organization, the unilateral veto power of each nation and the devotion of its members to their particular national interests, was clearly not going to prevent a determined aggressor from having his way. Hitler was able to abolish the Treaty of Versailles, to abrogate the Locarno Pact, to remilitarize the Rhineland, to capture Austria and Czechoslovakia without meeting any League of Nations opposition at all. The legitimate government of Spain received no League of Nations assistance as it battled against Fascist armies strongly supported by Germany and Italy. Similarly, the Japanese invasion of Chinese territory in 1937 elicited no response from the League. It is true that the League Council went through the motions of imposing "sanctions" against Japan in September 1938, but nobody seriously believed that they would ever be fulfilled.

Frustrated in its main purpose of defending a stable international system against aggression, the League turned more and more to the development of its economic and social role. But salvation could not be found here. World opinion could never forget that the motive for the existence of international organizations had always been the prevention of war, and a League which failed in this could not expiate that failure in other fields. As the tidal wave of the Second World War approached, the League of Nations, like the United Nations in later years, became progressively more ineffective. In the test of action it failed to arrest the tide of aggression. The founding members of the League, all of them European, transferred their effort from the harsh duty of resisting aggressors to the more comfortable notion of appeasing them. Appeasement of dictatorship was not unpopular in those days; it was ardently celebrated. "No conqueror returning from a victory on the battlefield has come adorned with nobler laurels," said the *Times* of London in hailing Neville Chamberlain after Munich. Learned jurists at Geneva pointed out that Munich represented the adjustment of boundaries according to ethnic composition and was therefore "compatible with the idea of self-determination." There was no less relief in Geneva about the Munich settlement than in the major Western capitals.

Even the representatives of small powers joined the prevailing euphoria in a total lack of solidarity with Czechoslovakia. The Peruvian delegate to the League Assembly said of Neville Chamberlain, "This knight of peace, who possesses neither hatred, envy nor fierceness, has attained the highest summit of human grandeur and acquired honour greater than that of all conquerors. His name is blessed today in all the homes of the Earth." This was typical Geneva oratory. It was left to an official of the League, its Deputy Secretary General, Sean Lester, to strike a note of candor. "What Chamberlain has done," he wrote in his diary, "is a logical sequence of the policy pursued by Britain and France during the past two years; they paralysed the League of Nations, they gave no help to the weak attacked by the strong, they ran away every time a threat was uttered. Now they have given Germany, for nothing but a temporary peace, the fruits of a great campaign. Democracy in a way does not matter, but the other [way] makes decent life for civilized man entirely impossible. There is still the garden and the river."

A few months later the critics of Munich were fully vindicated, but by then they could draw little comfort from their rectitude. The League of Nations, hailed two decades previously as "the great caravan of peace," had ground to a halt. Such trivialities as the Italian conquest of Albania and the German seizure of Memel evoked no echoes at Geneva. The contribution of the League to the drama of the Spanish Civil War consisted of giving shelter to the paintings previously exhibited in the Prado. In the first week of September 1939, when Hitler ravaged Poland, there were some routine-minded officials in the Foreign Ministries in London and Paris who, nurtured by habit, still remembered the existence of the League. They dutifully sent telegrams to the Secretary General of the League "informing him" that they were at war with Germany. It is quite possible that officials in Geneva had got wind of this interesting fact by the time the official notification reached them. But both powers justified their declaration of war by invoking the violation by Germany of the Kellogg-Briand Pact and the treaties with Poland; they were not prepared to quote the League Covenant, which had virtually ceased to exist. The Swiss government was so zealous in defense of its neutrality that it would permit the League Secretariat and other institutions to remain only if they ceased all activity. The League of Nations had, in effect, become a prisoner of war. Germany was too close to Geneva for comfort and could not be criticized. Soviet Russia, on the other hand, was relatively far away, and it was to give the League of Nations its last opportunity for self-assertion. When the Soviet Union invaded Finland, the League of Nations decreed its expulsion. All that this meant was that the Soviet Union had been banished from the deathbed of a moribund relic. Nearly four decades later a historian was to write an eloquent epitaph:

The League idea withered and died when each nation remembered that its holy mission was to serve itself and that all agreements, oaths, treaties and compacts are invalid when they conflict with that sacred cause; where patriotism is a virtue it is hard to espouse a brotherhood that laughs at boundaries.

In later years, however, historians would see the League experiment in a better light:

If the League of Nations is measured against a yardstick of hopes and possibilities of achieving world peace and cooperation, it fell short of its goal. If, on the other hand, it is measured by the standard of previous advances toward world order, it represented a breakthrough in the development of international organization.

There is much rationality in this indulgent judgment. Twenty years are too short a time in which to expect the full emergence of new forms of international integration and allegiance. Geneva, despite its fall from grace, had left enough impress on world opinion to keep the idea of international organization alive. The rhetoric of world community still had a strong hold, and the dramatic nature of collective diplomacy aroused more popular interest than was ever claimed by traditional diplomacy. Some of the major actors in the League had become well known to newspaper readers. When Austen Chamberlain of Britain, Gustav Stresemann of Germany, Maxim Litvinov of Soviet Russia and Aristide Briand of France came together in Geneva for frequent encounter, there was a relieved and complacent air. The business of peace was evidently not being neglected, and it was being transacted in the public view in terms which ordinary men and women could understand. The League idea even had a broad enough constituency to be politically rewarding for leaders such as Anthony Eden who seemed to take the idea seriously. Masses of citizens in many lands enrolled in League of Nations unions, creating a popular movement of a kind that had never been associated with diplomacy. It would be hard to imagine popular movements meeting in large and small halls to celebrate the Concert of Europe or the balance of power. And the League idea, like that of the United Nations in later years, had a special attraction for small nations. It gave them an opportunity to escape from parochialism. By their speech and vote their leaders could hope to influence issues that transcended the limits of their own countries. Since the proceedings were public, international statecraft came alive through being expressed and practiced by men of distinctive personality:

*That the League was indeed a reality seemed unarguable, as the delegates
gathered in 1921. Léon Bourgeois had grown stouter and wearier and
leaned upon his secretary, a woman almost equally aged. Balfour was as
jaunty as ever, with hat at an angle and walking stick under his arm. Paul
Hymans of Belgium was described by a correspondent as pirouetting grace-
fully to beam at myriad friends. Wellington Koo, President of the Council
at thirty-seven years old, carried an elegant light grey hat and nodded in
dignity at the elders about him, who so admired this cool and quiet spokesman for distracted China. In and out of the Palais corridors sped Sir Eric
Drummond, the Secretary General, shepherding his flock of statesmen, sum-
moning this one or that to private conferences to oil the machinery.*

On closer inspection, the make-up of this cast revealed the weakness
of the drama. The League remained a forum without ever becoming
a force because heads of state did not participate. Woodrow Wilson
was the only statesman of the first rank who ever made it the sheet
anchor of his policy, and he was disavowed by his own people. It never
occurred to Lloyd George or Curzon or Clemenceau to regard the
world organization as a place which they might actually grace by their
august presence. In most Foreign Ministries, excessive devotion to
international organization was regarded as a sign of doubtful virility.
Hardheaded masculine realists were on the side of the traditional
balance system, while woolly-headed utopian idealists, allegedly distrustful of the realities of sovereignty and power, would be found
devoting themselves passionately to the League. One of the architects
of the League and UN systems, Lord Robert Cecil, recorded of his own
country that "influential officials in the Foreign Office did not conceal
their suspicions of the League," while Cabinet ministers

*regarded it as a kind of excrescence which must be carefully prevented from
having too much influence on foreign policy. Geneva to them was a strange
place in which a new-fangled machine existed in order to enable foreigners
to influence or even control our international actions. For us to do anything
to help it, either with money or with diplomatic action, was, in their view,
an effort of national altruism which could rarely be justified. The League
was officially tolerated. It was never liked.*

There was hardly a capital of a major power about which these words
could not be written. As early as May 1919, a leading British economist, Sir Arthur Salter, foresaw the prospect that "Geneva will be a
suburb not a centre in the world's government." John Maynard Keynes
ascribed the difficulties of international organization to exhaustion:
"We had been moved already beyond endurance and needed rest. The
vitality necessary to change the tradition of international relations was

lacking. Safety and normalcy were the characteristic aspirations. Magnanimity and courage lay buried in the graves of the lost generations."

The Dawn of the United Nations

The hope that the new organization would have more success than its predecessor seemed to rest on strong foundations. The United Nations, unlike the League of Nations, would present a picture of the human family on a universal scale. All the world's power would be reflected in its membership. There were no signs of the American separatism that had spelled congenital weakness for the League. This time an American President had been the driving force in the plan for creating a world organization in the immediate sequel to the war and had not been repudiated, as Wilson had. Roosevelt had been much more enthusiastic about the UN than Churchill, who with what now seems uncanny foresight had thought it unrealistic to pass from nationalism to world order without an intermediate stage of regional integration. The United States was now in no mood for anything less than universalism. American statesmen and scholars had done most of the pre-Charter planning and research. The conference at which the basic text of the Charter was formulated was held at Dumbarton Oaks near Washington. The United Nations idea was popular in American public opinion, and Roosevelt with typical subtlety utilized this fact in order to win his countrymen over to a foreign policy based on international responsibility. The United Nations supplied the coattails on which he rode into battle against isolationism. At the same time the prospect of America's central involvement kindled a warm hope in European hearts. Since America's absence had always been regarded as the main cause of the League's failure, surely America's presence would be a major augury of the UN's success.

There was another consolation, even more potent. The United Nations would not be toothless like the League. While the League Covenant had spoken about resistance to aggression by the collective action of League members, no attempt had been made to carry the rhetoric into action.* No mechanism was ordained for the contingency which the Covenant claimed to meet. It was assumed that if action had to be taken, member states would contribute their national forces in accordance with a policy to be decided by the League Council when occasion arose. In the meantime they would make no commitment, earmark no contingents, establish no military framework. They were willing in

---

*This was not inadvertant. The French delegation under Léon Bourgeois had made a vigorous but fruitless attempt to provide for an international military mechanism based on advance planning and commitment.

principle to condemn conflagrations, but not to establish a fire brigade. The founders of the United Nations on the other hand proposed to remedy what they regarded as a fatal defect in the conception of collective security. They would not only announce the doctrine, they would make provision for its fulfillment. This idea came to expression in Article 43 of the UN Charter. A Military Staff Committee composed of the five Great Powers would work out a plan for the mobilization of United Nations forces to be held ready under the command of the Security Council. For the first time in history the idea of collective security would be institutionalized both legally and concretely. Chapter VII of the Charter developed a complex doctrine of sanctions culminating in military pressure, to be applied after the determination of a "threat to the peace, breach of the peace, or act of aggression." And in 1945 high military officers from the armies of the five Great Powers began to discuss the idea of United Nations military forces.

The conventional wisdom in the West, especially in the United States, tells us that there was a general desire to create this enforcement mechanism, but that it was frustrated by the Soviet veto. The argument on these lines was developed at the height of the Cold War in the early fifties. It is tendentious and inaccurate. The idea of an international military force broke down not only because of Soviet obstruction but also because of American reservations. The idea itself had rested from the beginning on such farfetched conditions that it is hard to imagine how anyone could have entertained it. The central assumption was that a concert of the Great Powers would cooperate at least in imposing peace on small and medium-size powers. This categorization, however, was fictitious. In the first place, there was no such thing as a concert of the Great Powers. The United States and the Soviet Union emerged from the war in such vast preponderance that the international system was marked by bipolarity, not by a pentagonal structure. Britain, France and China were not in the same league as the two giants. Thus Article 43 of the Charter in effect presupposed bilateral American-Soviet cooperation in international conflicts between medium-size and small countries. In fact, there was not cooperation, but competition. In almost every conflict between medium-size and small countries the superpowers would align themselves on opposite sides of the conflict. They would be fighting each other by proxy without involving their own troops. American and Soviet weapons would be in combat with each other in non-American and non-Soviet lands. Thus there was no reality in the idea of the superpowers moving together against a small or medium-size country bent on aggression. Nearly all the small or medium-size powers clustered around one or the other of the two giants, like planets around a sun. The idea that Washington and Moscow would show equal vigor or indulgence toward friends and foes was contradicted by the logic of their alliance systems. There were hardly any conceivable issues on which America and Russia would unite to decide who was to blame for a regional explosion and against whom, or on whose behalf, the United Nations should act.

The fallacies did not end there. Article 43 presented a scenario in which the United States and the Soviet Union would courteously invite each other into areas where their forces would not otherwise be. This was wildly improbable. It would soon emerge that a central aim of American and Soviet policy would be for each to exclude the other from any possible extension of its military presence. The only balance between Washington and Moscow was a balance of distrust. The Soviet Union feared that the United States, commanding a majority in the UN voting system, would have a dominant role in any United Nations force. This apprehension was strengthened when the United States blandly offered to contribute air forces while the Soviet Union would earmark land forces. In the realities of modern war this meant that the United States would always be first on the scene, with the Soviet Union restricted to a subsequent and subsidiary role.

The United States, for its part, feared that the Soviet Union, having once introduced its forces under an international letterhead, would be reluctant to remove them when the contingency had passed. There was nothing exaggerated in this suspicion. The Soviet Union had usually tended to move into areas more quickly than it moved out. The motives that each party ascribed to the other were reasonable and valid. What was not reasonable or valid was the failure of those who drafted the Charter to take such predictable possibilities into account.

Early in 1947, the negotiations on Article 43 collapsed. The only point that had been agreed on was that the military forces involved in Article 43 would be kept under national control until or unless they were called upon. The five generals and admirals, brilliantly uniformed and bemedaled, would hold ritual meetings of a few minutes at the beginning of each month. The chairman would call them to order, announce that no speakers were inscribed, and propose the adjournment. A new chairman would take office for the next month by alphabetical rotation. A talent for perpetuating nonexistent institutions was to bedevil the repute of the United Nations in future decades. In this case the monthly meetings were stopped before the farce became too blatant.

With the demise of Article 43, the United Nations had renounced the special quality that was meant to distinguish it from its predecessor. It had become, like the League, an arena of debate with a capacity still untested to promote settlements of disputes, not by coercion, but by consent.

The United Nations did not, however, easily renounce its dream of becoming a military power. The hope was revived in the summer of 1950 when, owing to the accident of Soviet absence (in protest over the nonadmission of the Chinese People's Republic!), the Security Council "authorized" enforcement action against North Korea. There was a double fiction here. In the first place, President Truman had ordered the deployment of American forces independent of United Nations approval. He was seeking sanction for a national policy already undertaken by the United States. It was thus euphemistic to call this a collective security initiative. If there was any UN legitimacy in the Korean action, it was won by a fortuitous circumstance enabling the Security Council to circumvent the veto provision. It would not happen again. On August 1, 1950, the Soviet Union returned to the Security Council, thus preventing any prospect of further decision by the Council without its consent. Insofar as the Korean War ended without advantage to the attacking power it may be accounted an international success. It is not, however, a success for international organization.

The United States was aware that the Security Council would not give it similar satisfaction again. It hoped that the General Assembly would fill the gap. The American Secretary of State convened the General Assembly and presented a resolution called "Uniting for Peace." It was adopted on November 3, 1950. Under the resolution, an emergency special session of the General Assembly could be called within twenty-four hours whenever the Security Council was deadlocked and failed "to exercise its primary responsibility for the maintenance of international peace and security in any case where there appears to be a threat to the peace, breach of the peace, or act of aggression."

This was nothing less than the transfer of the Security Council's most important powers to the General Assembly, circumventing the veto power which had been an indispensable condition for the adoption of the Charter. The usurpation of the Security Council's privilege went even further when the Uniting for Peace Resolution requested member states to designate and train armed forces for the service of the United Nations on the call either of the Security Council or of the General Assembly. The resolution also established a Peace Observation Commission and a Collective Measures Committee, both of which were to lapse into inactivity.

It was easier to evade the limitations of the Charter by paper resolution than in the field of action. The General Assembly would never call for collective military sanctions of the type envisaged in the Uniting for Peace Resolution. Emergency special sessions of the Assembly have dealt with conflicts when the Security Council was deadlocked, such as those in Hungary and Suez (1956) and the Six-Day War (1967). But these discussions never included an attempt to mobilize armed forces from within the member states on behalf of collective security.

It can be argued on strictly political grounds that the Uniting for Peace Resolution was a constitutional change effected by unconstitutional means. The realities of the power balance, however, have ensured that this change would have little influence on the efficacy of the United Nations in suppressing armed conflict. That aim continued to depend much more on the balance of terror and on diplomatic adjustment than on the threat or use of coercive power. Thirty-seven years have gone by without Article 42 of the Charter, providing for military sanctions, being invoked. Article 41, providing for economic sanctions, was applied partially against Southern Rhodesia in the Resolution of 1966. In 1968 the economic restrictions were extended to comprehensive sanctions. Twelve years later majority rule in Southern Rhodesia was achieved, but it would be farfetched to ascribe this in any large measure to the relatively weak effects of United Nations pressure.

There was to be one further sortie by the United Nations into the field of enforcement. It had all the spectacular attributes of classical drama without its coherence. The results were so traumatic that it is unlikely that the experience will ever be emulated.

The United Nations peacekeeping force in the Congo (ONUC) was the most ambitious effort ever taken in the name of collective security. The United Nations maintained military units in the Congo for four years; for three of those years they numbered between 15,000 and 20,000 men. Thirty-five countries participated in the ONUC, and other countries, including the major powers, contributed transport and logistical aid.

One of the bizarre aspects of the Congo force is that it never had a clear mandate. It was therefore at the disposal of an ambitious, dynamic and somewhat romantically minded Secretary General. The UN intervention arose out of the action by President Moise Tshombe of Katanga in proclaiming the independence of his province as a separate state. This would virtually have annulled the integrity of the Congo by tearing away the richest area with its great mineral deposits. The leaders of the Congo, President Joseph Kasavubu and Prime Minister Patrice Lumumba, requested aid from the United States, which referred them discreetly to the United Nations. On July 14, 1960, the Security Council adopted a resolution calling on Belgium to withdraw its troops from the Congo and authorizing the Secretary General to provide military and technical assistance to the Congolese government until the national security forces were capable of maintaining internal order.

It was under the July 14 resolution that Dag Hammarskjöld created the United Nations operation in the Congo. By July 15 more than

1,350 troops from Ghana and Tunisia had arrived in the Congo, and within a month the UN forces had exceeded 14,000. No units were accepted from permanent members of the Security Council or from any state that, in the judgment of the Secretary General, had a "special interest" in the situation. Priority was given to participation by African states, of which twelve contributed units. This was the golden period in the development of the Secretary General's office. Here he was— commander in chief of 15,000 troops acting on behalf of the whole world. If Hammarskjöld had had ten times more humility than he possessed, he would have been incited to exaltation by this unique situation. He would carry the UN flag into battle, keep the union of the Congo intact and put international agencies to work to build a model for a developing society.

This was easier dreamed than done. International action was no substitute for internal stability. The Kasavubu-Lumumba regime fell apart in savage dissension. Joseph Mobutu, the Chief of Staff, arrested the Prime Minister and took over the government in Kinshasa. By 1961 at least four separate governments were claiming legitimacy in the Congo. In February, Lumumba was murdered. Some of the Western powers, including Belgium, openly supported the secessionist movement in Katanga. There was sympathy for secession in Britain, France and, of course, Rhodesia. The Secretary General of the United Nations appeared as a modern international Abraham Lincoln, fighting the secessionists in the name of civil order and national unity. It was not so much as a United Nations officer as in his capacity as commander of a belligerent army that Hammarskjöld took a plane to meet his opponent, Moise Tshombe, in September 1961. He was killed in a plane crash. A playwright could not have invented a more dramatic climax. Even this did not end the fantasy of a UN Secretary General as a military commander. On November 24 the Security Council gave Acting Secretary General U Thant a mandate "to take vigorous action, including the use of a requisite measure of force, if necessary, for the immediate apprehension, detention and deportation of all foreign personnel and political advisors not under the United Nations command, and mercenaries." It was not until January 1963 that all military and political resistance to the central government ceased in Katanga.

It might be said that with this result the United Nations had achieved its purpose. But it left behind a country torn by dissension, seething with internal disorders and political upheavals. The circumstances were so particular and the results so ambivalent that the Congo operation was far from being an encouraging milestone on the road to collective security. On the contrary, it was a nightmare on which the United Nations looked back in apprehension whenever the idea of armed enforcement arose again.

Fallacies of Collective Security

The rapid eclipse of an idea held with such intense conviction by so many people for so long a time deserves analysis and scrutiny. Collective security was an international doctrine with wide popular support. It came on the scene at a time when public opinion was beginning to assert itself in what had been a reserved domain of specialized diplomacy. Previously, war and peace had not been matters to be decided by ordinary folk. As late as the nineteenth century, war between nations affected no more than a fraction of the peoples theoretically involved. There was no way for the general public to follow events as they occurred. In the War of 1812 the bloody battle of New Orleans in which Andrew Jackson rose to fame took place some fifteen days after the peace treaty had been signed between England and the United States. The news sent by fast packet was still en route from Europe when the dead were being buried, and neither the British nor the American forces received word in time to prevent the useless slaughter. Peoples who had little knowledge of how their wars were going would obviously be even vaguer and less knowledgeable about the course of peacemaking.

Even intellectual leaders in free countries developed little interest in international politics until the present century was under way. For example, a brilliant group of British thinkers used to meet in the decade before 1914; they included J. M. Keynes, Bernard Shaw, H. G. Wells, Leonard Woolf, the Webbs and others of the same intellectual stature. One of the participants has written that they "talked about every subject under the sun, and the contemporary state of society was never far from their conversation, but they hardly ever discussed international affairs. The international system, like the bones of a healthy person, was ignored because it gave so little trouble."

This complacency was cruelly shattered by two world wars which caused the loss of 100 million lives within three decades. In the preceding century, fewer than 4 million fatalities occurred in all the world's wars, half of them in the Napoleonic Wars and revolutionary movements. It is difficult in the twentieth century not to envy the wisdom and efficiency of nineteenth-century princes and ambassadors who practiced their art without disturbance for so long.

The eruption of public concern demanded a new flag around which masses of people could rally. It was unlikely that a populist movement would associate itself with elitist systems like the Concert of Europe or the balance of power. Collective security seemed to fit the requirements of a popular approach to international relations. Its rhetoric was universalist, democratic, respectful of the interests of small states, innovative and perfectionist. For half a century it was part of the ideological repertoire of liberals and progressive movements in all free countries, as well as being espoused with greater reserve in the terminology of the Communist world. For many years, collective security was submitted to very little criticism in the academic movement in the West. Yet now, after a brief florescence, collective security is discredited by empirical failure and no longer held in intellectual reverence. As one scholar has written: "It has lost its theoretical virginity; it has become in some degree subject to legitimate evaluation in terms of its practical as well as its theoretical validity."

One reason for the failure of collective security is that it has never really been tried. Like many sacred doctrines it has been more often invoked than practiced. The League Covenant had created a voluntary option for its application in case of need, but the League members had never seriously intended to create an international force of such intimidating strength that a potential aggressor would recoil before it. In the early history of the United Nations the contradiction between profession and practice was even more startling. At San Francisco in 1945, speaker after speaker referred ecstatically to the conference's "achievement" in creating an organization that would have coercive power. There would now be "real collective security," a "peace organization with teeth," a system under which an aggressor would encounter the unified and irresistible force of the world community. But when the delegates descended from the rostrum and went into their drafting groups, the idea of collective resistance to all acts of unprovoked aggression disappeared in a forest of reservations and restraints. The Charter itself by accepting the veto provision effectively ruled out any idea of military action against a Great Power or against any state that a Great Power would wish to befriend. Two years later, the residual possibility of military action against a state not falling into either of those categories was foiled by the collapse of Article 43 with its strange fantasy of American-Soviet forces acting with single purpose against a common foe.

Disappointed champions of collective security and of international organization have blamed the failure of their dreams on the veto provision (Article 27). Western writers have added a stern rebuke of the Soviet Union, without whose insistence it is alleged that the veto would not have been included in the Charter. Liberal critics have tended to regard the veto as a curse hanging over the idea of collective security and impeding the true working of the system. The mistaken attack on the veto is part of the reason for the failure of collective security. A system is unlikely to work well if its adherents refuse to understand it.

The veto was not a concession reluctantly accorded to an exigent

Soviet Union. It was the absolute condition for an international organization to be born. The United States also would not have given serious consideration to an international organization in which it did not have a power of veto over any action that might involve the commitment of its forces. Its representative, Cordell Hull, made this plain when he told senators in May 1944 that the veto principle was inserted in the Charter "primarily on account of the United States and . . . our Government would not remain there a day without retaining its veto power."

There is little doubt that the primary motive for the embrace of the veto power was the insistence of nation-states on the defense of their sovereignty. But there was an enlightened international logic at work as well. If collective security is taken to its logical conclusion a war anywhere can involve the whole international community in military action, thus converting a local conflict into a global war. As Hans Morgenthau has written: "Since peace is supposed to be indivisible, it follows that war is indivisible too. A device intent upon making war impossible ends by making war universal." Thus a critical analysis of collective security often leads the analyst to an expression of gratitude for the existence of the veto power. Inis Claude, Jr., the most lucid and powerful contemporary writer on this theme, vindicates the veto as a measure of international prudence:

> *The philosophy of the veto is that it is better to have the Security Council stalemated than to have that body used by a majority to take action so strongly opposed by a dissident great power that a world war is likely to ensue.*

In the light of this logic there is an acute paradox in the assault of liberals on the use of the veto. People who are patient and conciliatory in their approach to their own domestic and national policies become the advocates of uninhibited and ferocious enforcement when they talk of international institutions. When they speak of "strengthening" the United Nations they mean that the veto should be weakened and shunned and that the United Nations should have military force and a strong disposition to use or, at least, to brandish it. The assumption is that a multilateral organization is more to be trusted with dangerous firearms than is a national government.

Behind this illusion lies a widely held conventional view about the relation between force and order in a national society. The argument is based on the theory that force, or the effort to influence the behavior of others by the threat or use of armed coercion, lies at the root of the domestic order. The knowledge that disobedience of the law would bring him into collision with the police and the courts is assumed to be the motive that secures a citizen's acceptance of the social order. It "follows" that the absence of police power backed by force is the root cause of anarchy in international relations. The lesson appears to be plain. Police functions, which are the main pillar of the domestic order, must be reproduced in the international system. And the creation of police authority must be accompanied by an increase in the mandatory power of international law.

The analogy between individual lawbreakers and international aggressors runs persistently through the literature in favor of collective security. But the analogy is so imperfect that no useful conclusion can ever be drawn from it. In the first place, the exponents of this theory exaggerate the role of police coercion in ensuring domestic harmony in a well-ordered society. The most powerful cement in society is created by common values, mutual interests and a sense of common destiny. Domestic society is fundamentally consensual, with illegal violence existing on its periphery. It should be added that in domestic society, the police are fully identified with the social order, whereas in the international context, police forces would be acting against those with whom they feel no solidarity.

If we must seek an analogy, war should be compared not to individual crimes but to the problems presented by the disaffection of a large group comprising a very substantial portion of the population. If we think of the TUC in Britain or the AFL-CIO in the United States sponsoring a series of strikes in vital industries, it is obvious that the solution must be sought not in the police stations and law courts but in Parliament or the negotiation chamber, by conciliation, not by enforcement.

The most prudent course would be to shun the quest for analogy and to recognize the particularity of the international system as a complex of relationships standing uniquely on its own ground. International politics is politics without government and without law. Although some minor diplomatic politics are influenced by the etiquette of international jurisprudence, the crucial areas of global interaction lie outside any legal order. Inis Claude is not indulging in parody when he presents the idea of international "policing" in gentle irony.

> In schoolboyish fashion, one sees government as a legislature, a code of law, a policeman, a judge and a jail; those who misbehave are arrested and punished. The social discipline of government is located essentially at the end of the night-stick wielded by the cop on the corner. If this works in Kalamazoo, why should it not work on a world-wide scale, with a global cop intimidating potential criminals everywhere . . . ?

The paradox is that men of liberal mind, who would be offended by the idea that the police are the most important factor in assuring social cohesion, do not hesitate to become fierce police enthusiasts when they discuss the international system. The zealots of world community and collective security might have spared themselves these anomalies if they had been less despairing about the wide field of cooperation that lies open to international organizations, once the fantasy of coercion is laid aside. If there is not much to be done by law and enforcement, there are still the alternatives of politics and adjustment. The tragedies of our age should not blind us to the achievements of noncoercive diplomacy. Indeed, unrealistic dreams about enforcement may have led statesmen and diplomats to underestimate the promise and dignity of their task as conciliators. Even in our unsatisfactory world clashes of national interest are usually settled without the threat or use of force. Most of them are resolved by routine processes of diplomacy and conference. If coercion is abandoned, only persuasion remains; and in a world of sovereign nation-states, each devoted to its particular national interest, there is no substitute for persuasion. In the final resort, the prevention of war, like the prevention of civil strife within society, does not depend on legal procedures or police coercion, but on the art of adjustment.

Will collective security ever regain its pre-eminence as a central aim of international politics? Its fall from grace arose from a series of assumptions which were dogmatically asserted and not sufficiently scrutinized in the enthusiastic intellectual climate in which the idea was born.

The first assumption of collective security is that states will identify their own security with the existing world order to such an extent that they will be prepared to defend that order by sacrifice, including the loss of life, in places or situations remote from their particular national interests.

The second assumption is that states will be able and willing to agree on the determination of "aggression" and on the clear culpability of one of the parties to a conflict.

The third assumption is that the aggressor will be so weak or lonely that it will be possible to confront him with an international force vastly superior to his own.

The fourth assumption is that states, inspired by the austere, objective principles of collective security, will be willing to punish their closest allies as severely as they would proceed against their distant adversaries. The warm bonds of alliance, affinity and common culture will simply melt away.

The fifth assumption is that nation-states will renounce their sovereign habit of separate decision in the most sensitive area of all—that of national security—and give up their natural tendency to make their decisions independently and empirically, as and when the need arises.

There is nothing in international experience to indicate that any one of these five assumptions is even remotely correct, still less to encourage the belief that all of them together constitute a realistic model for international behavior. First, there is little evidence that many people living in the 160 modern nation-states feel strong mutual ties with the whole of humanity or share with them a common set of values. The sense of loyalty and identity built around the nation-state is not transferable to any notion of "world community." Nor are all actors in the international system willing to perpetuate the status quo.

Second, there is more obscurity than clarity in the definition of aggression, and there are few contingencies in which there would be unanimous agreement on the issue of culpability.

Third, the superpowers have such a large share of the world's military power that it is absurd to imagine them being intimidated by the prospect of an international force mustered against them. Even medium-size countries now have the sort of firepower which an international force would find it hard to overcome.

Fourth, since states are not immune from the general laws of human nature, they are not likely to react with equal and objective rigor or indulgence toward allies and adversaries alike. They base their judgment of culpability on their own interests and prejudices, not on objective analysis.

Fifth, statesmen will not easily surrender their capacity for empirical and discretionary response to situations which confront them, nor will they wish to tie themselves in advance to a preordained reaction. This fact can be convincingly adduced as an argument against any hard-and-fast contingency plan for response to crisis.

My conclusion is that collective security failed to take root as the central principle of international life, not because its adherents were unworthy of its vision or because its opponents were of small mind and ignoble disposition, but, more simply, because it is not a very rational idea. It came on the scene in a world of nation-states and called upon states suddenly to behave in a way in which states have never behaved in the whole of history.

One of the most tormenting aspects of collective security is that decisions which are of immaculate rectitude and logic in their own terms become harmful if they are isolated from the general chain of consequence. In the language and thought of collective security the League of Nations was justified in voting sanctions against Italy in 1936 after the Italian aggression against Ethiopia. But the overall result of the clash between Italy and Britain and France was to clear the way for the far greater threat of Hitlerism. Nazi Germany benefited in two ways. It secured Italian support through the alienation of Rome from its natural alliance with Paris and London, and it exploited the preoccupation of the Western Allies with Italian problems in order to plan and fulfill the German program for continental domination. Collective security, with its rigid, objective demands and its rejection of empirical discretion, committed its hesitant supporters to a course that was bound to lead to the weakening of the free world's essential confrontation with the danger that should have been its most urgent concern. Similarly, the United Nations action in the Congo, which could be justified legally in the terms of the Charter, undermined the possibility that the United Nations would face graver dangers to peace from a position of organizational strength. It is possible to be legally correct and politically imprudent within a single decision. Another example is the Anglo-French decision to resist the Soviet invasion of Finland early in 1940. This action, as well as the expulsion of the USSR from the League of Nations, was juridically correct in terms of the League Covenant, but Britain and France nearly found themselves simultaneously at war with Germany and Russia!

On the positive side of the ledger we must cite some of the lasting doctrinal effects of collective security. It expressed a moral revulsion from aggression, a notion of universal human solidarity in resisting it and a concept of global cooperation on behalf of world security. These are now a part of the ideology of international relations. The notion that nation-states are the sole judges of their own rights and duties has been weakened. On the negative side, collective security squandered a great deal of political and intellectual effort that could have been better spent in dealing pragmatically with each conflict on its own merits. The vain pursuit of a coercive system also detracted from the more salutary excitement which should have inspired international organizations to reinforce the techniques of conciliation and noncoercive settlement.

The UN and Pacific Settlement

There was a brief period in which the United Nations appeared to be fulfilling a central role without the illusion of coercive force. In 1946 the Security Council ordained the withdrawal of Soviet troops from Iran and of French forces from Syria and Lebanon. In 1947 it played a major role in the decolonization of Indonesia. It resolved a potentially explosive dispute over Bahrein. In 1948–1949, after some failures, it instituted a durable cease-fire followed by a prolonged armistice between Israel and its Arab neighbors. Meanwhile the General Assembly in 1947 had adopted a decision for the partition of Palestine which has been fiercely debated ever since but which cannot be denied its character as a strong, daring act free from the defects of obscurity and procrastination which public opinion usually seeks and finds in international organization. The future disposition of the for-

mer Italian colonies (Eritrea, Somalia and Libya) was decided by votes
in the General Assembly in 1949. Threats to the integrity and independence of Greece were repelled by the Truman Doctrine, and the United
Nations did not take direct action, but the General Assembly's vigilant
observation of the Greek situation did have some effect, as Soviet
irascibility at the time seems to confirm. The Universal Declaration of
Human Rights adopted at the end of 1948 may not have had direct
influence on the behavior of states, but it is a bold and proud document, illuminated by a bright vision of humanity in its more compas-
sionate and rational mood.

In the early 1950s, the United Nations seemed well on its way to a
recognized centrality in international diplomacy. A large press and
radio corps was permanently accredited to UN headquarters. Leading
newspapers published long excerpts from speeches in the general
debate. Foreign ministers spent two or three weeks listening to each
other's policy statements and conducting bilateral exchanges in their
hotels and delegation offices. United Nations associations proliferated
in free countries and often became potent lobbies to which Foreign
Offices had to give apprehensive respect. It seemed important to governments to win resolutions in United Nations meetings and to avoid
defeat or censure.

The years 1945 to 1955 were the UN's decade of prosperity, but
even then there was an approaching sense of marginality. Much of the
deferential publicity about the UN came from the United States. This
was not surprising, since the UN was giving steadfast support to
American policy. Even so, all the major powers including the United
States were determined to ensure that their own vital interests would
not be submitted to UN jurisdiction. The Marshall Plan and the establishment of the NATO alliance were carried through in total disregard
of the existence of the United Nations. The Security Council, with
great pomp and circumstance, established the Atomic Commission
and the Commission for Conventional Armaments, but by 1949 both
bodies had become inactive. It was evident that if Washington and
Moscow ever intended to discuss arms control seriously they would
seek each other out in the privacy of traditional diplomacy. In Europe,
the Common Market and the other institutions of the European Community were born without any relationship to the United Nations.

The years of an ascendant UN image in the United States were the
years of Soviet frustration. Even if the "successful decade" had been
prolonged, the United Nations was clearly headed for decline. Unless
its membership was broadened, it would have no claim to universality.
The Soviet Union might well have decided to leave what had become
a predominantly Western club in which it was condemned to the status
of a permanent minority. Thus if the tendencies of the early years had

continued, the United States would have retained its control, but over an even less effective organization than the UN would prove to be. As it happened, membership began to expand from 1955 onward. The United States now had to settle for a less predominant role in a more broadly based organization. Within another decade, the new nations in Africa and Asia had taken command of the voting system. Bipolarity was abandoned. Both the United States and the Soviet Union now had to woo the developing countries assiduously to win majorities or to avoid defeat. They do this dutifully, but they are both even less inclined than before to put their most crucial interests to a decision by an institution over which they have no control. The principle of universality has triumphed beyond previous dreams, but the victory is accompanied by a decline of the UN role in the major issues of international security. The UN structure is large and impressive, but the main currents of policy and action flow increasingly outside its walls.

The slide to marginality was arrested during the 1950s when the General Assembly considered security issues which had encountered deadlock in the Security Council. In 1956 two such dramatic explosions were under scrutiny by the General Assembly at one and the same time. The Soviet invasion of Hungary to suppress an eruption of independent nationalism led the General Assembly to address Moscow with injunctions, censures and orders of withdrawal that everybody knew would be ignored. The action taken by Britain, France and Israel against Egypt after Nasser's nationalization of the Suez Canal presented the United Nations in a more complex light. On the face of it, General Assembly resolutions "brought about" the withdrawal of the three armies that had entered Sinai. But the truth was different. Britain and France were acting under the multiple influences of domestic dissent, American pressure and Soviet rocket-rattling. It is certain that they would not have retired if a UN resolution had been the only obstacle to their plans. Israel withdrew from its conquests in Sinai and Gaza partly under the threat of American sanctions and Soviet violence, and partly because its war aims were successfully attained when the United States and other maritime powers acknowledged Israel's right to free navigation in the Straits of Tiran. The text conveying this understanding had been drafted by American, French and Israeli representatives in Washington and brought to UN headquarters for formal proclamation.

There are two ways of looking at the effects of UN action in the Hungarian and Suez crises. In strict realism it could be asserted that the UN was ineffective. The USSR refused to withdraw from Hungary at the behest of the UN agencies, while Britain, France and Israel withdrew under pressures and inducements registered outside the UN framework. In a deeper sense, however, this would be an underestimate of the UN role. The Soviet Union was concerned by the fact that so many nonaligned countries joined the West in the call for Soviet withdrawal, and some degree of moderation in its subsequent relations with the Hungarian reformists could be attributed to this uneasiness. In 1968, the UN was even less active in dealing with the results of the Soviet invasion of Czechoslovakia, but its highly publicized debates damaged the image of the Soviet Union in the world. The Soviet response was to make a virtual modification of the Charter's principle of sovereign equality by enunciating the Brezhnev doctrine under which the USSR frankly asserted a right of intervention in Communist states to prevent secession or heresy.

This was really the old spheres of influence formula in a new guise. It was by no means a purely Soviet theory. The interventions of the United States in Guatemala and the Dominican Republic was an expression of the same permissive interventionism that the USSR allowed itself on a larger scale in Hungary and subsequently in Czechoslovakia. The United States illustrated its embarrassment by concealing the real motives for its actions in Central America. It denied any direct role in overthrowing the Arbenz government in Guatemala and pretended that its 20,000 troops in the Dominican Republic were there for the purpose of protecting American citizens. In each case Washington moved quickly to transfer the discussion to the Organization of American States, in the spirit of the Monroe Doctrine, but even in the regional framework it found little sympathy for acts which clearly violated the nonintervention provisions of the OAS as well as the UN Charter. The United States was represented in the debate on the Dominican Republic by an eminent statesman, Adlai E. Stevenson, whose discomfort at having to defend a mendacious theory in a skeptical Security Council brought him to a crisis of morale with wide repercussions in the American intellectual community.

All in all, the policies of the two major powers in the decade between 1956 and 1966 refuted the illusion that international organization had superseded or even weakened the old notions of spheres of influence and balance of power. The United Nations, at most, was able to affect the climate of opinion in which the Great Powers indulged their traditional power politics. In the Sinai-Suez case of 1957, the very need of the parties concerned to bring their extra-UN formulas for UN notarization implied that the United Nations had a special status in the conferment of legitimacy; and the United Nations alone had the power to create the peacekeeping apparatus (UNEF) by which Egypt, Israel and the Western powers symbolized their understandings. The truth is that traditional diplomacy and multilateral diplomacy have worked in collusion and concert since the foundation of the United Nations, and the illusion of a "new era" has never had any reality. The UN, cured of utopian fantasies, is now willing to accept the idea that its role is not to impose solutions on its members but to help them fulfill solutions of their own making. UN peacekeeping deals with the consequences of conflicts, not with their causes.

The Secretary-General Legend

During the past fifteen years recourse to the United Nations as a primary method of conflict resolution has steadily dwindled. In 1959 the Security Council met only five times. In 1964 the General Assembly, gripped by a financial dispute which paralyzed the voting procedure, transacted no business at all, yet this omission caused no great alarm in the world's chanceries or in public opinion. It became fashionable to describe the debility of the UN in superficial terms as "an institutional crisis." The Security Council was deemed to be frustrated by Great Power tensions and the General Assembly by the nonmandatory nature of the powers accorded to it as well as by a cumbersome structure uncongenial to serious conciliation. Some UN enthusiasts believed that the Secretary General could fill the gap of initiative and authority and become a sort of secular Pope, radiating a message of faith and conscience which would give the organization a strong resonance by appealing to the peace-loving peoples above the heads of their cynical governments.

The first two holders of the office did what they could with their diverse gifts and temperaments to fulfill this fantasy. They had the UN's founding fathers on their side. The prevailing sentiment had been that the chief executive officer of the world organization should be more than an administrative functionary. Roosevelt had deemed the title of Secretary General to be too prosaic and restrictive. He thought that there should be a "World Moderator," while others spoke of a "Chancellor." It was agreed that the office should denote political leadership. It should become the focus around which a new race of supranational men and women would assemble in an effort to create devotions and solidarities transcending the nation-state. Each state and country had its spokesman; should not somebody speak and act for all mankind?

The Preparatory Commission which drew up the UN Charter had no doubts on this score. It declared that the Secretary General's office called for "the exercise of the highest qualities of political judgment" and that the man selected for the post "more than anyone else stands for the United Nations as a whole." Of even greater importance was the innovation expressed in Article 99 of the Charter which entitled the Secretary General to "bring to the attention of the Security Council any matter which in his opinion may threaten the maintenance of international peace and security."

The conventional wisdom tells us that it was the second incumbent,

Dag Hammarskjöld, who launched the adventure of an assertive spokesman of the international interest and that the idea was born and perished with him. The truth is that Trygve Lie preceded and excelled him in the scope of this ambition. In the earliest years of the United Nations we find Lie lobbying actively for implementation of the General Assembly's resolution on the partition of Palestine, condemning the entry of Arab armies into Palestine for the purpose of preventing the establishment of Israel, insisting loudly and vigorously on the admission of the People's Republic of China and strongly supporting armed action in support of South Korea. Thus within five years he had successively caused offense to Britain, the United States, the Soviet Union and the Arab group on matters crucially important to the offended parties. There was no question here of "quiet diplomacy," for Lie was a noisy man. His aspiration ran far ahead of his intellect; but he was sustained by a lofty, flamboyant sense of the potentialities of his office, and he put his vision to work with an intensity that might have had historic results for the international system—if it had not all been too good to be true and too swift to be lasting. One of his devices was to upgrade himself in the international hierarchy, meeting with heads of state and government amidst great flurry of protocol and breaking out of the UN building into spectacular diplomatic pilgrimages.

For a time the Soviet Union indulged Lie's pretensions. Andrei Gromyko even defended the Secretary General's decision to send representatives to Greece on his own responsibility if the USSR vetoed an official delegation. This may have encouraged Lie to make 1950 his most spectacular year. He made vehement efforts to get the USSR back into the Security Council by securing the admission of the People's Republic of China, and in March he formulated a "twenty-year program . . . to win peace through the United Nations." In April he called on the leaders of the Big Four, Truman, Attlee, Bidault and Stalin, and presented them with a ten-point memorandum, asking them for their comments.

It had an air of effrontery, but he seemed to be getting away with it. The spell was broken at midnight on June 24–25, 1950, when Lie received a report at his home in Forest Hills telling him that North Korean forces had moved southward across the demarcation line. The next day in the Security Council he took the floor with a statement which changed the history of the United Nations. He came out strongly for resistance to North Korea and went on in subsequent weeks to support the Security Council—minus the USSR—in its appeal to the United States to organize a fighting force under the UN flag. He had now become the object of a Soviet vendetta which was pursued implacably against him for three years. Ironically, his final downfall came not because of his audacity in the Korean debate, but because of his lack of courage in the administrative sphere. He made a craven surrender to the McCarthyist hysteria raging in the United States when he dismissed some UN officials arbitrarily suspected of "Communist sympathies." He was allowing the domestic complexes of the host country to violate the UN's international vocation.

Dag Hammarskjöld was elected because he was assumed to be without ambition or assertiveness. It was believed that he was adept at not giving offense. Nothing could have been less true. His character and temperament worked in quiet tones, but he was quick to develop a conception of his office which was bound to bring him into collision with forces outside his control. He would not be the servant of the UN's hierarchy of power; he would rather serve the abstract text of the Charter as he chose to interpret it. He would make himself the spokesman of those who had no voice—the new small nations with no independent diplomatic history behind them. He would insert himself into those conflicts that seemed manageable, not as a "force" or in any attempt at judgment, but—as he characteristically put it—as a "presence." Officials of the UN who had not been heard of before and would not be heard of very much afterward would embody the United Nations "presence" and keep violence at bay.

Hammarskjöld's emissaries would arrive in Jordan, Lebanon, Laos or Katanga with no explicit duty except to enunciate the principle that just causes were more likely to flourish in a climate of consent than in desperate gambles of power. A Secretary General with so many distinguished apostles was widely assumed to have some messianic qualities himself. Hammarskjöld developed an individual kind of rhetoric, obscure in its phrasing and metaphysical in its tone. He was acquiring an aura such as few people in diplomatic history have ever possessed. He was able to transcend national identity. Trygve Lie had continued to be parochially Norwegian even during the highest flights of his international fancy. Hammarskjöld said very little about being Swedish, and he was too unsentimental and aristocratic to present himself as the envoy of the "common man." He was fascinated by mankind as a spectacle, but he had little patience for human beings as individuals. He preached a theoretical compassion for mankind, without seeking to apply it to anybody in particular. His diplomacy was like a great iceberg of which only the top was visible. The rest of it was hidden in the convoluted language of his reports. In his final years, as his authority grew, he used the technique of publicly presenting an "interpretation" of resolutions or of the Charter and waiting to see if it was challenged. If it was not, he would later cite the point, often in a quite different context, as having been tacitly accepted. He was thus able to develop a remarkable set of precedents.

His careful wording aggrieved newspapermen who found it difficult to summarize statements as cunningly balanced as any mobile. He annoyed some of the ministers and diplomats with whom he had to deal. One statesman awarded him "first prize for ambiguity." Others, however, praised his calculated imprecisions. They were, after all, always calculated. They left room for maneuver, concealed temporary deadlocks and saved face all around, including that of some who complained of his vagueness.

Hammarskjöld appeared to thrive on crises, and this led to an unexpected enlargement of his powers. Although he had a dramatic sense of his own personality, he disliked anything that was spectacular or noisy. He thought that acrimonious debates in the General Assembly or Security Council did not deserve to be dignified by the name of diplomacy. He refused to believe that any serious business could be done in that way. He preferred to operate "behind the scenes." Indeed, he saw no reason for the existence of scenes except to do something behind them.

His ultimate failure was that of a man whose ambition was greater than his power. He tried to be more careful than his rambunctious predecessor, but the somewhat Napoleonic stance that he took as commander of the Congo expedition began by being vexatious to the colonial powers and ended, more dangerously, by alienating the Soviet Union. He spoke of the United Nations as "a dynamic instrument" for resolving conflicts, but his dynamism was more than the Soviet view of national sovereignty could stand. By the time that his plane crashed in the forests of the Congo he was cut off from all contact with the Soviet government. In August 1960 the Moscow press had launched an angry campaign of personal charges against him. In mid-September Valerian Zorin, the Soviet Deputy Foreign Minister, devoted two speeches at the United Nations to branding him as "a servant of the colonialists." On September 23, Khrushchev told the General Assembly that "the post of Secretary General should be abolished" and that there should be created instead "a collective executive body of the UN comprising three persons each of whom would represent a certain group of states." With the support of the Western powers and the nonaligned nations, Hammarskjöld was able to defeat Russian denunciations, but his power was sapped and his office had ceased to live before he met his physical death.

This seems to have marked the end of the Secretary General myth. The lesson of Trygve Lie and Dag Hammarskjöld was plain. A Secretary General who wishes to survive his term of office would be well advised to recognize the realities of power, to pretend modesty even if he does not possess it and to keep ambitions and possibilities within tolerable reach of each other. Under this interpretation, there is little scope for heroism in the Secretary General's role, and U Thant and Kurt Waldheim were able to pursue their missions to the end without crisis by acknowledging the limitations of their role. Today it would be difficult to imagine a Secretary General supporting an American military intervention in Asia as Lie did, leading an international army into Africa to preserve the unity of a threatened state as Hammarskjöld did, or taking sharply defined positions on matters at issue between the superpowers.

The Decline of Resonance

The meager results for conciliation under UN auspices must be considered against the achievements of conventional diplomacy. These have been more impressive than is commonly believed. It is natural for governments to be more preoccupied by existing deadlocks than by solutions achieved. But it would be salutary and accurate to recognize that the years since the end of World War II have been a relatively fruitful period for international conciliation and that most of the successes have been scored outside the UN. The Trieste agreement between Yugoslavia and Italy; the Austrian State Treaty; the termination of the Berlin blockades; the Treaty of Rome establishing the European Communities; the India-Pakistan accord at Tashkent; the end of the Algerian war; the American opening to China; the conclusion of the SALT I agreement; the Panama Canal settlement; the *Ostpolitik* agreements leading to the recognition of the European frontiers; the European Security Conference at Helsinki; the Rhodesia-Zimbabwe settlement; the Egyptian-Israeli peace treaty—all these together make an imposing list. They offer empirical evidence for the verdict that the public, multilateral approach has been less effective in conflict resolution than traditional negotiating techniques.

Apart from the fact that the major successes for conciliation have been scored outside its walls, the United Nations has had to face the harsh reality that there have been other dramatic events in which the UN role was either completely inactive or else only verbal and minimal. These include the Soviet entry into Czechoslovakia, the Vietnam war, the Biafran tragedy, the Kurdish revolts in Iraq, the atrocities of Idi Amin in Uganda and of Bokasa in the Central African "Empire," the Indian invasion of eastern Pakistan leading to the establishment of Bangladesh, the Cuban missile crisis, Turkish occupation of most of Cyprus, the seizure of American diplomats as hostages in Iran, the eruptions of violence in Ireland, organized terrorist assaults in every continent of the world and the Polish crisis of 1982. The assumption that the UN would be centrally involved in the pacific settlement of major disputes has been refuted by events.

Zealous supporters of international organization respond with the accusation that the Great Powers and others have transgressed against the UN by the tendency to bypass the United Nations. In this view, inspired by a large measure of institutional patriotism, it is almost better not to solve a conflict at all than to resolve it outside the United Nations. There is little to be said for this prejudice. Most people across the world deem it more important to defuse international tensions than to worry about where the defusing takes place. Moreover, the idea of bypassing is paradoxically inherent in the UN idea itself. The Charter (Article 33) entreats member states to seek a solution "first of all . . . by negotiation, enquiry, mediation, conciliation, arbitration, judicial settlement, resort to regional agencies or arrangements, or other peaceful means of their own choice . . ." One of the many contradictions in the UN's career is that its rhetoric elevates it to a pervasively dominant role while its Charter implores everybody to leave it alone and settle as many problems as possible without its intervention. When members take this injunction seriously and attempt direct settlements they feel reproachful charges of neglect flowing toward them from UN headquarters and UN associations.

The tendency of states to try their hand at direct settlement without risking procrastination or censure leads to a measure of injustice in the world's approach to the United Nations. There is a tendency to make the UN a dumping ground for disputes that cannot be solved elsewhere. To complain that most UN discussions are conducted in a pessimistic atmosphere is rather like asserting that most people in the emergency ward of a hospital look far from healthy or serene. Just as the rhetoric about collective security gave a wrong impression of what the UN could realistically achieve by coercion, so the ambitious claim to make the UN the decisive arbiter in regional conflicts ended in disappointment when the marginality of the UN in this sphere too became evident with every passing year. An uncomfortable division of attitudes has now taken root. States which want to solve a problem seek direct contact. Those which want to perpetuate a deadlock and to prove that their adversary is at fault find the UN a congenial arena.

There was still a hope that a strong moral and ideological influence would flow out of the United Nations and create a climate in which the idea of world community would take root. Some observers, making a virtue of necessity, even thought that this development would be to the advantage of international organization. Purged of the temptations and pride of earthly power the United Nations could articulate a vision that would be the more powerful for being disembodied and freed from the compromises of diplomacy or enforcement. Conor Cruise O'Brien, the Irish statesman who accompanied Hammarskjöld on the last part of his Congo adventure, wrote a book, pleading eloquently for this role:

> Since the United Nations makes its impression on the imagination of man-kind through a spectacle presented in an auditorium with confrontations of opposing personages, it may be said to belong to the category of drama. Since the personages, individually or collectively, symbolise mighty forces, since the audience is mankind and the theme the destiny of man, the drama may rightly be called sacred . . . The origin of the United Nations is essentially the same as that of all sacred drama, in fear and in prayer. In ancient drama the fear was of the gods, and the prayer was addressed to man. But the burden of the prayer—the aversion of doom—is as it was of old . . .

It is a lofty idea with many circumstances in its favor. O'Brien writes:

> In the sacred drama by the East River, the realities and fantasies of international life mingle, collide and take new shapes from interaction. The process ought surely to attract more attention than it has so far done. Sacred drama can be a preparation for war, or a substitute for it; or it can be dangerously ambiguous, a substitute so intensely felt as to merge into a disastrous reality. We need to know more about how the forces work that have proved so destructive and so salutary. It is in the theatre by the East River that they can be observed and studied.

The trouble with O'Brien's theatrical metaphor here is that drama, sacred or otherwise, can only have effect if someone is watching. One of the serious ailments of the United Nations is the diminution of public interest. The consoling reflection that even if UN agencies do not solve problems they do give a large resonance to international conciliation is no longer true. The UN can no longer sustain its claim to be the world's greatest microphone. The large press corps has dwindled, and few newspapers maintain a special bureau at UN head-quarters. Reporting of debates is rare and scanty. With the exception of the superpowers and states involved in particularly sensational vio-lence the spokesmen of member states are reconciled to the notion that the UN is no place to get headlines. The addresses of most foreign ministers in the General Assembly debate pass from the orators' lips into oblivion without a temporary resting place—even in the New York *Times*. A New York television station that once used to broadcast lengthy addresses from the General Assembly rostrum found that there was no listener interest, and renounced the experiment. In the first decade a General Assembly session was a major event at least in the host city. Today it is possible to arrive in New York in mid-October without finding any evidence that the General Assembly is in session at all.

In these circumstances the life of the UN community becomes parochially contained within itself. The round of identical cocktail parties bring the same people together in conditions so indistinguishable that the guests often forget who their hosts are. The UN building is not plugged into any social or human reality larger than itself. It is becoming more and more like a ship at sea—without means of communication with the shore.

Why has international organization moved so quickly from the center of international life to its outer edge? The answer takes us into two domains of analysis. The first shows us the contradiction between the real nature of international relations and the picture of them drawn by the founders of the United Nations. The second is concerned with procedural and methodological defects revealed by experience but prolonged by inertia.

Despite the growth of univeral interests and vulnerabilities, no loyalties or allegiances have yet weakened the exclusive appeal of the nation-state. With over 160 centers of sovereign decision, the international system is grossly decentralized and fragmented. The UN Charter makes modest demands for supranational action but even those that it does make are too much for humanity to bear in the present stage of its political evolution.

Great Power cooperation was built so deeply into the international idea that the structure could not bear the collapse of the central assumption. This reality has not substantially changed. The rhetoric of détente does not mitigate the rivalry of the superpowers, either in terms of their interests or of their missionary sense of destiny. Divergence of national aims is aggravated by a conflict of values.

International statesmanship has short horizons. National policies aim at immediate political and economic gains, and the promise of long-term benefits from international cooperation are met with impatience and skepticism.

The central theme of international organization has been collective security. This idea, as we have seen, never came to birth or serious trial. It requires nation-states to behave in a way in which they have never behaved in all their history. There is even a closed circle of logic. If states were able to act as collective security requires them to act, the international system would, by definition, be harmonious, not conflictual. In that case the punitive and coercive features of collective security would rarely be needed. Collective security is a device which would not be necessary in most of the conditions which would make it possible.

Whenever parties to a conflict have desired accommodation or compromise they have been able to achieve it without the bulky and strident processes of public debate. There has been no use of nuclear arms since World War II, the superpowers have avoided direct military confrontation, and some regional conflicts have been contained and brought to an end. The international system, controlled by the power balance and by negotiation, has not been ideal or reassuring, but it has not been so intolerable as to encourage states to seek new forms of conciliation involving a difficult sacrifice of national sovereignty. The prediction that the choice for mankind must be between international organization and world war has not become credible. Prudent diplomacy is a serious alternative.

The Limitations of Functionalism

Something has also gone wrong with the hope that the nonpolitical agencies would generate a universalist spirit that would have a perceptible influence on international stability and reduce the chance of war. A group of theorists once argued that since political and national rivalries were incurably virulent, they would have to be transcended by habits of cooperation in nonpolitical spheres concerned with economic and social welfare. Some writers considered that habits of cooperation and the recognition of common interests would "spill over" into the political arena and promote the creation of an integrated world community.

These claims appear to have been exorbitant. What has happened is that the acrimonies of the political arena have spilled over into the work of the Specialized Agencies. The superpowers have used these forums for the celebration and eulogy of their respective social systems. The Middle Eastern conflict and African disputes have occupied the time and attention of the Specialized Agencies with the same rhetoric that reverberates in the General Assembly and the Security Council. The anti-American tone of resolutions has led at various times to the suspension of United States support of UNESCO and the ILO. The United Nations Conference on Trade and Development (UNCTAD) was designed to be the point of encounter between the advanced and the developing countries. At an early stage this dialogue was embittered by confrontation. The poorer countries, rightly or wrongly, attribute all their difficulties to the heritage of colonialism and to the domination of the world economy by a few advanced states. This has led them to underestimate their own potentiality, to evade their responsibility for progress and to create a polemical atmosphere in the dialogue. The advanced countries have responded by a more cautious and parsimonious approach than is objectively justified. Most of them prefer to channel their development aid through bilateral programs over which they have national control. It is closer to the truth to say that political differences inhibit functional cooperation than to prove that economic cooperation has an alleviating effect on political tensions. It should not be forgotten that on the eve of the outbreak of World War I, Britain and Germany were each other's best customers.

The hundreds of organizations and groups working in nonpolitical fields are certainly a consoling element in a somber international landscape. But we do them no service when we pretend that they ameliorate the divisions in world society. There is no certainty that the loyalties which they inspire will be transferred to the political level. Thus, the claim of the functional theorist to have found a gradualist approach to world order through mutual interest has not stood the test of experience.

The Specialized Agencies have an autonomous claim to respect and admiration on their own ground. The alleviation of famine, disease and poverty are human ends of the highest moral order and need no justification in terms of other purposes. The trouble is that in the euphoria of the late 1940s and the 1950s their founders and sponsors linked them tightly to the aim of world security. The UNESCO constitution states that "ignorance of each other's ways and lives has been a common cause of war . . . and that peace must therefore be founded, if it is not to fail, upon the intellectual and moral solidarity of mankind." The WHO constitution proclaims that "the health of all peoples is fundamental to the attainment of peace and security," while the ILO constitution states that "universal peace can be established only if it is based on social justice."

The truth is that wars have only too often broken out between peoples who have all too accurate a knowledge of each other's ways and lives, while peace has prevailed among those totally cut off from the knowledge of each other's ways and lives. Nor could any serious scholar find a viable relationship between wars and the health of the belligerents. Those engaged in projects of international cooperation should celebrate the nobility of their vocations without claiming that they are the harbingers of a stable international order.

The same judgment must apply at this stage to the new dimensions of international cooperation concerned with planetary and environmental problems. The United Nations Conference on Science and Technology in Geneva in 1963 and the United Nations Conference on the Human Environment in Stockholm in 1972 were the product of immense preparatory labor. The Stockholm conference, in particular, came at a time when public opinion was awakening to the fact that ecological threats were real and could only be withstood by cooperation on a universal scale. This is the only Earth that we have, and the prospect of its devastation by neglect or avarice should draw all nations together above their parochial rivalries. So far, the most that can be said is that this and similar assemblies have had a useful effect in diagnosis and in the diffusion of consciousness. It cannot yet be claimed that they have advanced into the arena of remedy, still less that they have had a noticeable influence on the dialogue about world security and conflict resolution.

The test case may be the destiny of the Conference on the Law of the Sea, which has met intermittently since 1958. The breadth of the territorial sea, conflicting limits on fishing rights and the claims to the resources of the seabed seem ideal themes for the development of international law. It is a great sea battle waged on dry land and fought with words, and the stakes are the future of the 70 percent of the earth's surface occupied by the oceans. The alternative to "freedom of the seas" is "freedom of the seize." The international community is closer to a legal contract on this than on any other planetary issue, and it is paradoxical that the United States, which did most to inspire and promote the effort, should now be the country whose reservations are delaying a result worthy of celebration.

International Organization: Failures of Technique

Even while we admit that the difficulties of international organization lie deep in the soil of history and in man's political nature, there is now enough experience on which to base a rigorous critique of its methods.

A central defect is the vice of publicity. Public debate is not the only technique available to the United Nations, but it has enjoyed a virtual monopoly. Public diplomacy is not congenial to compromise. With television cameras focused upon them, the representatives of nations are less likely to show flexibility than to illustrate their heroic and virile nationalism. If diplomacy is dramatic and histrionic, it is more likely to evoke passion than reason. Seated on a stage with the whole world as their audience, the public diplomats speak to the outside world rather than to each other. Their aim is not to win agreement, but to gain multilateral condemnation of their adversaries. Here again, we have an account to settle with Woodrow Wilson: "The great things remaining to be done can only be done with the whole world as a stage and in cooperation with the universal forces of mankind." The word "stage" is significant. The idea of a public drama played out before a vast audience is not consistent with the deliberative principle. Hammarskjöld's plea "to give greater emphasis to the United Nations as an instrument for the negotiation of settlements, as distinct from the mere debate of issues" has been reechoed by his successors, but without effect.

Apart from its predilection for publicity, conference diplomacy is afflicted by a lack of clarity about its underlying principle of action. The tension is between the diplomatic and the parliamentary principles. These cannot easily be reconciled. The diplomatic principle tells me that I need my adversary's agreement. The parliamentary principle tells me that I do not need his agreement; I can secure his defeat and humiliation by a majority vote. The temperament and style necessary for these two exercises are totally divergent.

The parliamentary principle has put the diplomatic principle to rout in United Nations' practice, and the result is disastrous. At first sight, universal participation in conflict resolution sounds admirable. This is the first era of global history. It is hard to conceive of any event of significance taking place in one part of the globe without immediate repercussions over the whole human scene. A unitary framework of international relations seems to be the logical response to this new mutuality of human fate. But on closer reflection, there is more to be said for the settlement of disputes through dialogue between those directly affected by them; in other words, by those whose interests would be harmed by failure and served by success. As things stand, states not affected by events and not required to sacrifice vital interests can more easily take irresponsible attitudes than those whose security is in the balance. Nations with no crucial interests in a dispute may band together to outvote states whose very survival is at stake.

The voting habit is the greatest enemy of the United Nations system. The League of Nations was more rational in its restrained approach to the voting principle. The League Council was essentially a negotiating body. There was a strict rule of unanimity both in the Council and in the Assembly. This encouraged persistence in negotiation until a general consensus was achieved.* The absurdity of the UN voting system is aggravated by the almost grotesque inequalities of power between states having equal votes. China, Russia and the United States equal Fiji, Papua and the Maldive islands. The knowledge of this anomaly has deprived the voting process in the General Assembly of all solemnity and restraint. In the Security Council the veto power may well be a saving grace. The underlying idea was that if extreme or totally unacceptable resolutions were excluded by the threat of veto, the major powers would have to negotiate resolutions instead of merely seeking to impose them by majority vote. The veto is thus an incentive to compromise and realistic moderation, and the reluctance of the United States to use it for many years disrupted the balance of the Charter system by opening the way to extreme resolutions which

*Some scholars have pointed out that "the League resolved a greater proportion of the conflicts brought before it than has the United Nations" (Stanley J. Michalak, "The United Nations and the League," in *The United Nations in International Politics*" [Princeton: Princeton University Press, 1971], pp. 78–81).

had no chance of implementation. Recently, the United States has shown less inhibition about voting against extremist majority resolutions.

Nor is there any real paradox in the fact that those who cherish the parliamentary principle in national societies should be suspicious of it in the international context. The two realms are totally disparate. In free societies the parliamentary principle is validated by conditions that have no relevance to the United Nations. In national states conflicts are enacted within a common set of loyalties, interests and values. The contenders see themselves as partners in a mutual fate. Moreover, the final vote has a practical consequence for all of them, and the knowledge that this is so acts as a brake on recklessness. The distribution of votes in a national parliament reflects some real dimension of equity and power. In a democratic parliament no majority, however large, can expel any minority, however small, since the minority's right of dissent comes very close to being the essence of the system itself. None of these conditions is at work when hands are raised in General Assembly votes. Passions are free to rage without restraint of consequence, without a sense of common allegiance or patrimony, without a transcendental solidarity and without relevance to the realities of power.

Another defect of the parliamentary process in the international arena is that multiple participation encourages compacts and bargains which destroy relevance. A nation which seeks a result in one conflict pursues its cause by committing its attitude in another. If two countries have a dispute on a matter not involving the Middle East, they nevertheless tend to speak and vote in a way likely to win support from the large Arab bloc. If there is a debate on Cyprus, the Turkish, Greek and Cypriot delegations will each vote on African problems in such a manner as to win the maximum number of African votes. Thus the tensions of one conflict communicate themselves, under the compulsions of parliamentary bargaining, to another. Does a statesman have an ambition to become the chairman of a UN committee or the President of the General Assembly? If so, he may be tempted not to deal with international problems on their merits lest he incur the displeasure of a large voting bloc. Reciprocal bargaining obscures the specific context of each dispute and inhibits lucid and specialized study. No similar allurements exist within the compactness of a negotiation between a few interested parties outside the multilateral context.

International tensions are thus compounded in the United Nations system by faulty procedures and techniques as well as by a depressing habit of volubility, repetitiveness and documentary proliferation. There has also grown up a new jargon, particular and unique to UN resolutions and reports. The virtues of classical diplomacy have been gravely underestimated in the new vogue of multilateralism, and there is urgent need to restore the balance.

It is all too easy to dismiss procedural defects with the truism that the declining power of international organization is due to the divergent interests and values of governments. Without exaggerating the weight of procedure we can conclude that possibilities of influence can be squandered by failures of dignity and efficiency. The United Nations and the Specialized Agencies have not revised their method of work since they were founded, with far smaller membership, nearly four decades ago. There is little doubt that this kind of institutional conservatism has eroded their influence and efficiency beyond any degree that was objectively inevitable.

The United Nations as a source of public inspiration has suffered from the torrent of words that pours out of its principal organs. Delegates inflict a stunning quantity of discourse on each other without restraint or proportion. They often repeat their statements verbatim several times in the course of a single session, once in the committee discussion, later in the plenary assembly and finally in explanation of a vote. The normal reaction is for the listeners to seek refuge in sleep, but this incurs the prospect of being photographed several times by watchful cameramen in unflattering soporific postures. Some veterans of the East River have developed a talent for passing into coma with glazed eyes half open. Cases have occurred of chairmen of committees being unable to call on the next speaker through being dormant themselves. One eminent representative is rumored to have had the habit of speaking in one language while listening to the simultaneous translation in another in the hope, as he put it, of discovering what he himself was talking about.

The open agenda of the General Assembly results in issues being rehashed year after year without any intervening change in positions or circumstances which would make the renewed debate useful or instructive. Hundreds of resolutions have been adopted over the years, most of which leave no impression or consequence behind. UN language is a thing apart. It is a special idiom not identifiable in terms strictly equivalent to other forms of speech or writing. This semantic tone has even invaded the nonpolitical field in which a more pragmatic style might have been expected. A typical example is the Resolution of 1967 in which "the General Assembly urges member states to consider taking appropriate steps to intensify national and international efforts to formulate and implement a dynamic international policy for economic and social development of the developing countries to be pursued during the next decade." The world owes nothing but a debt of platitude to those who speak in this way. Loquacity is not the same as eloquence, and the failure of international organizations to express the pathos and nobility of the quest for international peace has been one of the self-inflicted causes of a diminished esteem in public opinion.

There is a theory that portrays debate as of intrinsic value in diplomacy: the more people talk to each other, the greater the chance that they will achieve mutual understanding. Most of us realize from personal experience that this is not necessarily true. If the style of rhetoric is self-laudatory, denunciatory of others and innocent of any element of compromise it is not unreasonable to conclude that debate can widen the gulf between nations and add to the difficulties of accommodation. The glib statement that it is better for nations to argue than to fight is superficial. The question is whether mere ventilation of grievances necessarily makes conciliation easier. Those of us who have worked in various fields of diplomacy cannot deny the assertion that "the least inhibited language in the annals of diplomacy is recorded at the United Nations." Diplomacy, traditionally associated with civility and courtliness, is turned on its head. Ventilation theorists allege that even these angry orations are beneficial since they are a substitute for physical violence. This is a nonsensical rationalization by those who cannot bear to hear a critical word about international organization. Descriptions of Americans as "bloodthirsty imperialists," of Russians as "godless, totalitarian oppressors," of Israelis as "Nazis" are an obstacle to conciliation, not a substitute for it. In the restraint of its discourse, as in many other attributes, traditional diplomacy has a better record than multilateral debate.

Institutional conservatism might not be so serious a matter if international organization were to achieve a substantive breakthrough in a domain which engages the concern of mankind, such as human rights or arms control. The obstacles to such an achievement are discussed elsewhere in this volume. To this date there has been no progress such as would balance the disappointing record or multilateral agencies in political adjustment. The functionalist school goes on to assert that if international multilateral agencies were to become decisive in the pursuit of economic welfare and social equality, the relative failure of political efforts would be significantly expiated. But even the most benevolent writers come back with a disappointed verdict in this sector as well. At San Francisco an eloquent delegate from Mexico declared:

> the Charter is also . . . an instrument of well-being and happiness against the horrors of a peace without hope in which men would be subjected to humiliating privations and injustice. Blood, sweat and tears comprised the glorious but provisional rule of war. It must not become the rule of peace.

This resounding appeal to human solidarities has not been translated into the kind of achievement that would compensate the UN for its political disappointments. In absolute terms the work of the Specialized Agencies of the UN shine forth as an impressive testimony to human solidarity and practical idealism. But in relation to the overall context of the international enterprise as well as to the UN's own stated goals, the effect is marginal. Here is the judgment of a sympathetic investigator:

> To pretend that the United Nations will certainly or even probably succeed in its aims of economic change and social modernization, expressed specifically in its proclamation of the first Decade of Development and the planning for the second, would be misleading and falsely optimistic. Whatever progress occurs, the point must be made that international organizations now constitute but one, and in some cases the least important, source of outside economic aid and influence . . . Whatever else can be said about the ambitious aims of the Decade of Development, it is clear that actual results have fallen far short of hopes and plans. Measured in financial terms alone, support for United Nations programs does not increase along a steeply rising curve; it does not even keep pace with the population increase in the less developed world . . . If present trends are projected ahead, there can be little confidence in UN programs of economic development and social change as a means for reconstructing the international system.

The standard text on the international development problem is now the Report of the Independent Commission on International Development Issues under the chairmanship of Willy Brandt. In its report, "North-South: A Program for Survival," the commission clearly favors the UN as the arena for negotiation between the advanced and the less developed countries. It suggests a summit for all groups dealing with development (OECD, Comecon, the nonaligned Group of 77). This dream, however, took a body blow at the Development Summit Conference at Cancun, Mexico, in December 1981. The Soviet Union refused to participate and the United States, wounded by adverse and sometimes defamatory resolutions of UN bodies, clearly preferred to keep the UN in the background and not the forefront of future development cooperation.

World opinion, or that part of it that hungers for the success of international organization, would have been grateful for some UN accomplishment in a specific crisis such as the capture of American diplomats held as hostages in Iran from November 1979 to January 1981. This problem seemed tailor-made for UN treatment. It was concerned with diplomatic immunity, which is an international issue, and no major power impeded the work of the Secretary General in an effort which was visibly humanitarian. Unfortunately the UN role was brief and humiliatingly ineffective. Such failures are particularly expensive in terms of prestige since they cannot be attributed to the enormity of the obstacles which the UN faces. A classic task of individual mediation in a limited domain was too heavy for the UN's fragile shoulders to bear.

Clearly, international organization must moderate its ambitions. It is more affected by the circumstances of modern international relations than influential in changing those circumstances. All that it can do is to create a mechanism to be placed at the disposal of states which may use it for whatever aims they wish. But if we are talking about a mechanism rather than about the force that puts a mechanism to work, it is surely worth while to perfect its working and to sharpen its efficiency. One of the few things that international organizations can do without waiting for far-reaching changes in the international system is to reform their methods and procedures.

The General Assembly should be convened no more frequently than every two years. This would break the repetitive cycle of routine into which it has fallen and give some chance for innovation and reflection.

Instead of the absurdly encyclopedic agenda that professes to solve every issue affecting the human condition, the General Assembly should select for each session a limited and feasible number of issues on which some prospect of useful advance is attested by a previous scrutiny.

The general debate in which a hundred speakers reiterate their foreign policy doctrines every year should be replaced by a more compact procedure enabling some thirty speakers to take the floor by agreements between blocs and groups delegating a few representatives to speak for many.

An agreement should be sought for limiting the length of speeches as in national parliaments so as to enable the biennial meeting to disperse within six weeks.

Except in matters of very specific definition, such as the budget, every effort should be made to reach conclusions by agreement, not by vote, which merely causes division. The United Nations must decide what it wants to be: an instrument for solving conflicts or an arena for waging them. Some bodies, such as the Committee on the Peaceful Uses of Outer Space and the Committee on the Elimination of Colonialism, have agreed that they will aim at conducting their work in such a way as to reach agreement without need for voting.

The Security Council should abolish useless ceremonies such as the habit for all fifteen members to praise the outgoing chairman and eulogize the expected virtues of the incoming chairman at the beginning of each month. One of the avoidable defects of international agencies is a tendency to behave grotesquely and thus to distance themselves from public understanding.

When a dispute is brought to the Security Council the first step should be to appoint a conciliator who would attempt to reach an agreed conclusion without public debate and vote. The UN would thus vindicate its role as an arena of negotiation, not of contest.

The huge conferences convened to discuss functional or planetary problems such as development, population, famine, population, environment, oceanic rights should be replaced by more compact committees in which realistic targets are defined for ratification by the plenary assemblies.

The New World Community

If we climb down from the rhapsodical expectations which doomed the supporters of international organization to disappointed gloom, it is possible to draw a more favorable balance. To do this requires us to acknowledge that international organizations have never been assigned a major role in a world dominated by national sovereign states. Nevertheless, the proliferation of international agencies and the multiplication of transnational contacts are helping to create a new consciousness of global responsibility and interdependence. The world is beginning to recognize that global problems require global solutions. An anonymous Irish pamphleteer in 1779 wrote that "the political body has no heart and nations have affections for themselves though they have none for each other . . . There is no such thing as political humanity."

This is not wholly true today. The movement toward a broader allegiance than the nation-state is slow, but not entirely without hope. When all disappointment is uttered, it remains true that a solution of the UN's crisis must be sought in reform, not in abolition or abandonment. It would be ridiculous if the first era of planetary interdependence were to find the world without a unitary framework of international relations. With all its imperfections the United Nations system is still the only incarnation of the global spirit. It alone seeks to present a vision of mankind in its organic unity. There was never a time in human history when so many people crossed their own frontiers and came into contact with people of other faiths and nationalities. Parochialism is becoming slowly eroded by the new accessibility. The dynamic of sovereignty is such that it resists all attempts to weaken it, but the compulsions of survival are bound to assert themselves in favor of new forms of integration.

Social history describes the expansion of a sense of community, from family to tribe, from tribe to village, from village to city, from city to nation-state. At every stage people have sought larger arenas in which to express a sense of solidarity and cohesion. In each case it was doubted whether the larger context would elicit the same loyalty and intimate sense of devotion as the smaller. De Tocqueville doubted if the United States would ever have a strong central government. Yet the social units to which people were ready to give their service and allegiance expanded across the generations. Why has the evolution of a sense of community got stuck at the crucial stage of transition with no capacity as yet to move beyond the nation-state?

This is a large question; indeed it is the largest of all. The failure of a sense of community to expand toward a world system should be the most intensive theme of research by the intellectual and diplomatic communities everywhere. It is true that ever since Adam and Eve ate the apple in the Garden of Eden mankind has never abstained from any folly of which it is inherently capable. And yet the idea of a world community lives on in the human imagination, even if it is not yet a full reality. The central truth about international society is well expressed by Teilhard de Chardin: "Everything that once made for war now makes for peace. Pressed against one another by the increase in their numbers and relationships, forced together by the growth of a common travail, the men of the future will have to form some kind of single consciousness." The statesmen of the future will need to act in a dual capacity, as the spokesmen of their particular national interests and as the representatives of a broader universal ideal. Something of this duality is kindled, however imperfectly, whenever nations encounter each other under an international flag. The paradox of international organization is that it has become indispensable before becoming effective or fully beneficial. But it is one of the few human enterprises in which the option of abolition does not exist.

Chapter 8

WAR AND PEACE
IN THE NUCLEAR AGE

The Sorry Record

Not one single atomic or conventional weapon has been eliminated by
all the disarmament negotiations conducted since the end of World
War II. Even the American-Soviet summit meeting at Moscow in 1972
did no more than limit the projected expansion of existing weapons
systems (SALT I). It involved no reduction or abolition.

If we go back to the period before World War II, the fate of the arms
control movement does not become much happier. At the First Hague
Peace Conference in 1899 and the Second Hague Peace Conference
in 1907 the nations represented (numbering twenty-eight in the first
conference and forty-four in the second) were unable to reach agreement on any specific formula. The Disarmament Conference at Geneva in 1932 was a fiasco. It was continued in the imminent shadow
of the Hitler wars, which can be said to have been caused to a large
degree by the lazy illusion of unilateral disarmament. If Britain had
built a few hundred more fighting and bombing aircraft, as Churchill
was constantly urging, Hitler probably would have halted his proces-
sion of violence before the Czechoslovakian crisis of 1938.

This leaves the history of disarmament agreements with only a single
"success." The Washington Conference treaties of 1922 for the limitation of naval armaments decided on an agreed distribution of naval
warships among the five major maritime powers. The ratio was 5 for
Britain, 5 for the United States, 3 for Japan, 1.67 for France, and 1.67
for Italy. Britain, the United States and Japan duly scrapped two-fifths
of their capital ships. But in 1934 when Japan demanded parity and was

refused, Tokyo embarked on a large construction program. Pearl Harbor was in the making.

The contribution of the United Nations to arms control has consisted largely of institutional proliferation. An Atomic Commission set up in 1946 was succeeded by a Commission for Conventional Armaments established in 1947. Having achieved nothing, the two bodies merged in 1952 into a single Disarmament Commission consisting originally of the members of the Security Council together with Canada. Zero plus zero of accomplishments still amounted to zero, and the situation was no different when the membership was subsequently enlarged. To carry the absurdity a stage further, the entire General Assembly constituted itself into a disarmament forum which last met —with a total absence of consequence—in May 1982. Bodies outside UN jurisdiction have met in Vienna, Geneva and Moscow with the aim of giving greater representation to Eastern European and Third World states. None of these organizational manipulations has had any substantial effect.

The sterility of the arms control movement is particularly astonishing when we consider some of the compulsions that ought to have worked in its favor. First, there is the atmosphere of sheer naked terror by which the arms control issue has been surrounded since the beginning of the nuclear age. The new epoch dawned in a kind of apocalyptic revelation. Celestial and infernal visions beyond Dante's imagination suddenly entered the common thought and speech. The destructive capacity of nuclear power made a stronger impact on world opinion than its potential for increasing economic welfare; the frequency and fervor of public demonstrations should have influenced political leaders in favor of a serious disarmament effort.

Yet this logic has not been fulfilled. There are more than 50,000 nuclear warheads in the world today, with a destructive power about 1.6 million times greater than the bomb which wrought such unforgettable devastation in Hiroshima. It is clear that a world with 50,000 nuclear warheads is a fundamentally different planet from anything that has existed in all of history. Human life goes forward in a shadow of vulnerability the like of which has never been known before. Since the fear inspired by the nuclear terror is universal, we might have expected a universal effort to bring about some reduction and limitation. Yet all that there is to show are two treaties: the first, between the United States, Great Britain and the Soviet Union, was concluded in 1963 for the cessation of nuclear tests in the atmosphere, underwater and in space, while leaving underground tests intact and all existing nuclear stockpiles unaffected. The second achievement is the Strategic Arms Limitation Treaty of 1972 (SALT I) freezing specified types of nuclear missiles and launchers without imposing ceilings on the number of warheads that may be carried by offensive missiles or on strategic bombers.

In 1979 a further agreement (SALT II) was signed by President Jimmy Carter for the United States and Leonid Brezhnev for the Soviet Union. However, ratification was blocked in the Congress of the United States, and when the Soviet Union invaded Afghanistan, the President withdrew the treaty from the Senate. The Reagan Administration has evidenced no interest in pursuing the matter. It has given SALT II a new name—START—but not a new hope of birth. The main lines of SALT II had been drawn up in 1975 when President Ford and Secretary Kissinger presided over U.S. foreign policy. The aim, in Kissinger's words, was "to put a cap on the arms race for ten years between 1975 and 1985." All this, however, involved no reduction of existing nuclear stockpiles.

The agreements so far concluded or envisaged are significant as symbolic illustrations of a mutual desire to reduce tension; they are not concrete measures of disarmament. The permissible ceilings under the SALT II agreement are so high (2,400 nuclear missiles and bombers on each side) that it would be sardonic to qualify the agreement as "disarmament" or "arms limitation."

It would be an instructive exercise for historians to inquire if there is any comparable instance in history of a problem so universally defined as grave and perilous with so little serious effort to achieve its solution or to diminish its virulence. The fear engendered by nuclear arms has inhibited their actual use without affecting their production or availability. There is no limitation on their political or psychological deployment. The fact that nuclear bombs have not been used in the postwar world does not mean that they have been irrelevant to diplomacy. In the Cuban missile crisis of 1962 the prospect of nuclear confrontation was a concrete issue. It was, in fact, the center and focus of the American-Soviet dialogue. In 1973 the United States did not hesitate to deter possible Soviet intervention in the Egyptian-Israeli war by a nuclear alert. In each case Presidents Kennedy and Nixon were not treating their nuclear arsenals as weapons of hidden reserve; they were actively deploying them in a contemporary international predicament. Since the United States had renounced any claim to predominance in conventional forces, its nuclear power was its only instrument of deterrence in times of global crisis. Far from regarding the nuclear fear as an incentive to abolition or reduction, the Great Powers have made a virtue of necessity and accorded to the nuclear bomb an accolade of peace. In this spirit Churchill declared as early as March 1949: "It is certain that Europe would have been communized like Czechoslovakia and London under bombardment some time ago but for the deterrent of the atomic bomb in the hands of the United States."

If the fear of vast death and destruction has had so little effect on the arms race, it is not unexpected to find that exorbitant wastefulness has been even less decisive as an argument favoring a limitation of arms. The world is spending over 6 percent of the planetary product, about $450 billion annually, on armaments. More than half of this expenditure is by the two major nuclear powers. Since 1945 the United States has shipped over $100 billion worth of arms to 140 countries across the globe. The amount being spent on armaments is more than the total revenues of all the Third World countries put together. It is nearly three times greater than what all the world's governments spend on health, nearly twice what they spend on education, and nearly thirty times what industrialized countries give in aid to developing countries.

Most of the arms traffic with Third World countries is in conventional arms, but there has been a swift proliferation of military nuclear capacities as well. At least ten countries are credibly regarded today as having a military nuclear option or as being able to create one within a brief period of time. Not reduction or limitation but escalation and proliferation are the current features of the nuclear predicament.

The record should disappoint all humanity, but it weighs with special intensity on those who have made the study of arms control negotiations their life work. It is hard to think of any sector of the diplomatic enterprise in which so much intellectual energy has been invested with so little consequence. The study of arms control, with its corollaries in the intricate theories of deterrence and miscalculation, has developed its own mathematics, and its own conceptual and systemic terminology. Scholars and statesmen such as Lord Cecil, Salvador de Madariaga, Philip Noel Baker, Alva Myrdal, Jules Moch, Garcia Robles, Lincoln Bloomfield, D. R. Richardson, Donald G. Brennan, Arthur Wohlstetter and B. G. Bechhoefer have made it something of an academic discipline in its own right.

Cause—or Effect

"In its own right." This may be the underlying explanation of the failure. The essential question is whether the arms race is an autonomous cause or a major symptom of political tensions. Many specialists treat it as a cause; indeed some of them tend to describe it as the "primary cause" of war. If only arms were reduced the international climate would be transformed, irrespective of the political conflicts and tensions between states. According to this school the ending of the nuclear arms race by a disarmament treaty would improve international relations, reduce tensions and facilitate the settlement of outstanding political disputes.

The more realistic view regards the accumulation of arms not as a primary cause of international tension but rather as one of its direct consequences. If this view is well-founded, disarmament negotiations in themselves will not be successful unless they are preceded or accompanied by some successes in the settlement of global or regional disputes. "Nations do not fight because they have arms," wrote Hans Morgenthau in a memorable phrase. "Nations have arms because they deem it necessary to fight." There is even a strong case for the theory that unbalanced disarmament unaccompanied by political solutions may actually increase the danger of war. It would not be an exaggeration to say that World War II—the most savage event in the history of mankind—was caused by such an imbalance of arms. The aggressive powers armed and the democracies remained weak.

It is all a question of proportion. Since total disarmament does not seem to be a feasible objective in the context of human and political nature, there is more to be gained by managing arms with a view to equilibrium than by a futile attempt to bring about total abolition. Many workers and negotiators, following in Churchill's footsteps, are even prepared to declare that the threat of nuclear destruction may have been the most important single factor that has prevented all-out war in the nuclear age. According to this theory disarmament without political progress is bound to fail. Arms control is not a separate discipline or a "subject" of autonomous importance in itself. The prophetic idea of "beating swords into plowshares" is integrally linked —even in the Biblical text—to the concept of a universally accepted vision of a human order based on human solidarity. In the absence of such a unifying vision there are always likely to be as many swords as plowshares in the world.

Like many chicken-and-egg discussions this one must end with a circular verdict. Arms are both a consequence and a cause of international tension. There is a vicious circle: it is impossible to reduce armaments without defusing global or regional conflicts. But the existence of large accumulations of armaments is one of the factors that prevent global and regional tensions from being defused. There seems to be no rational course except to cease regarding arms control as a separate and independent instrument for reducing international tension and to integrate it into a wider complex of causes and incentives that influence peace and war. There must be an urgent and simultaneous approach to arms control and the relief of major international tensions. In the meantime modern writers can only wonder at the matter-of-factness with which the nuclear presence is accepted—"the peculiar failure of response in which hundreds of millions of people acknowledge the presence of an immediate, unremitting threat to their existence and to the existence of the world they live in but do nothing about it—a failure in which both self-interest and fellow-feeling seem

to have died." The devotees of arms control end up in something close
to despair. As Alva Myrdal says: "We have accomplished no real disarmament. We can see hardly any tangible results of our work and the
underlying major cause must be that the superpowers have not seriously tried to achieve disarmament." It could be added that there has
not even been any success in avoiding the proliferation of nuclear
capacity among those who are not superpowers. Even though Moscow
and Washington may understand that nuclear war is unthinkable, there
is no assurance that a lesser power will be equally restrained. In June
1981 Israel was convinced that an Iraqi nuclear reactor near Baghdad
was designed for Israel's destruction, and Israeli air forces destroyed
the reactor. The only other purpose for the reactor would be to use
in an attack against Iran, which in fact had tried unsuccessfully to do
what Israel had achieved.

The Nuclear Dilemma

The overriding consolation is that since 1945 the United States and the
Soviet Union have avoided direct military conflict. The danger of
confrontation has undoubtedly moderated their behavior. Each nation
has drawn the same conclusions from the specter of nuclear warfare:
neither would be spared in the ensuing holocaust. This dilemma of the
nuclear era had been described by J. Robert Oppenheimer, who called
the superpowers "two scorpions in a bottle." A German author, W. W.
Schutz, referred to the relations between nuclear powers as "the interdependence of doom." The idea that human survival rests on a negative premise, not on a positive idea, has profound implications for
contemporary culture, but the strategist cannot deny its truth. Fear
plays a larger role than hope in the avoidance of war.

By the mid-1950s, the leaders of the United States and the Soviet
Union had frankly acknowledged the potential destructiveness of nuclear conflict. Eisenhower proclaimed that there was "no alternative to
peace," and Khrushchev declared that Lenin's prophecy of inevitable
war between Communism and capitalism had become outmoded
because of the unforeseen destructiveness of nuclear weaponry. In
their rhetoric, both nations recognized the nature of their choice:
coexistence or nonexistence; survival or extinction. The result was
seen in the caution and control which characterized the conduct of the
superpowers. The critical test of the nuclear age was not only to mobilize power for the advancement of national interest but to exercise that
power with restraint.

But if the need for a cautious foreign policy was grasped intellectually, this was not immediately manifested in superpower behavior. It
was only after the Cuban missile crisis in 1962 that the superpowers

began to take concrete actions to lessen the likelihood of nuclear catastrophe. Leaders of both nations, poised at the nuclear brink, came to perceive a common stake in the preservation of nuclear stand-off. The avoidance of direct confrontation and the beginning of negotiations for arms control were clearly a mutual interest. The United States no longer used inflammatory rhetoric as if it hoped to threaten existing Soviet interests; and the Soviets spoke increasingly of peaceful coexistence.

In the strategic dialogue the superpowers moved to an uneasy acceptance of the doctrine of "mutual assured destruction" (MAD). After the Cuban missile danger, they established a "hotline" between their capitals for direct communication during crises. They agreed in 1963 to a limited ban on the testing of nuclear weapons. In the United Nations they voted for a prohibition against nuclear weapons in outer space (1967), and in the nonproliferation treaty (1968) they agreed—without much effect—"to work together to prevent the spread of nuclear weapons." The process of bilateral negotiations led ultimately to the ABM treaty and the SALT I agreement of 1972 and to the SALT II treaty of 1979, which has not been ratified by the United States.

For the superpowers, arms control now had a compelling internal logic. Yet neither nation was willing to forgo changes in the nuclear balance in favor of its own national position. A state system based on national sovereignty, together with the existence of weapons capable of extinguishing life on earth, continues to pose the critical dilemma of the nuclear age. Both the United States and the USSR accept the paradox that the main justification for possessing nuclear weapons is to deter their use; yet both nations also seek through a variety of doctrines, strategies and policies to find means of expressing their nuclear power in political terms—whether through veiled threat or the elaboration of contingency plans and scenarios in which nuclear war is treated as a concrete and viable possibility. Thus, the global imperative of preventing a nuclear holocaust collides with the exercise of sovereign power and national interest. The destiny of this planet still remains fixed on the horns of this nuclear dilemma. The nations live in an atmosphere of duality. They understand the nuclear revolution but they conduct much of their behavior as though the revolution had not occurred.

Power Politics in the Nuclear Era

In the classic definition of international politics, nations have sought through the balance of power to achieve two objectives: the preservation of their own existence and, when possible, the maintenance of peace in the international system. The two goals are at times complementary; at other times they clash. While states generally would prefer both peace and national security, they have traditionally been willing to sacrifice the former for the sake of the latter. Security has mattered to nations even more than peace.

It is only in the nuclear age that the objectives of peace and security have become indistinguishable, so that war is a worse contingency than the situations which it seeks to correct. The balance of power and the maintenance of security still depend mainly on the relative military strengths of the superpowers, but the balance is now maintained by the threat of total force rather than by its actual employment in battle.

This does not mean that the superpowers or other nations possessing nuclear capacity have ended their struggle for political advantage. The dangers of atomic warfare remain unchecked. Although a nuclear holocaust may not result from a rationally premeditated attack, other factors could trigger the deadly sequence: miscalculation resulting from rapid and destabilizing technological changes, inept crisis management or the escalation of a limited war. A war fought between the superpowers would end international politics; it would in fact be the end of history.

In pre-nuclear times, any significant alteration in the balance of power usually resulted in war. The power that seemed to be losing the arms race was tempted to take pre-emptive action before its deterrent capacity was eroded. A breakdown in diplomacy was followed by war, described as "a continuation of politics by other means." Nuclear technology has, however, changed the degree in which military power can be used to restore balances of power or to prevent an expansionist nation from achieving hegemony in the international system. War, particularly between nations possessing a nuclear capability, can no longer be viewed as a rational method for solving disputes or for maintaining systemic balance. And yet war has become neither anachronistic nor obsolete. Something becomes obsolescent only when it is replaced by a better method of achieving the desired end. No absolute replacement for war as the arbiter of disputes between sovereign states has been invented for the nuclear age.

Thus, the present international system is left in an uneasy limbo. The specter of nuclear annihilation inhibits the resolution of disputes by war. Yet disputes between sovereign powers continue to exist and like a cancer left untreated threaten the health of the global body politic. As Einstein prophetically observed: "The unleashed power of the atom has changed everything save our modes of thinking, and we thus drift toward unparalleled catastrophes." As scientists, technicians and ordinary citizens we live in a nuclear world where we realize that our extinction as a species is an omnipresent threat. But as political actors we live in a pre-nuclear age, still believing that the clash of interests between sovereign states can be resolved by resort to violence. This incongruence remains, as it has since 1945, the greatest challenge for statesmen, philosophers and all who have a concern for moral and intellectual values.

The Deterrence of Nuclear War

Clausewitz wrote long before the advent of nuclear weapons: "Everything is subject to a supreme law which is the decision by arms." War, according to J. T. Shotwell, "has been the instrument by which most of the great facts of political national histories have been established and maintained . . . The map of the world today has been largely determined upon the battlefield. The maintenance of civilization itself has been, and still continues to be, underwritten by the insurance of any army and navy ready to strike at any time where danger threatens."

But nuclear weapons once and for all change the relationship between military means and political ends. Rather than helping to preserve civilization, the new instruments of violence threaten ultimately to destroy it. How can a nation employ nuclear weapons to defend its territorial integrity and national security if, in the very act of defense, it would sacrifice the lives of most of its own citizens? It is a misnomer to call nuclear conflict "war." While total wars may have been compatible with weapons of a limited destructive capacity, they are not compatible with weapons of total destruction. The "remedy" is more fatal than the disease.

The principal function of strategic military strength in the nuclear era has become the deterrence of an all-out attack. The aim of military establishments used to be victory. Today their chief purpose is prevention. An opponent is threatened with such massive and complete destruction that he dare not initiate an attack. Faced with the prospect of national suicide, a "rational" statesman would conclude that the costs of war far outweigh any conceivable gains. Herman Kahn, in *Thinking About the Unthinkable,* discusses the issue of "rationality": "It is sometimes stated that even an adequate deterrent would not deter an irrational enemy . . . As a result, we should want a safety factor in . . . deterrence systems so large as to impress even the irrational and irresponsible with the degree of their irrationality and therefore the need for caution." The paradox is extraordinary: military capacity must be overwhelmingly strong in the nuclear age in order that it may not be used. The sole utility of a strong nuclear arsenal is to make itself irrelevant in practical terms. Tens of thousands of nuclear weapons frighten their possessors no less than their potential targets.

Before World War II, states normally had standing military forces which they believed to be sufficient to deter enemy attack. If hostilities actually broke out, a major mobilization effort was required. Large mobilized forces prior to the outbreak of actual hostilities were both unnecessary and expensive. Plowshares were converted to swords only after an actual attack. This was particularly true of the United States, which, because of its insularity, had considerable time to mobilize for a war effort.

With the advent of nuclear weapons and the requirements of deterrence, however, readiness for retaliation became necessary in peacetime. The United States in particular could not give a potential adversary reason to doubt the credibility of its retaliatory capacity or its willingness to employ it. For deterrence to be stable and for peace to be ensured, nations would have to maintain a military capability sufficiently large to make a period of mobilization unnecessary. For the first time permanent military readiness became the price of permanent peace.

There are two alternatives to massive accumulation of nuclear weapons, but the wisdom of statesmen has not brought them into sight. One would be to have nuclear balance at a lower level. If each superpower had ten warheads rather than ten thousand, the balance would be just as effective. Another remedy would be to achieve a balance of conventional arms. These could threaten terrible havoc, but the planet itself would have a chance of survival.

Another change brought about by nuclear weapons has been the transformation of national defense from a concrete, military objective into an essentially psychological concept. A soldier's traditional function has been the application of force on the battlefield. The ultimate test of weaponry lay in its use. Today, the key word is deterrence. The only "rational" application of nuclear force is the threat of nuclear devastation to prevent a potential aggressor from striking first. Deterrence is a psychological concept. It aims to affect an opponent's perceptions and intentions. It is his state of mind rather than his war-making capabilities that must be influenced. The skills required to implement a deterrent strategy are not those traditionally associated with military leaders. This fact has created tension between military leaders—traditionally trained to use all available means to achieve victory—and civilian decision-makers seeking to constrain the means available to the military leadership. Since 1945, civilian strategists have had to battle on two fronts. They have been concerned not only to intimidate their foreign adversaries but also to impose the logic of deterrence on military thinkers who find deterrence more ambivalent and therefore less attractive than the actual utilization of strength.

In the nuclear age, the capacity to destroy totally another nation and the capacity to bargain are simultaneously necessary to the maintenance of peace. This contrasts with earlier periods when bargaining occurred after war. Military strategy used to be perceived largely as an alternative to negotiation, not as part of the process itself. The existence of nuclear weapons, however, has made the actual defeat of an enemy an unnecessary phase in the conflict. Both superpowers know that they can be hurt immeasurably in a nuclear exchange; this potential, therefore, can be taken for granted before and without the outbreak of hostilities.

Credibility in the Cold War

It is one thing, however, to influence an opponent not to resort to violence; the difficulty is to convince an opponent that you will actually go to war to achieve a crucial objective even if the cost is immense. How can an adversary be made to believe that a threat in support of a professed objective is credible? One method is by engaging a nation's honor and prestige, its bargaining reputation, and the confidence of its domestic public and allies. In the Berlin crisis of the late 1950s, for example, the United States felt that its reputation as a dependable ally and the credibility of its commitments were at stake. If the United States had given in to Soviet demands and withdrawn from West Berlin, then the Soviets would have been encouraged to make further outrageous demands, weakening in the process the United States commitment to the NATO alliance. The domino theory exists in the nuclear equation, not only in territorial disputes. Nations always ask: If I give in here, what will be the effects elsewhere? It is becoming desperately difficult to isolate any international problem for individual treatment.

Staking a nation's reputation forms the basis of a credible commitment because the cost of retreat from a given pledge would grossly undermine a nation's reputed power and influence in world affairs. In the bipolar world of nuclear power, this preoccupation with the credibility of commitments led to the proliferation of a global network of alliances, several of which had only a tenuous connection to the superpowers' vital national interests. The superpowers were thus trapped in a double bind of their own making. On the one hand, the exigencies of a bipolar world seemingly demanded a universal extension of commitments in order to contain the other superpower's influence. On the other hand, once a commitment was made, its credibility put all other commitments to the test.

The tenuousness of many of these commitments, particularly in Third World regions, made it unlikely that either superpower would risk nuclear annihilation to defend a pledge to a faraway land and people. But because the credibility of a commitment was at stake, it was necessary for the superpowers to find other means short of nuclear attack to demonstrate their resolve. The concept of limited war—using less than a nation's full military might in order to accomplish something less than an adversary's total defeat—provided one possible answer. Given the widespread nature of superpower commitment in the bipolar world, this type of limited, low-level conflict has proliferated. Thus, despite the absence of general conflict between the superpowers, the *pax atomica* has not ensured peace throughout the international system. A strong case can even be made for the proposition that peace in the northern industrial sector has been achieved by the "export" of limited wars to areas in which vital superpower interests have not been vitally engaged.

A second method of creating a credible commitment in the nuclear era has been by making a commitment somehow "automatic": a type of "burning one's bridges," making retreat literally impossible. If a commitment cannot be readily withdrawn, an adversary is less likely to test its credibility. In Western Europe, for example, the presence of American troops in forward positions in West Germany has sent a signal to the Soviets that any attack resulting in the loss of American lives would leave the United States no choice but to counterattack. This "trip wire" effect serves to underscore the strength of the American commitment to NATO. But for this limited military presence, which many Americans may at first sight deem useless and burdensome, the Soviet Union might easily take an aggressive measure on the assumption that "the Americans won't become involved."

The strategic underpinning of a rapid deployment force could likewise depend on sending a clear signal to Moscow concerning the degree of U.S. commitment to the stability of the Persian Gulf and assured access to its petroleum. Should the Soviet Union attempt to assert military control in the region, the rapid emplacement of a relatively small number of American forces—too small, in fact, to counter a determined Soviet attack—would serve as a warning to the Soviets that if the superpowers clashed directly, the United States might be forced to respond with nuclear weapons. This was the veiled threat behind the Carter doctrine. The ultimate (but imaginary) "automatic commitment" is the doomsday machine portrayed in the seminal movie of the nuclear era, *Dr. Strangelove*. The doomsday machine would function automatically to blow the world apart if any nuclear attack occurred.

In the actual practice of international politics, commitments are rarely irrevocable, and no pledge is ever totally watertight. France gave Israel a guarantee in 1957 that it could count on French support if Egypt blockaded the Straits of Tiran, where Israel had a Red Sea port —Eilat. In 1967, Egypt blockaded the waterway, and I went to Paris to "collect" the promised French "support." De Gaulle made clear that the support would not be forthcoming. When I asked, "What has changed since your assurance was given ten years ago?" De Gaulle replied: "The date has changed." He added: "Guarantees are not absolute. Things evolve."

Escape clauses are maintained in even the most resolute commitment, and even if the clauses are not written, they should be assumed. The United States Senate, for example, would never have approved U.S. membership in NATO if the sovereign power of making war and peace had been taken away from the President and Congress. Commitments are ambiguous; so are threats which are intended to sound firm yet are sufficiently vague to allow negotiating flexibility, especially when nuclear weapons are involved. It is also worth noting that the maintenance of commitments in the nuclear era depends on the communication of resolve and will, which are perhaps more important to deterrence in the nuclear era than the objective balance of capabilities. Your power is what your adversary thinks it is. An adversary's perception ultimately matters more than the actual nuclear arsenals. And each superpower's perception of the other's resolve is likely to fluctuate with time and specific circumstances. For example, Khrushchev's image of American determination was apparently damaged by Kennedy's early policies—allowing a neutralist government in Laos; the failure adequately to support the abortive Bay of Pigs landing; the inaction at the building of the Berlin Wall—so that he was "encouraged" to establish missile bases in Cuba despite Kennedy's warnings. Only after Kennedy firmly demonstrated his willingness to take the world to the brink of nuclear war was America's resolve clearly reestablished.

One of the factors in appraising the likelihood of a specific reaction is the personality of the leaders who have to make the decisions. The question of whether "Iran" or "Libya" might do this or that is meaningless. Khomeini or Qaddafi might do what "Iran" or "Libya" usually would not. Nasser's personality was decisive in creating the explosive situation that preceded the Six-Day War in 1967. There were no urgent or intrinsic reasons for changing the status quo. Israel's action in the 1982 Lebanese war would not have been carried out as it was if anyone but Ariel Sharon had been in charge of the defense ministry. Margaret Thatcher's personality was decisive in the reaction of Britain in the Falklands war of 1982.

The Beginnings of Arms Control

The balance of power is easy to calculate when the elements of a nation's power remain reasonably constant. But if power factors change rapidly, uncertainty is introduced into relationships between potential adversaries. This, in turn, can make miscalculation and hostilities more likely. The difficulty with the postwar balance of power has been that both elements in the equation—the actual military capabilities of the adversaries and their national resolve—have been in an almost constant flux. This dynamic has made it a complex task to calculate today's power balance, let alone forecast tomorrow's.

The hard logic of deterrence requires that the opponent must at all times be convinced that he can be destroyed. The need for an unchallengeable offensive capacity is constant, and this necessitates an unflagging concern for the effectiveness of nuclear delivery systems. Rapid technological progress in the respective delivery systems of the superpowers, however, affects the stability of the balance of terror. Since 1950, there have been several cycles during which technological innovation seemed to make a first-strike capability possible.

Even the early nuclear delivery systems tended to destabilize the postwar equilibrium. The ability of fast bombers to launch a surprise attack increased the perception of U.S. policymakers that they could destroy much of Soviet society. The Soviet leaders, on the other hand, had every incentive to attempt to destroy the American bombers in their own pre-emptive strike. The vulnerability of these bombers to a "nuclear Pearl Harbor" increased the incentive for both sides to strike first. Mere possession of atomic bombs was not enough to ensure that the existing balance would deter war. The possibility of eliminating the adversary's retaliatory capability—by destroying the relatively "soft" bomber delivery system—constituted a powerful incentive to strike before this occurred.

By the late 1950s, the superpowers began to realize the fragility of the nuclear balance. This led them to explore arms control measures which would stabilize mutual deterrence. Arms control proponents rejected the feasibility, and even the desirability, of "general" disarmament. They assumed that neither conflicts among states nor nuclear weapons could be abolished; the nuclear genie could not be put back into the bottle. Instead, humankind's best hope lay in the control of nuclear weapons and the strengthening of mutual deterrence. In a system of sovereign states, each seeking to defend its national interest and jealously guarding the prerogatives of its sovereignty, mutual deterrence was viewed by the first generation of arms control proponents as the only practical policy. Given this assumption, the foundation of deterrence needed to be strengthened and stabilized.

Arms control was thus intended to supplement more traditional defense policies. In fact, the aims of the old and the new systems were virtually identical—to protect national security by deterring war. Whereas disarmament stressed actual reductions in the capabilities of a nation's military forces, arms control emphasized the reduction of incentives to strike first. Although this limited goal has often been obscured by leaders of both superpowers in an effort to make their side appear more genuinely interested in actual reduction of armaments, the heart of arms control efforts since their inception has been the acceptance of weapons as a reality with an attempt to inhibit their use.

The remedy for the problem of a pre-emptive strike was to try to render each side's retaliatory forces invulnerable. One method was through the development of a second-strike capability. The vulnerable bomber delivery system was largely a first-strike force. If it were surprised on the ground, it would be wiped out. This created a dangerous situation of mutual "trigger-happiness." A secure capability that could absorb any initial blow and still retaliate was necessary in order to minimize the temptation of a first strike. A retaliatory force had to be so well safeguarded that the enemy could not possibly cripple it. The capacity to defend a retaliatory force thus becomes the crucial element of a nuclear power's defense. Without a consciousness of invulnerability for its retaliatory capacity, a nation becomes unsure of its own security and therefore less likely to be a stabilizing element in the world. It is essential for the adversary to believe that he cannot win on "first strike"—that he cannot destroy one's own retaliatory force. The logic of the arms race, if left to itself, is escalation. The vicious circle can only be broken by regulation and agreement. The absence of high-level contacts between the superpowers and the deadlock on ratification of SALT II have been disquieting realities in the early 1980s.

The best method of developing a well-protected retaliatory force is to disperse it, harden it and, if possible, make it more mobile. Solid fuel missiles, which can be fired instantly, meet these criteria. They can be dispersed more easily than bombers, and they can be "hardened" by burying them in concrete silos, or they can be made mobile by basing them on nuclear-powered submarines. The mobile delivery system of the nuclear submarine has been the single most important element in an assured second-strike capability.

The critical importance of the dispersal, hardening and mobility of missiles is that an adversary is deprived of the ability to conduct a surprise attack without overwhelming retribution. Moreover, the knowledge that one possesses an invulnerable second-strike capability reduces the need for hair-trigger responses to an aggressor's nuclear threats and provocation. Thus, given the assumptions of arms control, a secure retaliatory force which ensures mutual deterrence seems to be the best guarantee against nuclear war.

But stable mutual deterrence does not necessarily mean equality in numbers. A balance is achieved when both sides have second-strike forces able to inflict an unacceptable level of damage to the enemy's homeland after absorbing an initial blow. Whether one side has 5,000 warheads while the other side has 10,000 is not the crux of the nuclear balance. The ability to respond with a secure retaliatory force is the crucial element. "Arms control" does not necessarily mean a reduction in nuclear armaments, but it certainly does not receive a race for parity or beyond. Since its primary goal is to eliminate the incentives for attack, the number of weapons, after a capacity of overkill has been achieved, is secondary. This line of argument, of course, holds only for the maintenance of a stable system of mutual deterrence. There may exist other incentives for the superpowers to build nuclear forces in excess of the requirement for stable deterrence, including efforts to use a perceived advantage to extract political concessions and influence international events by threat, implied or direct. But for the maintenance of mutual deterrence only one thing is needed—a secure, assured and manifest capability of inflicting unacceptable damage on the aggressor.

The number of weapons each side possesses is not nearly as significant as the type of weapon and how it contributes or detracts from the stability of the deterrent system. In the context of arms control, weapons that threaten the second-strike capability of either side increase the incentive for *both* to strike first. Conversely, any means of making either side's retaliatory capability more secure decreases the potential for attack. Thus, if the two superpowers were interested solely in the achievement of a stable *pax atomica,* it would be in their mutual interest not only to avoid any destabilizing technological innovation, but actually to aid their adversary in maintaining the viability of his second strike capability. Unhappily, the superpowers have not followed the logic of arms control to this conclusion, seeking instead technological advantages that could be exploited for unilateral benefit.

Both superpowers have developed a process of signaling their intentions to the adversary by a series of cues, both open and tacit. This form of communication serves as an aid in preventing misunderstanding and resulting miscalculation during crises. In the United States, particularly, there is a great deal of information available from both public and private sources on America's nuclear posture. During the 1960s, for example, there were many speeches explaining why the United States was building up its land- and sea-based delivery systems and how this build-up was part of an effort to stabilize the deterrent balance, not to threaten the Soviet Union. What the United States says is clearly important, but what it does is paramount. Together, the two have been intended to influence Soviet perceptions of American military strategy and thereby achieve a stable balance of capabilities.

Perhaps the single most difficult problem to manage within the context of arms control has been the process of rapid technological change in the superpower arms race. With each technological innovation in weapons systems comes a new uncertainty as to who is "ahead" and how the system of deterrence can best be adjusted and adapted. The danger of miscalculation during these periods of flux in the strategic balance is great. Arms control negotiations have sought to stabilize the superpower relationship so that the "action-reaction" dynamic of the arms race could be moderated. In the SALT process, each side sought agreements that would create reasonable and verifiable expectations about the future of the arms race, codifying the nature of the competition. Neither side necessarily sought to reduce the level of nuclear arms.

The Superpowers and the Status Quo

In the nuclear era, preservation of the political status quo has become of increasing importance for the superpowers. Change, in whatever guise, has been viewed as destabilizing and a threat to the intricate web of balances that the superpowers have constructed. This complex network of mutual restraint serves not only to moderate superpower conflicts but also to preserve their own predominant position in the world system. Both in their intra-alliance relations and in their dealings with regional conflicts, the superpowers have attempted to preserve their hegemonic role. Clearly, the possession of vast nuclear arsenals helps each to maintain its paramount position both within its own particular bloc and astride the world system.

Dramatic change can threaten the stability of mutual deterrence, and it can threaten the involvement of the superpowers in a confrontation, with all the attendant risks of escalation to nuclear war. Thus, both nations should in strict logic favor the defense of the existing balance. Lines of demarcation have been drawn around the world, alliances formed and commitments tendered. The United States has been afraid of falling dominoes and has sought to contain Soviet expansion; the Soviets have feared capitalist encirclement and therefore have sought secure buffer zones on their eastern and southern borders. Unfortunately, neither side is convinced that the other side is satisfied with a given situation and is not seeking a more advantageous balance.

When violence has been employed by a superpower in the nuclear age, it has been mainly to preserve, defend or consolidate the status quo, not to transform it drastically. Nuclear weapons have played a large role in this conservative drift in superpower policy. They have provided a strong impetus to prevent change that could draw the superpowers into the vortex of nuclear confrontation. A new subspecies of war has developed and proliferated to fit the special characteristics of the nuclear age. "Limited" war, or war fought with less than a nation's full military capabilities, has become the general mode of interstate conflict. Just as it may be argued that the existence of nuclear weapons has contributed to the era of general peace in relations between the superpowers, so might it also be argued that nuclear weapons have stimulated the contagion of limited war in which the superpowers act out their conflict in areas where something less than their vital interests is at stake. Vietnam, despite its huge cost in blood and money, was vital neither to the interests of the Soviet Union nor to those of the United States, and Afghanistan constitutes a marginal strategic backwater in the struggle between the superpowers. Before December 1979, most Americans probably could not have found Afghanistan on a map. It is only on the margins of world politics that leaders in Washington and Moscow have felt it prudent to employ any part of their vast military arsenals and even then only in terms of conventional weapons. The existence of nuclear weapons assures them that their adversary will not react in full strength.

When a regional conflict erupts, as in Vietnam, the Middle East, the Falklands, the Indian subcontinent or elsewhere, the two superpowers are usually sentimentally on opposite sides. But because of their nuclear consciousness they have been careful not to take their partisanship too far. In the Middle East, for example, the Soviet Union has been candidly on the Arab side; but it has not used its full capacity to inflame tensions. Indeed we usually find Washington and Moscow coming together to support cease-fires and thus to deprive these conflicts of their full potentiality of escalation.

Crisis Management in the Nuclear Age

While nuclear deterrence has kept the essentials of a minimal peace between the superpowers, it has not meant the avoidance of United States–Soviet confrontations and crises. In the bipolar world of the immediate postwar period this was hardly surprising since each superpower viewed any gain by its rival as a loss to itself. The emergence of other significant and independent actors in the world did little to lessen the dangers of superpower confrontations. In many critical instances, the superpowers were drawn into local conflicts. While such conflicts in several instances held the potential of escalation to the nuclear level, the end result has always exposed the irrelevance of nuclear arms except as an ultimate deterrent. The possession of nuclear weapons has contributed very little to successful conflict resolution. For the United States in Vietnam and in Iran, and for the Soviet Union lately in Afghanistan and in Poland, the possession of vast quantities of nuclear weapons has not enabled a superpower to secure political goals.

In an international system characterized by its anarchical nature, crises and conflicts are unavoidable. Yet, crises may perform a kind of regulatory function for the international system. When a dispute erupts into a full-scale crisis involving one or both of the superpowers, it indicates that there is a systemic problem requiring immediate remedy. If the superpowers act with restraint and prudence, the crisis can be resolved and the system may return to a peaceful and a more stable condition.

Unfortunately, in the nuclear age there have been few true "settlements" of international disputes. The postwar problem has been not how to resolve disputes, but how to live with them. Dean Rusk, when asked whether he hoped to be remembered for having achieved a settlement of the Berlin crisis, replied that he was not that vain. He merely hoped to be remembered for successfully passing on the problem intact to his successor. Thus, "crisis management" in the nuclear age has often involved papering over fundamental disputes in order to defuse the escalatory dangers posed by superpower confrontation.

An international crisis, by definition, suggests that the existing balance of power in international affairs has been significantly disturbed. In 1958, for example—the year after Sputnik and the first Soviet ICBM test—Moscow perceived that the balance of nuclear capabilities was shifting in its favor, and it attempted to exploit this military advantage for political gain. At the very least, Khrushchev must have felt that the Soviet Union possessed sufficient nuclear strength to deter an American attack. At best, he hoped to use the perceived Soviet ascendancy to intimidate the United States. In American leadership circles, the Soviet technological achievement contributed to a new sense of vulnerability. The American nuclear arsenal, particularly its SAC bombers, was said to be extremely susceptible to a surprise first strike—a nuclear Pearl Harbor. American credibility was thus subject to some doubt, especially in Europe.

The Soviet Union attempted to take advantage of its new capabilities and suddenly demanded that West Berlin be "demilitarized" and turned into a "free city" by withdrawal of Western troops. If the Western powers did not agree to this demand by the end of six months, the Soviet Union would turn the problem over to East Germany, with whom the Allied powers would then have to negotiate. If the Allies refused to cooperate—a likely condition, since the West did not even recognize the East German government—and if the Allied nations attempted to break a subsequent blockade, the Soviets warned they would be forced to come to the aid of their ally. On the other hand, if the Allies negotiated new terms of access to Berlin with the East Germans, it was likely that East Germany and Moscow would seek further to erode the Allied position.

What was at stake in the Berlin crisis was the balance of power. Both superpowers perceived a change in each other's capability and resolve. The threat of escalation to the nuclear level was implied in the Soviet demands. While total war might not be a "rational" instrument of national policy, the Soviets hoped that the threat to escalate would prove to be a potent political weapon in its own right. Nuclear war may be "unthinkable," but to brandish the *threat* of nuclear war is not unthinkable at all. The potential of nuclear escalation endows the nation seeking to alter the status quo with a powerful bargaining device. The Soviets posed the issue in a series of limited challenges, none of which individually seemed acute enough to cause the United States to risk nuclear war. If the United States failed to respond, however, its position in West Berlin would be eroded inexorably. And by exerting pressure on the United States to accede to its demands, the Soviet Union placed the burden for initiating the use of force on the West. The Soviets merely posed the demands; the United States was forced to decide whether to stand firm or to yield, knowing full well that force, including the threat of nuclear confrontation, might be required to back up a defense of West Berlin.

The essence of this form of coercion is to force an adversary to choose between suicide and surrender in the hope that he will opt for the latter. The defender of the status quo is placed in the awkward position of yielding or of firing the first shot in anger. If the Soviet tactic worked and America acceded to the demands, it could have sounded the death knell for the Western alliance. The "Finlandization" of Western Europe would have become a more likely prospect. NATO and the Common Market might have disintegrated while their individual members sought accommodation and peaceful coexistence with Moscow. As President Kennedy presented the challenge posed by the Berlin crisis: "The fulfillment of our pledge to that city is essential to the morale and the security of Western Germany, to the unity of Western Europe, and to the faith of the whole free world." On the other hand, an attempt by the United States to confront the Soviets directly raised the prospect of escalation, and perhaps even nuclear war.

The manner in which the United States sought to handle this dilemma is revealing and may have led to a Soviet perception that American commitments elsewhere were not entirely credible. Despite affirming in resolute public pronouncements their commitment to West Berlin, American leaders continually attempted to negotiate their way out of the bind. The United States, perhaps for the first time, was forced to treat the Soviet Union as a coequal superpower, one whose newly developed nuclear capability posed a threat to the American homeland. As a result, the United States sought to make diplomatic concessions to forestall the prospect of nuclear confrontation posed by the Soviet challenge in West Berlin.

By 1962, the Soviets had apparently become convinced that the United States would not resort to force to honor its commitments. Khrushchev talked openly of America's failure of nerve. The reluctance of the United States to support the abortive Bay of Pigs invasion provided evidence, and so did the West's passive acceptance of the Berlin Wall in August 1961. This perception that the United States lacked the resolve to use military force to back up its obligations may even have encouraged Khrushchev to install Soviet missiles in Cuba. On the basis of past American behavior, Moscow might have expected that after much public outcry and demands for the missiles' withdrawal, the United States would accept the *fait accompli* presented by the Soviet Union. In any test of will the Soviet leadership felt that it would triumph.

On this occasion, however, the United States did respond directly to the challenge. The threat to America's position in the world, as well as the perceived threat to the American mainland, was too direct, too clear, too menacing to be negotiated away. A failure of American will in the face of such a clear hemispheric challenge would have had dire consequences for America's position in the world. While an objective calculation of the strategic balance might not have been altered very much, as Defense Secretary Robert McNamara suggested at the time, the perception of that balance would have been altered dramatically in favor of the Soviet Union. The spillover effects of such a change would have affected U.S. interests and commitments everywhere. In Cuba the Soviets had violated a fundamental "rule of the game," which required a clear and authoritative American response.

There was little choice for Kennedy, then, but to demand the withdrawal of the missiles. Why was the United States more successful at compelling the Soviets to remove their missiles from Cuba than it had been at defending a frontier in Berlin? One reason was that many of the more hysterical fears over the so-called missile gap had been stilled by 1962. The United States had embarked on an intensive build-up of its nuclear arsenal; many of the Soviet claims of weapon and rocket production were discovered to have been exaggerated. The failure of the Soviet attempt to place missiles in Cuba demonstrated that the missile gap was ephemeral. When confronted by this reality in Cuba, the Soviets not only withdrew their missiles, but they also assumed a more conciliatory tone on negotiations generally, as evidenced by the test ban treaty of 1963.

A second reason for the American success in Cuba was that neither superpower wanted an actual nuclear showdown. Neither nation wished to breach the nuclear threshold or take any action that would inexorably lead in that direction. Thus, in each crisis the "compeller" held the clear advantage. During the several Berlin crises, Moscow thrust the responsibility for potential escalation upon the United States. In Cuba, Washington was able to reverse positions on Moscow by imposing a blockade ("quarantine") of Cuba. The Soviets would have to attempt to run the blockade; this meant that the initiative for the use of force was left with Moscow, and the United States by passive resolve was able to compel the withdrawal of the Soviet missiles.

A more general point needs to be made on crises in the nuclear age. Crises often erupt when the balance of capabilities and resolve is in a state of flux or when one side perceives itself to be ascendant and seeks to profit politically as a result. Conversely, after a crisis period, a new era of stability often ensues as the implications of the new balance become clearer. Thus, from 1958 to 1962, the Soviet-American strategic balance—both in capability and resolve—was extremely fluid. The Soviets sought political gains from their perceived ascendancy; the United States, somewhat uncomfortably, sought to cope with its new vulnerability. After Cuba, however, American superiority in both elements of the balance was firmly reestablished; the world had gone to the brink of nuclear war but had not tumbled into the abyss.

Following the missile crisis, both superpowers sought negotiated agreements that would lessen the prospects of future crises degenerating into nuclear war. The establishment of a "hotline," the limited test ban treaty and the ban on orbiting nuclear weapons in space all signaled a greater stability and order in the nuclear balance. Thus, the crises of the 1958–62 period revealed the central issues of the nuclear age: the superpowers learned that, of necessity, they would be forced to live with each other and avoid confrontations that posed the risk of nuclear war. This realization, however, did not—indeed could not—end the superpowers' struggle for political advantage. In the jargon of arms control, nuclear weapons were only useful to deter their very use. But since the dawn of the nuclear age the superpowers have also sought to devise strategies to give their weapons political weight and meaning.

U.S. Doctrines and Strategy in the Nuclear Age

Following World War II, the United States enjoyed virtual immunity from attack. The Soviets did not explode their first atomic bomb until 1949; they did not begin to develop a long-range bomber capability until 1954. On the other hand, the Soviet Union was vulnerable to SAC bombers for the entire period. Yet even under such apparently favorable strategic conditions, and with the United States firmly committed to resisting Communist aggression, the U.S. threat to respond to limited encroachments by attacking the Soviet homeland did not seem wholly credible. Nowhere was this more clearly demonstrated than in Korea. Not only was the U.S. nuclear arsenal ineffective as a deterrent to the North Korean invasion; it also did little to prevent the Chinese from entering the war when American forces approached the Yalu River.

Up to the early 1950s, the United States had yet to develop a coherent strategy for its nuclear arsenal. In Henry Kissinger's words, the United States "added the atomic bomb to [its] arsenal without integrating its implications into [military] thinking." In a sense, the nuclear age had not arrived. The American store of atomic weapons was small; the Soviets had yet to develop a deliverable atomic capability.

In 1953, however, the Eisenhower Administration tied together hardware and doctrine, creating a strategy for America's nuclear arsenal. The "New Look" attempted to find some means of employing nuclear weapons for national purposes. While it was acknowledged that the ultimate role for nuclear weapons should be to deter their use, U.S. policymakers sought at the very least to use the threat of nuclear attack to deter Soviet expansion. The answer, provided in its most authoritative form by Secretary of State John Foster Dulles, was the doctrine of "massive retaliation." Local defenses against Communist subversion would be reinforced by "the further deterrent of massive retaliatory power." The United States would deter Communist aggression by having the "capacity to retaliate, instantly, by means and at places of our own choosing."

By the late 1950s, however, inadequacies in the doctrine of massive retaliation were becoming apparent to American statesmen and strategists. While the threat of massive retaliation was an adequate deterrent to a Soviet attack against the American homeland, it had little credibility in deterring limited Soviet provocations around the world. Challenges to United States interests in Korea and in Indochina confronted U.S. policymakers with the impossible choice of humiliation or holocaust. Henry Kissinger, in his classic work *Nuclear Weapons and Foreign Policy,* summarized the situation this way:

> *At a time when we have never been stronger, we have had to learn that power which is not clearly related to the objectives for which it is to be employed may merely serve to paralyze the will . . . If the Soviet bloc can present the challenges in less than all out form . . . it . . . will then pose the appalling dilemma of whether we are willing to commit suicide to prevent encroachments, which do not, each in itself, seem to threaten our existence directly but which may be steps on the road to our ultimate destruction.*

Thus, prescriptions for a new type of "graduated" or "proportional" deterrence emerged. The idea was that in view of the wide array of military and political challenges posed by possible Soviet aggression, the United States should be prepared to respond flexibly, consistent with the nature of the threat. General Maxwell Taylor, in his book *The Uncertain Trumpet*, argued for a "strategy of flexible response" to provide "a capability to react across the entire spectrum of possible challenge, for coping with anything from general atomic war to infiltrations."

In the early 1960s, under the guidance of Secretary of Defense Robert McNamara, the United States adopted an essentially two-track nuclear strategy. The problem of containing "conventional" Soviet aggression in Europe was separated from the requirements of deterring a strategic Soviet attack on the American homeland. The policy of flexible response called for a renewed emphasis on American conventional military strength; for a declared willingness to "escalate as necessary" in order to repel aggression; and the forward placement of tactical nuclear weapons and conventional capabilities that would permit the United States to escalate its response gradually in proportion to the provocation. In Europe, this implied a readiness to breach the nuclear threshold if NATO faced the possible defeat of its conventional forces.

During this period, the requirements of deterring a strategic nuclear attack on the American homeland remained essentially unchanged, although the problem was compounded by the increases in the Soviet nuclear arsenal. According to McNamara, American nuclear forces needed to have "the ability to survive a first blow and respond with devastating power." Mutual assured destruction (MAD) became enshrined as America's chief deterrent strategy. McNamara, however, did not intend that MAD should obviate all attempts at military planning. Though nuclear war was unthinkable, one needed a strategy nonetheless if it should come, and this strategy was called "counterforce." McNamara noted: "Principal military objectives, in the event of a nuclear war stemming from a major attack on the NATO alliance, should be the destruction of the enemy's military forces, not of his civilian population."

Toward the end of the Ford Administration in 1976, CIA Director George Bush asked a number of experts on Soviet affairs and defense to prepare an alternative to the agency's National Intelligence Estimate. The nongovernmental team, the B team, concluded that between 1965 and 1975 official intelligence estimates had consistently underestimated Soviet military spending as well as Soviet nuclear and conventional capabilities. Members of the B team took their case to the public, arguing in books, periodicals and on editorial pages that the Soviet Union was bent on limitless nuclear expansion that would provide it with the capacity to launch a disarming first strike against the

United States, to fight a nuclear war to a successful conclusion or to use the threat of either event to coerce the American leadership into making major political concessions. Reconstituted under the Committee on the Present Danger, the "hawks" on the B team fought tooth and nail against the Carter Administration's proposed SALT II treaty, which they regarded as "fatally flawed." With help from the Soviet Union in Cuba and Afghanistan, the militant school in America's strategic community managed to derail SALT II. Then in 1980 a President was elected who promised a thorough overhaul and modernization of U.S. strategic forces.

Ronald Reagan called on America to shake off the syndrome of Vietnam and the debacle in Iran, and to reassert itself as a global power. In nuclear weapons development, Reagan proposed a six-year, $180 billion program, including the construction of the MX missile, the B-1 bomber, the Trident II missile, air-, land- and sea-based missiles, as well as more exotic weapons such as hunter-killer satellites and laser weaponry, in order to shift the strategic balance back in favor of the United States. Arms control, notably the SALT II treaty, was allowed to languish. In nuclear doctrine, the Reagan Administration continued the strategy adopted in 1980 by Carter in Presidential Directive 59, which called for the increased targeting of Soviet missile silos, command facilities and shelters for Soviet leadership.

The most recent Pentagon five-year survey of American defense capabilities advocates that the United States develop the strategies and weapons systems for waging a "protracted" nuclear war. The United States seems to have completed the gradual shift in U.S. nuclear strategy from MAD to NUTS (nuclear utilization target selection). Some American planners now contemplate the use of limited nuclear weapons in a variety of war-fighting contexts, and some spokesman of the Reagan Administration has scared to death a goodly portion of humanity, including the American public, with offhand remarks about nuclear warning shots and limited nuclear war.

The idea that we continue to live in a "MAD" world increasingly threatened by the prospect of nuclear war is perhaps most subtly understood by the Europeans, who have lived for the better part of the postwar period both under the protective umbrella and under the potential stormclouds of nuclear weapons. While American insistence on its own nuclear strategy is often well founded in practical terms, the United States has shown little psychological understanding of European anxieties. The rhetoric in which the United States talks as if a nuclear war were a rational possibility may or may not intimidate the Soviets. It certainly frightens Europe to death. On balance, much would be gained by greater reticence.

NATO and Nuclear Strategy

Since NATO's founding in 1949, the defense of Western Europe has rested on America's nuclear guarantee, buttressed by the presence of United States and European conventional forces. During the early years of the alliance America's overwhelming superiority in deliverable nuclear weapons gave great credibility to the American commitment. But as evidenced by the Sputnik launching in 1957, the Soviet Union had acquired its own capability to launch nuclear weapons against the United States. This new capability forced a reexamination of NATO doctrine. For every member of NATO, the critical question posed was whether the United States would defend Western Europe if the Soviet Union could threaten a direct attack on American cities. Was defending Hamburg, for example, worth the risk of a Soviet nuclear attack against New York?

The NATO response to this new Soviet threat was the "flexible response" of the Kennedy Administration: an increase of U.S. conventional forces in Europe and a huge deployment of American tactical nuclear weapons. By the late 1960s, some 7,000 such weapons were present in Europe. NATO's flexible response strategy emphasized "controlled deliberate escalation," including explicitly the first use of nuclear weapons in response to a Soviet invasion. NATO strategy once again rested on America's lead in nuclear arms. The use of tactical medium-range weapons in the European theater was linked to the possible use of American strategic nuclear weapons. If the threatened use of tactical nuclear weapons failed to deter Soviet attack, then the United States would be forced to attack the Soviet Union directly with its strategic capability.

Whether the Soviets found this threat credible is impossible to say; clearly no war occurred in Europe during this period. In fact, some of America's NATO allies seemed to doubt the American commitment more than the Russians did. France, under Charles de Gaulle, not only withdrew from NATO's military arrangement but developed its own nuclear capability, the *force de frappe*.

In the 1970s, Soviet military gains once again necessitated more strategic adjustments by NATO. Improved Soviet conventional forces and the seeming possibility of a Soviet blitzkrieg-style attack compelled NATO to adopt a long-term plan in 1978 for 3 percent annual increments in NATO defense spending, with particular emphasis on resupply and mobilization of NATO resources. A Brookings Institution study posed the issue with blunt candor: "The credibility of

NATO strategy . . . rests, in large measure, on the certainty of timely U.S. reinforcements."

In the area of nuclear doctrine, NATO strategy reflected the growing American preoccupation with Soviet advances in "theater" weapons targeted on NATO military installations. In the late 1970s, disputes arose between some European NATO members (particularly the Low Countries) and the United States over the deployment of new weapons, specifically the neutron bomb and theater weapons such as the cruise missile and the Pershing II intermediate-range ballistic missile. Designed to counter the new Soviet theater nuclear missile, particularly the SS-20, the cruise and Pershing II missiles met a storm of controversy. Many Europeans fear that America is preparing to fight a limited nuclear war on the European continent. Though all the NATO governments approved the theater weapons modernization plan in December 1979, the unease in European public opinion since then reflects a growing fear that the new round of the nuclear arms competition increases the danger of general nuclear war. As former SALT negotiator Paul Warnke observed, "A tactical nuclear weapon is one that goes off in Germany."

Disarmament and the Nuclear Freeze

The fear of nuclear war in the 1980s has spurred wide public interest in the movement for nuclear disarmament. Begun in Europe as a response to the proposed deployment of new U.S. theater weapons, the movement has now spread to American shores in the form of a suggested "freeze" on the level of nuclear weapons. One proposal from the grass-roots freeze campaign calls for "a mutual freeze on the testing, production, and deployment of nuclear weapons" and of nuclear delivery systems. In short, a cease-fire in place in the arms race; the Senate resolution sponsored by Edward Kennedy and Mark Hatfield is closely modeled on this version of the freeze.

Another major proposal is the resolution put forward by Senators John Warner and Henry Jackson. Supported by advocates of a strong defense, this freeze proposal argues for "a long-term and mutually verifiable nuclear forces freeze at equal and sharply reduced levels of force." The key word is "equal," implying that a freeze in place would be of greater benefit to the Soviet Union at this time. In this proposal, endorsed by the Reagan Administration, the United States calls for some leeway to replace obsolete weapons systems in order to ensure the stable preservation of mutual deterrence. This is the traditional approach expressed in the SALT process and the START negotiations which began in June 1982.

The Soviets, for their part, also support general freeze proposals. In

November 1981 President Reagan offered his zero option on inter-mediate-range nuclear weapons in Europe. This essentially canceled deployment of Pershing II and ground-launched cruise missiles if the Soviets would agree to dismantle their SS-4s, SS-5s and 300 SS-20s. The more recent Reagan proposal for starting a new round of negotiations on strategic weapons, including a substantial reduction in the number of nuclear warheads and long-range missiles each side could possess, has met with a lukewarm response in Moscow, although it was well received by some European governments. Since he is proposing cuts in Soviet land-based missiles while failing to address curtailment of American advantages in submarine-launched missiles, long-range bombers and cruise missiles, Mr. Reagan's suggestion appears as no more than an opening gambit in the negotiating process. And, to the disappointment of disarmament advocates, neither the Reagan START proposal nor any of the Soviet offers prevents any new weapons testing or any contemplated weapons deployment.

The public outcry over the dangers of nuclear war cannot be ignored. Seven hundred thousand nuclear demonstrators marched in New York in June 1982 in the largest political demonstration in U.S. history. In Britain, West Germany and Holland the anti-nuclear movement is massive. There are even anti-nuclear stirrings in the Soviet bloc which the officially sanctioned Soviet Peace Movement cannot always control. For the first time in the nuclear age, the general public has taken a strong interest in the subject of nuclear weapons and their accompanying doctrines. Something of this atmosphere has begun to pervade establishment circles. There is no other explanation for the surprising call by Robert McNamara, George Kennan, Gerard Smith and McGeorge Bundy, in April 1982, for a unilateral gesture by the United States, renouncing the idea of "first use" of nuclear weapons before any real progress has been made in strengthening the relative power of the West in conventional arms. It is difficult for an outside observer to understand at first sight how any form of unilateralism could strengthen the deterrent power of the Western alliance at a time when that power is not as convincing as it was before the USSR developed a capacity to strike at American cities.

On the other hand, these authoritative spokesmen would probably not have intervened if they did not feel that official American policy was obscure about its central aim. Does the United States aim only at deterrence through the massive power of second-strike retaliation? Or does it secretly seek a first-strike option? The Administration's policy of stationing multihead MX missiles in vulnerable silos seems to give credence to the latter belief.

It was a European anxiety rather than a superpower initiative that stimulated the sudden movement in nuclear diplomacy in 1982–1983.

After a period during which the Reagan Administration in the United States evinced a skeptical and cautious attitude to arms-control agreements, the pressure of American public opinion and of the European allies forced American policy into a more mobile posture. The background reality was the reluctance of some NATO allies to accommodate cruise and Pershing intermediate-range nuclear missiles on their soil to counterbalance the Soviet SS-20 missiles. In some European countries this reluctance was enunciated by governments; in others, such as Britain under Margaret Thatcher and West Germany under Helmut Kohl, the governments were favorable to the American policy but they encountered large-scale protest movements and resistance by opposition parties. It was plain that without some evidence of flexibility in negotiation the United States would be unable to enlist all its allies in the next stage of nuclear deterrence. European statesmen were making an enlightened use of their bargaining power within the alliance; they were trading their readiness to receive the nuclear missiles for an American readiness to enter meaningful negotiations. President Reagan's "zero option" of November 1982 proposed complete abstention from the installation of the cruise and Pershing missiles in return for the dismantling of the Soviet SS-20 missiles already targeted on West European population centers. The USSR response included a proposal to allow the Soviet Union to retain a number of intermediate-range missiles equivalent to the British and French nuclear weaponry. The idea of a "balance" between Soviet and Anglo-French weaponry aroused derision in Washington, but pressure on President Reagan to offer compromise on his utopian "zero option" mounted. Early in April 1983 Mr. Reagan acceded to this idea; he proposed mutual agreed reduction of intermediate-range missiles as a stage of progress toward ultimate abolition.

It is still not clear whether any agreement is imminent, but the last phase of the nuclear debate has illustrated two significant political facts: the increase of European influence in what had been a bipolar U.S.A.-USSR dialogue; and the inexorability of governmental response to public opinion in democratic countries even when governments consider the public opinion to be uninformed.

While public opinion on this matter generally incites governments toward greater flexibility, it is necessary for the sake of accuracy and fairness to mention the opposite viewpoint. This rests on traditional ideas of negotiating psychology which have never been proved obsolete. In its immediate application to the nuclear controversy, this thesis states that the Soviet Union is very unlikely to accept a compromise involving the non-installation of cruise and Pershing missiles unless there is actually a beginning of their installation. When President Reagan was asked to comment on this idea he said: "If you're going to negotiate, you have to have some strength on your side . . . You have to have some reason for them to look at and weigh the value of reducing their own weaponry."

The general experience of negotiation supports this view. It is more difficult to dismantle a reality than to renounce an intention. It follows that a promise to abstain from a projected action has less weight than a spectacular removal of something that already exists. This was one of the substantive reasons for the Soviet disdain of President Reagan's zero-option proposal. The American "zero" was already extant; the Soviet "zero" had to be painfully manufactured. And the Soviets still hoped to prevent the installation of cruise and Pershing missiles without reciprocal concession, by fomenting the anti-nuclear unilateralism in vogue in some Western countries. One has to be an incurable illusionist to imagine the Soviet leaders, of all people, paying for something that might be obtained free of charge.

The anguish of Europe in the face of its own role as the "host" of new American nuclear weapons (cruise and Pershing) came to expression in reaction to the memorable speech by Kissinger in Brussels in which he declared that

> Our European allies should not keep asking us to multiply strategic assurances that we cannot possibly mean, or if we do mean, we should not want to execute, because if we execute, we risk the destruction of civilization.

One of the European interpretations of this explosive remark was that America would hesitate to make a nuclear response even to a danger of Europe becoming overwhelmed by the conventional forces of the Soviet Union. This strongly confirmed the wisdom of France and Britain in maintaining their own independent nuclear deterrent.

Another convincing statement in support of an independent European nuclear capacity came from an authoritative British source, Lord Zuckerman, who has advised successive British governments on scientific and strategic problems:

> On the positive side, there is another reason why the United Kingdom should retain its nuclear arsenal, and which to the best of my knowledge has never been deployed. Paradoxically, its continued possession could help in the process of world disarmament, not because the U.K. might be allowed to argue the case in the conference chamber but because the scale of what it has, and what France has, is an indication to the two superpowers of the forces that are adequate to maintain a nuclear threat.

The notion that the two superpowers could maintain a nuclear balance at an immensely lower quantitative level is the kind of simple truth that becomes self-evident as soon as it is enunciated clearly. The objective is, after all, balance, not any particular quantity beyond the capacity to inflict vast destruction. Yet this simple veracity has been lost from view in all the talk about "parity," "superiority" and "who is ahead of whom?"

The fallacy arises from the idea that the nuclear balance is a military matter susceptible to military advice. It is not a military issue at all. On the contrary, the familiar criteria for military judgments are so irrelevant to nuclear problems that they should be set aside. In the history of conventional war, quantity has mattered very much indeed. So also has the capacity to advance far into the enemy's territory. If the generals had their way we should all have to keep a garrison on the moon to defend us against a possible attack from Mars. And we would never agree voluntarily to let our adversary have a numerical advantage in any weapon. There is nothing discreditable in this kind of advice from military establishments; military commanders have a professional commitment to anxiety. They should be encouraged to give worst-case analysis. But their advice should not become the only automatic source of decision. Statesmen and diplomats, in danger of being overwhelmed by the authority of uniforms, should heed the directive sent by Lord Salisbury to one of his envoys:

> If I took your gloomy view, I should commence immediate inquiries as to the most painless form of suicide. But I think you listen too much to soldiers . . . You should never trust in experts. If you believe the doctors nothing is wholesome; if you believe the theologians nothing is innocent; if you believe the soldiers nothing is safe. They all require to have their strong wine diluted by a very large admixture of insipid common sense . . .

A nuclear balance at a lower level would not exclude the theoretical possibility of a disaster greater than any in the history of war. A small fraction of the existing number of warheads could devastate the planet but the psychological effects of a reversal in the insane dynamic of quantitative escalation might be very great. Few things are more improbable than a nuclear war between the superpowers, but on this issue improbability is not enough. The constant fluctuation in a race for numerical predominance gives the impression that what should be inconceivable is being seriously conceived.

Is There an Alternative to Deterrence?

However unattractive the ethical implications may be, it is certain that the nuclear fear has had an inhibiting effect on the outbreak and scope of wars. Great Power involvement in military operations, although alarming and deplorable whenever it occurs, has been less frequent and more controlled than the number and intensity of unsolved politi-

cal conflicts would have dictated in a previous age. Yet the disarmament and arms control conferences have not contributed significantly
to this result. They have mainly been manipulated for purposes of
propaganda. There is now a familiar technique: any plan proposed by
any party usually includes one set of proposals designed to appeal to
world public opinion and another set of proposals that the other party
is certain not to accept. Each party then accuses the other of neglecting
a possibility of real disarmament.

The problem of arms control is not the problem of arms control
alone; it is, in a deeper sense, the problem of the organization of the
world community. There is an undoubted revulsion on the part of the
nuclear powers to use their destructive capacities, but no way has yet
be found to institutionalize that revulsion. The only rational course is
to accept military power as a reality, and instead of a vain attempt at
abolition, to try to manage it successfully so that wars become less
likely and frequent and more susceptible to limitation if they do break
out.

The first question to ask is whether nuclear war is inevitable. The
pessimists point out that there has never been an accumulation of
armaments without the arms being put to use sooner or later. According to this view the inevitability of war is inherent in the very existence
of the weapons and, more especially, in their vast multiplication and
diffusion.

The weakness of this argument lies precisely in its recourse to experience. Nothing is more fallacious than to deduce nuclear conclusions
from non-nuclear precedents. It is true that nations have always regarded certain interests and causes as superior to peace; but when a
particular form of war becomes not only murderous but suicidal, the
list of objectives that can rationally be regarded as worth the risk of
nuclear attack becomes so drastically reduced that reference to the
past is of small relevance. The probability of war with the use of the
total capacity of the belligerents is less than it was in the period when
the consequences of war were capable of remedy. Nuclear weapons are
a revolution and not merely just another stage in weapons development. There may well have occurred what one authority has called "a
break in the continuity of history," as a result of which "victory has
been drained of its content."

Diplomacy usually appeals to tradition and comparative analysis for
a solution of its problems, but no such help is available in nuclear
issues. The contingencies and choices are new and unique, so that the
intellectual challenge is correspondingly more acute than ever before.
It is true that it has been notoriously difficult to make accurate predictions about the likelihood of war or about its possible scope; optimistic

theories have usually been discredited. In 1931 a British enthusiast of disarmament and collective security, Lord Robert Cecil, declared that "war has never been less likely than today"; a week later the Manchurian battle broke out in what has since been considered to have been the beginning of World War II. But in any real sense a contemporary comparison is irrelevant precisely because of the new restraints created by weapons development.

The fact that bombs were actually used at Hiroshima and Nagasaki seems to confirm the deterministic view that all weapons invented are destined to be used; but it is obvious that the American decision in August 1945 was not inevitable. The choice of a deterrent demonstration was not taken as seriously as it would be today. In 1945 there was no restraining fear of retaliation, so that the decision-making process in that case is not a viable point of departure for estimating the likelihood of a similar decision today. It is hard to believe that Truman's decision would have been taken so firmly if Japan had been capable of withstanding a first strike and returning the nuclear fire. It can be argued that what made Hiroshima possible was not the existence of nuclear weapons, but the lack of a deterrent inhibition. Today the probability of a nuclear strike must be discussed in a climate of balance, or near balance, not of monopoly. Whereas in the conventional age a Great Power could say, "Accept my demands or I shall destroy you," today it can only say, "Accept my demands or I shall destroy myself—and you." It is axiomatic that the credibility of such a threat is almost negligible.

The pessimists might retort that even in the era of balance a nuclear war was an imminent possibility in October 1962 and that something that nearly happened cannot be dismissed as improbable. The answer to this is that the exemplary effects of the Cuban missile crisis are more likely to serve both parties as deterrent warnings rather than as models for emulation. Moreover, there is reason to doubt whether the nuclear factor was decisive in the evolution and termination of that crisis. An American authority has convincingly concluded:

> *Our capability for limited war—that is, our supremacy in conventional and naval forces—had more to do with the successful outcome of the crisis than our overwhelming superiority in strategic nuclear weaponry.*

In October 1973 the Nixon Administration ordered a nuclear alert in response to Soviet threats of intervention on behalf of Egypt to halt Israel's advance in Sinai. The psychological and symbolic aspects of this action predominated so strongly over its potential military consequence that we may safely say now—as was felt at the time—that the risk of actual nuclear confrontation was not substantial. The Soviet

Union showed a capacity for graceful retreat. It pretended that the dispatch of UN observers from Eastern and Western states would have the same effect as that which Brezhnev had proposed to achieve by unilateral Soviet intervention! This conclusion retrospectively proves that Kissinger, who controlled the American crisis moves while Nixon agonized over Watergate, was exercising a deterrent strategy with courage but not with excessive risk or audacity. Like Kennedy in 1962, he must have known that there was only one way in which the diplomatic confrontation could end once the picture of American resolve was imprinted on the Soviet mind. There is no evidence as yet to sustain the demonological view that the Soviet Union is more eager than any Western country to become involved in nuclear war.

Moralists might prefer a more enlightened and altruistic motive for the avoidance of nuclear war than the fear of retribution. But if no other motive exists we might as well cherish what we have. The abolition of nuclear weapons is not a viable alternative. Scientific and technological innovations are not reversible; the genie cannot be put back in the bottle. Deterrence is morally unattractive but it is more realistic than abolition.

No less futile than the call for abolition of nuclear weapons is the appeal for world government. This approach sounds loftily utopian, but it is in fact defeatist. Nations are not about to surrender their power of individual decision in matters of security. To make the avoidance of tragedy dependent on a condition that has no chance of fulfillment is a counsel of despair.

More serious than these messianic dreams are proposals of more limited scope designed to mitigate the heavy, brooding atmosphere surrounding the nuclear problem. One of these is the idea of nuclear-free zones. They have been suggested for Central Europe (the Rapacki plan), Latin America, Scandinavia and the Middle East. These proposals have important symbolic value as indications of a desire to reduce tensions, but they are not strictly relevant to the strategy of avoiding nuclear conflict. To be without nuclear weapons is not a guarantee against being attacked by nuclear weapons; after all, Hiroshima and Nagasaki were nuclear-free zones. A region declaring itself "nuclear-free" is very similar to a nation declaring itself "neutral." If some neutral countries have not been invaded, such as Switzerland in the two world wars, it would be hard to prove that this was because of their declared neutrality. It was either because there was no strategic necessity for a belligerent to violate their frontiers, or because the neutrality was useful to the belligerents or because they had prudently modeled themselves on the example of the porcupine; bristly animals are not a tempting target for a wrestling match. Nuclear-free zones, like neutrality, are a unilateral hope, not a prescription for safety.

Even a drastic lowering of the level of the central nuclear balance such as I have advocated here is an alleviating measure in the psychological sense rather than a guarantee against nuclear attack or intimidation. Given the ease of concealing a few nuclear warheads as against the difficulty of hiding large quantities of conventional weapons, it could even be argued that in an atmosphere of reduction a deceitful country that kept very few nuclear devices could achieve a power of assault or intimidation in a way that would have been difficult in the conventional age. In pre-nuclear days it was virtually impossible for any country to carry out a serious rearmament program in secrecy. The processes of manufacture, to say nothing of the products themselves, are so bulky and visible that effective concealment is impossible. Britain and France had exact knowledge of Hitler's "secret" rearmament; if they drew no adequate conclusions, it was because of a failure of will, not of forewarning. There have been many surprises in the anticipation of attack but hardly any surprises concerning an adversary's strength. With conventional weapons it is easier to conceal intention than to conceal capacity. In the era of nuclear weapons systems a reduction agreement would require more detailed and stringent verification than some governments would regard as compatible with their domestic structure. To sum up: although it is by no means a panacea, an agreement to maintain a nuclear balance at a lower level would furnish the best psychological background for what must remain the ultimate hope of nuclear peace—the fear of reprisal accompanied by the possibility of conciliation.

Here diplomacy faces another paradox. It used to be thought that there was a direct relationship between the avoidance of war and the solution of problems that provoke tensions. This is no longer self-evident. The nuclear age does not offer strong incentives for radical conflict resolution. The possibility of preserving peace without eliminating the issues that threaten it is greater in this era than in the past. Governments are tempted to avoid the painful compromises required to solve conflicts; they take refuge in the thought that the balance of prudence will prevent major conflagration even if the basic problems remain unresolved. The nuclear age is more congenial to partial settlement than to radical solutions.

The advantage of the balance of terror—or the "balance of prudence," as Raymond Aron has called it—is that it is self-implementing; it does not depend on written agreements or institutions. It operates, if at all, through the intrinsic self-interest of the parties. It presupposes enough rationality to preclude suicidal adventure. But even if there is an unwritten agreement to maintain it, there is need for preventive measures in some directions. What happens if there is an accidental development, so that war breaks out without conscious deliberation?

There are imaginative scenarios both in literature and in war-games-manship in which nuclear warfare becomes feasible even if there is a mutual desire to avoid it. Some of these scenarios are concerned with technical breakdowns. A code signal for nuclear attack is wrongly transmitted and acted upon; a crazy commander of a submarine or aircraft decides to avenge his country's honor; a missile goes off accidentally and the avowal of error is not believed by the adversary; a false alarm leads country A to take defensive preparations which country B, knowing that it has no aggressive designs, assumes to be preparation for an unprovoked attack.

These nightmares afflict the arms controllers, and they have done well to dispel them. The measures for avoiding war by misunderstanding are diverse and reassuring. They include direct communication between the leaders of the superpowers, reciprocal advance notice of maneuvers and troop movements, military missions in each superpower capital and abstention from bomber flights in areas or periods of tension. The system seems able to absorb and neutralize an error or miscalculation, and the melancholy view that a single nuclear weapon would inevitably start the entire chain of universal destruction underestimates the will and capacity of the nuclear powers to halt a nuclear process before it escalates beyond control.

Surprise Attack

The trouble is that the statement that a surprise attack with nuclear weapons is "very improbable" does not have the same reassuring effect as would a corresponding statement on conventional war. The stakes are so awesome that there must be a search for something close to complete certainty. The safeguards must be detailed and sophisticated. This means that adversaries must develop the kind of intimacy that usually prevails only among friends, who—if they were friends—would not need the safeguards. Adversaries are especially sensitive to the possibility of surprise attack. Both superpowers carry traumatic memories of having been surprised by the most dangerous assault that each has ever suffered in its history—the United States by Japan at Pearl Harbor in December 1941 and the Soviet Union by the German invasion of June 22, 1941.

The usual thinking about the problem of surprise attack revolves around the idea of the invulnerable reprisal capacity. If the surprise attack is not going to be a "knock-out" and will invite a massive counterblow, it loses much of its appeal. Another means for safeguarding oneself against surprise attack lies in improved intelligence and warning systems. These are adversarial approaches. But if we presuppose a mutual desire to avoid the consequences of surprise attack, there

would also seem to be room for a cooperative approach to the problem. Various attempts to reach such understandings have been made,
beginning with the Geneva meeting on surprise attack in November
1958. The obstacle lay not so much in the subject itself as in the
ostensibly extraneous issue of "closed" versus "open" societies. The
United States proposed extremely thorough and rigorous mutual inspection by air, sea and land, including the sensational idea of each
power maintaining radar installations on the territory of the other. The
Soviet Union accepted some control stations in the Warsaw pact area,
but without free movement! It also required a linkage between this
measure and the acceptance of Soviet proposals of a substantive nature. No concrete agreements have yet been reached, but there is a
hopeful atmosphere in the discussion precisely because there is a
reciprocal interest. Of all the possibilities of progress, an agreement
to prevent surprise attack seems to be the least arduous.

Living with Nuclear Weapons

The world is destined to live dangerously, but this does not mean that
it will not live. The prospects for the rest of the eighties may not be
encouraging, but they are at least predictable. Nuclear arms will not
disappear, and it is not certain that they will even be diminished. Their
overall effect will be to set limits and restraints on the use of armed
force. The superpowers will cooperate in the avoidance of surprise
attack and may reach agreements on balances such as those illustrated
by the SALT agreements. Apart from the two major nuclear powers,
France, Britain and China will preserve their nuclear option, and some
smaller countries may keep a nuclear weapon in the background of
their consciousness—or in more concrete places—even if they do not
proclaim, confess or brandish their capability. After thirty-seven years
without any war between any two major powers it is impossible to
dismiss the Churchillian rhetoric which told us that "safety will be the
sturdy child of terror."

The effects of nuclear weaponry on the psychology and culture of
the next generations are harder to predict. There are signs of melancholy engendered by a sense of vulnerability in a world where everything is volcanic and nothing appears stable. Against this background
the public revolt against the nuclear arms race is bound to escalate and
to force itself upon the attention of governments and parliaments.

The mass pressure for unilateral renunciation gained ground
dramatically in the early 1980s. The motives and justifications for
unilateral renunciation of nuclear weapons are not uniform. They
range from strictly pragmatic assertions to counsels of apocalyptic
despair. The pragmatists assert that Soviet power should not be exag-

gerated; that Moscow has abandoned its revolutionary vocation and would not try to spread its ideology by force; that the Soviet Union would not seek to annex a defenseless Europe since it would find its conquest indigestible; that all that the West needs is a credible capacity for retaliation—which already exists; and that a Soviet Union faced by a Western world voluntarily stripped of its nuclear weapons would be shamed into joining the movement. Some unilateralists go further; they are frank to admit that even if the Soviet Union applies its monopoly of force against an unarmed Europe, "Better Red than dead"; even subjugation to Soviet rule would be a lesser evil than the results of a nuclear war.

The British unilateralists, including the Labour Party, compromise the moral argument since they are prepared to rely overtly and explicitly on the American nuclear deterrent while keeping their own country nuclear-free. In Japan and in the United States itself there are demonstrations against any visible or audible plan for nuclear modernization. In theory these are demonstrations against all nuclear weapons, but in fact it is only the American bomb that incurs opposition, since Soviet ears are not assailed by the demonstrators.

A complicating factor in this debate is the claim of one of the schools of thought to moral superiority over the other. It is hard to see why the advocates of unilateral renunciation are more "moral" than those who seek to prevent war by a reciprocal balance of deterrents and incentives. If the abolitionists and the balancers are both sincerely trying to prevent war, it would seem that they ought to be judged only by the effectiveness, not the virtue, of their solutions. Why is the prevention of conflict by effective deterrence less moral than the invitation to conflict by avoidable imbalance? In the history of conventional conflict it has been empirically established that unilateral disarmament can end in war, not in tranquillity. Statesmanship must be judged by consequence, not by intention. In the late 1930s Neville Chamberlain almost certainly wanted peace and detested war more passionately than Winston Churchill did, but his appeasement of dictators provoked war, whereas Churchill's call for a timely rearmament program, if heeded, might have secured peace. Since peace is a moral value, the warrior was more "moral" than the pacifist.

It would be incongruous if the protagonists of the two approaches were to fall apart in acrimony like separate and mutually hostile nations. Living with the nuclear anguish is a universal predicament, and it deserves a universal and cooperative preoccupation. If this is described as a classic confrontation between ends and means, the end of avoiding nuclear war is so transcendent that it must claim priority over the means by which it is achieved. The test of unilateral renunciation is whether it would achieve its end more effectively than the balance theory, which has worked for thirty-seven years. The tendency of the unilateralists to pre-empt the moral argument was reinforced in 1982 by a remarkable discussion in religious movements and especially in the Catholic Church. A draft pastoral letter prepared by the Bishops' Commission of the Catholic Church in the United States seemed to align the church with such ideas as "no first use" and a prohibition of injury to civilian populations. Although the Washington meeting of the bishops in November 1982 conducted the debate on moral and Biblical premises, some of the results brought the bishops into collision with official U.S. and NATO policy. The immunity of civilian populations virtually annuls the use of nuclear weapons and goes against the deterrent philosophy of Mutual Assured Destruction. And the draft pastoral letter, in denying first use, goes on to say that "Non-nuclear attacks by another state must be resisted by other than nuclear means."

These views, whatever the origin of their formulation, constitute frank interventions in the strategic nuclear debate. It seemed as if the very morality of deterrence was being threatened on the grounds that if it is immoral to do something, it must be immoral to threaten it. Under the influence of second thoughts and of Administration persuasion, the bishops amended their formulations in the direction of less rigor and greater flexibility. Pope John Paul II himself, addressing the United Nations Special Session on Disarmament in June 1982, caused relief in U.S. and NATO circles when he declared that "in current conditions 'deterrence' based on balance, certainly not as an end in itself but as a step on the way towards a progressive disarmament, may still be judged morally acceptable." Protestant churches and Jewish rabbinical organizations issued declarations against nuclear war but without condemning deterrence. Secular opinion was not intimidated by the intense activism of the clergy in the nuclear debate. Some commentators pointed out that there was a lack of symmetry in the whole exercise; the churches were able to influence opinion in the West but not in the Soviet Union, and there was thus an intrinsic imbalance in the consequences of their activity. Others pointed out that if there is a moral judgment on deterrence, there should be an effort to examine the moral consequences of the alternatives. Is it immoral to commit an evil (deterrence) in order to prevent an even greater evil (nuclear war)? In the end, the clerical speakers and writers found themselves dividing up according to the spectrum of views held outside the churches. Morality, like political judgment, is surrounded by ambiguity, not by dogmatic certainty. The prevalent views in the churches, as expressed in their resolutions and declarations, do not rule out the principles of balance and reciprocity.

Yet however logical the idea of a nuclear balance may be, defense leaders in the West find it more and more difficult to win the understanding and sacrifice that they need from their own people. Defense is not a popular theme in democracies. This has many explanations. First, particularly in modern times, the costs of defense are so prohibitively high that national economies have great difficulty in sustaining them. The nuclear age has made the choice between "guns or butter" particularly difficult. Second, there is doubt whether war achieves anything, so that the difference between victory and defeat is blurred. Third, and most decisive, is the fact that defense is too often discussed in its own limited terms without reference to the larger purpose for which defense may be worth the effort and resources needed to sustain it.

The notion that all war is totally ineffective is a fallacy based on a half-truth. But a strong case can be made for the proposition that wars that are not fought for defensive aims usually end badly for those who initiate them. John G. Stoessinger goes so far as to say that "no nation that began a major war in this century emerged a winner."

The list of wars that seem to validate this view is impressive. Germany began two wars in this generation and both ended in unconditional surrender; Japan failed in its attack on the United States in 1941; North Korea did not destroy the independence of South Korea; the Arab states began a thirty-year war for the purpose of destroying Israel's statehood and lost many territories while Israel became progressively more secure and established; Pakistan believed that "weak" Indian leadership after Nehru offered a chance of punishing that country for its encroachment in Kashmir and ended up mutilated and in diminished pride; in Cyprus, it was an ambitious Greek leader who initiated the assault on the Turkish minority which has ended with Turkish predominance; Iraq attacked Iran with high hopes of success and has reached a low point in its fortunes; the Soviet Union has nothing but trouble to show for its assault on Afghanistan. Yet this very record proves that defending countries *did* have reason to be thankful for their military power.

A moralistic view of history would see a divine hand at work here. A more secular interpretation will lead to the conclusion that in this age defense is the only aim that war can successfully accomplish, so that military plans which are not strictly defensive end up in frustration and loss.

Military power can prevent a nation from losing its territory or its sovereignty or its national independence. It can sometimes substitute the lesser evil for the greater and thus enable the stream of history to flow in a direction that it would not have taken if threatened rights and interests had been allowed to go by default. But it can rarely go beyond its crucial preventive role in order to create new harmonies, to shape human emotions and to alter the pattern and texture of interstate relations. Defeated nations can be forced to stop fighting, but they cannot be forced to love or to cherish, to respect or to understand, to cooperate in positive adventures or, least of all, to make peace in the deepest and truest sense of that unfathomable word. That is why any military enterprise must be succeeded as soon as possible by politics and diplomacy, in which the key lies in persuasion, not coercion.

If the transforming effects of conventional war are deemed to be limited, it is not surprising that nuclear issues arouse emotions so despairing that public opinion in many parts of the world is ready to renounce the whole nuclear theme rather than incur the labor and stress required for a modulated response based on reduction and balance. This attitude of apathy and frustration about defense matters would be less acute if there was less discussion of missile and bomb capacities and more attention to the values that are worth defending and that would be lost if the Soviet Union were to become the only repository of power. Democracy seems to have no proselytizing spirit. It has lost its rhapsodic sense. It is diffident about celebrating its values. Political and social freedoms are not the subject of assertive advocacy, and yet democracy has had its successes. In these four decades six nations—Germany, Japan, Italy, Greece, Spain and Portugal—have emerged out of totalitarianism into stable democracy while few of the new nations in the developing world have shown much interest in Marxist-Leninist ideas. Germans try to leave East Berlin for West Berlin, but nobody has heard of a movement in the opposite direction. Yet the West has shown a tendency for unilateral ideological disarmament and faces Communism in an apologetic mood. Thus the debate on defense is enacted on a technical level without being illuminated by the exalting potentiality of the ideas and systems that lie in the balance.

It may well be that the democracies are retreating far beyond the point of any pursuit. Soviet leaders would respond pragmatically to evidence that their ideological adversaries have principles and interests that they regard as worthy of devotion and risk. There is no objective case for arguing that unilateralism is the only course open to the West. The Soviet Union has traumatic memories of war and is vulnerable to the economic implications of the arms race; in a word, it has an interest of a compelling nature in seeking an agreed balance. Western nuclear diplomacy has options other than defeatism on the one hand and a virulent refusal to communicate on the other. Nuclear decisions are so vitally dependent on high-level decisions that the fact that American and Soviet presidents have met only once in seven years must be regarded as a failure of Western diplomacy. Superpower agreements on this issue are more crucial and therefore more possible than on any other.

Yet the nuclear problem is not an island unto itself. Indeed the major fallacy in the recent eruption of agitation and writing on the nuclear question has been the tendency to isolate that question from its surrounding context. A nuclear disaster could only arise through war. War could only break out through the aggravation and subsequent escalation of a regional dispute in which the superpowers were engaged on opposing sides. Interventions by one superpower that the other superpower considers to be unacceptable are possible in the Middle East, in the Gulf, in Africa or in Central America. A mutual understanding between the United States and the Soviet Union on the limits of permissible intervention would be at least as important as any arms control agreement. If the peace marchers would call for such an understanding in place of their obsessive concentration on nuclear issues, they would be addressing themselves to causes as well as symptoms. If the nuclear problem is capable of solution, it will be a solution broader and deeper than the nuclear issue itself.

Chapter 9

DIPLOMACY
Old and New

D EAN G. ACHESON, former Secretary of State of the United States, arrived in Paris from Washington on October 22, 1962. A car with no official markings took him to a street corner opposite the Élysée Palace. Looking around somewhat furtively, he crossed the road together with an official of the U.S. Central Intelligence Agency. They entered the palace by a side door and made their way through rooms and passages that were more functional than impressive. A few minutes later Acheson was in the President's private office being greeted courteously by Charles de Gaulle. "Your President has done me great honor in sending me so distinguished an emissary," said De Gaulle.

The Soviet Union had installed missiles in Cuba within range of American population centers. President Kennedy had decided not to accept this encroachment; the United States Navy would be ordered to intercept Soviet vessels to Cuba. The world trembled on the brink of confrontation between two nuclear superpowers. The United States had a right and a duty to seek the solidarity of France and other European allies in a common cause. On the other hand, if the support from Europe was absent or hesitant, an immense boost would be given to Soviet audacity. The encounter in Paris therefore had to be kept secret until its outcome was certain.

This was diplomacy at work. In one sense it was very traditional. A special envoy bearing messages between sovereigns had been the normal method of communication between governments since ancient times. What was particular to the twentieth century was the speed with which the meeting had been concerted. Acheson had not had time to collect spare clothes, money or passport before rushing from a meeting with Kennedy in the White House to the airport. Another modern feature was the intense care that had to be taken to evade media attention. The fact that ambassadors were not involved in the encounter reminds us of another predicament of contemporary diplomacy: heads of state (in this case Kennedy acting through Acheson) are taking matters into their own hands with diminished use of intermediate and specialized levels of contact.

The enormity of the issues that hung in the balance that day was also unique to the twentieth century. States and nations had risen and fallen, empires had flourished and declined, but never had statesmen and diplomats had to deal with anything that could be called the problem of human survival. Yet although the cause that brought Acheson and De Gaulle together was charged with the most urgent gravity, it was necessary for them to behave as if something illicit and disreputable was afoot.

The Old Diplomacy

The ambivalence surrounding the popular view of diplomacy has never changed. Back in 1777 a French writer, Le Trosne, had described diplomacy as "an obscure art which hides itself in the folds of deceit, which fears to let itself be seen and believes that it can exist only in the darkness of mystery." Nearly two centuries later we find an eminent British diplomat, Sir William Hayter, remarking that "sometimes . . . oppressed with the futility of much of diplomatic life, the fatiguing social round, the conferences that agree on nothing, the dispatches that nobody reads, you begin to think that diplomacy is meaningless . . . But it seems that states will always need to organize their relationship with each other." Diplomats are even heard to wonder whether their vocation is really necessary. An Italian ambassador leaving London at the end of his career in 1980 wrote an imaginative scenario in which electronic devices situated in empty buildings will one day beep out their communications to heads of state and prime ministers from one capital to another without any ambassadorial intervention.

A similar sense of futility can be discerned in a modern example. In 1977 an American official who had served his country in many responsible posts was approached by President Jimmy Carter with the offer of a choice of diplomatic posts in major capitals. In earlier times such a prospect would have been appreciatively accepted by anyone who wished to influence his country's destiny. But this is what George W. Ball replied:

I quietly declined . . . I refrained from saying what I really felt—that jet planes and the bad habits of presidents, national security assistants and secretaries of state had now largely restricted ambassadors to ritual and public relations. I did not wish to end my days an innkeeper for itinerant congressmen.

When diplomats are not complaining of their impotence they are reduced to listening to reflections on the moral defects of their profession. These come from every part of the ideological spectrum. It was Stalin who once said that to speak of honest diplomacy is "like speaking of dry water."

These bleak utterances give the impression that diplomacy is not very important or very honorable or very necessary. If such lamentations were well-founded it would be hard to understand why diplomacy continues to attract the devotion of its practitioners and the constant attention of scholars and the mass media. One can rarely open a newspaper or switch on a television or radio program without encountering a headline or an opening story concerned with a diplomatic process, such as a meeting of heads of state or an exchange of ministerial visits. The spectacle of a dignitary from one country emerging from a limousine in another country is deemed to symbolize a hope or anxiety worthy of prominent record. So perhaps we should not take the rhetoric of self-deprecation too seriously. It may be nothing more than a defensive shield behind which lurks a guilty pride. After all, the avoidance of war and the development of a world community should not logically rank among the least worthy of human pursuits. If peace is a higher goal than war, there is no reason why generals should be so complacent, or diplomats so dejected.

The Tradition

It can certainly be said of diplomacy, as of few other human occupations, that mankind has never been able to live without it. "Diplomacy" as a word is relatively young. It is based on the Greek *diplomata*, meaning "folded documents." The word begins to occur in English at the end of the eighteenth century. Before that time diplomats were called heralds, messengers, orators and, most recently, negotiators. But if the word is modern, the system whereby groups seek agreements with other groups whom they regard as alien to themselves is as old as social history. A Western writer with more imagination than precision conjures up a scene in which Neanderthal cave dwellers fighting each other for hunting grounds would sometimes require a respite from their exertions and losses. They would send messengers. It would be obvious that if the messengers were captured and eaten before delivering their messages, the chances of a successful negotiation would be sharply reduced.

Whether this pleasant fantasy is well-founded or not, it is certain that the tradition of safeguarding an emissary from the impact of the dispute that he is trying to resolve is very ancient. The idea of immunity, which ancient civilizations interpreted as a form of sanctity, is the first condition of a diplomatic system. In two classical languages, Hebrew and Greek, the words for messenger ("*mal'ach*" in Hebrew and "*angellos*" in Greek) convey the idea of sacredness as well as of secular mission. In the biblical literature the "messenger" or angel is often sent by God to announce a divine justice. These angels or messengers are sacred beings of mysterious appearance who, in the words of the Jerusalem Talmud, act as "mediators who fill the intermediate space between the earth and the infinitely distant realm of the Divine Presence." But there is a great deal of political and military diplomacy in the biblical narrative as well. Kings, queens, generals and other dignitaries are portrayed as sending messengers to adversaries in the region, usually with such unwelcome tidings that they would need every ounce of immunity that they could get. A classic case is of the Assyrian-Judean war in the year 701 B.C.E. Isaiah recounts how the Assyrian ruler Sennacherib sent messengers to the Judean king, Hezekiah, to argue the case for Judean submission and to warn against the perils of resistance. The envoys asked the Judean king why he was so confident of his power and how he thought that salvation could possibly come from alliance with "the broken reed" of Egypt. It might well have been a German envoy talking to Czechoslovakia in 1938 about the futility of relying on France and Britain.

The numerous references to messengers in the Old Testament say nothing about their character or appearance, or the qualifications which led to their appointment. But the very frequency of such references implies that diplomatic missions were a familiar part of ancient civilization; they were not confined to the area in which the Assyrian, Babylonian and Egyptian empires sought to achieve their aims by war mingled with threat and inducement. At the very time when Sennacherib's envoys were intimidating the tormented Judean king, an elaborate system of diplomatic ritual was being developed in the multistate kingdoms of China. These kingdoms dealt with each other as communities of equal status. In his standard work, Richard Louis Walker writes:

Each emissary had to go through a rigid pattern in presenting to the ruler of the state where he had been sent his proper credentials . . . The envoys also had to be able to respond in proper manner to the toasts given at the banquets in their honor. This usually involved the ability to select for the occasion a fitting verse from the well-known songs of the time.

Few modern ambassadors would be able to match this melodious virtuosity. Even the United States has not yet appointed a Frank Sinatra as an ambassador. Perhaps contemporary envoys would complain less sharply about their hardships if they had to follow the ancient Chinese practice in the signature of treaties:

> *After long discussions about the terms of the treaties to be signed, the representatives participated in a very solemn ritual in which an animal— usually a calf—was sacrificed at some holy spot outside the walls of a city. The left ear of the sacrificial victim was cut off and was used to smear with blood both the document bearing the articles of agreement and the lips of the principals. One copy of the document was buried with the sacrificial beast and each of the signatories kept a copy.*

Although diplomatic processes are found in all civilizations, it is accepted that modern diplomatic traditions have been influenced primarily by Greece. Diplomacy can only flourish in conditions of fragmentation, pluralism and formal equality of status. In such situations there is hope of achieving goals by persuasion, eloquence, inducement, threat or deterrence, and not only by physical domination and war. The ancient Greeks lived within a multistate system. It is not surprising, therefore, to find ancient Hellas evolving a complex diplomatic tradition. Here too we find a tendency to sanctify diplomacy by giving it a religious legitimacy. In the Homeric poems, heralds are accorded the patronage of Zeus, although their particular source of authority and emulation was Hermes, the god of cunning ruses and pretenses, who is probably more responsible than any other historic or mythical figure for giving diplomacy a reputation for deceit.

By the time that the Greek cities leave the center of history they bequeath a rich legacy of diplomatic experience as well as a refined vocabulary of terms for various aspects of conciliation, such as "arrangements," "truces," "conventions," "alliances," "commercial treaties" and "peace." Arbitration is a favorite diplomatic device of the Greek cities; in the two centuries before 100 b.c.e. we have records of nearly fifty cases of arbitration, including a treaty between Athens and Thebes secured by arbitration of the city of Lamia. Sometimes an eminent citizen would be named as arbitrator, such as a writer or a hero of the Olympic Games. Contrary to popular belief about the importance of internal political institutions in the foreign policy of the city-states, ideological differences had little effect on the alliances or rivalries of Greek cities. No city had such a deep faith in its own political system as to encourage it to convert others to its ways with missionary zeal. Some polarization of democratic and oligarchical communities around Athens and Sparta respectively was apparent in the fifth century, but each of those states was prepared, if convenient, to work with regimes of differing complexions. In any case, democracy and oligarchy were not regarded as opposite terms, and there were many varieties of each form of constitution.

The central fact of Greek diplomacy was patriotism: my city right or wrong. Greek cities were intensely devoted to their own pride and interests and contemptuous of other Greek cities as well as of the external "barbarian" world. Their egotism was tempered by restraints and taboos which they attributed to divine revelation, but which were probably equally inspired by humane instinct and rational self-interest. Some customs and principles applying to the Greek community and others were of universal application. War was a recognized part of the Greek system, but it was restrained by a code of rules, such as those which forbade undeclared and unheralded attacks and crimes against the wounded.

The weakness of the Greek method, as of much modern diplomacy, arose from failures of reticence and cool judgment. There were no Foreign Offices, and everything was decided by elected assemblies given to unbridled oratory and to the swift punishment of unsuccessful envoys. Ambassadors were called "elders" and had to be at least fifty years of age. Whatever their age, they would feel at home in modern public diplomacy, since they had a touching faith in the capacity of eloquence to influence the policies and attitudes of adversaries. There is something very modern in Thucydides' description of a long speech made by the delegate of Corinth to the Spartan Assembly outlining the complaints of his city against Athenian actions and urging the Spartans to invade Athens. An Athenian mission, in Sparta on other business, decided to ask for a hearing, which was granted. The Athenians spoke sober words: "Think of the great part that is played by the unpredictable in war . . . think of it now before you are too far committed."

It is clear from the long speeches reported by Thucydides that Greek diplomacy was concerned more with public advocacy than with negotiation. Unfortunately, Greek diplomats were so enthralled by their own intercity squabbles that they did not give enough notice to a small "detail": an anti-Greek power was at the gates waiting to overwhelm all the Greek cities one by one, irrespective of their relations with each other.

With all these failures there is a strong probability that Hellenic diplomacy did prevent many internecine wars and thus gave Greek civilization a longer opportunity to display its gifts.

The Greek experience would have been even more fruitful in the long run if the Roman Empire had been disposed to inherit it and take its development some stages further. This did not happen. The implication of the Greek procedures was that the parties at issue, however disparate in their power, were equal in their status; there was therefore some point in argument and persuasion. The Roman Empire, as a hierarchical system, had little respect for the idea of "sovereign equality." Imperial goals were to be achieved by force or not at all. There was little taste for institutionalized diplomacy. Roman ambassadors (*"nuntii"*) made short visits to other lands, came home to report to the Senate and returned to their normal pursuits. Foreign ambassadors to Rome seldom went away with agreeable recollections. They had to pass suspicious scrutiny before obtaining right of entry, often had to wait for long periods before addressing the Senate, waited even longer to receive the imperial reply and were "encouraged" to leave with all possible dispatch. Courtesy to foreigners was not the distinguishing feature of imperial Rome. The soul of the diplomatic idea is reciprocity, and this was an unfashionable notion in the domineering environment of Roman politics after victories in war. But if the Pax Romana was not congenial to the more amiable refinements of diplomacy, it did develop legal and contractual relationships in the external as well as the internal realm. By the third century B.C.E. a tradition of legal diplomacy had entered Roman theory and practice, and it was administered by a college of officials known as the fetiales. They served as the custodians of good faith in international relations and as the living depositories of archives.

Roman law was to have a strong impact on Western diplomatic culture. Evidence of the Roman influence is to be found in the history of modern Europe, where treaties have long been drafted on the model of Roman contracts.

The Byzantine courts in the twelfth century were the first to use ambassadors not only to make supplication or proposals but also to report on conditions in countries to which they were sent. Envoys sometimes involved themselves dangerously in the life of the foreign countries in which they worked. The candid Byzantine practice of including the gathering of information among the tasks of embassies gave birth to the reputation of ambassadors as spies. They have never recovered from this suspicion. It is generally accepted that Byzantium had a corrupting influence on the evolution of diplomacy. But although Byzantine culture has few admirers, historians are on firm ground when they confess that it reveals what one of them calls "an astute and all-pervading sense of the value of stylised forms as ordering principles of thought and action."

Despite the universal respect for immunity, ambassadors in medieval times had good reason to worry about their personal safety while attending to their business. It is often difficult to understand why anybody sought the job. Here, for example, is a description of a credentials ceremony at the Turkish court:

> *In the inner court of the Seraglio, surrounded by delicate marble pillars, was the Sultan's chamber, guarded by ushers in robes of gold and silver. The ceremony required that the ambassador pay his respects to the Sultan by kissing his skirt. At the door two attendants seized the envoy's arms and wrists, and introduced the pinioned man to the sacred presence . . . The pinioned ambassador kneeled and kissed the imperial robe; then the breathless envoy was made to retreat backwards step by step. At the opposite end of the chamber, near the exit, the diplomat made his quavering address to a motionless, bored and cold Sultan. If his Majesty was pleased he deigned to murmur in reply: "Giozel (very well)."*

In his superbly documented study *Renaissance Diplomacy*, Garrett Mattingly goes beneath the outer forms of the medieval system to explore its underlying principles and its moral environment. The salient fact is that by the fifteenth century diplomacy had become secular. It could no longer operate within the assumption of obedience to a supreme authority embodied in a canon law which transcended the particular interests of states. The church had ceased to command the behavior of princes. The Holy See had bequeathed its meticulous spirit, its reverence for hierarchies and its constructive obsession with the preservation of archives, but diplomacy had broken loose from its ecclesiastical bias.

The Italian institution of resident ambassadors was far more than a procedural innovation; it symbolized the tendency to regard diplomacy as preventive and permanent, not merely as a sporadic exercise in situations of emergency. By the end of the fifteenth century, resident ambassadors were common among the Italian states, though almost unknown in the rest of Europe. It was through them that Italian statecraft maintained a degree of stability within the fragmented peninsula.

The medieval ambassadors, like their predecessors in Greece, served the "sacred egoism" of their sovereigns. There was nothing ecumenical about them. Thus one of the earliest literary commentators on diplomacy, Ermolao Barbaro, does not tell us that the business of the ambassador is peace. Instead he says quite explicitly that the duty of the ambassador is "the same as that of any other servant of a government—to do, say, advise and think whatever may best serve the preservation and aggrandizement of his state." And the state and the state alone is the judge of what its own vital interests are and how they may best be protected.

Little has changed since then. The supreme ethic of the diplomat has always been *raison d'état*. The origins of diplomacy are rooted in the acceptance of rivalry as the natural condition of interstate relations, and diplomats have always had to be single-minded in defending their national interest against all others. Machiavelli, who had diplomatic experience in the service of his Florentine prince, was merely more candid than his contemporaries in the sharpness with which he separated the morality of power from individual ethics. In his *Discourses* he emphasizes that the standards whereby people measure the morality of an individual act cannot apply to the acts of a state. Conduct that would be regarded as sinful in any religious or social context, such as cheating, stealing, killing, lying, might be accepted and even praised when performed in the name of the state. Machiavelli is emphatic and unreserved:

> *For where the very safety of the country depends on the resolution to be taken, no consideration of justice or injustice, humanity or cruelty, nor of glory or of shame should be allowed to prevail, but putting all other considerations aside, the only question should be what will save the power and the liberty of the country.*

In all succeeding ages, leaders and spokesmen of states have been unable to escape from this moral predicament. To this very day we condone certain types of behavior undertaken on behalf of the state, while condemning similar acts committed by an individual in his personal interest. Diplomats at all levels operate in a world of competing sovereignties in which it is not easy to uphold uncompromising morality.

Yet it would be an exaggeration to say that the medieval world, any more than our own, regarded diplomacy as totally free from restraints. Contrary to conventional belief, corruption, assassination and conspiracy were not the common tools of fifteenth-century Italian diplomacy. They were used on occasion, as they have been in every age and place. But the happy paradox was that self-interest could sometimes prevent self-interest from being carried too far. It was already clear in medieval times that a diplomat who succeeded by deceit and mendacity more than once or twice would acquire the kind of reputation for himself or his country that would make it impossible for him to function in the future. There was thus a pragmatic and unsentimental reason for honesty. If deceit were only immoral, it could be condoned; if it were also impractical, intelligent men would recoil from it.

Even when the church could no longer impose its unifying authority, the residual effects of its hegemony and its preference for conciliation lived on in the European diplomatic community. Ambassadors still saw their victory to lie more in the prevention of war than in military conquest. Since it is impossible to prove that something was prevented that might otherwise have ensued, most of the victories of deterrence are always a matter of conjecture. But there is no doubt that medieval diplomacy prevented war from breaking out more often than it did, and its structural achievement in the fifteenth century has never been superseded.

When Charles VIII of France crossed the Alps into Lombardy in 1494, the Italian balance-of-power system collapsed. The small Italian states never had a chance of resisting the powerful monarchies, first of France, then of the Hapsburgs. But the methods, procedures and atmosphere of Italian diplomacy were taken over by the new monarchies and came to constitute the normal pattern of interstate relations. Nor was progress limited to the procedural realm alone. A new ideology evolved in the writings of jurists and scholars who sought a non-religious justification for international peace. Hugo Grotius, the Dutch jurist, invoked what he called "a sense of justice and of right reason" as the motive for interstate cooperation. The growing diplomatic community was the trustee of this new secular ideal, and behind the shield of its immunity it developed a deepening sense of solidarity. Grotius argued that "although law and equity required equal penalties for equal crimes, the law of nations made an exception of ambassadors because their security as a class was more important than their punishment as individuals."

In the seventeenth century the professional status of diplomacy became firm. In 1626, Cardinal Richelieu, as diplomatic adviser to Louis XIII, established a Ministry of External Affairs to centralize the management of foreign relations under a single roof. The practice was followed all over Europe, where French diplomatic leadership was now generally recognized in every sphere, including the recognition of French as the vernacular of diplomacy. When the Congress of Vienna established the rules and customs of diplomacy by its Règlement of 1815 it was ratifying established practices rather than embarking on a process of innovation.

In the nineteenth century, after the Napoleonic Wars, diplomacy entered its period of grace. For exactly a century between 1815 and 1914, war was marginal and peace seemed to be the normal condition of mankind. Stability was maintained through the informal but effective system of the Concert of Europe. It was a remarkable achievement; peace was secured for long periods in an age in which war aroused no moral revulsion. War had not ceased to be regarded as a legitimate and appropriate instrument of policy, and the rationality of peace was not moral or legal; it was entirely pragmatic. The European system responded to the enlightened self-interest of the five major powers—Austria-Hungary, Britain, France, Prussia and Russia—who held a predominance of armed force and influence. Each of them considered that the maintenance of the existing balance offered greater power and safety than could be obtained by its disruption.

It was a frankly hierarchical system. The self-appointed concert would meet and decide whether to accept consultation with lesser states and how to avoid explosions of hostility among its members. Whenever rivalry became too intense, the major powers would compensate each other at the expense of the territories and peoples in which there were no recognized sovereign states. For colonialism was quite legitimate in the theory and practice of the nineteenth-century international system. Sovereignty was still the possession of a few privileged communities, and the inequality between the few dozen sovereign states and the masses of dependent peoples evoked no legal reservations or moral discomfort. Thus after its defeats of 1870 and 1871, France was in a disgruntled mood. Bismarck feared that the cooperation of France with the Concert of Europe would be fragile unless it received some redress or consideration. He urged France to annex Tunisia. When Britain and France quarreled dangerously over Fashoda, a village on the Upper Nile, in the last years of the nineteenth century, they composed their differences by recognizing each other's spheres of influence in Egypt and Morocco. In fact, the Entente Cordiale was built on that foundation: Britain and France were simply paying each other off with tribute from the Egyptians and the Moroccans. This habit of ensuring European stability by diverting expansionist ambitions into Africa and Asia continued well into this century. When the leaders of France and Britain met Mussolini at the Stresa Conference in 1935, their decision to accept his aggression in Ethiopia was directly related to their hope of keeping Italy as a satisfied member of the European system. Robert Tucker has summed it up well:

It is only in retrospect that we can fully appreciate the extent to which such moderation as the balance of power introduced in Europe depended upon the immoderation of its working in the world outside Europe.

For the aim of diplomacy in the nineteenth century was European stability, not universal equality; and this aim was achieved. The period 1815–1914 was an era in which power and responsibility, force and interests were brought into harmony. Apart from the Crimean War, England, France, Prussia, Austria, Russia and Italy engaged in war with one another for a period totaling only eighteen months. The previous two centuries had shown an average of sixty to seventy years of major wars among the principal powers.

But the "one hundred years of peace," nostalgically evoked by statesmen and diplomats in later generations, rested on exceptional conditions. The stability could not last, still less could it be taken as a precedent for emulation. The balance of power operated behind the shield of British naval predominance. There was a network of mutual interests in the development of trade. The effective actors in the international system were few, and the compactness of the European continent gave them a possibility of swift and convenient interaction. European nations, crowded together as they were, could hardly fail to know what each of them was planning or plotting. Even after the decline of direct Christian authority, the consensual atmosphere of the Roman Empire and the Holy See lingered on. There was a great diversity of interest, but not of philosophy. European powers had no desire to impose their own regimes or social ideas on each other. The affinities between statesmen and diplomats transcended national frontiers. Together with the royal courts, which were particularly active in diplomacy, the statesmen and ambassadors formed an aristocratic transnational community. This was their golden age. Economic and technological progress, together with the proven durability of peace, created a utopian mystique. Victor Hugo could write of "the death of war" and Andrew Carnegie, in establishing his foundation, gave his researchers simple advice: They were to begin by solving the problem of war, and "once that was settled they should go on to something else."

It would soon become clear that the problem of war was far from "settled," but there was enough success in the prolongation of stability to give the diplomats a sense of achievement. In France, Britain and other European states, diplomacy emerged as a distinguished vocation with specialized professional skills and a particular appeal to social and intellectual elites.

The world was to know many upheavals between the Congress of Vienna and World War II, but until recent years there was little change in the method or atmosphere of diplomacy. The power balance might change; preoccupation would shift from one part of the globe to another; but for many decades the diplomatic method seemed to have a versatile relevance to every contingency.

As the twentieth century took its course it became evident that the international system would be marked by convulsion and change, not by harmony and stability. The traditional order had been dominated from the beginning of the twentieth century by the seven great empires of Europe, those of Austria-Hungary, Czarist Russia, Ottoman Turkey, Germany, Britain, France and Italy. The first four of these empires were swept away by World War I, and the supremacy of the other three was eroded by World War II and the struggles that came after it. All the seven empires except that of France had been headed by royal houses, of which only the British monarchy survives today. Diplomacy, essentially traditional in its nature, now had to adapt itself to a revolutionary age.

The most decisive innovation in the twentieth century has been the end of the European monopoly through the entry of the United States into the small group of senior members in the diplomatic community. It is easy to forget how slow and reluctant this process has been. In its early formative years America would have preferred not to have a foreign policy at all. The New World was obsessed with the ecstasy of separation from the Old. Its rhetoric constantly celebrated the joys of distance. The central purpose of American life was to put the European experience behind, especially the memories of conflicts and wars. The first definition of American foreign interests was suspicious and restrictive. "The business of America with Europe is commerce, not politics or war," declared John Adams. The American Revolution had engendered a sharp suspicion of any external entanglements. Most of the Founding Fathers shared the austere view of Adams, "I confess I have sometimes thought that after a few years it will be the best thing we could do to recall every minister from Europe and send embassies only on special occasions." Others echoed a common view, not completely eradicated up to our own times, that those who represented their countries abroad might easily forget whence they came and fall under the seduction of alien ideas. John Quincy Adams insisted that diplomats should always be recalled after a few years "to be renovated by the wholesome republican atmosphere of their own country." For many decades there was no inclination in America to make diplomacy a specialized profession. It was simply an extension of domestic politics. Four of the first six Presidents had held diplomatic posts before their accession, and diplomatic service was often an honorific episode in the lives of eminent citizens. The American habit of appointing ambassadors for reasons other than diplomatic talent dates back to this tradition.

Diplomats were far from popular in the rugged psychology of the American pioneer society. Benjamin Franklin was an inspiring exception; his diplomatic function in France was expiated by his status as a Founding Father and by the special place that France occupied in the trust and affection of the American colonists. But Americans still did not want diplomacy to become revered. There was a grudging attitude toward the diplomatic enterprise. Diplomacy seemed to have a great deal to do with foreigners, and foreigners with their guile and experience were likely to get Americans into trouble. For long periods diplomacy was something to be accepted if there was no alternative, but it was kept on a short leash and was awarded few resources of money or manpower. One of the early secretaries of state, Edward Livingston, observed that diplomats "are considered as favorites selected to enjoy the pleasures of foreign travel at the expense of their people; their places as senators; and their residences abroad as a continued scene of luxurious enjoyment." Jefferson expressed the modest hope that a Secretary of State would always have enough assistants or advisers to "insure that somebody was available in the office when his colleagues were at luncheon." In 1833, Secretary Livingston querulously remarked that he could hardly carry out his duties efficiently if he did not have a qualified interpreter or secretary. In 1832 a resolution of the House of Representatives had ordered an inquiry "into the expediency of reducing the number of our Ministers resident abroad to three, that is to England, France, and Russia." In 1859 a member of the Congress was to argue: "here is the evil, the fungus, the excrescence of a pinch-beck imitation of the pomp and pageantry of royalty and we should put the knife to it and cut it out." In 1906 the United States had only nine embassies abroad, the rest being legations. Until 1893, there had not been a single American diplomat abroad with a rank higher than that of Minister. The number of those enrolled in the foreign service of the United States up to the end of World War II was less than eight hundred, and fewer than half of the serving heads of mission were career diplomats.

The idea of diplomacy as a creative and honorable profession rather than a disagreeable and somewhat dangerous necessity is not more than a few decades old in the United States; but once the United States joined the diplomatic community in full momentum and responsibility, it readily adapted itself to a tradition largely fashioned and developed in Europe. American statesmen and envoys made no attempt to rebel against the pomp and formalities bequeathed by the Congress of Vienna. They sought no change. The old traditions have a way of imposing themselves on all newcomers to the diplomatic world. After the Russian Revolution in 1917 the Soviet government made an abortive attempt to create its own diplomatic usage and procedures. The word "ambassador" had an aristocratic or royal sound and it was duly banished for a time from the Soviet vocabulary. The USSR tried to call its envoys "polpreds." It was soon discovered, however, that obscurity of title prevented Soviet envoys from asserting their precedence in diplomatic corps composed of "ambassadors" and "ministers plenipotentiary." Within a short time, Moscow obediently adopted the conventions and titles formulated in aristocratic Europe a century before.

By the time that we reach the modern age we find diplomats everywhere characterized by many of the attributes that are only now beginning to fall into disuse: reticence, discretion, universal professional solidarities, a strong insistence on immunity, and a capacity to transcend the passions and prejudices of domestic politics.

It would be well to pause here for an attempt to describe the character of diplomats as they were generally perceived up to the Second World War. There had been vast change in the method of waging war but very little change in the method of conducting negotiations. Diplomacy was more tied to a uniform cosmopolitan tradition than any other significant human pursuit. The governments of nation-states were the only important actors in the international system. They held a monopoly of physical force and unlimited power to decree its use. The development of international organization had not kept pace with the rhetoric by which it had been surrounded, and its effect on diplomacy was still marginal and subsidiary. Nations sought their security in their own military power, in the strength and credibility of their alliances and in the advantageous use of their geographical situations. The world's diplomatic community was relatively intimate and compact; it comprised no more than forty or fifty sovereign states, of which fewer than a dozen were regarded as "important." In most countries diplomacy was a reserved domain springing to the attention of public opinion only in rare moments of crisis and emergency. The greater part of diplomatic intercommunication went forward in discretion and reticence. Meetings between heads of state and heads of government before World War II were so rare as to create a sensation when they occurred. For the most part, ambassadors and foreign ministers conducted their business with occasional parliamentary supervision but without being the focus of tense public emotion. Since travel was more arduous and prolonged than it is today, negotiations were conducted mostly by resident ambassadors. They were not exposed to the intrusion of the media during the initial or intermediate stages of their negotiations. Diplomacy was recognized everywhere not as a science, but as an art. It achieved its goals, if at all, by reference to tradition, to historical precedents and to the results of trained intuition. Doctrines shaped policies less than facts. Yet diplomats were aware that history in general and diplomatic history in particular are essentially unpredictable; the soundest appraisals can be disturbed by elements of chance and contingency. International relations had not yet become recognized as a formal academic discipline. There was no great proliferation of research institutes or "think tanks" seeking to complement or challenge decisions of governments. Half a dozen European countries together with the United States formed the apex of the international diplomatic hierarchy. Diplomacy was preoccupied mainly by questions of strategy, the avoidance or termination of war and the resolution of territorial issues. Organized propaganda had not yet emerged as one of the central diplomatic pursuits. The vast mass of humanity, not yet organized in sovereign states, lay outside the world of diplomatic action. There was little international economic cooperation, and nonpolitical problems were regarded as "low politics" to be enacted at the junior levels of the diplomatic pyramid. Matters of protocol, precedence, ceremony and ritual were a large part of the diplomatic enterprise.

In all countries, envoys abroad were conscious of their subordination to policymakers at home; they tended to accept the distinction between determination of policy by ministers and its implementation through ambassadors. Diplomacy was hampered and confined by its own formality. And with all its institutional prestige, it operated in an apologetic mood. Balance of power and collective security, which had been the two salient doctrines of diplomacy in the earlier part of the twentieth century, had been discredited for the simple reason that they had failed to keep the peace or to organize a systematic or automatic resistance to aggression. Despite many marginal successes, diplomacy had not been able to avoid such disasters as World War I or the collapse of international stability under the hammer blows of Nazism and Fascism leading to World War II. The time was ripe for change.

The New Public Diplomacy

Any discussion of changes in the diplomatic system must begin with the most potent and far-reaching transformation of all: the collapse of reticence and privacy in negotiation. The intrusion of the media into every phase and level of the negotiation process changes the whole spirit and nature of diplomacy. The modern negotiator cannot escape the duality of his role. He must transact business simultaneously with his negotiating partner and his own public opinion. This involves a total modification of techniques. Whether this is a favorable development or not is irrelevant; it is certainly irreversible. There is no way of putting the clock back to an era in which the early and intermediate stages of negotiation were sheltered from the domestic constituencies of the negotiators.

The first portent of this transformation came long before the present era in diplomatic history. The biblical text for open diplomacy was formulated by Woodrow Wilson in the first of the Fourteen Points, published in 1919:

> *Open covenants openly arrived at, after which there should be no private international understandings of any kind, but diplomacy shall proceed always frankly and in the public view.*

There is a startling extremism in this famous formulation. Openness here is celebrated both as a means and as an end. Reticence is excluded with austere totality; and the definition is absolute: "no private international understandings of any kind."

Woodrow Wilson was doubtless reacting against the conspiratorial tradition in which a few major powers used to decide the future of smaller nations without their knowledge, let alone their consent. His dictum had a brief rhetorical triumph but was not followed by any operative results. Soon after declaring his fidelity to "open covenants," Wilson locked himself in a room in Paris with leaders of Britain, France and Italy in a peace conference more secretive in its procedures and less respectful of the views of nonparticipants than most of the conferences that had preceded the Fourteen Points. Wilson himself never thought to reconcile this inconsistency. In the words of a close observer, "He and his conscience were on terms of such incessant intimacy that any little disagreement between them could be arranged."

Shortly after the enunciation of his doctrine of "open covenants," Woodrow Wilson attempted a tactical retreat which has been insufficiently noted by writers and scholars ever since. In a meeting with the Senate in 1918 he declared,

> When I pronounced for open diplomacy I meant not that there should be no private discussion of delicate matters but that no secret agreement should be entered into and that all international relations when fixed should be open, above board and explicit.

This was a major revision of doctrine. It indicates that Wilson himself was worried by the possible consequences of his earlier rhetoric. Unfortunately, however, the explosive slogan had sent its repercussions into modern thought with such power that his subsequent interpretation of it was to have little impact. The idea that open negotiation has a higher level of morality than traditional diplomacy has never been erased from the public consciousness.

Diplomats and scholars with a professional approach have usually regarded the intrusion of the media into negotiations as a major disruption of the diplomatic process. They argue that "negotiation" can never break out of the mercantile context implied in the word itself. Negotiation presupposes bargaining. A negotiator must be prepared to come out of the bargaining process with positions different from those which he espoused in the beginning. If initial positions are widely published the negotiator is inhibited in his capacity to move to other proposals. The legitimate mobility of negotiation becomes interpreted in the public mind as a failure of credibility.

Nobody can challenge the need to present agreements to public scrutiny before they are put into force. It is quite another thing, however, when negotiators have to present to their constituencies not only the agreement for which they seek approval but every tactical phase, trial balloon or tentative proposal, including those submitted for the purpose of provoking a response. It can be demonstrated that international agreements have been endangered through premature exposure to domestic scrutiny.

It is interesting that Dag Hammarskjöld, who might have been expected by reason of his UN office to be the high priest of public diplomacy, left a legacy of disillusion behind in his final report:

> *The best results of negotiation cannot be achieved in international life any more than in our private world in the full glare of publicity with current debate of all moves, unavoidable misunderstandings, inescapable freezing of positions due to considerations of prestige and the temptation to utilize public opinion as an element integrated into the negotiation itself.*

This single sentence is a lucid refutation of the doctrine of "open covenants." But Hammarskjöld's warnings have gone unheeded both in the United Nations and in the general arena of interstate diplomacy. The "freezing of positions" through the "full glare of publicity" is one of the hazards which most negotiators have to try to overcome.

The insistence of the media on knowing every stage of a negotiation has become more aggressive in recent years as a result of events in the United States. The American media, after all, have celebrated great triumphs of exposure in the issues of Watergate and Vietnam. These experiences have strengthened the assumption that secrecy is intrinsically sinful while publicity is inherently virtuous. The effect has been to create a fallacious identity between privacy and conspiracy. It is assumed that anything honorable should be capable of instant exposure to public view and, conversely, that anything that is kept in even temporary discretion must somehow be unscrupulous.

Nobody involved in the quest for international peace can possibly accept so sweeping a generalization. The hard truth is that the total denial of privacy even in the early stages of a negotiation has made international agreements harder to obtain than ever in past history. Here we find a built-in conflict of interest between the diplomat and the journalist. What one seeks to conceal the other seeks to reveal; and each is acting within the guiding principle of his vocation. As a general rule, revelation has a better sound than concealment. But if the journalist has the better of the argument about the means, the statesman can reply that peace is a higher social value than the satisfaction of curiosity, so that he often wins the argument in terms of ultimate ends.

But the polemic is about much more than the efficacy or legitimacy of a particular diplomatic method. Most people will decide their attitude according to their perception of mass opinion as a factor in determining grave and complex issues. Is the public wise or foolish, virtuous or imprudent? Those who advocate open negotiation and uninhibited press coverage generally believe that peoples are intrinsically wise and relatively pure of heart, whereas leaders are fallible, vain, power-greedy and insensitive to humane impulses. The argument about diplomatic method becomes an argument about public virtue.

The exaltation of popular wisdom was a common theme of Enlightenment thinking and is sustained by many of the progressive ideologies that have arisen in subsequent generations. It was in the name of that assumption that men like the philosopher De Condorcet in the eighteenth century proclaimed that agreements and contracts should always be submitted to public decision. From eighteenth-century writers the habit of obeisance to the public will spread throughout political literature and came to offer serious challenge to the reticent school of diplomacy. The rectitude and idealism of peoples were contrasted with the qualities of ambitious rulers whose egotism, vanity and ambition might lead them to support or initiate wars.

By the same token the critics of open diplomacy are not prepared to idealize mass opinion. They know that public emotions are not always kindly or prudent; they are often savage and reckless. Between the two world wars nobody did more than Walter Lippmann to dethrone public opinion from the deference which it traditionally evoked. He managed to combine a reputation for liberalism with a scorchingly severe contempt of the public mind. His theme was simple: the choices and predicaments faced by a democracy could only be grasped by people of mature judgment and specialized knowledge. Later in the complex international environment of the 1950s, Lippmann reached the extreme conclusion that public opinion is nearly always wrong in international affairs.

> *Public opinion compels governments which usually know what would be wiser or more necessary or more expedient to be too late with too little or too long with too much, too pacifist in peace or too bellicose in war, too appeasing in negotiation or too intransigent. Mass opinion has a growing power in this country but it has shown itself to be a dangerous master of decisions when the stakes are life and death.*

This negative view of public opinion is generally upheld by those who have a professional or scholarly commitment to diplomacy. The argument is that parties to a negotiation have to reach a result on a level of expectation lower than that on which they started. Publicity has an inhibiting effect on this process. Morgenthau writes, "To publicize such negotiations is tantamount to destroying or at least impairing the bargaining position of the parties in any future negotiations." He goes on with increasing vehemence:

It is for these reasons that in the free market, no seller will carry on public negotiations with a buyer; no landlord with a tenant; no institution of higher learning with its staff; no candidate for public office will negotiate in public with his backers; no public official with his colleagues; no politician with his fellow politicians. How then are we to expect that nations are willing to do what no private individual would think of doing?

Quincy Wright, the author of the standard work *A Study of War,* believes that statesmen may often have a good motive in aspiring to secrecy; they desire to achieve compromise, and this ambition is liable to be thwarted by public opinion clamoring for nationalistic victories and the total humiliation of adversaries. "Parliaments are usually more nationalistic and belligerent than executives, and people than parliaments, because they are less aware of the risks."

Experience does not confirm that public opinion invariably works in favor of bellicosity. It sometimes takes the opposite direction. During the 1930s the fear of retribution from a pacifist public opinion caused the British government to abstain from the rearmament necessary to deter the expansionist aims of Hitlerism. Prime Minister Stanley Baldwin admitted this frankly. The large section of public opinion represented by the Labour Party stood simultaneously for resistance to Hitler and for opposition to British military reinforcement! In the late 1960s, American public opinion exercised pressure on United States negotiators against persistence in the Vietnam war. Henry Kissinger has recorded that the Administration's bargaining position was weakened by evidence that public opinion would settle for unconditional withdrawal without even making demands on Hanoi for reciprocal concessions. In 1956, Britain's Suez expedition was foiled by clear evidence that public opinion was against the war, although there is room for the belief that if the military action had been successful and if it had earned more international support, public opinion would have approved it heartily. On the other hand, when Argentina seized the Falkland Islands in April 1982, British public opinion almost compelled the government to strike a pose of extreme rigor and to undertake an expensive and hazardous naval expedition. Left to themselves, the governing elite might well have renounced the islands in view of their blatant marginality.

A surging public opinion in all Western countries has recently claimed the right to intervene in government decisions on the production and location of nuclear weapons. Perhaps this illustrates the predicament of public diplomacy more vividly than anything else. On the one hand, it can be claimed that a problem so dependent on technical knowledge and on the psychological refinements inherent in a deterrent strategy cries out for solution by people of long training with particular skills and experience in decision making. How can such

judgments possibly be left to those whose only equipment is the reading of newspapers and an occasional glimpse of a television debate?
On the other hand, the pathos and tragedy inherent in the nuclear
debate strike at the very heart of the human condition, and nobody
alive on the planet would be safe from the consequence of an erroneous choice. How then can it be said that these issues should be left
for decision by a small group of experts and scientific specialists? An
"expert" is a man who understands everything—but nothing else. He
sometimes becomes immune to the intangible but powerful human
impulses that lie beneath the surface of his discipline.

The dilemma is more acute in conflicts that admit of no clear-cut
solutions and require compromise, ambivalence, reciprocal concession. A diplomatic solution is usually one in which no party may claim
total victory or suffer the humiliation of total defeat. This is all very
well for the diplomats, but when war breaks out the public often likes
clear and swift results. It is taught by its leaders to see the human
spectacle in terms of a conflict between light and darkness; once these
images are fixed, national leaders hesitate to persuade public opinion
to move toward a more flexible stance. American opinion was quite
willing to sustain the Vietnam war when there was a prospect of fairly
quick victory. But when the war became bogged down in a quagmire,
most Americans preferred withdrawal to a tedious perseverance in
pursuit of what was called "honor." Victory is more popular than
defeat, but withdrawal is preferable to deadlock.

Most American statesmen were convinced by the end of the 1960s
that the United States should make an effort to correct its relations
with China, but the effort was delayed for several years because successive administrations had created a circular dilemma. First, they had
nourished a fierce hostility to China which they had imposed on a
public opinion traditionally friendly to the Chinese people. Subsequently, when the leaders were ready to change their position, they
assumed without much evidence that the public would not welcome a
change of course. They thus subordinated themselves to a passion
which they themselves had generated and which they wrongly believed
to be deep-rooted and tenacious. They erred twice: once in creating
the prejudice and once in underestimating their own capacity to eradi-
cate it. They would have suffered no great damage in public opinion
by making the opening to China at an earlier date.

A similar predicament faced American statesmen in their effort to
promote détente. In justifying containment and military and economic
aid to Europe, American leaders had presented their strategy in ideological and moral terms. They portrayed what was really a "normal"
conflict of interests as an incurable collision of ideas and principles.
This transformed the Cold War from a classical power struggle be-

tween states into a worldwide crusade by the "free world" against "international Communism." Each of the two protagonists was presented in simplistic, monolithic terms. Once public opinion had been taught by national leaders to see the contest in such sharply polarized images, those same national leaders hesitated to lead a movement toward a more flexible attitude. In retrospect, it is evident that Soviet policy shifted significantly as early as 1952 with Stalin's conciliatory proposal for a neutralized and unified Germany. Despite a number of promising gestures by the post-Stalin Russian leaders, including a moderation of Soviet attitudes to Turkey, Iran and Greece, American leaders made no effort to persuade their constituencies that it would be worthwhile negotiating with Moscow and that the entire Communist "world" was not united against the West. American public opinion had been driven by its leaders into an intense anti-Communist mood, but it might well have responded to a call for revision when circumstances seemed to have changed. Political leaders in the United States did not put this flexibility to a test until many years later when the Nixon Administration, with its strong anti-Communist credentials, felt that it could lead the American public in the direction of détente.

If public opinion sometimes leads policy astray against the best judgment of leaders, it is usually because leaders allow themselves to be petrified into exaggerated reverence of something that they themselves have created. A case in point is the British decision to join the European Community. When this idea was debated, the public attitude, as reflected in polls, was overwhelmingly negative. When Edward Heath's government took the decision first and submitted it to ratification afterward in a plebiscite, the action was emphatically endorsed.

The futility of consulting public opinion too slavishly is illustrated by the French referendum in 1972 on the question of British admittance to the Common Market (EEC). President Pompidou organized a bizarre procedure under which electors would enter a voting booth where a learned memorandum on the French and British economies awaited them. Those who had received academic training as in one of the Grandes Ecoles might have absorbed this erudition. A fisherman from Normandy would have been baffled—and, indeed, 60 percent of the electorate simply stayed away. Sometimes "public opinion" would like to be left alone. It is unrealistic to expect political leaders to ignore public opinion. But a statesman who keeps his ear permanently glued to the ground will have neither elegance of posture nor flexibility of movement.

The case histories do not point to a simple verdict on the role of public opinion in diplomatic history. Most objective historians would agree that the leaders of Western democracies should have ignored the pressure of public opinion in favor of ill-considered disarmament and appeasement in the 1930s. On the other hand, if public opinion helped to save Great Britain from a hopeless adventure in Suez in 1956; or forced the United States to abandon its ill-fated commitment in Vietnam in the 1970s; or compelled many governments seriously to reconsider the utility of an unrestrained nuclear arms race—it may be accounted on those occasions to have played a positive role. The dogmatic assertion that public opinion never gets anything right is far too sweeping. If public opinion has obstructed some wise decisions, it has also prevented or curtailed many follies. Walter Lippmann's judgment that "mass opinion has showed itself to be a dangerous master of decision when the stakes are life and death" is much too absolute and one-sided.

The idea that folly and irresponsibility are the prerogatives of "mass opinion" while virtue and prudence are the monopoly of statesmen and diplomats does not emerge from a close study of the fateful case histories of the past few decades. When statesmen yield to "public opinion" they are usually interpreting that opinion apprehensively and not always with accuracy. It is not at all certain that the American people would have withheld their support for a longer sojourn of troops in Europe immediately after World War II if they had been told that this was necessary to save the peace, but the Administration believed that "bring the boys home" was the final wisdom of public opinion. It is questionable whether British opinion would really have resented a serious armament program in the 1930s, but the governments of that period "assumed" that the public wished to avoid burdens. If the United States had decided to end the Vietnam war at an earlier date, public opinion might well have acquiesced, but the responsible negotiators "assumed" that the people wanted a face-saving formula that would be consistent with "honor" and that they would be prepared to pay a heavy price of blood while this quest was pursued.

Arab governments "assumed" that a wrathful public opinion would exact terrible punishment on rulers who presumed to explore the prospect of peace with Israel, but when Anwar el-Sadat took this plunge he received a hero's welcome in the streets of Cairo. His subsequent assassination was for reasons of domestic rivalry unconnected with the Camp David process, which his successor has continued without interruption. Israeli leaders anticipated an enraged reaction to the dismantling of settlements and military installations in Sinai, but when the test came, public opinion accepted the renunciation with little traumatic reaction. Successive French governments believed that the abandonment of North African possessions would drive public opinion to "mutiny and rage," but when Mendès-France and, later, De Gaulle took their courage into their hands it turned out that Frenchmen could well live without control of Tunisia and Algeria.

The common error is to regard public opinion as immutable, static and endemically foolish and to underestimate its tendency to follow rather than to control the judgment of policymakers. Even those who question the way Kissinger solves problems admire the way he defines them. What he has called the "core question of leadership in a democracy" is linked to the problem of relating policy to opinion:

> *To what extent must a national leader follow his conscience and judgment, and at what point should he submit to a public mood, however disastrous for the nation or the peace of the world he considers it to be? The question admits of no abstract answers. The extreme cases are easy. The dilemmas arise in the gray area where the national consensus is itself vague and likely to lead to a debacle.*

The exclusion of the public from negotiation is not an absolute principle of diplomacy, but it is reasonable to regret the total eclipse of secrecy. There has hardly been a success for international conciliation in our time without the option of secrecy having been used at a crucial stage of the negotiating process. Many breakthroughs in conciliation would have been impossible if the negotiators had not found at least temporary shelter from public scrutiny. In some cases, such as the Austrian State Treaty and Trieste, the privacy was secured by abstention from spectacular summit diplomacy, leaving the agreements to be hammered out by patient diplomacy conducted by skilled ambassadors. In others, such as the Egyptian-Israeli agreements at Camp David, a measure of secrecy was obtained by ensuring physical seclusion. President Carter simply extended an invitation to the negotiating parties and withheld it from representatives of the media, who could do little more than congregate below the hilltop whiling away the hours in apprehensive speculation, There have been occasions when leaders sought privacy by practicing elusive deceit, as in the case of the Acheson mission to France in 1962 and Moshe Dayan's visit to Morocco in disguise in 1979 to make the first contact with Egypt, which later led to the peace treaty.

One method of defusing the anticipated anxiety of public opinion is to delay disclosure of commitments until there is a good chance of getting public acceptance of them. In the Cuban missile crisis of 1962 it was helpful for the American people to know the President's response to the crisis before the existence of the crisis was widely known. Thus when President Kennedy first apprised the American people of their danger, he was able at the same time to communicate the spirit and attitude by which he would seek to avoid it. He announced that he would apply a blockade but avoid military reaction. It is probable that if the American public had been told of the danger without being simultaneously informed of the proposed remedy for it, its reaction would have been anxious and perhaps even hysterical.

Even when negotiators understand that they will have to reveal their activities in the last resort, it is often important that they should maintain some option about the timing of their disclosure. In the Egyptian-Israeli negotiation at Camp David both major participants—Prime Minister Menachem Begin and President Anwar el-Sadat—offered far-reaching concessions which would in all probability have caused them difficulty in their domestic constituencies. Sadat would have had to risk alienation from the main body of Arab nationalism as well as astonished indignation in those sections of the Egyptian public which clung to the traditional anti-Israeli ideology. Begin, for his part, had agreed that Israel would renounce a naval base, airfields, access to a neighboring source of oil, towns and villages in which thousands of Israelis had built their homes, and the sense of space and distance which had reassured Israel about its strategic security for over a decade. If the two leaders had been compelled to reveal their concessions before being able to point to the compensating advantages, it is probable that they would have been repudiated. By secretively delaying the disclosure of concessions until an integral settlement had been achieved, the negotiators increased the chance that their concessions would be ratified.

If the media force diplomats to reveal their concessions before explaining the advantages for which they are made, they virtually ensure that prospects of peace will be lost in waves of domestic antagonism. The desire of diplomats to delay revealing their negotiations until the full results are known serves the human cause more than the ambition of journalists to put everything on immediate record. The ambition to make total and immediate disclosure of every phase in negotiation responds to the "sacred" principle of the "right to know"; but the question is whether the right to know is sometimes counterbalanced by the "right to peace." At some point the journalist and the editor must decide whether they are judges and commentators of society from outside or whether they are also an organic part of it, bound up with its destiny and committed to its fate.

Negotiators working for the avoidance of war are often conscious of representing a higher social principle than journalists working for the avoidance of secrecy. Unfortunately, however, the diplomatic cause becomes heavily compromised when secrecy is harnessed to aims which would never be accepted in open debate. The intention of the Kennedy Administration in 1961 to bring about the downfall of the Castro regime in Cuba by force was known by a New York *Times* writer, James Reston, before the invasion of the Bay of Pigs took place. The unhappy adventure was not prevented. Most Americans and indeed most of humanity would now agree that it would have been better if it had been foiled by exposure. We end up in dilemma. In some cases, premature public disclosure works against peace. In the case of the invasion of the Bay of Pigs, it might have worked against an aborted war.

Peace and war are not the only contexts in which the predicament arises. In a world full of totalitarian states there are many cases where governments are ready to do good only by stealth. Thus in 1972 and subsequent years the Soviet Union was prepared to allow the free departure of tens of thousands of citizens, especially Jews, provided that not too much was made of it in the public media. At this point the media faced another harsh choice. What was more important: to save lives by relative secrecy or to endanger them for the sake of journalistic success? In this case the harmony was not disturbed by the media alone. American legislators who had worked hard to secure the humane concession from the USSR could not resist asking for reciprocity. The Jackson-Vanik amendment was published. It made economic and commercial concessions to the Soviet Union dependent on Soviet leniency in allowing emigration from the USSR. The Soviets resentfully closed the tap of emigration. It was one thing for the USSR privately to agree to make a concession in order to improve its trading conditions in the United States. It was quite another thing to confess in public that a superpower was moderating its domestic policy for the sake of its own commercial benefit.

Sometimes the problem becomes so intricate that governments must use secrecy not only to defeat their adversaries but also to delude some of their own departments. An essential aspect of the secrecy of the SALT negotiations was the celebrated "back channel" negotiating that took place between Kissinger and Anatoly Dobrynin in Washington, of which their official delegations in Helsinki or Vienna were totally unaware. Progress in the negotiations and the breaking of deadlocks were due far more to the communications on the back channel than to anything done at the formal proceedings.

One of the most spectacular uses of the back channel was in April 1972. Washington was alive with a rumor that an important meeting, presumably about Vietnam, would be held at Camp David during the weekend. Everyone, including most cabinet officers and the White House staff, assumed that such a meeting had taken place, until it was announced on April 25 that Henry Kissinger had just returned from Moscow, where he had been negotiating with the Soviet leadership for four days. The secrecy had been perfect. While Kissinger was actually in Moscow, everybody assumed that he was at the fictitious Camp David gathering.

Diplomacy was always involved in a tension between international interests and domestic consensus. It is not a modern predicament alone. Far back in history we find Demosthenes complaining about the manner in which popularly elected assemblies defeated the refined compromises of diplomats by insisting on black-or-white decisions. But the tension between international and domestic consensus was never as pervasive as it is today. It obviously has the greatest effect in democracies. Tocqueville once wrote, "Democracies only do external things for internal reasons." He may not have been exaggerating as much as has been believed. But the conversion of international negoti- ation from a reserved pursuit into a public spectacle has been particu- larly intense and rapid in this generation. Traditionally the phase of negotiation was separate from the phase of public discussion. First one would negotiate an agreement with an adversary in conditions of reti- cence until a draft agreement was reached. At that stage it would have to be submitted for acceptance or repudiation by the domestic con- stituency. Today the news media follow every phase in the evolution of agreements or discords. This makes compromise difficult. Since it is conventionally believed that fair solutions lie somewhere midway between the positions of contending parties, negotiators are com- pelled to invent fictitiously excessive demands in order that their real positions should later appear moderate to public opinion. The hard test comes when concessions have to be made. To your negotiating partner you describe your concession as so painful as to be almost beyond endurance. Simultaneously you whisper to your suspicious constituency that your concession is inherently trivial and that only your own virtuosity and your adversary's gullibility have given it some importance. The trouble is that in the modern world, with close press surveillance and instant communication, the wind carries the two voices in both directions; your adversary and your constituency each hear what you say to the other.

It is too easy for the moralists to say that this merely proves the intrinsic duplicity of the diplomatic exercise. A measure of ambiva- lence on the part of a mediator is inherent in any quest for agreement between parties who have divergent interests. The difficulty would be reduced if parliamentary leaders and journalists could be convinced that negotiation is not a zero-sum game. It does not follow that what you give to your adversary is necessarily a loss for yourself. That a concession can be useful on balance both to one's self and to one's rival is a truth that responds to the dialectic of real life.

Is there a solution? I have quoted Dag Hammarskjöld as speaking with regret of "the temptation to utilize public opinion as an element integrated in the negotiation itself." It might be more fruitful to follow Talleyrand's advice: to define that which is inevitable and then to cooperate with it. However startling the prospect might be to traditionalists, we may yet live to see negotiations in which foreign ministers, ambassadors, diplomatic officials, and newspaper editors sit together on negotiating teams, with the editors authorized by their professional colleagues to promise phases of secrecy in accordance with volatile shifts in the negotiating prospect. Until then the battle will be drawn on the basis of an agreed conflict of interests.

There have been cases in which negotiators have felt more sympathy with their foreign negotiating partners than with their own journalistic compatriots; and it should not be assumed that the public is invariably on the side of journalistic exposure and against diplomatic secrecy. There was no evidence of popular enthusiasm in America for the premature exposure of positions in the SALT I negotiations; and public opinion in all the countries concerned revealed no compassion for the frustrated commentators and interviewers who were kept on the wrong side of the fence during the Middle East negotiations at Camp David in 1979. Secrecy is not to be embraced for its own sake, but there are many in the world who would prefer peace with secrecy to secrecy without peace. The professional media are not always the same as "public opinion." It may well be that public opinion stands intermediate between the diplomats and the journalists, and that each of them has a case.

No foreign policy establishment has ever emerged with ease from the dilemmas created by the modern need to take account of public opinion. It is recorded that Secretary of State Dean Rusk "made it clear to his subordinates early in his administration that he did not want them to take domestic political views into account in making decisions at their level." Bernard Cohen points out that "nonresponsibility for public opinion may be a noble sentiment for professional specialists, but nonresponsiveness to it is unrealistic for most of them since they are supposed to be—from their job standpoint—politically sensitive, hard-nosed, practical realists."

The problems created by publicity do not operate with equal effect across the whole international system. Communist and other authoritarian governments do not impose this problem on their representatives. A Soviet negotiator is not under the pressure of a liberal conscience, nor is he assailed by public pleas for moderation in his home country. He gets the best of two worlds. He is immune from the effect of domestic public opinion in his own case, and he can play on public opinion in the country of his democratic negotiating partner, behind the back of the delegation with which he is bargaining. Democratic negotiators may bemoan this discrimination, but they cannot escape their handicap by useless longings for immunity from public opinion. They can only hope to compensate for their disadvantage by

utilizing some of the assets which a free society accords, and a dictatorship denies, to those who negotiate in its name.

The Age of Summitry

Apart from the vogue of publicity the most conspicuous major change
in the diplomatic process is the widespread practice of summitry. The
traditionalists have usually deplored the growing habit of heads of
government to negotiate with each other frequently and directly instead of relying on their accredited intermediaries. This was considered in classical diplomatic mythology to be a dangerous pursuit. It is
natural for ambassadors to be especially resentful of a process that
erodes their own negotiating status. Most of them look back with
wistful yearning to the age when they were immune from persistent
ministerial usurpation. Thomas Jefferson as President of the United
States once wrote the following memorandum to his Secretary of State:
"We have heard nothing from our ambassador in Spain for two years.
If we do not hear from him this year, let us write him a letter."

This splendid utterance reflects the leisured atmosphere of an age
in which the title "ambassador plenipotentiary" was much more than
a fiction. The history of the United States contains the most salient
example of diplomatic agents taking momentous decisions on their
own account. Robert Livingston and James Monroe were empowered
to purchase New Orleans and West Florida for $10 million. They
ended up by buying half a continent for $15 million—doubling the
area of the United States and adding a tract of 820,000 square miles
between the Mississippi River and the Rocky Mountains. Most people
today would agree that this was an excellent real estate investment
even if the envoys did exceed their constitutional powers. In our age
they would have been able to make a telephone call to their department, which would have sternly ordered them to stay within the limits
of their instructions and to avoid wasting money on extra-budgetary
luxuries.

The argument against excessive summiteering is that it involves the
prestige of the negotiating parties at a level on which compromise is
most difficult. Heads of state are by the nature of their office prevented
from undertaking the detailed, careful exploration from which precise
agreements emerge. They are a court of last resort. They cannot
therefore launch tentative noncommittal ideas in a free play of intellectual initiative. It might also be said without cynicism that there is a
grave danger that they might get to know each other personally. This
is probably why Philippe de Comines in the fifteenth century wrote:
"Two great princes who wish to establish good personal relations
should never meet each other face to face, but ought to communicate

through good and wise emissaries." Much more recently Dean Rusk has written:

> *Summit diplomacy is to be approached with the wariness with which a prudent physician prescribes a habit-forming drug—a technique to be employed rarely and under the most exceptional circumstances with rigorous safeguards against its becoming a debilitating or dangerous habit. The experienced diplomat will usually counsel against the direct confrontation of those with final authority.*

The Congress of Vienna, sitting for ten months in 1814–15, and the Congress of Berlin, dominated by Bismarck and Disraeli in 1878, would qualify for the definition of summit meetings, although the phrase was not coined until our own times. The Congress of Berlin shocked traditionalist diplomats when Disraeli addressed it in English instead of the conventional French. When he ordered his train to be made ready for departure as a sign that he was not prepared for further concession, he was inaugurating a psychological device that has often been used since then. The most populated summit conference of all times was that which brought President Wilson, the British Prime Minister Lloyd George, the French President Clemenceau and the Italian Prime Minister Orlando to a meeting in Paris in 1919 in which some thirty other countries were represented by prime ministers, foreign ministers and emirs. In Acheson's words, "The eminence of the participants was equalled only by their failure . . . None of the Big Four perceived the true nature of their problems or the consequences of their actions, or the strength of the forces which they were attempting to control, or their own weakness." Occasional summit meetings were not unknown before the present age. What is particular to this generation is their frequency, with a consequent eclipse of other forms of diplomacy.

The phrase "summit diplomacy," like much of our modern diplomatic vocabulary (e.g., the Iron Curtain), goes back to Winston Churchill, not in his rhetorical glow during the Second World War but in the exceptional lucidity and imaginativeness of his later career in the 1950s. Having laid the ideological foundation for détente ("the idea appeals to me of a supreme effort to bridge the gulf between the two worlds so that each can live their life if not in friendship at least without the hatred and maneuvers of the Cold War"), he went on to propose East-West negotiations at the highest level. Between 1955 and 1960 he proposed such negotiations on more than forty occasions. His persistence was resisted by many of his own colleagues and especially by leaders of the United States. There was even a churlish tendency to attribute his insistence to his advanced age and personal vanity.

Nevertheless he had coined the durable phrase: "If there is not *at the summit of the nations* the wish to win the greatest prize of peace, where can men look for hope?" But while eloquence was Churchill's weapon, real power lay in Washington, where President Harry S. Truman was austerely reluctant to indulge the dramatic temptations of summitry. He was attached to more traditional methods. From Potsdam in 1945 to Geneva in 1955 no American President took part in a summit meeting. Moreover the first summits were not very fertile. The major heads of state came together in Geneva in 1955, at Camp David in 1959 and in Paris in 1960. It would be hard to prove that they left the international scene in greater serenity or security than they found it. The reservations of professional and academic experts were consequently reinforced.

It must, however, be admitted that skepticism about summitry is in direct proportion to the personal distance of the skeptic from the summit. Thus in 1957, when he was perched on the lower slopes, Henry Kissinger could write that many of the arguments advanced on behalf of summit diplomacy were "fatuous in the extreme." The proposition that only heads of state could settle intractable disputes was not borne out by experience. Problems of great complexity which had divided the world for a decade and a half were not likely to be resolved in a few days by harassed men meeting in the full light of publicity. Kissinger believed that summitry would give birth to a vogue of intellectual frivolity—"the evasion of concreteness, the reliance on personalities, the implication that all problems can be settled with one grand gesture." The arguments appear sound, but their fragility is illustrated by the speed with which they are relinquished whenever the theoretician becomes a practitioner. When this occurs, "reliance on personalities" no longer seems to be a vice. Kissinger's criticism of summitry vanished quickly when he himself qualified as a summiteer. Earlier Anthony Eden had opposed an East-West summit meeting in 1955 when Churchill was in power—but when Eden became Prime Minister he urgently sought a summit meeting with Soviet leaders.

As communications become easier the nomadic instinct is given greater scope. In less than two years between Yalta in February 1945 and the Paris Peace Conference of July to October 1946, Secretary of State James F. Byrnes traveled 77,000 miles. In a similar period of time John Foster Dulles traveled 178,749 miles. In his three years as Secretary of State, Kissinger traveled 650,000 miles, 564,000 of them to fifty-seven foreign countries. He was no longer afraid of "reliance on personalities." When the dispute erupted between Great Britain and Argentina about the Falkland Islands in April 1982, the United States Secretary of State, Alexander M. Haig, traveled 34,000 miles within a period of five days. In the European Community, heads of government and foreign ministers can count on having to meet each other several times a year; their encounters are celebrated without pomp or sensation.

The plaintive protests of ambassadors appear to be futile. As with the vogue of publicity, so with summitry the best course is to abandon learned denunciation and bow to the inevitable. Negotiation at several levels of authority was inevitable in the eras of limited communication. In the early part of the eighteenth century, for example, it would take several weeks for the French ambassador to Stockholm to go from Paris to take up his post. It was impossible to do anything but give him general guidelines on how to proceed. Once he arrived he could only depend on his intuition and resourcefulness. The first substantive change came with the invention of the telegraph, allowing home governments to give their ambassadors more precise instruction and to receive more exact information. Even then monarchs, presidents and foreign ministers could make their views and attitudes felt only by indirect influence, not by personal contact. It was in World War II that summitry came into its own with the publicized and dramatic encounters of Churchill, Roosevelt and Stalin. Yet the hardships and hazards of prolonged travel were still so acute that each occasion gave hostages to fortune in the physical as well as in the diplomatic sense. Indeed, only the emergency of war could have impelled these elderly men and their leading associates to accept such frequent toil and risk. Today there is not much risk and very little toil. In April 1982 a British Foreign Minister took off from London at eight o'clock in the morning and was conferring in Washington on the Falkland crisis at eight o'clock in the morning on the same day. There is now a constant "monarchization" of government under which ambassadors, foreign ministers and heads of governments upstage each other, carrying the level of negotiation upward every year. The result is that the policy-makers are convinced that they do not need so many intermediate levels of mediation.

They do have a case. The wholesale deprecation of summitry seems tendentious and, on the whole, ill-founded. We have noted that heads of government conducted their intercommunication through several diplomatic levels only as a matter of necessity arising from the compulsions of distance. It is not intelligent to behave in diplomacy as though the communications revolution had not taken place.

The balance sheet is ambivalent and confused. There have been occasions when summit meetings have left the international atmosphere even more disturbed than it was before. (Such was the Khrushchev-Eisenhower-Macmillan-De Gaulle summit in Paris in 1960, which exploded on the U-2 issue.) But this would have been the case even if the powers had met at a different level of representation. It is difficult to believe that the errors of Yalta would have been avoided if the powers had negotiated at any level below that of heads of government. The obscurities were dictated by policy; they were not the results of inadequate skill. And there have been successes for summitry. The American opening to China was only conceivable if it could be enacted conspiratorially at high levels of decision. The Camp David Accords of 1979 with their sensational climax in an Egyptian-Israeli peace treaty could never have been concluded without the intimacy of three leaders in secluded and continuous encounter, free, at least for a time, from the pressures of their domestic constituencies. The *Ostpolitik* in 1976, culminating in an established and legitimate security system in Europe, went forward at great speed largely because it became the personal vocation of an authoritative head of government in the German Federal Republic. If Willy Brandt's efforts had been fragmented along routine, bureaucratic lines, it is unlikely that they would have reached a successful climax.

Summit meetings have now lost their emergency character and are not confined to functional necessities. They have also invaded the symbolic and ceremonial domain of diplomacy. The heads of state and government in major capitals such as Washington, Moscow, London, Paris, Bonn and Rome can all expect to receive from a dozen to a score of their opposite numbers each year. There is a personal acquaintance-ship among them similar to that which used to prevail among the "royal cousins" in European courts. In the late 1930s it was possible for a statesman to be Prime Minister of Britain or France without ever having met the President of the United States. (This was actually the case with Neville Chamberlain, who never set eyes on Franklin D. Roosevelt.) Today a pilgrimage to the capitals of the major countries —especially Washington—is the first care of a newly elected, appointed or self-appointed leader. Thus ambassadors are upstaged not only in negotiation. Even their symbolic and ceremonial role in the representation and articulation of interstate friendship has been largely taken over by their political chiefs.

The strongest argument for summitry, apart from its inevitability, lies in the integral character of modern diplomacy. When negotiations are held at a lower level, representatives are limited by their departmental capacities. They are each in charge of a narrow sector of their national responsibility and cannot offer package deals. On the other hand, prime ministers or presidents can trade an economic concession for a military advantage or a political agreement for a financial compensation.

The paradox is that if summitry has its dangers, these become reduced by multiplication. When a summit meeting was a rare, conspicuous and dramatic event there was always a chance that its failure would generate universal despair. The lack of positive results would become the subject of polemical discussion between Great Powers about responsibility and blame. A device that was designed to alleviate world tensions would thus end up by aggravating them. Now that summit meetings have become more or less routinized their failures, if not too frequent or drastic, can be absorbed without undue shock.

The spectacular increase of frequency in summit meetings can be illustrated by the experience of the United States. Throughout the whole of American history up to 1939, fewer than thirty high level visits had been paid to Washington by heads of foreign nations. In this age, a similar number takes place every year. Even countries with lesser responsibilities and burdens do not lag far behind, especially if their leaders consider themselves to be world figures. In the eighteen months between January 1955 and July 1956, nineteen heads of state and foreign ministers made official visits to Prime Minister Jawaharlal Nehru in New Delhi. Most of the adverse criticism of this trend comes from professional diplomats or their supporters in the press and the professional literature. The principal accusation is of superficiality arising out of haste. There is no time for the careful, meticulous study of problems with any of the thoroughness that serious work should demand.

The denunciation of summit meetings would be more convincing if it were confirmed by some case histories. A more moderate criticism is that summit meetings lead, if not to danger, then at least to superficiality. Being unable to solve intricate problems in a few brief, harassed days, the statesman, eager to give the impression of success, lends his name to communiqués and declarations which celebrate the "solution" of subsidiary or trivial problems while the more obdurate and central issues are swept under a carpet of delay.

It is possible that the professionals and scholars who inveigh against the improvisations of heads of state may be overstating the importance of meticulous planning. No planning of a conference could ever have been more meticulous than that of the Paris summit meeting in 1960, yet once Khrushchev had decided to lose his temper over the U-2 incident, no amount of preparation could save the encounter from fiasco. On the other hand, the Nixon-Kissinger mission to China on February 21, 1972, seems to have been very unprepared in any technical professional sense; yet most historians would call it a success.

One of the difficulties in the controversy about summit meetings arises from the ambiguity surrounding the ideas of "success" and "failure." What do these words mean? The critics of summit meetings appear to believe that "success" has something to do with amiability. Thus, if the encounter of powerful leaders ends up on a contentious note, it is assumed that injury has been done to the cause of international understanding. This may not necessarily be the case. A frank knowledge of difficulties arising from the conflicting temperaments and personal traits of leaders might be a useful result even if it creates a somber atmosphere. It cannot be a disadvantage for those who have to make decisions to achieve an intimate knowledge about their colleagues or adversaries. It did no great harm for President Kennedy in Vienna in 1961 to become aware of the dark and threatening side of Khrushchev's character, or for the Soviet leader to discern that behind the young President's air of inexperience was a hard sense of power and resolve. A serious scholar believes that "the coldly grim and formidable impression left by De Gaulle on Khrushchev before the abortive Paris summit meeting in 1960 may have tipped the balance against a Soviet move on Berlin." The idea that success is proved by an atmosphere of geniality and that candor implies failure responds more to the concepts of public relations than to those of diplomatic craftsmanship. The idea that a summit meeting is successful if it ends in fatuous declarations of harmony ought surely to have died a permanent death after the Munich Conference of 1938. Similarly, the rhetoric of the Nixon-Brezhnev summit in 1972 invited disappointment. On the face of it the two superpowers promised to avoid any competitive activity against each other anywhere in the world. Their rhetoric outran their intentions and from the Yom Kippur War of 1973 onward it became evident that their communiqué was a document of illusion.

The critics of summitry are on strong ground when they prefer traditional diplomacy in enterprises which require patient study of intricate problems. Thus, the Austrian State Treaty is said to have required the United States representative Ambassador Llewellyn Thompson to undertake more than three hundred days of negotiation. The United Nations diplomat Ralph Bunche spent many hundreds of hours in infuriatingly detailed discussions to bring about armistice agreements between the Middle Eastern states in 1949. When war broke out in Lebanon in 1982 involving Israeli and PLO forces, a persistent, detailed negotiation conducted by an American envoy, Philip Habib, was necessary in order to secure a cessation of hostilities. No amount of glorified summiteering would have been of any use amid such complexities. There are other examples of occasions in which heads of state, meeting ceremonially, could not possibly have advanced a negotiation toward success. It would be internationally harmful if professional diplomats were to lose their sense of vocation through being constantly outflanked by their political masters.

The Decline of the Ambassadorial Function

By the time that Roosevelt and Churchill established their summitry practice in World War II, the dignity and efficacy of Foreign Offices had already been eroded through constant interference by political leaders. The French and British governments ignored accurate and ominous reports reaching them through normal diplomatic channels. Heads of government felt, then as now, that they were born with a special genius for diplomacy and had no need for the tedious, pedantic warnings of experts. Gordon Craig goes so far as to suggest that this was one of the contributory factors in the escalation leading to the war:

> The British Foreign Office was never perhaps reduced to the mere technical apparatus that the German Foreign Office became after Hitler. But throughout the period it was subjected to more interference than any other service department; it was often by-passed; periodically it was inadequately informed on meetings between economic experts, military advisors and labour officials, and deprived of any opportunities of evaluating the findings of such meetings; and with distressing frequency, the right of its permanent staff to be considered as the expert advisors on foreign policy was contested or ignored. There was a recurring tendency on the part of political leaders of the state when matters of high moment were pending, to believe that the professionals in the Foreign Office were incompetent to deal with them because of their narrowness of view, dependence on traditional concepts or lack of realism. Lloyd George believed this, Ramsay MacDonald believed this and it became dogma with Neville Chamberlain.

Across the Channel in the autumn of 1935, French diplomats were sending predictions to Paris about an imminent German reoccupation of the Rhineland, and three years later, in October 1938 after the Munich agreement, the French ambassador in Moscow, Robert Coulondre, was reporting that a Russian rapprochement with Germany could now be expected. Craig admits that "it is not clear whether these reports reached the decision makers. What does seem clear is that statesmen often gave their confidence only to reports which matched their preconceived notions and their wishful thinking."

It is hard to avoid the conclusion that the French and British governments were ill-advised in their neglect of professional diplomacy after World War I. Yet the practice of bypassing Foreign Offices and giving preconceived ideas priority over intelligence from the field has attracted little criticism; it is still very much a part of democratic practice in foreign affairs.

There is a functional relationship between the complacency of political leaders and the more skeptical rigor of Foreign Offices. Bad news is generally not something that politicians want to hear. Their natural reaction is to resent the bearer of evil tidings and punish him for disturbing their serenity. A more sophisticated device is to dismiss the diplomat's nervousness as a sign of weak character or inadequate national feeling. Many diplomats have cooperated in the decline of their profession by obsequiously sacrificing truth on the altar of popularity. When they do this, they become a danger to their own peoples. Thus, in the late 1930s, the British ambassador in Berlin, Neville Henderson, strove mightily to console his masters with the idea that Hitler's appetite would really stop short at Czechoslovakia and that he would not go on to devour Poland as well. This is what Chamberlain wanted to hear.

Fortunately, totalitarian diplomacy is even more prone to these illusions. In the early part of World War II, the Nazi German ambassador in Dublin was comforting Hitler with reports that Churchill was becoming unpopular in England and would soon be succeeded by a leader willing to compromise with Hitlerism. This fantasy seems to have played a part in causing Hitler to delay the launching of what could have been a successful invasion of the British Isles. What was the point of accepting all that risk if British resolve was going to collapse of its own accord?

The American ambassador in London in the early part of World War II, Joseph P. Kennedy, had described Britain with such hostile contempt that his dispatches must have strengthened all those in the United States who believed that it would be worthless for America to invest its strength and fidelity in what was manifestly a lost cause. Ambassadors tend to forget or ignore the occasions on which governments did well to reject their advice.

But while governments may sometimes have suffered through taking too much notice of ambassadors, the greatest affliction has arisen from taking too little notice of them. A prominent example is the refusal of Western governments to believe their ambassadors in Tehran who were convinced in the late 1970s that the Shah's regime was more fragile and insecure than the dogma of "Iranian stability" would allow them to believe. George Ball has written: "Not only was the State Department being excluded from the management of our policies towards Iran [in 1978]. I soon found out that our ambassador in Tehran, William H. Sullivan, was being similarly bypassed."

One of the handicaps of diplomacy is that while it is admired as a profession, it is not yet plugged in to any recognized science. It cannot intimidate the amateurs by requiring them to prove their credentials after a specific training process. Indeed, those in political control of international relations are less likely to have recognized qualifications in that domain than their own junior officials. Ernest Bevin is said to have remarked that the only job he could ever have obtained in the British Foreign Office was that of Foreign Secretary; he could never have become a junior officer or a fourth secretary, since those posts were subject to examinations in history and French. The conviction of politicians that international relations are an open field is strengthened by the fact that diplomacy does not hide behind an inaccessible vocabulary, although this will change if the "science" of international relations increases its authority.

The shaping of high policy is now moving away from the embassies, and few ambassadors would claim to be filling as formidable a role as in the past. There has been an enormous growth in the world's diplomatic community as a result of the proliferation of states and the functional expansion of the themes that fall under the heading of "international relations." Up to World War II the number of people bearing full ambassadorial titles could be counted in the hundreds. Today by rough estimate there are now fifty thousand officials in the world exercising diplomatic functions in Foreign Offices, embassies and international organizations. But the increase in numbers has been accompanied by a sharp decline in influence and prestige. With political leaders encroaching both on the operative aspects of negotiation and on the ceremonial and symbolic functions of diplomacy, the embassies have become increasingly harassed and forlorn. They face a psychological crisis arising from the blatant disparity between their external pomp and their dwindling sense of power.

Diplomacy has developed across the centuries as a sacred calling requiring early discipleship and constant devotion. Its members live in a kind of subsidized international aristocracy, whose studied mannerisms and lavish style are becoming irrelevant to the tone of twentieth-century life. Since the ambassador is often distant from his own country and thrown into close contact with people from other lands, he tends to develop a closer affinity with his professional colleagues than with his own fellow citizens at home. He is very vulnerable. On the one hand he is an authoritative champion of his country's interests; indeed, his basic function is to get as much as possible for his country while giving as little as possible in return. But he is more obliged than any other public servant to perceive the limitations of national positions and to seek legitimacy for his country's policies in terms of a broader universal ideal. Public opinion and his own fellow citizens are liable to make the diplomat the scapegoat for the nation's inability to get its own way. Since governments are usually constituted with an eye on domestic policy, the public is accustomed to expect a link of consequence between what a government decides and what ensues from that decision. In international life no such automatic consequence is possible since the power and sovereignty of the state do not extend into the external realm. Foreign policy is "foreign," that is to say, remote from the intimate consciousness of the people. The foreign minister and ambassador tend to become the targets of criticism for the frustrations created by foreign resistance or competition.

The professional diplomat faces an ordeal of alienation. The very collegiality that binds him to other diplomats separates him from the common touch which colors the life of citizens who stay at home. The cosmopolitan solidarities of diplomats are no longer as intimate as they were in the nineteenth century, when the number of sovereign states was small, when nearly all of them were European and when the international diplomatic community was composed of men who shared a common culture and form of expression. With the growing numbers and diversity of states there goes a deeper schism between politics, traditions and cultures. "The·decline of professional diplomacy may prove to be both a cause and a result of a wider decline in the conditions of international order in this century."

The discomfort about the ambassadorial function can be illustrated by a discussion in one of the historic centers of the diplomatic tradition. A document entitled *Review of Overseas Representation* was published in 1977 by a British government think tank. Taking a profoundly defeatist view of their country's strength, influence and likelihood of recuperation, the writers suggested a drastic reduction in the number of missions, in their size and their budgets. They poured the coldest possible water on the illusion that any but a superpower could take meaningful initiatives in the international arena. They asked their readers not "to exaggerate the extent to which the U.K.'s past world experience gives it an ability on occasions to play a bridge-building role and [not to] ignore the fact that it no longer has the influence to play a decisive part in solving international disputes . . . Its efforts . . . to help solve international problems by diplomatic or military means—Rhodesia, Cyprus, the Middle East, South Arabia, Vietnam, the problems of its own dependent territories—have not been conspicuously successful." This report did consider whether diplomacy might help a country remedy the causes of its decline, but it reached a negative answer. "It is misleading and dangerous to think that the U.K. can maintain its position in the world by keeping up appearances."

The report was condemned by the foreign policy establishment in Britain as unduly mercantile and defeatist, and was hastily shelved. But the phrase about "keeping up appearances" continues to echo long after the document was consigned to embarrassed oblivion. It reflects a popular belief that diplomacy is more a symbol and façade than an element of strength in a nation's armory. Nothing does more insult or injustice to diplomats than to traduce their function in this way. In general, they are a hard-working, dedicated group with an ideology of service and, in recent years, even of sacrifice. Nothing could be more absurd than the popular tendency to contrast the efficiency with which soldiers win battles with the failures of diplomats to win similar victories at the conference table. To adduce this argument is merely to say that it is easier to "persuade" an adversary by pointing a gun at his head than by laboriously arguing with him. This fact is so axiomatic that the recitation of it has a grotesque touch. It is precisely because military force is able to "solve" so few problems that the diplomatic agenda becomes crowded with deadlocks.

Personal diplomacy by heads of government and foreign ministers has effectively destroyed the traditional distinction between the making of policy and the negotiating of agreements. Any rational definition of diplomacy today must include the entire process whereby policy is determined, formulated, enunciated and implemented. Nor is there much intellectual profit in discussions of diplomatic techniques and procedures in isolation from the substantive movements of power and ideas within the international system. The whole policy-making community from heads of government and foreign ministers through ambassadors and their staffs is caught up in every phase of the process. There are differentiations in the degree of their influence and responsibility, not in the scope of their preoccupation. The division between those who decide what to do and those who decide how to do it has little relevance. Prime ministers and foreign ministers do much hard negotiating, and ambassadors often have a strong influence on policy.

Whatever changes take place in diplomacy, the professional ambassador is the loser on all fronts. His political masters do much of the negotiation and usurp some of his symbolic function in celebrating and dramatizing international friendships. Miniature foreign ministries spring up in prime ministers' offices; and in the United States a new layer of intervention interposes itself between policymakers and embassies—the "personal representatives" of Presidents.

The word "ambassador" would normally have a professional connotation but for the American tradition of political appointees. The bizarre notion that any citizen, especially if he is rich, is fit for the representation of his country abroad has taken some hard blows through empirical experience. But it has not been discarded. Nor should the idea of diluting a rigid professionalism with manpower from less detached sectors of society be dismissed out of hand. The diplomacy of the United States was adorned in the 1960s by scholars and writers such as the liberal economist John Kenneth Galbraith. However one of the benefits of allowing outsiders to penetrate a professional domain is that it allows the transient member to reveal some of the secrets of the guild. Galbraith must have discomfited many career diplomats by exposing the inequalities of their burdens. Not all of them are equally hard-working. Galbraith writes: "In India during my time there were some fifty ambassadors . . . They were a spectacular

example of what economists call 'disguised unemployment.' The ambassadors from Argentina and Brazil could not have had more than a
day's serious work a month. The more deeply engaged diplomats from
Scandinavia, Holland, Belgium or Spain could discharge their essential duties in one day a week." The myth of the "valuable cocktail
party" also crumbles before that corrosive pen: "I never learned anything at a cocktail party or dinner that I didn't already know, needed
to know or wouldn't soon have learned in the normal course of business. The emphasis that diplomats of all countries in all capitals accord
to entertainment is the result of a conspiracy by which function is
found in pleasant social intercourse and controlled inebriation."

It would be fair, on this point, to draw attention to the fire-brigade
role of embassies. After months of routine and lethargic ease a crisis
can erupt which places an ambassador in the center of a sudden turmoil. In the meantime his presence contributes to the symbolism of an
evolving world community. But it is undeniably true that the only
overworked embassies are those of major powers with universal and
competitive interests and, even more, those of countries which are
plunged in controversy or conflict or whose legitimacy is challenged
by their neighbors.

Galbraith rightly concluded from his experience that the main injustice of nonprofessional appointments lies in the obstruction of ascent
in the promotion ladder for professional ambassadors who find themselves stranded in the lower reaches while undeserving but politically
favored amateurs inherit the challenging peaks. When the strongest
nation in the world appoints a tycoon or a wealthy hostess to head an
embassy, the discredit and frustration spread throughout the entire
diplomatic corps in the country concerned.

It might be asked whether anybody should worry about who does the
negotiating so long as it gets done. The answer is that the world
community would lose an asset if the decline of the ambassadorial
function were to proceed too far. There is no lasting substitute for the
exercise of trained, professional minds, accustomed to the alleviation
of international conflicts and afflicted with a "dangerous" tendency to
understand the reactions and attitudes of foreign nations. These qualities depend on constant immersion in the daily life of a foreign society;
they cannot be acquired in a brief descent of statesmen from airplanes
for periods of two or three days. In particular, the kind of subterranean
rumblings which often precede changes of power balances can be
discerned, if at all, only by those who have a sustained contact with the
country of their accreditation.

In the present populist mood of public opinion, professional diplomats are not going to find much help outside their embattled embassies. They can look back with nostalgic wonder to the time when

ambassadors conducted the Louisiana Purchase at their own discretion, when Benjamin Franklin from his legation in a Paris suburb negotiated the adherence of France to the fight of the American colonies against George III, or when a British ambassador of dominating temperament in Constantinople, Stratford-Canning, made a personal "decision" to warn all concerned that Britain would fight against Russia or Austria if either of them attacked Turkey. His country was as good as its ambassador's word. It would have taken at least two months to explain the whole issue by courier to and from London, and who had time for such "formalities"? While the issue was debated through "regular channels" the war might have erupted through Russian or Austrian miscalculation. Since no war did break out between Turkey, Russia and Austria, nobody can prove that the daring ambassador did not pull off a successful operation of deterrence. No ambassador is likely to have such a sense of power again.

The Dangers of Formalism

Most of the criticisms which have been brought against the diplomatic services in all countries are summarized in a report to the British Foreign Office contained in a White Paper in 1943. This document asserts that the diplomatic service

> is recruited from too small a circle, that it tends to represent the interests of certain sections of the nation rather than those of the country as a whole, that its members lead too sheltered a life, that they have insufficient understanding of economic and social questions, that the extent of their experience is too small to enable them properly to understand many of the problems with which they ought to deal and that the range of their contacts is too limited to allow them to acquire more than a relatively narrow acquaintance with the foreign people amongst whom they live.

The historian Herbert Butterfield has written of diplomats in a similar mood:

> There is something in the history of diplomacy which inclines to be cold and forbidding and lacks the full-blooded leap of the larger story of human life. Like the history of institutions it will tend to concern itself with the development of a system abstracted from its human context. There is much that proceeds out of the logic of the situation, there is much that seems to come by an automatic interaction. Sometimes in rationalization one can almost forget that there are human beings at work with play of mind and mood and impulse; acts will not seem to cry out for an explanation in personality

but will be referred to some logic of policy; and history will fall to her greatest
temptation, hearing the tick of the clock, but failing to feel the pulse.

This is undoubtedly what masses of people think about diplomacy
and diplomats. International diplomacy would be held in greater public respect if it could refute these stereotyped impressions. Diplomacy
is separated from popular comprehension by its reputation for formal-
ism in matters of protocol and prestige. There was a time when these
protocolar sensitivities aroused more passion and violence than they
do in modern times. In 1661, the French ambassador in London attempted to outrank the Spanish ambassador by pushing his coach
ahead of that of his rival. When the Spaniards offered physical resistance, the Frenchmen fell upon them with drawn swords and poured
gun shot upon them. The Spaniards defended themselves, hamstrung
two of the Frenchmen's horses, mortally wounded a postilion, dragged
the coachman from his box and took the coveted place of honor. On
learning of this incident, King Louis XIV ordered the Spanish ambassador to leave his kingdom and sent instructions to his own representative in Madrid to demand redress, including an undertaking that
Spanish ambassadors would in future yield precedence to those of
France at all foreign courts. In case of a refusal, a declaration of war
was to be made. This "problem" continued to fester for a whole
century, until on August 15, 1761, it was agreed that at Naples and
Parma, where the sovereigns belonged to the Bourbon family, the
French ambassador would always have precedence, but at other courts
the relative rank was to be determined by the date of arrival. If both
arrived on the same day, then the French ambassador would have
precedence.

Preoccupation with this kind of triviality was very slow to die down.
Thus, at a court ball in London in 1768, the Russian ambassador,
arriving first, took his place in the most prestigious seat. The French
ambassador came in late, and climbing onto the second bench,
managed to slip down between the Russian ambassador and the envoy
of the Emperor of Austria. An altercation took place followed by a duel
in which the Russian ambassador was severely wounded. These clashes
are avoided in modern times by an objective order of precedence; the
relative seniority of ambassadors, and consequently their precedence,
is determined simply by the date on which they presented their credentials. Yet even under this system, envoys are often jealous of their
precise rank and have been known to leave important functions if they
were not seated properly.

It is too easy to say that an obsessive concern of diplomats with
precedence, style of address and outer forms is so frivolous a matter
that it cannot have any consequence. It would be more honest to admit

that flummery does, in fact, do a great deal of harm by presenting diplomacy as a picturesque but obsolete ritual deriving its forms and memories from the past. These practices obscure the fact that modern international relations are a serious, pragmatic and usually prosaic business closely anchored to the needs and hopes of contemporary society. The stilted forms of credential ceremonies, the residual use of glittering diplomatic uniforms, as well as the obsession with precedence and titles give the general public a sense of detachment from the concerns of diplomacy. Diplomats would earn a warmer understanding in public opinion if they would renounce such customs as meeting each other at airports, sometimes with guards of honor, and living in residences which are more like institutions than homes; and if they would adapt their bearing and procedures to the normative standards of late-twentieth-century life. Since the gap between their profession and the understanding of it by the public contributes to their sense of alienation, it would be reasonable for them to cooperate in an effort to take artificiality out of their conduct.

Something of this simplification is already at work among the political and diplomatic representatives of Western European countries. The very frequency of their meetings would make it impossible, or at least tedious and absurd, for them to go through all the formalities traditionally associated with international exchanges. They come and go with no more fuss than in meetings between businessmen or professionals in any field. In other areas, a stage has been reached in which it would be eccentric for ambassadors, in presenting their letters of credence, to dress themselves up in the picturesque uniforms full of gold braid and feathers which used to be part of their professional equipment. The sacrifice of mystique is rewarded by a deeper public understanding of the real interests which diplomacy seeks to serve.

There are, however, occasions on which issues of ceremony, form and prestige are invoked not on behalf of pride or sensitivities but in support of specific political attitudes. A relevant case was the ten-week delay in the 1968 negotiations in Paris for ending the Vietnam fighting. The participants were the United States, the governments of North and South Vietnam, and the Vietcong (the "National Liberation Front"). The United States refused the normal procedure of having a series of tables, or a round table, at which all participants would be seated contiguously. This would have implied equal status of all conference members, including the Vietcong. To meet the American objections a variety of devices were discussed: two half-oval tables placed against each other to form a broken oval; two half-circular tables to form a broken circle; two half-circular tables adjoining the Secretariat table on condition that the Secretariat table would jut out a few inches on either side of the curved table. In the end there was agreement on

a circular table without flags or nameplates. In order to avoid identifying the Vietcong, all the participants renounced visible signs of identity.

All this appears absurd in cold print. But it is less frivolous than it
sounds. The United States wished to recognize the Vietcong not as a
separate actor but only as a tool of the North Vietnamese government.
If the Vietcong formed a separate delegation, then the Vietnam conflict was obviously a civil war. If, on the other hand, the Vietcong was
merely a subsidiary of North Vietnam, then the war was a war of
invasion and aggression on the part of North Vietnam against South
Vietnam. Thus the United States was not fighting for mere pride; it was
upholding and defending a substantive position on the nature of the
war and the purpose of the conference. The shape of the table was
deemed to prejudge the fundamental issue on the basis of which the
conflict had been joined.

This was an understandable attitude for those trained in complex
symbolism. But the end result was a defeat for diplomacy. Bombs and
shells were falling during the ten weeks of protocolar contention.
Newspaper readers were fed with the diverse permutations of the
furniture at Paris while lives were being lost. Diplomacy was made to
appear grotesque and inhuman. The American reservation about the
status of the Vietcong could have been convincingly explained at the
conference table itself, without a ten-week altercation on formal procedures.

An analogous situation developed at the Middle East Peace Conference held in Geneva in December 1973 after the Yom Kippur War.
This was the first peace conference attended by Israel and Arab states
with the participation of the United States and the Soviet Union. The
very symbolism of foreign ministers from Israel and some Arab states
at the same table excited world opinion; and the conference was destined to lead Egypt and Israel on the road toward disengagement
which eventually led to peace. But on the opening day the Egyptian
Foreign Minister insisted on the interposition of an empty table between himself and the Israeli Foreign Minister, in an effort to indicate
that Israel was a form of contagious disease. In the Israeli view, such
a spectacle would have made a mockery of the idea of a "peace conference." In Israel itself, the idea of the conference, already attacked by
the opposition as a cover for territorial concession, would have been
discredited. The symbolism of ministerial proximity was all that Israel
could show as a gain to offset the territorial renunciation that it would
have to make. Israel refused to cooperate with the Egyptian proceedings, and the conference, as well as millions of television viewers, was
held in suspense until the problem was resolved. This argument only
took a few hours. The eventual solution was for the Israeli and Egyp-

tian delegations to be seated on either side of the Chairman's table, occupied by the UN Secretary General, with no insulting gap between the participants, but also with no Egyptian-Israeli contiguity.

Visitors to the stately Metternich Room in Vienna will observe that there are five doors where strict architectural logic would require only four. This device enabled all the five sovereigns who participated at the Congress of Vienna in 1815 to enter the hall with simultaneous pomp and primacy. Much later, at the funeral meeting to commemorate Chancellor Konrad Adenauer's death in Bonn in 1967, simultaneous entry to the Bundestag Chamber was arranged for President Lyndon B. Johnson and President Charles de Gaulle, to the satisfaction of American and, more especially, of French honor.

Diplomats of the eighties are becoming impatient with these maneuvers of prestige. They resent the degree to which the word "diplomacy" is equated in the public mind with the external forms rather than with the living content of their craft. The impatience with some of the old conventions applies to one of the oldest and most fallacious habits of the diplomatic system: the habit of treating diplomatic relations as a grace to be awarded or withheld rather than as a convenience to be universally employed. Nothing could be more full of anomaly than the "breaking off" of diplomatic relations in moments of crisis. It is precisely when there is conflict that there is most need of such relations, and it is in such conditions that they are often eroded. For many years the United States denied itself the opportunity of conducting its dialogue with China through the diplomatic channel. A similar negligence disrupted the relations between many Western countries and the Soviet Union shortly after the Russian Revolution. This tradition reflected the erroneous belief that diplomatic relations have a moral rather than a utilitarian significance.

In June 1967, at the height of the Six-Day War between Israel and the Syrian-Egyptian-Jordanian alliance, the Soviet ambassador in Israel called on me to announce the decision of his government to break relations with Israel. The motive of this decision was the existence of "far-reaching differences of outlook and policy between the Soviet and the Israeli governments." In reply I suggested that if our differences were really as great as the ambassador alleged, we ought to strengthen and reinforce our embassies, adding new personnel on both sides in order to cope with the tensions that were disturbing our relations. I said that it is in conditions of conflict that diplomatic relations are needed; if there is no conflict there are only cocktail parties. The ambassador made a historic reply: "What Your Excellency is saying is very logical. But I have not come here to be logical. I have come here to tell you that we are breaking relations." The consequence was that the Soviet Union, having no discourse with one of the parties in the

Middle Eastern dispute, lost all possibility of influence. It had awarded the monopoly of influence to the United States. Soviet emotion and Soviet interest had collided with each other, and emotion had won.

It is doubtful if anyone could recount a single instance in which a rupture of diplomatic relations has ever brought any benefit to the government initiating the break. An interesting example of the doctrine of universality is to be found in the policy and practice of Rumania under President Nicolae Ceausescu. He maintained relations with the United States, China and the Soviet Union irrespective of the conflicts and tensions between them, and he stubbornly kept regular diplomatic channels open with both Israel and its Arab adversaries even during shooting wars. It would be a service to diplomacy if a doctrine on the universality of diplomatic relations between states were adopted in an international convention, thus liberating individual governments from the temptations of sterile decisions. The only exception should be an actual abuse of the diplomatic function itself; and even here a selective approach such as dismissing a particular diplomat would be preferable to the abolition of the entire function.

The Qualities of Diplomats

The literature on diplomacy deals copiously and perhaps disproportionately with the personal qualities with which envoys are supposed to be endowed. The classic text comes from de Callières, the senior diplomat at the court of Louis XIV:

> The good negotiator must have an observant mind, a gifted application which rejects being diverted by pleasures or frivolous amusements, a sound judgment which takes the measure of things as they are, and which goes straight to the goal by the shortest and most natural paths without wandering into meaningless refinements and subtleties.
>
> The good negotiator must have the gift of penetration such as will enable him to discern the thoughts of men and to deduce from the least movement of their features which passions are stirring within.
>
> The diplomat must be quick, resourceful, a good listener, courteous and agreeable. He should not seek to gain a reputation as a wit, nor should he be so disputatious as to divulge secret information in order to clinch an argument. Above all, the good negotiator must possess enough self-control to resist the longing to speak before he has thought out what he intends to say. He must not fall into the mistake of supposing that an air of mystery in which secrets are made out of nothing and the merest trifle exalted into an affair of state is anything but the symptom of the small mind. He should pay attention to women but never lose his heart. He must be able to simulate dignity even if he does not possess it, but he must at the same time avoid

all tasteless display. Courage also is an essential quality since no timid man can hope to bring a confidential negotiation to success. He must have a calm nature, be able to suffer fools gladly and should not be given to drink, gambling, women, irritability or any other wayward humours and fancies. The negotiator, moreover, should study history and memoirs, be acquainted with foreign institutions and habits, and be able to tell where, in any foreign country, the real sovereignty lies. Everyone who enters the profession of diplomacy should know the German, Italian and Spanish languages as well as the Latin, ignorance of which would be a disgrace and shame to any public man since it is the common language of all Christian nations.

He should also have some knowledge of literature, science, mathematics and law. Finally, he should entertain handsomely. A good cook is often an excellent conciliator.

De Callières was under no doubt that diplomats should be reticent and secretive:

One of the most necessary qualities in a good negotiator is to be an apt listener; to find a skillful yet trivial reply to all questions put to him and to be in no hurry to declare either his own policy, still less his own feelings; and on opening negotiations he should be careful not to reveal the full extent of his design except as far as is necessary to explore the ground; and he should govern his own conduct as much by what he observes in the faces of others as by what he hears from their lips.

Few of the works on diplomacy published since de Callières's tract in 1717 have deviated very far from these precepts. It is evident that the qualities held to be essential for a diplomat are not likely to flourish except in an aristocratic, elitist atmosphere. The accent is on the diplomat's remoteness from the broad base of his national society, not on his rootedness within it. Harold Nicolson is aware of the functional defects that diplomats may therefore develop. He refers to the risk that the diplomat may be so "inured to the contrast between those who know the facts and those who do not know the facts, that he forgets that the latter constitute the vast majority and that it is with them that the last decision rests."

Diplomats are entitled to indignant rejection of the popular myth about their pampered, luxurious life. Theirs is not a profession to be recommended for people in search of tranquillity. In recent years there is even a tragic, heroic dimension. Ambassadors and other diplomatic personnel have been murdered, maimed or kidnapped in the United States, Britain, France, Germany, Italy, Turkey, Brazil, Uruguay, Guatemala, Sudan, Lebanon, Iran, Ireland, Somalia, Cyprus and other states, old and new. The Iranian fundamentalists and the PLO have headed the list of assailants, with other terrorist organizations helping to spread the infection. Since diplomatic immunity is one of the earliest principles of international law to have been put into effect, there is something profoundly depressing in the passivity of the world community in face of this assault on a cherished achievement. Apart from a pallid show of solidarity by America's European allies in the Iranian hostages case, the practice has been for the countries not affected by specific assaults on diplomats to remain docile spectators of each other's distress. There has not even been a symbolic demonstration of concern such as the convening of signatories of the 1961 Vienna Convention on Diplomatic Relations.

Many diplomatic historians seem convinced that the personal attributes of statesmen and envoys have a decisive influence on the outcome of negotiation. This idea may have been exaggerated. In most cases, nations make accommodations to each other not because they are impressed by their adversaries' rhetoric but because they believe that making a concession will be more useful or less harmful than refusing it. Thus the business of a diplomat is not so much to be eloquent in defense of his nation's rectitude as to define incentives and deterrents so convincingly that his rival will identify a concession with his own self-interest. This means that the diplomat at the negotiating table or in the international arena must rely for his effect not so much on his gifts of personality or expression as on the pressures and inducements which his government can mobilize outside the negotiating room. It follows that elegant books sparkling with anecdotes which define diplomacy in personal terms tend to be more entertaining than realistic. Most of international history indicates, unfortunately, that the logic of force is often more effective than the force of logic.

Since the interests of states are, to a large extent, incompatible, while some states are more powerful than others, it follows that there is no absolute prescription for successful diplomacy. Success is relative to perceived possibilities, and diplomacy is the art of appraising the feasible. For each state, the outcome of the practice of diplomacy is at best the avoidance of those conflicts that are more costly than the value of what might be gained. A diplomatic process begins as an exercise in contest, not in problem-solving. Since the contest is between states and not between their representatives, the outcome will be determined far more by the relative power of states than by the relative capacity of diplomats. There is, in fact, a danger of illusion in the belief that personalities count for too much. Diplomats who take this view are likely to compare the predicaments of international conflict with the familiar interactions of individuals. The truth is, however, that the behavior of individuals within societies is not a guide for the behavior of states within the international system. Individuals representing their nations are governed by a totally different framework of principles, inhibitions and scruples than that which governs their conduct as citizens of their own countries. Sociology, which is concerned with the behavior of groups, is much more relevant to international relations than is psychology, which is concerned with the behavior of individuals. The fact that a statesman is markedly humanitarian in his private life will not always affect his decision for or against using nuclear bombs. The Truman experience illustrates this paradox.

When all is said and done, diplomacy is a profession like other professions; it has a status which grows in proportion to the ignorance of those outside it about the specialized knowledge and skills required to practice it. It becomes less awe-inspiring the more that is known of it. But it is quite unprofessional in any scientific sense, and it is candidly pragmatic in most of its functions outside the routines of diplomatic administration and protocol—where it usually excels.

Diplomacy has to be empirical, pragmatic and intuitive, since it cannot rest its assumptions on any rigorous mathematics. It depends, in the last resort, on the way in which its practitioners react to opportunities and dangers as they arise. The favorite method of reaction is to refer to accumulated case histories on the assumption that nations have been in conflict and competition with each other so often and for so long that very few situations are likely to arise for which some precedent and tried solution cannot be found. Yet reliance on analogy and experience has led many statesmen and diplomats into blind alleys. Policymakers who base their intuitions on analogy and experience are on dangerous ground in this age of transition. Their experience is of a pre-nuclear era in which many of the present-day sovereignties were still living under foreign rule and in which Europe dominated international diplomacy. The intellectual context in which they were trained is not relevant to the issues of our times. J. W. Burton points out that in these conditions "languages and history are no longer sufficient as equipment [for diplomats]. Practitioners now require, in addition to their traditional skills, some basic propositions and theories to ensure that nuclear-age decision-making is at least as efficient in the field of peace and war."

International events, like fingerprints, are marked by particularity, not similarity. "History," as Paul Valéry reminds us, "is the science of things that do not repeat themselves." Yet statesmen who have undergone either a traumatic or an ecstatic experience early in their careers constantly take their memories with them into negotiations of which the context and implications are totally different. Anthony Eden always remembered his "heroic" epoch when he—undeservedly—symbolized resistance to dictators in the 1930s. When Nasser nationalized the Suez Canal, an event which few historians would regard as epoch-

making, Eden instantly and absurdly compared the situation to that
which arose from appeasing Hitler and Mussolini in preparation for
the catastrophe of World War II. On the other hand, when John Foster
Dulles used the "Rhineland argument" to justify the use of force
against the insurgents in Indochina, Eden primly retorted: "I was not
convinced by the assertion which Mr. Dulles then made, that the situation in Indochina was analogous to the Japanese invasion of Manchuria
in 1931 and to Hitler's reoccupation of the Rhineland." Everybody
sees the fallacies of other people's analogies.

When he ordered American resistance to North Korea in 1950,
President Truman admitted that he thought intensely about the Japanese invasion of Manchuria as one of the prior causes of World War
II. The advocates of American intervention in Vietnam constantly
sought popularity for their decision by comparing it with the Korean
decision, which was relatively acceptable in American public opinion.
The habit became so rampant that a farsighted opponent of the Vietnam war, Under Secretary George Ball, felt bound to make a patient
analysis of the differences which disturbed the analogy. He noted that
the Korean intervention—unlike that in Vietnam—had been sanctioned by the United Nations; that the United States, as a result, had
active support from other countries, including fifty-three that contributed troops, whereas in Vietnam "we are going it alone." South
Korea, unlike Vietnam, had a stable government. The South Koreans
were ready to fight for their independence, whereas the South Vietnamese, having been at war for twenty years, had no such energy or
commitment. The Korean War, explained Ball, was a classic land invasion by 100,000 troops across a recognized frontier; it therefore gave
the United States "an unassailable political and legal base for counteraction." In South Vietnam, on the other hand, the insurgents had
broad popular support, so that the insurgency was, in fact, an internal
rebellion. In South Vietnam, there had been no invasion, only a slow
infiltration.

These differences are so self-evident that it is disturbing to think of
the highest officials of a Great Power standing in need of laborious
explanations. Yet at no time did the policymakers concerned with
Vietnam manage to liberate themselves from the Korean analogy,
which was never relevant in any degree.

The Vietnam and Munich syndromes have become deeply rooted in
the consciousness of this generation. They are used in contemporary
diplomacy as an alibi for the refusal to make a meticulous and specific
analysis of separate cases. The argument runs like this:

Munich was an attempt to solve a crisis by concession and compromise.

Munich was a failure.

Therefore any attempt to solve a crisis by concession and compromise is to be avoided.

Vietnam was an attempt to solve a problem by resistance.

Vietnam was a failure.

Therefore any attempt to solve a crisis by resistance is to be avoided.

If compromise and resistance are both excluded from the repertoire of diplomacy, there is precious little left.

In the formation of post-nuclear public policy, nothing is quite as lethal as a faulty pre-nuclear analogy. Failures of this sort are apt to be failures not of will but of understanding.

Theory and Practice in Diplomacy

All around them, statesmen and diplomats observe the evolution of disciplinary techniques supported by scientific method, statistical analysis, electronic calculation and other resources that offer the glowing promise of swift breakthroughs. These methodological advances have revolutionized social and behavioral research. Amid all this achievement the practitioners and theorists of international relations have a sense of being left behind. They seem to be stuck with an outmoded technique, with history and intuition as their only instruments of work and thought. Teachers and students of international relations, who have proliferated mightily in recent decades, are even more restless than the diplomats. As Raymond Aron has pointed out, "Intellectuals cannot tolerate the chance event, the unintelligible; they have a nostalgia for the absolute, for a universally comprehensive scheme." So many writers now ask why there should not be an algebra of international relations—equations and distinctions that would be applicable in various situations, liberating them from the laborious duty of exploring particular cases.

In the early sixties an explosion of scholarly activity began in the United States directed toward making the study of international relations more rigorous and systematic. The new quantitative and behavioral approach was expressed in a prolific literature aspiring to the creation of a theory of international relations whose propositions would be mathematically verifiable. The scholars engaged in this intellectual adventure have turned away from the discussion of specific countries and conflicts and plunged into an austere preoccupation with formulas and general doctrines. The student no longer sees the

landscapes and hears the languages of foreign nations; he finds himself
in a world of mathematical symbols and a jargon inaccessible to
nonspecialists.

The major theories and approaches pursued in this exercise include
theories of balance and imbalance; integration theory; strategic theory;
game theory; influence theory; interaction analysis; crisis as an analytic
focus; image as an organizing concept; learning theory; and field theory. Morton Kaplan, starting from the assumption that "some pattern
of repeatable or characteristic behavior does occur within the international system," has built six alternative "models" of international systems. In some fields, such as factor analysis, the style of the
"international science" becomes even more recondite. Rudolph J.
Rummel writes in a discussion of the foreign behavior of nations:

> Let me denote the economic development of a nation by E, its power capabil-
> ity by C and its participation in the system by P. Then the theory is that
> $P = \alpha E + \beta C$ where α and β are constants.

If he wants to "denote," let him denote, but let him not expect much
understanding.

This kind of treatment involves such a revolution of style and
approach that its critics are justified in asking the most searching
questions about its validity and usefulness. The traditionalists are eloquently led by Hedley Bull, who defends the classical approach derived
from philosophy, history and law, which holds that "general propositions cannot be accorded more than tentative and inconclusive status."

Those who wish to study this controversy will find the confrontation
formulated with precision in a single work, *Contending Approaches to
International Politics*, edited by Klaus Knorr and James N. Rosenau.
Hedley Bull objects that Morton Kaplan's models are lacking "in internal rigor and consistency, but even if they possessed such qualities,
they would not provide the illumination of reality that Kaplan claims.
He has provided an intellectual exercise and no more." Kaplan retorts
heatedly in the mood of an innovator recoiling from the conservatism
of traditionalists. He scores his strongest points when he makes modest claims for the new science of international relations. He admits that
the approach is in its infancy and that it is both premature and intellectually unacceptable to deny its potentiality. There is no doubt that "the
early attempts at a scientific approach to international politics are
guilty of crudities and errors," but "the self-correcting techniques of
science will, however, sustain orderly progress in the discipline." If it
is too early to pass a final judgment on the search for a theory of
international relations, accuracy compels us to agree that this research

has not yet had any impact on concrete issues of diplomacy. The traditional documentary approach still holds the field.

An advocate of the scientific method, Herbert McClosky, complains that there is a tendency for the traditional approach to be mainly concerned with "the investigation of individual phenomena, instead of *classes* of phenomena, treating events as though each of them were unique instead of searching out among them the uniformities and the parallels required for generalization."

"*As though* each of them were unique." That is the crux. Surely all evidence indicates that most international situations really *are* unique. Since they deal with contingency and purpose, they cannot be traced by rigorous formulas. A scientific system can, at best, calculate and predict how governments and statesmen might act if their processes of decision were always rational and if they were always prone to act in their own interest. This is not the case. A system that makes no allowance for contingency, emotion and personality is unlikely to lead to better solutions than the admittedly imperfect classical method has been able to achieve.

A more immediate question is the impact on diplomacy of the widening academic study of international relations. The cooperation between governments and academic institutions in this field has become more intense in recent decades. Most governments, no matter how convinced of their own omniscience, have the habit of calling for academic analysis and advice. Members of the academic profession move impressively between their chairs and the centers of power and authority. The reputation of intellectual pursuits in government has risen. Even for working politicians a discreet measure of literacy is no longer an insuperable handicap; it can with time and patience be lived down.

The idea that intellectuals are of any use in politics and statecraft has a formidable adversary in the great Arab writer of the fourteenth century, Ibn Khaldun. Let us, for the sake of humility, remember what he says in Chapter 6, Section 41, of *Introduction to History, the Mukaddima*:

Scholars of all people are those least familiar with the ways of politics. The reason is that scholars are used to mental speculation and to a searching study of ideas. They tend to compare things with others that are similar to, or like them, with the help of analogical reasoning. But conditions existing in civilization and society cannot be compared with each other. The intelligent and alert segment of civilized people falls into the same category as scholars. They seek ideas, analogies and comparisons; therefore they commit errors. The average person of a healthy disposition and a mediocre intelligence judges every situation by its particular circumstance. His judgment is *therefore not infected with analogy and generalization. Such a man has the right outlook for political activities.*

If Ibn Khaldun considered mediocre intelligence to be the best qualification for statecraft, it is unfortunate that he is not alive today to draw consolation from the spectacle of the contemporary international scene.

There are, in fact, few disciplines in which the tension between theory and practice is more acute than in diplomacy. Governments have done more than universities to keep the two perspectives in balance. Most governments and foreign ministries use the services of academic experts, but few faculties of international relations understand the need to have a working ambassador in their midst. Ideal or fanciful notions about how the diplomatic process works re-echo across many campuses on the basis of theoretical models without ever being subjected to comparison with that which is illogical but real. It is hard to imagine a professor of surgery who has never performed a single operation, but there are many professors of international relations who have never negotiated an agreement or argued a case in an international forum.

Scholars and diplomats are engaged in a constant polemic, and each of them has a case. Working diplomats tend to doubt whether any fixed doctrines are applicable to specific cases. They are convinced that theories have a lesser role in shaping policies than facts, and that those who come to diplomacy with fixed conceptual systems in their minds do not have the freedom of maneuver essential in a changing world. The scholars vigorously respond that diplomats, by professional deformation, tend to sanctify the situations to which they are accredited. They are reluctant to admit that ostensibly stable conditions of power are liable to swift and radical change. Since they are accredited to existing regimes, revolutionary currents are outside their scope of duty. They are therefore surprised when the regimes to which they are accredited "suddenly" explode.

Scholars also deride the degree to which diplomacy is tied down by rigid formalities. They point out that traditional procedures and ceremonies take such heavy toll of a diplomat's time that he becomes functionally incapable of innovation. The diplomats respond that if their thinking is inexact, this is not because of intellectual indolence, but because diplomacy really is an inexact science. In the words of one of them, "Men act in diplomacy because they must. Their alternatives are restricted, their choices hedged about, and the ground on which they stand is not wholly of their own choosing. Decisions are made oftentimes not for want of other more desirable intentions but because the range of practical choice excludes them."

The fact that an intrinsic antagonism separates the theoreticians from the practitioners seems to lay a special responsibility on those who have been able to move between the academic and the diplomatic arenas. But even they do not always find it easy to resolve the conflict. On the contrary, they feel the conflict between theory and reality raging uncomfortably inside their own minds and emotions.

What is clear is that historians and political scientists who aspire to exercise influence on practical diplomacy must fight their way inside the governmental structure and not deceive themselves with illusions about their power to control events from the seclusion of their campuses. The story of the most celebrated academic consultant is vividly and candidly told by Henry Kissinger:

> *The very nature of an outside consultancy, and my own academic self-centeredness, as yet untempered by exposure to the daily pressures of the Presidency, combined to make this a frustrating experience on all sides. A regular consultant is too remote to participate in fast-moving decisions, and yet too intimately involved to maintain the inward distance and mystery of the outside adviser. He becomes almost inevitably a burden alike upon those who must assist him and those whom he advises. With little understanding then of how the Presidency worked, I consumed my energies in offering unwanted advice and, in our infrequent contact, inflicting on President Kennedy learned disquisitions about which he could have done nothing even in the unlikely event that they aroused his interest. It was with a sense of mutual relief that we parted company in mid-1962.*

A modest verdict must also be returned on the direct effects on foreign policy of the abundant labors undertaken by think tanks, faculties of political science and international relations, institutes and foundations dedicated to peace research or area studies. The volume of output is prodigious, but the direct input into policymaking is still scanty. The utility of these activities must be measured by their long-term influence on students destined to be connected with the foreign policy establishments of their countries and, of course, by the possibility that public opinion will be enriched by the publications of insights coming from the academic system. If the influence is not as direct or potent as the academicians would like to believe, it is because in any contest for influence in decision-making, those who have the fullest information will carry the day against those who merely have opinions.

Private Diplomacy

Public anxiety about the issues of peace and war has led private organizations and individuals to enter the diplomatic arena with offers of mediation. This habit is especially prevalent in the United States, where the professional status of diplomacy is less established than elsewhere. Quakers, church leaders, heads of peace research institutions, professors, members of parliaments and journalists have all attempted to solve or alleviate conflicts which have eluded the efforts of officially accredited emissaries. The Pugwash conferences became significant at the moment when the Soviet Union sent scientists and academicians who stood relatively high in the Soviet political hierarchy. The Dartmouth conferences organized by Norman Cousins, editor of the *Saturday Review*, seemed to have the prior benediction of President Eisenhower, who thought that "private citizens who enjoyed the confidence of their governments might help prepare the way for official negotiations." If that was an accurate description of Eisenhower's attitude, he must be accounted an exception to a general rule; most government leaders did not disguise their feeling that the unofficial mediators were well-meaning but troublesome meddlers.

The main experiences in this field have been brought together in a thoughtful and realistic collection of studies, *Unofficial Diplomats*. The final claim is modest:

> *At the moment the effects of transnational activities appear largely indirect and long term . . . Nongovernmental groups have played a key role in raising the salience of such issues on the international agenda, in offering expert advice on these issues and in demonstrating to national and international authorities that there is public support for long-term and global approaches.*

The reasons for so meager a harvest from so much disinterested toil are not complicated. What gives a negotiator his chance of success is not so much his skill or sincerity as his visible authority. A negotiator of limited skill and wisdom who can commit his government is likely to be more effective than a man of great virtuosity who lacks that mandate. The value of the unofficial diplomats lies more in the creation of a climate of confidence than in any operative capacity of breakthrough.

The difficulty of appraising the exact value of these private activities is a consequence of the obscurity surrounding the whole theme of motivation in international conflicts. Governments solve conflicts for as great a variety of reasons as they wage them with, and it is impossible to evaluate the contribution of each grain of influence that is brought to bear upon them. What is certain is that there is little to be gained from unofficial contacts that are totally alienated from the official communications system. When Harry S. Ashmore, an official of the Center for the Study of Democratic Institutions in Santa Barbara, attempted to mediate between Washington and Hanoi in 1967–68, McGeorge Bundy of the National Security Council in the Johnson

Administration told him pointedly that "he did not feel that foreign policy was a proper matter to be handled in an unofficial forum over which those who had ultimate responsibility had no control." It should have been clear at that moment that the mission was bound to fail irrespective of the rectitude or fallacy of Bundy's argument.

On the other hand, when the Soviet Union in its face-saving frenzy during the missile crisis in Cuba in 1962 desired to communicate with the United States by sending a junior diplomat to talk to an American newspaperman in a Washington coffee shop, the Kennedy Administration was wise to indulge the quirk and to use the services of the United Press correspondent John Scali as the intermediary for the exchange of formulas.

Diplomacy and War

If diplomacy tends to be apologetic, it is largely because it has failed to meet the test of unreasonable expectations. Whenever war breaks out it is assumed that diplomacy has failed. Since the end of World War II some fifty eruptions of violence between states have been recorded. None of these has involved the likelihood or reality of direct clashes of arms between two superpowers, but those who believed that atomic fear would have a stabilizing effect clearly underestimated the tenacious hold that war has on human consciousness and culture. Peace has not yet become the natural state of mankind, nor was it even a goal of international diplomacy until the present century. War has persisted not only because of irrationality and sin, but also because until the nuclear age it stood the empirical test of social utility; it performed functions for which there were no effective alternative devices.

Scholars who have specialized in the study of war are constantly involved in a tension between what they would like to believe and what they are commanded by their intellectual integrity to record. Thus Clyde Eagleton observes with stark precision that "for centuries war has been regarded as a means of remedying unjust situations, of settling disputes, or enforcing rights." James Shotwell states with cruel candor:

War has been used as an instrument against criminal aggression itself. It has played a beneficent role in history as well as a criminal one . . . Where would this nation be now, or for that matter any other civilized nation, if it had not met oppression with force and asserted its determination to maintain as against the world those institutions which embody its political career? Are we of this generation to take the strange position that, after having made thorough use of the war tool to establish liberty, to secure democracy and to create our modern states, we are now to deny ourselves those uses?

It is not only a question of securing democracy. Lenin in a celebrated passage predicted a series of "frightful collisions" between the Soviet Republic and the bourgeois states, while Mao Zedong wrote that "the central task and the highest form of revolution is to seize political power by force, to solve problems by war . . . Political power emerges only from among the guns."

Yet to the question "Are we now to deny ourselves those uses?" the ideology of the modern international system answers, "Yes." In abrupt deviation from centuries of experience and intellectual habit our modern age defines war as a "scourge." This attitude responds partly to a refined moral sensibility and more largely to the prudent awareness of what war could now mean if it took its extreme nuclear form. Unfortunately this affirmation of the illegitimacy of war has not been accompanied by alternative methods of solving the problems to which war has traditionally been an answer. Stanley Hoffmann correctly states that "no problem is more important than that of knowing to what extent the invention of nuclear weapons opened a totally new phase of history—of knowing whether the 'state of war' was drastically transformed . . . or whether, on the contrary, the traditional competition persists, although at a higher level of risk and with new rules."

The conventional belief that there has been a transformation of the "state of war," whereas in fact there has only been a modification, has worked unfairly against the diplomats. If the atomic fear has diminished the chance of Great Power confrontation, it has, for that very reason, given greater scope for limited wars within local parameters. One of the inhibitions against limited armed action used to be the fear that small wars would escalate into global confrontations. In our day there is a tendency to trust the superpowers to avoid this contingency by their own mechanisms; thus medium-power war is "safer" than before. Since modern war is "limited" both in its scope and in its objectives, diplomacy enters the picture more obtrusively and at an earlier stage than in the classic descriptions of war as a substitute for diplomacy or a denial of it. It was commonly held that the duration of war in its full intensity is a period of passivity and suspense for the diplomats. *Inter arma silent leges.* In modern limited war, however, the question of how to end a war arises as soon as, or even before, it has begun. Robert Osgood, who more than any other modern writer has illuminated the particular problems of limited war, goes so far as to suggest that modern war is not essentially a military problem at all. The object of war is not military—the destruction of the enemy—but political—the attainment of a result by negotiation and compromise.

It is "more broadly the problem of combining military power with diplomacy and with the economic and psychological instruments of power . . ." The consequence of this conception is that war is merely a form of coercive diplomacy and should therefore be conducted at every stage by political leaders, not by generals. The military establishment should be "the controllable and predictable instruments of national policy . . . It would be a dangerous error to apply the whole complex problem of harmonizing military policy with national policy to the far simpler imperatives of the battlefield . . ."

If we accept the notion that the object of war is to induce a certain frame of mind in the consciousness of the adversary and not to destroy him or to render him helpless in the determination of the postwar settlement, it follows that diplomacy is never in suspense. It has a three-phased task: to prevent war when possible; to control its course once it has broken out; and to end it as soon as possible in conditions likely to prevent its renewal. It must be confessed that notwithstanding the doctrines of analysts such as Osgood and others who stress the political nature of modern war, the diplomats will have a hard time taking over from the soldiers in most countries. They will have to overcome a contrary tendency—to regard diplomacy and politics as functions of an incessant military operation. The United States in the Vietnam war and Israel in the war around Beirut are two countries in which military advisers went beyond the conduct of the war into the task of determining its aims and desired consequences. General MacArthur's action in the Korean War is the classic example in his generation of the subordination of diplomacy to military momentum.

If it is inequitable to ask the diplomats why they have not prevented war, it is more legitimate to ask why they never seem to give due warning of its eruption. Here we come up against an extraordinary record of surprise. There appears to be something built into the international consciousness that prevents it from seizing, ahead of events, that which seems clear and obvious in retrospect. Much of the resentment of public opinion against the world diplomatic community arises from the failure of diplomacy, even when allied to military intelligence, to protect the international system from the shock of constant surprise. Despite all the devices of modern technology, despite the communications revolution and the license which diplomatic practice now allows to those seeking information in foreign countries, the hard fact is that there is much more surprise than foresight in the international history of this century.

The Soviet Union suffered strategic surprise when invaded by Germany in 1941. So did the United States in the same year at Pearl Harbor when Japan attacked its forces. The United States was again surprised in 1950 when North Korea invaded South Korea, and subsequently when China intervened in the Korean War. India was surprised in 1962 when Chinese forces crossed the boundary between the two states. Israel was surprised by the sudden blockade and troop concentrations initiated by Egypt under Nasser in May 1967. A few weeks later Egypt was surprised by the timing and power of the Israeli response, especially in the air. Before World War II, British leaders had been surprised by the Soviet-German pact leading to the attack on Poland and a world war. After the war the United States was surprised by a series of crises precipitated by the Soviet Union over Iran in 1946, over Berlin in 1948, 1958, 1959 and 1961, and over the Cuban missiles in 1962. Israel was surprised by the Egyptian and Syrian attack on Yom Kippur, October 6, 1973. Egypt was surprised by the Israeli crossing of the Suez Canal, enabling Israel to recuperate from the surprise of Yom Kippur. The United States was surprised by the landing of Turkish troops on Cyprus in 1974, by the Soviet-Cuban intervention in the Angolan civil war in 1975 and by the Soviet intervention in the Ethiopian-Somali conflict in 1978. For its part, the Soviet Union was surprised by the intensity of the American reaction to the placement of missiles in Cuba in 1962. Back in World War II, the Soviet Union had been surprised by the strength of Finnish resistance in the Winter War of 1939–40. The French army was surprised by the violence of the German tank breakthrough in May 1940. The United States military leaders underestimated the strength of North Vietnam in the 1960s.

The frequency with which governments are surprised in matters affecting their most vital interests has been the subject of much research, which remains inconclusive. The reason does not lie in inaccurate information. In nearly every case, the physical facts about troop concentrations and political hostility were known. Yet those who were threatened by them lent themselves easily to lenient and complacent interpretations. In some cases there was successful disinformation: for instance, in the summer of 1973, Egypt spread many stories about its own unpreparedness and weakness in the hope that Israel and others would not regard its subsequent troop concentrations in October as proof of imminent assault.

But the deepest and most universal reason for surprise lies in the psychological structure of governments and statesmen. Their habit is to formulate an appraisal about enemy intentions and capacities, and thereafter to reject any prediction that contradicts the sacred text. There is also a tendency to believe that habits and tendencies of an adversary diagnosed in the past are bound to arise in the future. Thus in 1962 the American intelligence services, despite all evidence to the contrary, initially refused to believe that the Soviet Union was installing missiles in Cuba, largely because Moscow in previous years had scrupulously avoided placing missiles in situations in which they could threaten targets in the United States. Similarly, Israeli intelligence agencies declined to believe that the Egyptian troop concentrations in October 1973 were an augury of war, for the simple reason that similar concentrations in May 1973 had not been followed by war. The American surprise at the Turkish invasion of Cyprus in 1974 was sustained by the fact that in previous and similar crises, Turkey had concentrated troops in various ports and issued threats of intervention in Cyprus without ever executing the threats. It was, accordingly, assumed that Turkey would threaten without taking action this time as well.

Thus experience and analogy might well be described as the most dangerous ailments of diplomacy. The emphasis on history and precedent in the training of diplomats may well mean that they will not be alert for the unpredictable, original and innovative factors in international conduct. The significant elements in human experience are to be found not in those domains in which events are similar to each other, but in those where they are particular and unique.

The Role of Rhetoric

"Ambassadors," said Demosthenes, "have no battleships at their disposal, or heavy infantry or fortresses. Their weapons are words and opportunities." The disposition of diplomats to weigh their words with excessive precision used to be held against them by the "hardheaded" school. Words break no bones, move no armies, conquer no territory.

This is no longer strictly true. In the age of deterrent strategy the importance of rhetorical talent and semantic precision has increased. Deterrence deals not with facts but with impressions. Everything depends on what the adversary reads into one's intentions. A bluff that is believed is more effective than a sincere threat which is dismissed with incredulity. Since much of diplomacy is now conducted through public communication, the significance of pictures of intention conveyed in words has never been greater. Words do move armies—or prevent them from being moved. They are part of the substance, not the form, of the diplomatic enterprise.

It cannot be doubted that Neville Chamberlain's disastrous words in 1938 describing Czechoslovakia as "a faraway country about which we know nothing" made Hitler's conquest inevitable. Who need fear intervention on behalf of a country held in such evident contempt and apathy? In 1950 the Soviet Union had a right to believe that the United States would be unlikely to come to the aid of South Korea since Secretary Acheson in a speech in January had failed to include South Korea in his definition of the American "defense perimeter." Statements by American leaders about the offshore islands of Quemoy and Matsu in the late 1950s had been sufficiently ambiguous to give China the impression that they could be taken without drastic reaction. In the 1960s the United States gradually escalated and sharpened its rhetoric, and the islands were left alone. In the classic case of the Cuban missiles the Kennedy Administration played mostly with words. It successfully conveyed an ambivalent message: on the one hand, it would insist on the removal of the missiles; but, on the other hand, it would do everything to avoid the appearance of Soviet humiliation.

The case histories, however, are ambiguous, since there are also precedents for the successful defiance of what seemed to be effective warnings. In 1953 John Foster Dulles threatened an "agonizing reappraisal" of American policy if France refused to ratify the plan for a European defense community. France did refuse and no reappraisal ensued. The West German government warned all states during the operation of the "Hallstein doctrine" that it would break relations with any government which established diplomatic relations with the East German regime at Pankow. Yugoslavia established relations with East Germany, probably believing that Bonn would not break with a Balkan state against its own interest. But the West German government attached such great weight to the credibility of its rhetoric that it proceeded with the rupture of its relations with Yugoslavia in 1957 and with Cuba in similar circumstances in 1963. In 1982 Great Britain "invited" an Argentinian invasion of the Falkland Islands chiefly by removing its capital ship *Exeter* from the coast, but also by a rhetoric that gave no sign of rigor in its concern for the islands.

The history of the Middle Eastern conflict is full of unsuccessful use of rhetoric, in the sense that the parties at issue brought about results contrary to their interests. The Arab states constantly spoke of the "destruction of Israel." At no time after the late 1940s were they really in a position to accomplish this grisly goal, but the psychological effects of this verbiage against the background of the Jewish experience in the Nazi period generated an Israeli determination to take the threat seriously and to develop a pre-emptive strategy. No nation can afford to face liquidation twice in a generation.

The present Israeli Prime Minister, Menachem Begin, respects rhetoric so much that he has reacted to Arab speeches by legislative enactments. In 1979 when the Egyptian National Assembly, which is not a very important body, adopted a resolution against Israel's sovereignty in Jerusalem, Mr. Begin supported a law enacted in the Knesset reiterating Israel's sovereignty. This did not change Israel's position, which was already established in 1967, but a dozen embassies were withdrawn from Jerusalem by governments which wrongly believed that Israel had taken new action. Similarly, the Israeli law providing for the annexation of the Golan Heights by Israel in 1981 was adopted in response to a speech by President Assad of Syria announcing that he would "never make peace with Israel." Assad thus weakened the argument in Israel and elsewhere in favor of leaving the status of Golan indeterminate as an incentive for future negotiation. On the other hand, a speech by Anwar el-Sadat early in 1977 announcing that he would "never" meet an Israeli leader so long as a single Israeli soldier was on Arab soil was ignored by Israel and turned out to be an idle boast refuted by Sadat's courageous voyage to Jerusalem a few months later.

It was Sadat who illustrated the positive dynamic of oratory in November 1977. By announcing in a public address his desire for peace with Israel and his renunciation of the Arab doctrine of irredentism, he created a movement culminating in a peace treaty which marks a revolution in Middle Eastern history. The important point is that he achieved this result with words alone, for no accompanying action was either undertaken or required.

Except in extreme cases involving a nation's crucial interests, it has been established empirically that it is wise for statesmen and diplomats to leave an escape clause in their rhetorical warnings. Once credibility is weakened by a single failure it is not easily re-established. The salient example in this generation takes us back to the Khrushchev period; he constantly tried to bully the Western powers into the evacuation of their armies from West Berlin by threatening, in a series of tense deadlines, to recognize the East German government, thus preempting an agreed solution of the German problem such as did eventually take place. One deadline after the other expired without the threat being fulfilled. It is more than probable that Khrushchev's loss of credibility, together with a later collapse of his ominous noises about Cuba, moved the Soviet leadership to think that it was time for a change at the head of the Soviet state.

The conclusion is that in the modern diplomatic era, a capacity to use words with precision and a highly developed sense of their potential effect on listeners are of substantive importance and are not merely a matter of ritual elegance. The semantic obsessions of diplomats deserve more respect than they generally receive. What statesmen and diplomats say is often as vital as what they do. It would not be farfetched to go further and declare that speech is an incisive form of action.

Yet speech loses its incisiveness when it is contradicted by actions that go against its purport. This is a particular weakness in democratic societies, where the occasions for speech-making are infinite and habits of cross-checking are lax. It is hard to know what a puzzled Kremlin could have made of American policy on April 24, 1982. The Secretary of State, Alexander M. Haig, was telling a conference of newspaper editors that the Soviet Union was the source of every international tension and that the United States would refuse to put up with Russian occupation of Afghanistan. Almost at that very hour President Reagan was announcing that the grain embargo imposed by his predecessor on the very grounds of the Soviet occupation of Afghanistan would now be lifted. It is possible to justify each of the two utterances separately in their own contexts, but taken together they illustrate the languid charm of easygoing democracies rather than their consistency or serious purpose.

Paradox in the International System

The international spectacle, despite vast efforts to explore its workings, remains mysteriously incoherent. This is meant in the literal sense: things do not hang together. There is far more paradox than logic.

First, there is the political paradox. Never was the world more united in its destiny—and more fragmented in its structure. In theory the individual nation-state should be in eclipse. It is not a viable unit of security. It does not function as an autonomous economic system. It cannot solve environmental problems within its own limits. Yet there has never been such a swift proliferation of nation-states as in the last quarter century. The international system is so decentralized, through the existence of more than one hundred sixty units of decision, that it can hardly qualify to be called a system at all. The multiplicity of nation-states in a world where sovereignty has lost a great part of its meaning is the central political anomaly of our age. The need for men to be identified with a social group seems to be as elemental as the need for food, shelter and the perpetuation of the species, and no collective idea exerts a more potent hold than the nation-state as a source of inspiration, solidarity and sacrifice. Despite the growth of regional and supranational institutions, there is no sign that the individual nation-state is about to be superseded as the focus of allegiance and social pride.

Those who predicted that the sense of nationhood would decline based their judgment on the inadequacy of the nation-state as an expression of military or economic independence. They gave too little weight to the fact that nationhood is largely a spiritual ideal, and is thus immune to the erosion of its secular and material relevance. In the words of the French historian Ernest Renan: "A nation is a soul, a spiritual principle. A common glory in the past, a common hope for the future. To have done great things together, to want to do them again—these are the conditions for the existence of a nation."

Yet there is a paradox within the paradox. Together with the multiplication of the nation-state as the most important actor in the international system, there goes a tendency to transcend nationhood through larger units of solidarity and cooperation. The world is fragmenting and integrating at one and the same time. Regional and multilateral bodies, such as the EEC, the OAS, the OAU, the Arab League and OPEC, proliferate in the diplomatic arena, and multinational corporations are making national frontiers irrelevant in the organization of economic power. In traditional representations of the international system interstate relations are portrayed as the only significant ones. Very little attention is paid to nongovernmental activity. Arnold Wolfers calls the traditional system "the billiard ball model." It portrays the international community as composed only of states each of which "represents a closed, impermeable and sovereign unit completely separated from other states." It is assumed, according to this model, that international life consists of the collisions and separations of identically shaped units. The political reality today, however, tells us that the interaction of governments is only one level of international relations. There are many other areas of interaction—between trading partners, scientists, scholars, tourists, and business and technological enterprises. Indeed, one of the difficulties in the study and practice of international politics lies in the immense expansion of their range. A cobweb would be a better model than a set of billiard balls for representing the way in which actors in the international system relate to each other. International relations comprise a greater number of actors and a broader variety of functions than could have been imagined a generation ago. Yet the nation-state still holds most of the cards, and international politics is largely the story of interstate relations.

Then there is the military paradox. Never has so much military power been concentrated in the hands of so few; yet never has military power been less effective as an instrument of policy. Those who possess vast military strength do not necessarily enjoy a feeling of overwhelming political power. The major components of their strength are so awesome in their destructive effects that there is little credibility in the threat to use them. The question then arises whether power that is unlikely to be used continues to be power. The current theme of the power system is deterrence. The capacity for deterrence requires three conditions: the existence of power; the willingness to use it; and the reflection of those two conditions in the consciousness of potential adversaries.

When any of the three conditions is absent or doubtful, the entire structure of deterrence collapses. If nobody believes that the nuclear powers will ever use their power, their capacity to coerce or intimidate nations becomes no greater than it would have been in the absence of their nuclear forces. The nuclear powers are cut down to size, and smaller nations feel free to go their own way. In the disputes of the

United States with Cuba, Panama, Vietnam, Cambodia and Iran, a vast preponderance of power in favor of the United States did not assure it of political victory. Nor did Soviet military predominance prevent deviationist or independent tendencies from asserting themselves in Yugoslavia and Rumania. In a fishing dispute between Britain and Iceland, a small country with no military power at all came out very well against a nuclear power. In 1972 Egypt proved itself able to defy the Soviet Union even to the extent of expelling its advisers. The paradox under which the powerful become politically weak and the weak become politically powerful has had confusing intellectual and psychological results. In many sectors of the international system, and especially in Western Europe, the fact that the use of nuclear power has little effect on local or subsidiary conflicts has been taken to mean that military power as a whole is ineffective in the modern world.

This would have been a reasonable view if only it had been shared by the Soviet Union. This was not the case. While Western military thinking became defensive and skeptical, that of Moscow became dynamic, global and not merely protective. In Hungary, Czechoslovakia, Angola, Ethiopia and Afghanistan the Soviet Union and its allies achieved results through military power such as the Western powers had not been able to realize in Suez, Algeria, Vietnam or Iran. Wars between Iran and Iraq, Argentina and Britain, and hostilities involving Israel in Lebanon, where the Palestine Liberation Organization had established a revolutionary enclave for terrorist assaults on Israel, were not prevented by Great Power influence or speedily terminated by Great Power pressure. The fact that two powers have immense predominance over all others does not give them total control of international life. In all sectors of the world system that lie beyond the central nuclear balance, there is now a more permissive atmosphere for limited, local war than ever before. Limited war means conflict in which a state uses less than its total power to achieve less than the total destruction of its adversary. This implies that neat definitions of victory and defeat are less categorical than they used to be. Since the prevention or limitation of war is still the main ambition of diplomacy, the lack of clarity about the place of war in the international system will continue to be the main challenge of the diplomatic community throughout the eighties.

The arms control dilemma is not as central to this issue as was once believed. Arms are more a result than a cause of international tension. Technical arms control discussions conceived as a separate discipline without a political context have been sterile and frustrating.

A similar air of paradox dominates the international economic scene. There is a greater availability than ever before of resources for the promotion of welfare and the elimination of poverty, together with a new consciousness of the need for international cooperation in the distribution of wealth. Yet the gap between the rich and the poor, represented by the North-South syndrome, grows constantly wider. The rich are growing richer at a pace which the developing nations will never be able to overtake, while the standard of living in poorer countries, although slightly improving in absolute terms, seems paltry in relation to the potentiality and the need. The consequent frustration is explosive. Equality is the keyword of twentieth-century life. People are no longer prepared to put up with traditional conditions of inequality, either as individuals within society or as nations in the international community. The expansion of political independence has not been accompanied by corresponding gains in economic and social advancement.

The human rights paradox also arises from the disparity between consciousness and achievement. The recognition of international responsibility for the freedoms of individuals has never been more acute. It was sharpened by the horrors which the Nazi-Fascist era brought to millions of innocent victims. But the movement for human rights comes up against two obstacles. The idea of sovereignty works against obtrusive international criticism, while external pressure for human rights tends to increase tensions between those who intervene and those who resent the intervention. This creates a conflict between the cause of human rights and the cause of international conciliation. Détente causes Western public opinion to moderate its criticism of discrimination within the USSR. Advanced countries have a guilty deference toward nations recently released from colonialist domination. They are therefore reluctant to criticize new nations for their absolutist and charismatic versions of government.

Science and technology are the success stories of this generation, but even in this realm we cannot escape the prevalent air of paradox. Man has become endowed as never before with the power to generate energy, to increase productivity, to conquer distance, to disseminate skills and to bring the entire human race close together in mutual accessibility. The space age has given humanity a new sense of mastery and adventure. Yet across this hopeful scene there is the brooding fear lest the destructive and polluting qualities of scientific progress may prevail over its potentiality for increased welfare and abundance.

There is a legal paradox, too. There is much lip service paid to the idea of applying the restraints of law to the relations between states. International law has developed a copious literature and an impressive cluster of institutions. Yet it would be idle to ignore the reluctance of states to organize their relationships in accordance with legal principles and procedures. International law was not mentioned in the League of Nations Covenant and was also left out of the Dumbarton

Oaks draft of the UN Charter. In the Charter itself it has a meager and parenthetical mention. Governments are more prone to solve their disputes by war or diplomatic compromise than by committing themselves in advance to accepting an objective juridical verdict. In the sorrowful words of C. Wilfred Jenks, a prominent international lawyer:

> *There is increasing scepticism concerning the relevance of legal processes to the fundamental needs of society in a world of cataclysmic change; there is persistent reluctance to refer important matters to international adjudication; there is continued suspicion of the law-making treaty as an encroachment on national and personal freedom; the widespread hostility to entrusting wide regulatory powers to international bodies in any but the most limited fields remains unabated.*

Many of the contradictions between expectations and realities in international politics can be attributed to a lack of clarity about the moral element in these relations. Ideas of what is right and what is wrong are fairly well developed in the domestic consensus and national cultures of most countries, however imperfectly they are carried out. In the international field, there is not even a theoretical consensus. Jenks, who has brilliantly illustrated the theme of paradox in international relations, concludes that "the unity of mankind in peace, brotherhood and freedom under law is essentially a moral vision of the social order, but moral purpose is not the characteristic temper of the world . . ." Three scholars, Michael Walzer, Stanley Hoffmann and Michael Howard, have recently probed deeply into the moral implications of international politics, especially in relation to war and peace; but the most that they can prove is that states are sensitive enough to seek moral justification for what they have already done or decided to do. This is not the same as abstaining from advantageous decisions on moral grounds. Legal advisers in foreign ministries are not expected to tell their governments that what the governments propose to do is illegal. Their task is to find a legal justification for whatever the governments intend to do. Since there is no compulsory adjudication in international relations as there is in domestic affairs, everybody's interpretation is as good as anybody else's.

The Future of Diplomacy

Diplomacy is called upon to bridge gulfs and to defuse tensions in a world where there is no effective restraint on the policies of individual states and no development of enforceable international authority. And when diplomacy does succeed, its successes are often invisible. They must, of necessity, go unheralded. They consist for the most part of dangers avoided, not of concrete changes achieved. Yet, despite conventional pessimism in the diplomatic community, the fact remains that most of the conflicts in the relations between states are resolved through the routines and procedures of diplomacy. Problems thus solved do not earn any headlines. The media thrive on confrontations, not on compromises. Tolstoy pointed out that "happy families have no histories."

Sometimes a sharp dispute subsides by being allowed to fade from view. The choice is not a tidy one between "solution" and "eruption." A classic case is that of the Berlin crises of 1958–61. After many episodes of ominous threat, the Soviet Union under Khrushchev simply accepted the division of Berlin as a reality, just as it had accepted the idea of a divided Germany, since there was no way of solving the problem in its favor except by an unwanted war.

If there is hope of avoiding catastrophe and creating new harmonies, it is not so much because diplomacy is becoming popular as because the alternatives appear increasingly insane. In a world in which there are 50,000 nuclear warheads, each capable of immense devastation, the central nuclear balance is held together by the instinct of avoiding suicide. Meanwhile the old ideological divisions between capitalism and socialism are becoming less sharp as new generations, oblivious of the immediate postwar "crusades," begin to examine their predicaments with more pragmatism than religious zeal. The Soviet empire is less closed from the world than in its earlier days, and it is under sporadic pressure to liberalize its internal regime and its methods of international intercourse. Communism has been a success in power politics but a failure in ideology. Instead of transforming the world the Soviet Union by the end of the Brezhnev era has been transformed; from being the center of world revolution dedicated to the downfall of existing social and political order, it has evolved into a mature global power whose interest in stability balances its revolutionary zeal.

The explosive envies and resentments of the Third World are real. But they are mitigated by the simple fact that they are acknowledged and not resisted by the advanced nations. The discussion is about how to satisfy the aspirations, not about how to deny them. This places the North-South dialogue on an empirical plane with a theoretical basis of consensus. Moreover, the confrontation itself is blunted by the fact that what is called the Third World is a historical fiction nourished by a common experience in the past but with little common identity in the present. For the present and the future the salient fact is that the Third World contains several states of vast opulence and economic power which are incongruously grouped together with countries living in semi-starvation. Kuweit, Saudi Arabia, Venezuela, Nigeria are not really of the same economic family as Ruanda-Urundi, Haiti, Mali and

Bangladesh. Thus any attempt at a unifying definition of the Third World is bound to be inaccurate.

There is a great deal of literature about the need for the renunciation of the nation-state system as a means of ensuring world peace. While these statements are couched in utopian rhetoric, they are in fact a source of pessimism. To make survival depend on conditions that have no realistic prospect of coming into existence is a counsel of despair. The task of statesmen is to understand what is real and concrete in the international environment and to seek the maximal chance of peace within that context. That the abolition of state sovereignty would bring about a new and peaceful order is, in any case, problematical. Wars can arise within political units as well as between them, and supranational organizations are just as capable of reckless decisions as are individual governments. Ireland, Lebanon and Cyprus are modern examples; they show that national sovereignty may often be a façade behind which there is as much discord and hostility as that which disturbs the relations between separate states. In any case, a debate about what would happen if there was a world government is superfluous, since the human race shows no sign of replacing the sense of nationhood by an overriding allegiance of another kind.

The best hope lies in enlarging some of the positive experience of the post-1945 era. The transition from extreme Cold War to various forms of East-West dialogue; the reconciliation of old enemies such as Germany and France in Europe and Egypt and Israel in the Middle East; the new harmony between China and the United States despite conflicting social structures and ideas; the generally peaceful emergence of many new states from colonial domination; the civility with which the North-South dialogue is conducted; above all, the avoidance of general war despite the proliferation of regional conflicts; the slow but promising growth of the habits of transnational contact and cooperation—all this encourages the belief that even a world of nation-states is not inevitably or totally anarchic.

The most promising feature of modern diplomatic literature is its restrained mood. There is little self-delusion. Those who seek Grand Designs for the immediate transformation of the human condition are likely to suffer, and to deserve, disappointment. Yet the traditions and institutions of diplomacy, developed in a long sweep of history, may have a protective role if they are put to work wisely and well. Problems of war and international rivalry may never be "solved," but there is a rational hope that they can be kept in restraint. War prevented is a kind of peace, perhaps the only kind of peace that nations will ever know. This may sound unambitious and unattractively sober in comparison with messianic yearnings for perfect peace that fill many of the noblest chapters of literature. But diplomats, scarred by their own experience, have few choices but to inhabit a middle emotional ground between excessive skepticism and exaggerated hope. Once we come to terms with the fact that international politics are fundamentally different from any other kind of politics, we shall at least enjoy the shelter of realism. The central fact about international politics is that power is not controlled, since there is no authority capable of controlling it.

To imagine the rule of conscience or the growth of order and justice beyond the limits of the nation-state requires the kind of innocent credulity for which diplomats are not famous. But if there is an evolution, however slow, in that direction, it will probably owe much to the presence of some thousands of trained people in every part of the globe whose calling requires them to look over the fence in which their own allegiances are confined in an effort to explore the impulses that move other sectors of mankind. In a world of more than one hundred and sixty nation-states, the number of potential armed conflicts is far greater than the number of those that have actually broken out. Diplomacy must be judged by what it prevents, not only by what it achieves. Much of it is a holding action designed to avoid explosion until the unifying forces of history take humanity into their embrace.

Source Notes

1 / The New International Era: The Curtain Goes Up

PAGE

5   United Nations Charter, Preamble.

6   Roosevelt quote on the Russians in John L. Gaddis, *The United Nations and the Origins of the Cold War, 1941–1947* (New York: Columbia University Press, 1972), p. 6.

6   William C. Bullitt, "How We Won the War and Lost the Peace," *Life*, August 30, 1948, p. 25.

8   U.S. Department of State, *Foreign Relations of the United States, 1945* (Washington, D.C.: Government Printing Office, 1955), pp. 679–80.

9   George F. Kennan, *Memoirs, 1925–1950* (Boston: Little, Brown, 1967), p. 253.

9   W. Averell Harriman and Elie Abel, *Special Envoy to Churchill and Stalin, 1941–1946* (New York: Random House, 1975), p. 236.

10   Cordell Hull, *Memoirs*, Vol. II (New York: Macmillan, 1948), p. 1170.

2 / America and the World

15   George Washington, Farewell Address, 1796. See Felix Gilbert, *To the Farewell Address: Ideas of Early American Foreign Policy* (Princeton, N.J.: Princeton University Press, 1961), Appendix, p. 145.

15   Thomas Jefferson, Inaugural Address, 1801.

16   Gilbert, *loc. cit.*

17   Henry Steele Commager, *The Age of Enlightenment* (New York: Doubleday, 1977), p. 175.

PAGE

19   Schlesinger quote in George Schwab, ed., *Ideology and Foreign Policy* (New York: Cyrco Press, 1978), p. 129.

19   George F. Kennan, *American Diplomacy, 1900–1950* (New York: New American Library, 1951), p. 82.

19   Wilson quote in Woodrow Wilson, *The New Democracy: Presidential Messages*, ed. Ray Stannard Baker and William E. Dodd (New York, 1926), p. 104.

20   Cordell Hull, *Memoirs*, Vol. II (New York: Macmillan, 1948), pp. 1314–15.

23   Harry S. Truman, *Year of Decisions*, Vol. I (New York: Doubleday, 1955), p. 82.

24   Frederick L. Schuman, *Cold War: Retrospect and Prospect* (Baton Rouge: Louisiana State University Press, 1962), p. 15.

25   Thomas T. Hammon, ed., *Witness to the Origins of the Cold War* (Seattle: University of Washington Press, 1982), pp. 28–33.

37   Robert Divine, *Eisenhower and the Cold War* (New York: Oxford University Press, 1981), p. 154.

52   Henry A. Kissinger, *For the Record* (Boston: Little, Brown, 1981), p. 265.

68   Jimmy Carter, *Keeping Faith: Memories of a President* (New York: Bantam, 1982).

74   Jeane J. Kirkpatrick, *Dictatorships and Double Standards* (New York: Simon & Schuster, 1982), p. 86.

78   Kissinger quotes in Laurence W. Martin, ed., *Strategic Thought in the Nuclear Age* (London: Heinemann, 1979), p. 7.

82   Norman Podhoretz, "Kissinger Reconsidered," *Commentary*, June 1982, p. 24.

85   Colin Gray, "Presidential Directive 59: A Critical Assessment," *Parameters* (The Journal of the U.S. Army War College), March 1981.

86   Richard Pipes, "The Soviet Strategy for Nuclear Victory," Washington *Post*, July 3, 1977.

86   Taylor quote: Washington *Post*, June 30, 1981.

87   George F. Kennan, *The Cloud of Danger* (Boston: Little, Brown, 1977), pp. 228 ff.

88   Barbara Tuchman, *Practicing History* (New York: Ballantine, 1981), pp. 305–6.

3 / The Soviet Union in World Politics

98   "troubles in Poland and Hungary": Philip E. Mosely, *The Kremlin and World Politics* (New York: Knopf, Vintage Books, 1960), p. 324.

99   "breaking the Atlantic alliance": Marshall D. Shulman, *Stalin's Foreign Policy Reappraised* (Cambridge, Mass.: Harvard University Press, 1963).

PAGE

102   Joseph L. Nogee and Robert H. Donaldson, *Soviet Policy Since World War II* (New York: Pergamon Press, 1982), p. 124.

107   "and now by China": Adam B. Ulam, *Dangerous Relations: The Soviet Union in World Politics, 1970–1982* (New York: Oxford University Press, 1983), p. 42.

111   "Nixon did not even sound": Gerard Smith, *Doubletalk: The Story of the First Strategic Arms Limitation Talks* (New York: Doubleday, 1980), p. 21.

112   David Riesman, "The Danger of the Human Rights Campaign," in Fred Warner Neal, *Détente or Debacle* (New York: Norton, 1979), p. 56.

116   David Holloway, *The Soviet Union and the Arms Race* (New Haven, Conn.: Yale University Press, 1983), p. 106.

118   Coral Bell, *The Diplomacy of Détente* (London: Martin Robertson, 1977).

121   Holloway, *op. cit.*

122   George Arbatov and Wilem Oltmaus, *The Soviet Viewpoint* (New York: Dodd, Mead, 1983), pp. 93–94.

125   Mosely, *op. cit.*, p. 3.

130   "The orthodox school": This important classification is convincingly made in Lawrence T. Caldwell and William Diebold, Jr., *Council on Foreign Relations* (New York: McGraw-Hill, 1981), pp. 80–82.

132   "Using outside events . . . ," in Robert Dallek, *The American Style of Foreign Policy* (New York: Knopf, 1983).

132   "Western Europe's inability . . . ," in Ulam, *op. cit.*, p. 315.

4 / The New Europe and the Alliance

134   Barbara Ward, *The West at Bay* (New York: Norton, 1948), pp. 9–10.

140   Raymond Aron, *A New Europe* (Boston: Houghton Mifflin, 1964), p. 60.

151   Dean Rusk, "American Foreign Policy in the Eighties." LTV Washington Seminar, 1980, Washington, D.C.

151   Henry A. Kissinger, *The Troubled Partnership* (New York: McGraw-Hill, 1965), p. 40.

152   Henry A. Kissinger, *For the Record* (Boston: Little, Brown, 1981), p. 160.

152   "Where are the Allies?": New York *Times*, November 14, 1979.

154   Theodore Draper, "The Western Misalliance," *Washington Quarterly*, Vol. 4, No. 1 (Winter 1981), p. 56.

163   Stanley Hoffmann, "Fragments Floating in the Here and Now," in "Looking for Europe," *Daedalus*, Winter 1979, p. 23.

168   Michael Howard, "Reassurance and Deterrence," *Foreign Affairs*, Winter 1982–83, p. 322.

169   "Some observers believe": William Wallace, *Foreign Policy Making in*

Western Europe: Old States and New Circumstances (Saxon House, England, 1978), pp. 34–35.

5 / The Third World: Asia, Africa, Latin America

171   *Barnhart Dictionary of New English Since 1963,* quoted in William Safire, *Safire's Political Dictionary* (New York: Random House, 1978), p. 724.

176   Fuad Asami, "The Arab Road," *Foreign Policy,* Summer 1982, p. 24.

177   John Stuart Mill, Dissertations and Discussions (Boston: William Spencer, 1864–67), pp. 251–52, quoted in Robert W. Tucker, *The Inequality of Nations* (New York: Martin Robertson, 1979), p. 10.

177   Shlomo Avineri, in *Karl Marx on Colonialism and Modernization* (New York: Doubleday, 1969), pp. 132–33.

182   See P. T. Bauer, "Western Guilt and Third World Poverty," *Commentary,* January 1976, and Peter L. Berger, "Speaking to the Third World," *Commentary,* October 1981.

183   Karl Borgin and Kathleen Corbett, *The Destruction of a Continent* (New York: Harcourt, 1982).

186   "at the end of the war": David MacEachron, "The United States and Japan," *Foreign Affairs,* Winter 1982–83, pp. 406–8.

6 / The Unending Conflict: The Middle East

193   "The peoples of the North . . . ," in Abba Eban, *Tide of Nationalism* (New York: Horizon, 1959), pp. 42–43.

193   Bernard Lewis, *The Arabs in History* (London, Hutchison, 1970), pp. 164–65, and *The Muslim Discovery of Europe* (New York: Norton, 1982), p. 68.

201   Walid Khalidi, "Thinking the Unthinkable: A Sovereign Palestinian State," *Foreign Affairs,* July 1978, p. 695.

217   Henry Kissinger, *The White House Years* (Boston: Little, Brown, 1979), p. 341.

230   Albert Hourani, "The Decline of the West in the Middle East," *International Affairs,* April 1953, p. 166.

7 / International Organization: Myth and Reality

238   Quoted in George Scott, *The Rise and Fall of the League of Nations* (New York: Macmillan, 1973), p. 300.

240   Quincy Wright, *A Study of War,* Vol. I (Chicago: University of Chicago Press, 1942), p. 254.

241   "The actual system . . . ," quoted by Ernst B. Haas, "The Balance of Power: Prescription, Concept or Propaganda," *World Politics,* Vol. 5 (July 1953), p. 453.

PAGE

241   "It will be shown . . . ," quoted by Inis B. Claude, *Power and International Relations* (New York: Random House, 1962), pp. 11–93.

242   Mowat quoted in Kenneth W. Thompson, *American Diplomacy and Emergent Patterns* (New York: New York University Press, 1962), p. 152.

242   Winston Churchill, *The Gathering Storm* (Boston: Houghton Mifflin, 1948), pp. 207–8.

243   Harold Nicolson, *The Congress of Vienna* (New York: Harcourt, 1946), p. 123.

245   "The balance of power": Claude, *op. cit.*

245   "to preserve an uncertain balance . . . ," in James Brown Scott, ed., *President Wilson's Foreign Policy* (New York: Oxford University Press, 1918), p. 238.

245   ". . . the future tranquility of Europe," quoted from Guglielmo Ferrero, *The Reconstruction of Europe* (New York: Putnam), pp. 178, 261.

246   ". . . major force of mankind," *Public Papers of Woodrow Wilson*, ed. R.S. Baker and W. E. Dodd, Vol. I. Reprint of 1927 ed. (Kraus Reprints).

250   "This knight of peace . . . ," in Elmer Bendiner, *A Time for Angels: The Tragicomic History of the League of Nations* (New York: Knopf, 1975), p. 393.

250   Sean Lester quoted, *ibid.*, p. 394.

251   Scott, *op. cit.*

251   A. LeRoy Bennett, *International Organization* (Englewood Cliffs, N.J.: Prentice-Hall), p. 37.

252   Bendiner, *op. cit.*, p. 171.

259   "talked about every subject . . . ," Rupert Brooke, quoted in F. S. Northedge, *The International Political System* (London: Faber, 1964), p. 81.

260   Claude, *op. cit.*, p. 151.

261   Hans J. Morgenthau, *Politics Among Nations* (New York: Knopf, 1974), p. 422.

261   Claude, *op. cit.*, p. 160.

278   Conor Cruise O'Brien, *The United Nations: Sacred Drama* (London: Hutchison, 1968), p. 10.

284   Leon Cordenker, *UN in International Politics* (Princeton, N.J.: Princeton University Press, 1971), pp. 172–74.

8 / War and Peace in the Nuclear Age

288   "on any specific formula": John G. Stoessinger, *The Might of Nations* (New York: Random House, 1975), p. 376.

290   Address at the Massachusetts Institute of Technology, March 31, 1949.

291   "outstanding political disputes": Philip Noel Baker, *The Arms Race* (New York: Oceanna, 1958), pp. 119–20.

PAGE

292   "war in the nuclear age": Stoessinger, *op. cit.*, p. 374.

292   "the peculiar failure . . . ," in Jonathan Schell, *The Fate of the Earth* (New York: Knopf, 1982), p. 4.

296   Herman Kahn, *Thinking About the Unthinkable* (New York: Avon, 1979).

310   Henry Kissinger, *Nuclear Weapons and Foreign Policy* (New York: Norton, 1969.)

311   Maxwell Taylor, *The Uncertain Trumpet* (New York: Norton, 1964).

317   Henry A. Kissinger, *For the Record* (New York: Little, Brown, 1981), p. 240.

317   Solly Zuckerman, *Nuclear Illusion and Reality* (New York: Viking, 1982), p. 142.

319   "a break in the continuity . . . ," in Y. Harkabi, *Nuclear War and Nuclear Peace* (Jerusalem: Scientific Translations, 1966), p. 167.

320   Peter W. Rodman, "The Missiles of October," *Commentary*, October 1982, p. 40.

327   Stoessinger, *op. cit.*, p. 206.

9 / Diplomacy: Old and New

331   Le Trosne, *De l'Ordre Social* (Paris, 1777), p. 395.

332   George W. Ball, *The Past Has Another Pattern* (New York: Norton, 1982), p. 452.

333   Richard Louis Walker, *The Multi State System of Ancient China* (Hamden, Conn.: Shoestring Press, 1953), p. 77.

334   *Ibid.*, p. 82.

334   "Greek cities": Harold Nicolson, *The Evolution of Diplomacy* (New York: Collier's, 1966), p. 11.

335   Frank E. Adcock, *Diplomacy in Ancient Greece* (New York: St. Martin's, 1975), pp. 139–40.

337   "at the Turkish court": Adda B. Bozeman, *Politics and Culture in International History* (Princeton, N.J.: Princeton University Press, 1960), p. 338.

337   Garring Mattingly, *Renaissance Diplomacy* (New York: Penguin, 1973), p. 24.

340   Robert Tucker, *The Inequalities of Nations* (New York: Basic Books, 1977).

346   "He and his conscience . . . ," in Harold Nicolson, *The Evolution of Diplomacy*, p. 30.

348   Walter Lippmann, *The Public Philosophy* (Boston: Little, Brown, 1955), p. 20.

349   Hans J. Morgenthau, *Politics Among Nations*, 5th ed. (New York: Knopf, 1978), p. 543.

349   Quincy Wright, *Problems of Stability and Progress in International Relations* (Berkeley: University of California Press, 1954), pp. 22–23.

353   Henry Kissinger, *Years of Upheaval* (Boston: Little, Brown, 1982).

357   "made it clear . . . ," in Robert A. Aliano, *The Crime of World Power* (New York: Putnam, 1978), p. 326.

PAGE

357 Bernard C. Cohen, *The Public's Impact on Foreign Policy* (Boston: Little, Brown, 1973), p. 189.

359 Dean Rusk, "American Foreign Policy in the Eighties." LTV Washington Seminar, 1980, Washington, D.C.

365 Gordon Craig, "The Professional Diplomat and His Problems, 1919–1939," *World Politics*, January 1952, p. 151.

368 "The decline of professional diplomacy . . . ," in Hedley Bull, *The Anarchical Society* (New York: Macmillan, 1980), p. 179.

368 Central Policy Review Staff, *Review of Overseas Representation* (London: Her Majesty's Stationery Office, 1977), pp. 9–10.

369 John Kenneth Galbraith, *A Life of Our Times* (New York: Ballantine, 1981), p. 391.

371 Proposals for the Reform of the Foreign Service (CMD 6420), 1943, p. 2.

371 Herbert Butterfield, *The Peace Tactics of Napoleon* (Cambridge: Cambridge University Press, 1929), p. 232.

376 François de Callières, *On the Manner of Negotiating with Princes* (South Bend, Ind.: University of Notre Dame Press, 1963).

377 Harold Nicolson, *The Evolution of Diplomatic Method* (New York: Macmillan, 1954), p. 208.

379 J. W. Burton, *Systems, States, Diplomacy and Rules* (New York: Cambridge University Press, 1968), p. 208.

380 "I was not convinced . . . ," in Fred Iklé, *How Nations Negotiate* (New York: Harper & Row, 1964), pp. 158–59.

382 Rudolph J. Rummel, "Some Dimensions in the Foreign Behavior of Nations," in James N. Rosenau, ed., *International Politics and Foreign Policy*, rev. ed. (New York: Macmillan, 1969), p. 612.

382 "The traditionalists": Richard Snyder et al., *Foreign Policy Decision Making* (New York: Free Press, 1962), p. 189.

382 Julius Knorr and James N. Rosenau, eds., *Contending Approaches to International Politics* (Princeton, N.J.: Princeton University Press, 1969).

385 Henry Kissinger, *The White House Years* (New York: Little, Brown, 1979), p. 9.

386 Maureen Berman and Joseph E. Johnson, eds., *Unofficial Diplomats* (New York: Columbia University Press, 1977). (See also Oran R. Young, *The Intermediaries: Third Parties in International Crises* [Princeton, N.J.: Princeton University Press, 1967].)

387 James T. Shotwell, *War as an Instrument of National Policy* (New York, Harcourt, 1929), pp. 15–16.

388 "Mao Tse-tung and Confucianism," in Mao Tse-tung, *Selected Writing* (Harbin, Manchuria, 1948), pp. 114, 131.

388 Stanley Hoffmann, *State of War: Essays on the Theory and Practice of International Politics* (New York: Praeger, 1965), p. viii.

389 Robert E. Osgood, "Postwar Strategy of Limited War," in Laurence W. Martin, ed., *Strategic Thought in the Nuclear Age* (London: Heinemann, 1979), pp. 99 ff. (See also Robert E. Osgood, *Limited War:*

PAGE

     The Challenge to American Strategy [Chicago: University of Chicago Press, 1957].)

395   Arnold Wolfers, *Discord and Collaboration* (Baltimore: Johns Hopkins University Press, 1962), pp. 3–24.

398   "There is increasing scepticism . . . ," in C. Wilfred Jenks, *The World Beyond the Charter* (London: Allen & Unwin,), p. 132.

398   "the unity of mankind . . . ," in *ibid.*, pp. 132–33.

398   Michael Walzer, *Just and Unjust War* (New York: Basic Books, 1982); Michael Howard, *War and the Liberal Conscience* (New Brunswick, N.J.: Rutgers University Press, 1978).

Index

Truman Doctrine, 22, 27, 97, 139,
214, 266
Tshombe, Moise, 257–58
Tucker, Robert, 177, 340
Tunisia, 197, 198, 199, 200, 201,
212, 258, 340
Turkey, 191, 194, 204
Soviet relations with, 21, 22, 87,
127, 139
U.S. relations with, 12, 22, 27,
28, 43, 55, 87, 216, 218
Turkish court, credentials
ceremony at, 337

Ulam, Adam, 107
Uncertain Trumpet, The (Taylor),
311
UNESCO, 277, 278
United Arab Republic, 200
United Nations (UN), 3–5, 80, 97,
219, 253–58, 265–86
Arab-Israeli wars and, 36, 99,
115, 206, 221, 225, 265
Atomic Commission of, 266,
289
blindspot about, 9–10, 20–21
Charter of, 5, 6, 7, 92, 105,
191, 238, 246–47, 253,
254–55, 257–58, 260–61, 265,
269, 274, 276, 398
China and, 13, 29, 254, 256,
270, 280
Commission for Conventional
Armaments of, 288, 289
in Congo crisis, 257–58, 265,
272
defects of parliamentary process
in, 280–81
diminution of public interest in,
275–76
Disarmament Commission of,
289
early hope for, 237–40
failures of technique in, 279–86
founding conference of, 3–4,
191, 238, 260, 283
General Assembly of, 13, 101,
103, 176, 206, 237, 239n,
256–57, 265–66, 267, 269,
275–76, 280, 282, 285
impotence of, 237–38, 273–74
Khrushchev and, 100–101, 103,
272

in Korean War, 13, 30, 126,
191, 256, 270–71
League of Nations compared to,
246–47, 251, 253–54, 255,
280
military framework of, 253–56,
261
nation-state vs., 245–46
Pacific settlement and, 265–69
Preparatory Commission of,
269
reform of, 285–86
Secretary-General legend in,
269–73
Security Council of, 13, 22, 103,
126–27, 137, 200, 206,
246–47, 254, 256, 257–58,
265, 266, 267, 269–70, 280,
285–86, 289
Specialized Agencies of, 13,
277–79, 282, 283–84
Third World's role in, 175–76,
179, 180, 267
Uniting for Peace Resolution of,
256–57
veto power in, 13, 254, 260–61,
280–81
visionary role of, 274–75
United Nations Conference on
Science and Technology
(1963), 278
United Nations Conference on the
Human Environment (1972),
278–79
United Nations Conference on
Trade and Development
(UNCTAD), 174, 178, 277
United States, 12–88
commitment problem in policy
of, 87
diplomatic tradition in, 342–43
economic power of, 13–14,
15–16, 41, 58–59, 135–36,
154, 155
elections and campaigns in, 33,
46, 73, 75, 83
expansionism of, 15, 19
history of summitry in, 363
interrelation of foreign and
domestic policy in, 57–58, 73
interventionist policy of, 35–36,
43–44, 74, 268; *see also*
Vietnam war